CW00970198

A BROAD PLACE

Praise for *A Broad Place*

"Jürgen Moltmann introduces the reader into the broad space of his inspiring life.... The famed theologian answers all the questions about his life and work in an amazingly open, fair and irenic way.... A lucid book, opening on wider spheres."

—*Zeitzeichen*, Berlin—

"In no other of his books does Moltmann manifest his existential Jesus-spirituality as directly as in this autobiography, composed as an expression of his belief.... His theology here appears...as the self-expression of a pious soul who consciously chooses against the nihilistic signature of the modern age."

—Friedrich Wilhelm Graf, *Neue Zürcher Zeitung*—

"The global theological player par excellence takes the reader with him on many theological forays and speaking trips around the world.... This autobiography confirms the unbroken relevance and contemporaneity of Moltmann's turn from fear-driven and confining theologies in support of 'the reign of God and his righteousness on the earth.'"

—*Zeitschrift für die Evangelische Landeskirche*—

A BROAD PLACE

An Autobiography

JÜRGEN MOLTMANN

Translated by Margaret Kohl

"Thou hast set my feet in a broad place."
—Psalm 31:8

FORTRESS PRESS
Minneapolis

A BROAD PLACE
An Autobiography

First Fortress Press edition 2008.

Translated by Margaret Kohl from the German *Weiter Raum: Eine Lebensgeschichte*, published by Gütersloher Verlagshaus, Gütersloh, copyright ©2006.

Photos courtesy Gütersloher Verlagshaus, Jürgen Moltmann, and Christopher Morse (plate 22).
Cover design: Josh Messner
Book design: James Korsmo

Library of Congress Cataloging-in-Publication Data
Moltmann, Jürgen.
A broad place : an autobiography / Jürgen Moltmann.
p. cm.
Includes bibliographical references and index.
ISBN 978-0-8006-6214-1 (alk. paper)
1. Moltmann, Jürgen. I. Title.
BX4827.M6A3 2007
230'.044092—dc22
[B] 2007008176

The paper used in this publication meets the minimum requirements of American National Standard for Information Sciences—Permanence of Paper for Printed Library Materials, ANSI Z329.48-1984.

Manufactured in the U.S.A.

12 11 10 09 08 1 2 3 4 5 6 7 8 9 10

This life story is dedicated to
my grandchildren

Jonas and Christoph
Malte and Jakob
and Eliza

CONTENTS

part I

Youth

part I

Youth

ONE

THE SETTLEMENT

Seventy-five years ago, anyone who took the Waldörfer train from Hamburg to Grosshansdorf and got out at Buchenkamp station found himself alone among open fields. Left and right, arable lands stretched away, divided not by fences but by hedgerows, banks of earth called *knicks* or *breaks*, grown over with hazelnuts, birches, and all kinds of bushes, which were roughly cleared every seven years. At that time there were no proper roads in the area, but simply paths or tracks for farm carts, and these were generally soft and muddy. If one arrived at nearby Wulfsdorferweg—a Weg, or path, of the same kind—one found oneself in front of four similar, long double houses, red roofed and built of bricks. In a side road with the curious name Im Berge, 'in the mountain' (although there was nothing but flat ground far and wide), there were two similar detached houses. This was the shared 'settlement' of a few teachers who, in the wake of the youth movement of the time, were enthusiasts for 'the simple life' (propagated by Ernst Wiechert) 'on their own soil'. They were led by the indefatigable visionary Helmut Hertling and his practical neighbour, the socialist Alfred Schär.

The gardens were grouped round a common playground and sports round, with a shared water supply and cesspit. A community hall, where music was to be taught, and a poultry farm had been planned, but these soon evidently proved to overtax the public spirit of the participants. However, there was a kindergarten (which I attended) and shared festivities, sports groups, neighbourly help—everything, in fact, which at that time belonged to a real community. There were many experiments, but not everything lasted. My parents joined in 1929 and built their house, 'Im Berge 4', although they didn't have a penny in their pockets and their relatives thought them mad and offered no help. They wanted to escape from the 'grey city walls', and also from the housing shortage in Hamburg, and sought fresh country air and 'the basics' of life, a garden of their own and the fruits of their own labours. They neither drank nor smoked; there was only decaffeinated coffee, fruit juice, and margarine from the health stores. Every free moment was devoted to the garden. And my mother preserved beans, peas, and carrots for the winter.

My childhood was coloured by the spirit of this 'settlement', and by its problems as well. There was a group of boys about the same age (and at least four of them were called Jürgen, the name being a favourite at the time). We made expeditions to the neighbouring woods and marshes, and at ten years old, of course we all wanted to be forest rangers. In spring we leapt over the fires lit on Easter morning, singing the folk song 'Winter Adieu', and burning winter's effigy. We played football, volleyball, and hockey on our sports ground. We had a game of our own called 'Kippel-Kappel', which we played in the road with sticks (there were no cars); we played hide-and-seek in the cornfields and vied with each other in climbing the highest oak trees. We were country boys, and accordingly unkempt. There were annual sports days, under the supervision—no, 'together with'—the grown-ups. In 1937 I won the 'Olympic pentathlon', which consisted of high jump, shotput, horizontal bar, a board game, and musical exercises. It was the tenth anniversary of the founding of 'our settlement'. A sports teacher was engaged for the school holidays, and this Mr Sörensen gathered us together for early morning gymnastics and took us on bicycle tours. His sister taught the girls and their mothers a special form of gymnastics (Loheländer gymnastics) about which they were particularly enthusiastic.

Everyone was supposed to contribute actively to the community. Our neighbour Kurt Gaebeler (later my English teacher) drew us into his poetry writing. He put together a settlement magazine, which, however, died after only a few numbers. My later Latin teacher Arthur Kracke enchanted me with his violin in family concerts, although, like my father, I counted as 'unmusical'. The Stefan George enthusiast Maschmann never taught me himself (luckily for us both). He wrote a poem with the words: 'At dawn the spade already breaks the sod of the barren ground …' Helmut Hertling was also my teacher later at the local school. His visions were far beyond my childish comprehension, but they impressed me greatly. One day he wanted to drain the Mediterranean and water the Sahara instead. He was the only pacifist in the settlement, and kept to it even throughout the Nazi period and the war. After the war, he led the peace movement in Hamburg.

All of us children were made by our parents to work continually and steadily in the garden. That was the miserable part of this humane community. We followed our fathers with hoe and spade. We planted peas and beans, we picked gooseberries and red currants, we cleared the paths and cut up vegetables—above all on Sunday mornings. My father solemnly called this 'Sunday work'. Two of his maxims made a deep impression on me: 1. 'Illness is a matter of the will,' and 2. 'First think and then speak'. There was no church in Volksdorf, nor would anyone have gone to it. As a reward for our Sunday work, we were allowed to learn swimming in the nearby bathing pool and were occasionally—but only exceptionally—given a 10 pfennig ice. Ever since that time I have loathed gardening and hated rewards.

My favourite neighbour was a painter, Fritz Beyle. 'Uncle Fifi' was a great and irreverent wit and, after all the solemnity of the 'settlement', could always make us laugh again. Unlike my father, he was a practical man. I was permitted to help him make built-in cupboards, and I admired him greatly. I often visited his workshop of an evening, and under his instruction made nesting boxes for the birds, fretwork objects, and once a complete doll's house for my sister Marianne. He rather liked me, and developed my manual skills. When he was made director of an art school in Hamburg in 1935, he built himself a studio in the garden, was given commissions for extensive murals, and often got me to sit (or more usually, unfortunately, stand) for him as a model. He could undoubtedly be grumpy and was not always an easy neighbour for my peaceable parents. Nevertheless, the friendship lasted for 40 years.

The settlement survived the Nazi period and the war. Apart from Arthur Kracke, who indulged in a theatrical flirtation with the Nazi party because he hoped for a career in the cultural sector, no one became a Nazi in 1933. Nor did any of the boys and girls become leaders in the Hitler Youth or the League of German Girls (BDM). People behaved in public as they were compelled to do, and otherwise lived privately for themselves, somewhat cut off, in our secluded area. This may well have been partly due to the shock over the fate of Alfred Schär. He was killed by the SA in the Fuhlsbüttel concentration camp in 1937. It was said that he had tried to help other victims of the Nazi movement, but he was also a member of the International Socialist Task Force (Internationaler Sozialistische Kampfbund), led by the Göttingen philosopher Leonhard Nelson, and that was the first to be persecuted. Not much was said about this in front of us children, but we undoubtedly strongly sensed the sinister character of the story.

My parents married in 1923. My father was powerfully built—over six feet tall—and was pledged to a life of 'plain living and high thinking'. My mother, in contrast, had a cheerful and happy nature, and wherever she went, the clouds lifted. The two were remotely related, and their families in Hamburg and Schwerin knew each other well.

My father was his parents' seventh child and was born in 1897 in Hamburg, at a time when my grandfather was already very ill. He suffered from tuberculosis, the pulmonary scourge of the Hanseatic cities. My grandfather Johannes was a freethinker and lived in the optimistic spirit of the opening years of the German empire. He moved to Hamburg from Schwerin as a private teacher and soon opened his own private school in the Harvestehude quarter of Hamburg. He became a Freemason and Grand Master of the Heinrich zum Felsen Lodge. He wrote school books and pamphlets in the spirit of the Enlightenment, directed against the church.[1] Like Lessing, he believed firmly in the education of the human race for good, and for his gravestone in the Ohlsdorf graveyard he chose this verse:

> It will come, it will surely come,
> the time of perfecting,
> When man will do the good
> because it is the good.

The maxim is taken from §88 of Lessing's essay on the education of mankind. Johannes Moltmann took for his Göttingen doctorate a historical subject, the Empress Theophano. Feuerbach's 'Enlightened' writings robbed him of his family's belief in God. Like all Hamburg citizens, he welcomed the establishment of the German empire through Bismarck, which turned Hamburg's harbour into a world port, but he despised William II and his martial posturings. He had a portrait of Friedrich III, the '99 days emperor', hanging in his room. When he fell ill of tuberculosis, he could no longer teach. He had to give up his school, and his family was reduced to poverty.

In the upwardly-thrusting, middle-class society of the time, social decline was the worst thing that could happen. He still tried to invent new games and to write the histories of Hamburg families, but what concerned him inwardly were the philosophical questions of monism and the morally imperative idea of the good, which called for a heroic life. I still have a copy of Ernst Haeckel's book *Die Welträtsel* (popular edition of 1949), which came from his library. He died in 1910 and through his early death became the model for my then 13-year-old father, who all his life tried to come to terms with his father's philosophical writings. The children had to break off their education, and the private school became a boarding house for foreign students. Nevertheless, by giving private lessons on the side, my father was still able to attend the Johanneum school until the war broke out in 1914.

Like his brother Alex and his sister Irmi, my father was seized by enthusiasm for the 'free German' youth movement. True, as he himself wrote, the transformation from bookworm to 'child of nature' was physically difficult for him, but the idea of the alternative life fascinated him. He joined the 'League of German Ramblers' but liked best to go on walks by himself. My father was a born historian. He often stood outside himself, observed the life he was living, and took note of it. This gave him sovereignty but also made him lonely. In 1914, as a 17-year-old, he volunteered for the army and came back in 1918 with severe wounds, the scars of which we children saw with a shudder on his great body. He could tell fantastic stories. According to his version of 'the Flying Dutchman', in the end the pirates threw him overboard, and he drowned in the sea. We children gazed at him open-mouthed.

After a short time in the Bahrenfeld Freikorps (volunteers) in the fight against the Spartacus revolt in Hamburg, he wandered far and wide through Germany, sometimes with others belonging to the same youth movement but generally alone, this being his way of shaking off his experiences during the war. For a short, happy time, he studied in Heidelberg and then applied to the school authorities to take the necessary examination in Hamburg. No course certificates or the like were asked for. At that time, students were treated as 'academic members of the public' who arranged their studies for themselves. They were not, as they are today, treated as immature people unable to make use of their own reason without the guidance of someone else. He did not wish to take a doctorate, so as not to be cut off from ordinary people by a title. He then soon became a teacher at the famous

Lichtwark school, where he taught Helmut and Loki Schmidt, among others,[2] until this democratic institution was closed by the Nazis—the first school to be so—and my father was moved to an uncongenial school for girls. After 1933 the closer and more remote family went over to the Nazis, which left my father lonely. He fled into the military and forced himself to undergo the drill required of a reserve officer. But of this I shall have more to say later.

My mother came from Schwerin, and that was my youthful paradise. There was the dream castle on the lake, the Kaninchen and Ziegelwerder islands, Zippendorf, where people came to escape the summer heat, and the elevated atmosphere of a little duchy. My loving and good-natured grandfather, Friedrich Stuhr, was the director of archives and at all times a stalwart servant and upholder of the state. My grandmother, Anna Stuhr, came from the family of the Forest Director Dankwart in Schönberg and was always very much aware of who she was. My mother grew up in accordance with her position. Illness prevented her from completing her grammar school education, which proved to be a disadvantage to her when she married the learned teacher. For a time she worked happily in the museum and in Schwerin Castle and could tell us all the ghost stories in which it was shrouded. My mother was unusually easily roused to enthusiasm and entered so warmly into the lives of other people that many went away with lighter hearts after an encounter with her. During the war she read all Ernst Wiechert's novels and recounted them at table, so that I know them all without ever having read them. There is no doubt that all her life she felt inferior to my all-knowing, all-determining father, but we children realized later that it was she who supported him, not he her. Without my mother, my father would probably have sunk into solitariness and melancholy. She put a new heart into him through her admiration and praise.

My mother was my first love. When my father was called up in 1939, I was proud and happy to take over many of his tasks in home and garden and to queue for hours in all the shops with our ration books. Sad although the reason was, I blossomed and came to myself once my father was away. For me, 1939 brought the end of a childhood in which I had suffered through a lack of orientation. I woke up out of my childish dream worlds, and my mother—now alone—and my brother and sisters helped me into real life. They trusted me to do things my father would never have trusted me to do, and I was able to do what I had never expected of myself.

That gave me confidence. Life with my mother without my father from 1939 until 1943 was a great time for me; yet I missed my father for all that. During my adolescent years, I didn't know what was the matter with me, and I had no one who might have explained it to me a little. I shrank back from girls and was afraid of my unfamiliar feelings. I was never unconcernedly self-confident but was often plagued by fears of failure.

I was born on 8 April 1926 and grew up with a two-year older brother, Hartwig, and a three-year younger sister, Marianne. In 1937 my brother Eckhart was added to the family, and in 1941 my sister Elisabeth. I never knew my brother Hartwig, but he was always present to us. The day after he was born, he began to have convulsions and then developed meningitis, which after a week had damaged his brain so severely that he was unable to recognize anyone. My parents kept him with them until he was three, but this then proved to be no longer possible, and they put him in the Friedrichsberg hospital. He had no awareness of any kind. He must have been a sweet child, for the nurses called him 'our little prince'. Our parents visited him every Wednesday afternoon, and every time came back silent and with stony faces. They never took us children with them. In 1940, either just before or already during the Nazis' first euthanasia action, he died of pneumonia, as my parents believed. But that was what was always given out at the time. His fate and our parents' consequent suffering made a deeper mark on my youth than I realized. When I was born, my father wrote, 'Everything that was missing in Hartwig was with him a matter of course, good things and bad. After the terrible years, life was given to us parents afresh. For that reason we called our little Jürgen "Dankwart". That was the strange family name of Grandmother Loycke, and only we parents really understood the reason for it.' Our parents had Hartwig buried between their own graves, so as to have him with them in eternity.

In 1929 my sister Marianne was born. I was no longer alone, although the baby disappointed me by not being able to walk. But she was 'my' sister, and when curious neighbours' children gaped at her through the French windows, I defended her from them by breaking the glass. Marianne was a happy little girl who liked to join in all the boys' pranks. She swung on the horizontal bar in the neighbour's garden much more fearlessly than any of the rest of us. When we went to school, differences admittedly emerged. She was attentive, industrious, and successful, whereas I had my difficulties. She kept her Easter eggs for months, whereas mine were gobbled up by the same evening. She learnt the piano, and with her long plait and her violin was a charming sight. In my case, my parents didn't even attempt any such musical training. So there was also a degree of rivalry in the struggle for our parents' recognition and affection. But that ended effortlessly when war broke out in 1939 and my father was called up. From that time on we were both there for our mother and our younger brother and sister, and we complemented one another harmoniously. There was always much to do, and we could rely on each other.

Now that I have described the context in which I grew up—the settlement we lived in, my parents and brothers and sisters—I must finally come to myself. For me, childhood was not an entirely happy time. It was often one in which I 'didn't know what to do'. Compared with my tall father, I was too small. Sent to school too early, I was always the youngest in the class and the least mature. As compensation I was probably endowed with an undue measure of imagination. When I walked through the woods with my mother, I saw dwarfs and elves everywhere and invented the wildest stories, which she very much enjoyed because she liked to imagine similar things too. I was supposed to be 'sociable' and play outside with the other boys, but I was often alone, and gladly so, dreaming of far-away things as I sat in front of the window. In the local school there was no teacher who awakened my enthusiasm, nor did my teachers find in me a pupil who could awaken theirs. I was untidy, was seldom attentive, and found it difficult to keep my mind on what I was doing. The flight of a fly in the classroom fascinated me more than what was written on the blackboard. In the primary school and my first two years in grammar school, my teachers clearly found me a trial. My marks were accordingly poor, and at the bottom of my reports was often the perfidious comment: 'Could do better.' This regularly enraged my father. 'Why don't you do what you are able to do?' He didn't see that I no doubt wanted *to be able* but couldn't manage the *wanting*.

When I was about 12 and had arrived at the lowest point in my development, my Schwerin grandmother intervened like an angel in time of need. She didn't put me down, like my father, but believed in me and encouraged me. In the school holidays she arranged for me to have riding lessons in the royal Schwerin stables, and looked on. For every 'A' I got at school, she gave me a riding lesson worth two Reichsmarks. So I learnt self-control on the back of a horse. In her highly cultivated home, I learnt table manners and to pay attention to my appearance. She had silver tea and coffee pots, had a table laid in the garden, and in the house had the dishes brought up from the basement kitchen in a lift. She took me with her to the bathing beach at Göhren on the island of Rügen, and I even accompanied her when she joined the ladies belonging to Schwerin's society, with whom she played bridge. She was a proud woman and a beautiful one; I respected her greatly. In this way the Duchy of Schwerin became for me the opposite pole to the country 'settlement'. In Schwerin the pavement was called the *trottoir*, one walked round the *carree*, went onto the *peron* (platform) in order to get into the *coupee* (compartment), and waited for the *conducteur*. My grandmother even trained the wire-haired terrier Bonzo with French words such as *allez hopp*. French counted as the language of society at the ducal court, and to this society my grandfather Stuhr, the director of archives, belonged as a matter of course. French was a survival of the great world of the eighteenth century and was still cultivated in provincial Schwerin in order to distinguish its upper class from the ordinary people, who spoke dialect.

For me, Schwerin's bliss meant driving a scooter on made-up roads, rowing and swimming in the lake, taking Sunday afternoon trips to Zippendorf in the steamer *Pribislav* or *Obotrit*, and going on long horseback chases on the Grosser Dreesch, which was still a parade ground and not yet built-up. I played with my cousins, and liked one of them, Wolf Wagner, particularly. He was killed in Breslau in 1945 at the age of 17. It was in Schwerin, in 1932, that I had my first experience of politics: we were playing in a sandpit when a bigger boy came up to us, taught us to raise our clenched fists and shout 'Rotfront'. We stamped enthusiastically after him, raised our fists and cried 'Rotfront' until my aunt opened the kitchen window and called energetically: 'We are not Rotfront at all. We are Black-White-Red.' And so the communist revolt in the sandpit was crushed by the German National Party.

Above his writing desk my grandfather had a large mural showing the homecoming of wounded soldiers. Two hunting knives hung on his wall. My father got on very well with his father-in-law. The two were passionate genealogists and could trace our families back to the fifteenth century. Admittedly not much can be discovered about the name Moltmann. It means 'the man' of a farmer 'Molt' belonging to the Parchim region and is of Slavic origin, like 'Molotov', the hammer. My grandfather died before the end of the war, and my grandmother moved to the west, to Hamburg, together with my mother's sister and her family. When I arrived in Hamburg with my first motorbike in 1953, she could not be dissuaded, 83 years old though she was, from jumping onto the pillion and letting herself be driven about. She lived to a great age because she was always interested in life—even though she drank as many cups of coffee during the day as she took sleeping pills at night. She left me a kind of religious testament which ends with the heroic sentence: 'In the end I shall enter into the eternal nothingness.'

My father was an authority in German, Latin, and history. With his fabulous memory, he was a walking encyclopedia, and let the less proficient person feel it. When I gradually emerged from my nadir and picked myself up, I threw myself into the subjects about which he knew nothing—mathematics, physics, and chemistry. I worked through mathematical textbooks on my own so that I could appear competent in lessons. In the top class I encountered a teacher of genius, Mr Magin, who only talked to the members of the class who showed an interest, and singled me out to be his pupil. Chemistry was occasionally the fashion in our school. We experimented on our own in our cellars with Bunsen burners and test tubes. A friend and I once blew up a tool shed in his garden with potassium chlorate and red phosphorous. There were even boys who hurt themselves badly through similar experiments. In pure physics, I advanced as far as Louis Broglie's book *Matière et Lumière* (Matter and Light), which appeared in German in 1943 with a foreword by Werner Heisenberg. I was in the middle of it when I was called up. My talent for languages was not much developed, but my school English was sufficiently voluble when I was taken prisoner by the British in February 1945. When I was 15, my feeling for lyric finally awakened. I read Goethe's poems and learnt them by heart; I read Novalis's 'Hymn to the Night' by moonlight on the heath and was completely transported. The German Romantics were music to my ears. In addition, I fabricated attractive silhouettes, until this artistic vein slowly ran out. But that was also due to the events which intervened in my life and changed everything. The sciences I took so seriously did not at that time make a realist of me. I remained a dreamer and longed for fresh horizons. I could surf for hours in the dream worlds of impossible possibilities, forgetting everything around me.

TWO

JULY 1943

Operation Gomorrah

Apart from school, my youthful years were marked by the state youth movement, the Jungvolk (for younger boys) and the Hitler Youth, by confirmation classes, and a dancing class. All three were intended to contribute to our maturity, and for all three I was wholly unsuited and somewhat too young.

In 1936 my parents sent me to the Jungvolk. I found it frightfully tedious, and after the first training hour I was sent home: I couldn't march in step and confused right and left. But because participation was obligatory, I joined a band. I had to try to play Prussian marches on the piccolo. But I failed hopelessly all round. I played wrong notes and was never at home in the group. Once a patrol leader snapped at me—it was Dietz Pohl, who was later shot down with his Stuka in Russia: 'After all, you want to be a leader one day.' But no such idea had ever entered my head. I hated the drill and the pre-military training, although shivers of religious emotion went up and down my spine at the heroic song: 'Holy Fatherland, in danger will thy sons surround thee.' So my career in the Jungvolk was inglorious. When I was 14, I advanced to the mounted section of the Hitler Youth. This was a somewhat elitist group that was more concerned about its horses than about Hitler. Once I had to attend a Hitler Youth camp on the Darss peninsula in Mecklenburg. It was an appalling time. Ten 'comrades' shared a single tent and were continually made to march or run in step. The experience strengthened my conviction that I was not born to be one of a mass, and my determination to be alone rather than to be ordered about. In 1943 the Nazi hullabaloo was over for me and was replaced by the military lunacy.

My religious education was deficient. Once a year the whole family attended a service in the school hall (because Volksdorf had as yet no church). That was on Christmas Eve and, as my father later admitted, was not out of reverence for the birth of the Saviour but in order to celebrate the holy family—that is, the holiness of our own: father, mother, and her youngest child in the crib. With the rest of my school class I was sent to Pastor Hansen Petersen for confirmation classes. After the war Petersen made a certain name for himself as a television pastor. His teaching made no impression on me. I can only remember some abstruse Germanic stories from the Edda, and some of Jesus' parables, as well as the Sermon on the Mount. He belonged neither to the (Nazi-sympathizing) German Christians nor the Confessing Church but after the war joined the Bernechener movement for liturgical reform and laid great stress on elaborate services. When in 1948 he no longer allowed the congregation to pray the Lord's Prayer but had it sung by the choir, I felt deprived of my responsibility and left the Lutheran church. In Göttingen, I joined the Reformed congregation for the gospel's sake. During my youth, religion and the church remained completely alien, and I would never have dreamt that I would find my calling there.

As was the custom, my confirmation in 1940 was followed by dancing classes, which were supposed to make grown-ups of us. I went with my school class, because it was the expected thing, and the similarly aged girls' class joined as well. Every week I had to put on my black confirmation suit, slick down my hair with brilliantine, and present myself in the Stadt Hamburg Hotel. At first I didn't find it easy, but I was curious, too, and for the first time began to be conscious of the opposite sex. I arranged to go to the final ball with Ingeborg. Afterwards she enjoyed taking me to the concert hall in Hamburg (for she was a passionate violinist), and I went with her gladly. I well remember the shock that went through us when we listened to Beethoven's Third Symphony, the Eroica, after Stalingrad in 1943. In Volksdorf during those years it was the fashion for girls to sit at the spinning wheel again and to spin wool. That gave me the chance to watch Ingeborg and to read aloud to her. We were close friends, and when I was 'on active service', as the phrase went, we exchanged letters and told each other what had been happening to us. She even once visited me in my prisoner of war camp in England, having applied to help get in the English harvest. When I came back from the camp in 1948 as a Christian and theology student, we drew apart, for her family, especially her dominant mother, belonged to the neo-Germanic Ludendorff movement, which took its bearings not so much from the old field marshal as from his wife, the 'seer' Matthilde Ludendorff. There would have been no future for Ingeborg and me together, but in those years of chaos, and in exile, I was able to think of someone who thought of me, too, and that did me good and was a wonderful experience that gave me support.

In February 1943 our school class was conscripted and made air force 'auxiliaries'. Together with boys of similar age from the St George's high school, we were stationed with the Alster anti-aircraft battery in Schwanenwieck. This 8.8 cm battery stood on stilts on Hamburg's large lake, the Outer Alster, probably so as to have a wide firing range in all directions. I was put on the firing platform together with Gerhard Schopper, the mathematical genius from the other class. We felt that we were already soldiers, but all the same we had not left school behind us: teachers came to the barracks and taught over-tired 'warriors' who had been on the alert during the night. There were frequent night-time air raid warnings, but in Hamburg nothing happened. We found it quite exciting, and at night could look through the powerful telescope on the firing platform and see the Jupiter moons. So we industriously learnt how to identify the constellations. It was at this time that I struck up my great youthful friendship with Peter Schmidt. We often wandered arm in arm through the battery at night and dreamed together about a better future and about the great things we were going to do. Peter was a little older than me and came from a teacher's family in Schmalenbeck. In 1944, after our time together as air force auxiliaries, our ways parted. He fell in love with my sister Marianne, but in 1944 was sent to labour service in Riga, whereas I was sent to Kaunas. Peter was killed near Magdeburg in May 1945, in the last days of the war.

For me the high spot of 1943 was a week's leave at the beginning of July. I wanted to go walking, like my father, and I travelled to Coblenz and walked from castle to castle and from bank to bank of the Rhine, upstream as far as Bingen, through the gloriously blossoming and peaceful Rhine valley. Then I visited Heidelberg and bicycled up the River Neckar as far as Wimpfen and down as far as Schwetzingen. My grandfather and my father had studied in Heidelberg, and I wanted to do the same. Heidelberg has remained my dream university down to the present day, but unfortunately I was never invited to a chair there.

When I returned to the anti-aircraft battery, the deadly terror of this year began, for on 24 July 1943 'Operation Gomorrah' was launched.[1] That was the name the biblically versed English gave their planned destruction of the first big German city. I can remember every detail of the first night. Bomber squadrons approaching over the North Sea set off air raid sirens. We manned the equipment and the guns and waited. The bombers were already over Flensburg, and we thought their goal was Berlin. But then they turned in our direction. Searchlights went on and we were prepared, when suddenly the NCO who was manning the radar came rushing down crying, 'I can't see anything any more, I can't see anything any more.' On his screen everything had gone white. He was blinded by a mass of fine aluminium strips which, for the first time, had been thrown down from the bombers. We found them everywhere the next day. With this device the whole of Hamburg's defence against air attack was eliminated. And then it began. There were more than 1,000 aircraft in the attack. Round about us explosive and incendiary bombs rained down, most of them falling in the water. Helplessly we looked on as St George's began to burn, and then the city hall, and finally Hamburg's churches, which flared up like torches. The RAF's tactics were simple: first explosives, then incendiaries. What had been chosen as a target was the densely built-up working-class area of East Hamburg. The bombs set off a firestorm with a temperature of about 1000°C, which burnt up everything, even the people in the air raid shelters. All the houses from Hammerbrock to Barmbek were destroyed, so that later some parts of the city, or what was left of them, were simply walled up. This inferno was repeated night after night, nine nights long.

The first night we followed an officer into the residential district nearest to us and tried to fight the fire and to help. We climbed over charred bodies in the burning houses and pulled down incendiaries from the roofs, but in the morning we saw that it was useless. Survivors sat beside the Alster with a book or whatever they had been able to save in a hurry and stared in front of them completely apathetically, with empty eyes. They had lost everything. The landing stage that led to the battery had been partly destroyed. Some of our barracks had burned down. By day, heavy clouds of smoke hung over the city and it went on burning. Fortunately, we were allowed to go home briefly during the day, to see how things were and to show that we were still alive. But in the evening we had to report back. It was on the last night, or the last but one, that an explosive bomb hit the platform where we were standing with our useless firing device. The mass of splinters destroyed the firing platform and tore apart my friend Gerhard Schopper, who was standing next to me. He hadn't got down quickly enough. I stood up as if anaesthetized, blinded and deaf, with only a few splinter wounds in my shoulder and one on my cheekbone. Everyone looked at me as if I were a miracle, someone risen from the dead. I didn't know myself how I came to be still alive. The others took Gerhard Schopper's body away—his head had been torn off—and disappeared, so that I was left alone in that place of death. More bombs fell on the battery and destroyed the platforms and landing stages. Finally, I found myself on a plank in the water and pulled myself out with the help of one of the stilts. During that night I cried out to God for the first time in my life and put my life in his hands. I was as if dead, and ever after received life every day as a new gift. My question was not, 'Why does God allow this to happen?' but, 'My God, where are you?' And there was the other question, the answer to which I am still looking for today: Why am I alive and not dead, too, like the friend at my side? I felt the guilt of survival and searched for the meaning of continued life. I knew that there had to be some reason why I was still alive. During that night I became a seeker after God.

Operation Gomorrah cost the lives of more than 40,000 people, most of them women and children. The idea had been to incite the workers to rebel against Hitler because of the destruction of their homes; that was what German immigrants had prophesied. They overlooked the fact that most of the able-bodied men had long since been sent to the front. It was only after those nine days of mass destruction that American B-23 bombers, the Flying Fortresses, came and attacked the submarine yards in the harbour, which were so important for the war. Because there was no longer any German defence against such attacks, we were all convinced that the war would be over in a few days. But it lasted for two more years and cost further senseless millions of victims.

Operation Gomorrah: Was Hamburg a sinful city like the Bible's Sodom and Gomorrah? During the Nazi period more than 40,000 people were put to death, in Neuengamme concentration camp near Hamburg, and about 30,000 Hamburg Jews died on the fields of White Russia. As a survivor of 'Gomorrah', I am a survivor of these Hamburg catastrophes, too, and feel 'guilty' and in duty bound to the dead because of my survival.

When the destruction came to an end after nine days and nights, our Alster battery had become useless. It was demolished, and we were moved to another in Bahrenfeld. There, too, there was, I think, some school teaching, but we were inwardly moved by very different questions. At least I cannot remember any actual lessons. We stood to the guns at night and gazed into the dark nothingness of that destructive time.

On 8 February 1944 Flight Sergeant Freitag dismissed our class of air force auxiliaries with the comment that, when all was said and done, we had had a good time. I thought he was being cynical. But he probably knew what was ahead of us, and in that sense he was right.

I was soon to have a taste of this when I was quite superfluously drafted for labour service, and in Lithuania was forced to put up with the vilest humiliations. But before that I had a few weeks free, and I pushed my way into Hamburg University. There, with my wartime Abitur[2] of 1943 in my pocket, I sat with wounded soldiers and a few female students and heard lectures in chemistry and physics which I found quite comprehensible. When I came back from labour service and waited to be called up, I again had the good fortune to immerse myself once more in this different world, the life of the mind.

THREE

PRISONER OF WAR, 1945–47

War stories are not tales of adventure. They are stories about destruction and death. That is why anyone who was involved does not like to talk about it. I had no desire for these experiences, but they put their stamp on my life, and so I shall say something about them.

Many people who were forced to do labour service before they were called up tell of the same things: pointless drill, brutal harassment, inhumane humiliations. With some boys of my own age belonging to my school class, I was sent via Gumbinnen in East Prussia to Kaunas in Lithuania, where we were put up in a school. Footcloths with army boots were distributed, which slipped on every march and gave us huge blisters on our feet. We were given spades, not so that we could dig something but so that we could polish them like glass and drill with them as if they were rifles. Although there had never been a gas alarm anywhere during the war, we had to run and crawl, march and stand to attention wearing our gas masks. The men in charge were small fry from East Prussia who had managed to avoid being sent to the front. We thought they were all the dregs of society, for why else would they have gone into the labour service? They revenged themselves on us arrogant grammar school boys with every conceivable torment. If we came back at midday, exhausted from some senseless exercise, we found our beds pulled apart, the lockers emptied out and the contents thrown on the floor: the beds had not been made properly and the lockers were allegedly in a mess. It was pure despotism. Anyone who rebelled was made to run through the neighbourhood wearing his gas mask. This and nothing else went on for three months. I cannot remember ever once having performed a useful piece of work during the whole time.

Anyone who voiced a criticism risked being condemned in Königsberg as a traitor. When my father came to visit me—he was meanwhile a major in a unit of the home defence in Minsk—I was not given a single hour's leave. I took it for myself and walked through Kaunas with him. He had come in order to entrust me with a frightful discovery. In Minsk he had heard about the mass murder of Jews and had seen the mass graves for himself. He didn't know what the consequences ought to be for him personally, but he wanted me to know as well. This completely put a stop to my willingness to serve in the war. Ever since the catastrophe in Hamburg, I had known that the war was lost, but that it was the cover for crimes such as this embittered me with a sense of my own helplessness. In the summer of 1944 we at last went home. In the Gumbinnen camp the first Russian leaflets had been dropped. The front was coming inexorably closer.

During the war my father suffered from an inner conflict, which he was unable to solve. On the one hand he felt in duty bound to defend his country, but on the other hand in no circumstances did he want Hitler to win the war. He was unable to grasp the fact that by defending his country until the end of April 1945, he was helping to prolong Hitler's war. Does one have a home country at all in a dictatorship?

In July 1944 I then received my call-up and travelled to the barracks in Delmenhorst. I had been assigned to the heavy weapons company of an infantry battalion. Here we really did have military training in the use of rifles and machine guns. Occasionally we also had shooting practice. But the main thing was that senseless Prussian drill—marching, wheeling, standing to attention, eyes right, eyes left, and so on. We learnt to distinguish all the army ranks from lance corporal to general. We learnt how to salute our superior officers when we met them: three steps before the salute and three steps after. But I cannot remember that we were ever shown what a Russian, English, or American soldier looked like. Since we were infantry, we were not taught how to recognize an enemy tank either. We 'enjoyed' peacetime Prussian barrack-square drill, quite remote from any experience related to the war. On 20 July, the day when the attempt was made on Hitler's life, there was an alert during the night. The English had allegedly landed in East Frisia, and we marched aimlessly for hours through the area with live ammunition, until the alert was called off. During the following days, the battalion commander was transferred to the eastern front. He had links with the men behind the 20 July plot. From that time on, the military salute was replaced by 'Heil Hitler'. Very little of what had really happened filtered through to us. What we were told was propaganda. Gradually I became skilled in the use of my machine gun—at all events I was the quickest in taking the thing to pieces and putting it together again. That won me a few days' leave and some free hours, which I spent with my mother and my sister Marianne in Delmenhorst.

In August 1944 the middle section of the German eastern front collapsed. In Delmenhorst 50 men of our battalion were suddenly equipped and set on the move, I being one of them. In Siegen, together with some others, we were formed into a new company and were put on the train. It was a wonderful summer. I can still see myself lying on the grass in front of the barracks in Siegen, tracing the movement of the clouds, and later, through the open door of the railway carriage, admiring the peaceful Thuringian landscape in the evening sun. When we got to the old German frontier to Poland, the non-commissioned officers began to get drunk, which seemed to me odd, and not just because, following my father's example, at that time I drank no alcohol. The men probably knew what was ahead of us. At the Lietzmannstadt/Lodcz station our train came to a standstill and remained there for two days. We watched the weapons and tanks belonging to the 'Grossdeutschland' division being loaded. Beside the tough types belonging to this elite unit, we felt like little boys playing at soldiers. But then our train suddenly went back again. We arrived at Siegen once more, and our group was sent back to Delmenhorst. The intention had probably been to send us for training close to the front against the Red army, but after the front had collapsed this no longer seemed a good idea. I probably owe my life to the unknown general who apparently arrived at this insight. Our youthful unit would not have survived at the front for long.

On 17 September 1944 things became serious. The British operation 'Market Garden' began, with parachute landings in Eindhoven and Arnheim. We were now equipped for battle, of course, with the superfluous gas masks as well as with spades and revolvers, which we had never seen before. Then we were sent to the railway station and travelled all day towards the west in cattle trucks. In the evening we were made to get out in Venlo and marched all night as far as Asten—a march of more than 35 kilometres—and met scattered soldiers who were falling back, some of them wounded. In the morning we were spread out along the bank of the Albert Canal, and had to dig ourselves in. In the evening all at once things started. We came under heavy fire, which lasted about two hours. I lay in my dugout—and went to sleep, until I was woken by our corporal shouting, 'Out and back.' Since we couldn't see anything and didn't know anything, we ran after him into a little wood and in complete darkness arrived at the village of Asten. All night long, grenades howled over our heads and rained into the village, and there was the sound of fighting on the bridge. Since there was no longer anyone in command of us, we moved hither and thither individually, trying to find our unit. When we gathered together the next morning, only half the company was still alive. All the men who had lain closer to the bridge than us were dead. Then in the early morning British tanks rumbled up, followed by the 30th Corps of airborne troops. Towards evening we decamped over the dark fields. In a farmhouse someone slaughtered a pig and cooked it. But it still wasn't ready when the British arrived and we made tracks. We heard later that our commanding officer had taken refuge in a cellar in Asten, waiting until he could surrender to the British. This was my first experience of war, and it was repeated later. I was always shot at but never fired a shot myself. And that was all to the good.

From September 1944 until February 1945, we were in South Holland, in the Reichswald Forest and in Cleves, allegedly at the front. But since I had no overview, and never arrived at one, I never knew where we were, and I have only unrelated shreds of remembrance. But the same can probably be said of every ordinary soldier in a war. I can remember various forest positions, and that I once saw an American prisoner, an officer, who had probably got lost. A more considerable battle took place in the region of Venrai. Later I read in a British war report that this was 'the battle of Venrai'. That must have been on the morning when I and some others were hiding in a farmstead and a broad swathe of British tanks advanced towards us; however, they turned off shortly before they reached us, and thundered past. Relieved, I looked through the glass in the open door and saw English soldiers on the other side who probably got as great a shock as I did when they saw us through the reflection in the glass. We ran out the back door, through the pigsty, and were shot at with submachine guns until we took refuge behind a haystack. When night fell, we crept past the occupied village, in front of which the British had set haystacks on fire so as to give them a light. I was then assigned to a reconnaissance troop. We set off at night but found no enemies until we came to an open path. There a Red Cross ambulance had hit a mine. The two British drivers lay beside it, dead. A little farther on, on a small hill, was an English tank which had been knocked out. We crouched down behind it and listened for a while. We were close to the British lines. We all came off unscathed but without discovering anything. It was simply a pointless action during the battle of Venrai.

Our territory beyond the Maas contracted slowly but surely under British pressure. This went on until December. Then we withdrew over the Maas to the other bank. But shortly before that, I once again had the painful experience of losing a companion. Günther Schwiebert and I were sitting in the sun one morning on the edge of a wood. In front of us were some shallow bunkers. Suddenly, out of a clear sky, grenades began to rain down on us, and we made a rush for the bunkers. I reached them, but Günther had only got as far as the entrance when the grenades fell on us. All at once the roof of the bunker above me was open, and a splinter hit the back of Günther's head. I tried to bandage him and pulled him into the wood, but he only screamed and stammered. I finally got him onto a cart and brought him to a dressing station, but he died in my arms. He came from Worpswede and was supposed to take over his father's well-known hotel there one day. Again I came face-to-face with the insistent question, Why him and not me? What am I going on living for?

In January there was a light snowfall. Nothing better occurred to our commanding officers than to send us out on a reconnaissance again, on the other bank of the river, in order to discover which villages were occupied by the British and which were not. One night it was my turn. We put on snowshirts and rubber boots and were led by Fritz Goers. Pioneers put us quietly over the river in their rubber dinghies. Then we walked through the white landscape into the next village. It looked quite peaceful. We searched the first houses but found nothing. As we walked farther along the main road into the village, suddenly a flare went off which had been fastened to a mast. We threw ourselves into the next field and were shot at from the houses until Fritz Goers raised himself a little and called in a loud voice, 'Englishmen, help me; I am wounded.' I don't know whether they understood him or merely heard the sound of English, but at all events the shooting stopped as suddenly as it had begun. Roland Pundt and I crept away and came, very much cast down, to the place where the pioneers were drawn up. I wrote a letter of sympathy to Fritz's parents, for we thought he was dead. But in 1948, in the university canteen in Göttingen, I saw him in the flesh, sitting at another table. The English had picked him up, bandaged him, and taken him to a field hospital. It emerged that he had led us to the wrong village. So this unsuccessful undertaking had a happy end. But the shock of the flare followed me in my dreams for a long time.

However, war is not just made up of a series of extraordinary events of this kind. Its everyday lunacy consists of the fight against dirt, lice, and sickness. From September 1944 until February 1945, I never slept in a bed but only in dugouts, either dug by myself or already made—at best on dry straw. When we were sent reinforcements from the army in the east, they brought lice, and we couldn't get rid of them. German de-lousing stations were helpless and could only provide showers and clean our uniforms. So we sat in the trenches and 'cracked' lice, which proliferated more quickly than we could kill them. The daily orderlies brought us our food, which was typical army grub. The pea soup was the best of it. I suffered from boils on my neck and generally went round with a gauze bandage. The medical orderlies painted my neck with some unidentifiable tincture, but the boils refused to disappear. By candlelight I read whatever I could lay hands on. My sister had given me Goethe's *Faust* to take with me, in a pocket army edition. That was the comfort of another world. I have the yellowing edition still. Otherwise we played cards until we were silly, and wrote longing letters home. At Christmas in 1944 there was plenty of brandy, but, following my father, I strictly refused it, which of course isolated me from the rest. On New Year's Eve the German front put on a kind of fireworks display, but it did not impress the British particularly.

At the beginning of February 1945, British and Canadian troops started the offensive that was to take them into the Ruhr by way of Cleves and the Reichswald Forest. We were alerted and set on the march to Cleves. We passed through the deserted town, arrived at a previously prepared trench, came under heavy fire there, turned back, and were led to a hill with an observation tower where parachutists were already in position. There we came under heavy artillery attack. When the rifle fire came closer, we shot back but couldn't see where we were shooting. In the evening the first heavy British tanks then drove up the hill through our positions and occupied the tower. It became plain that we were shut in. The next morning we congregated in little groups—the officers and most of the parachutists had already decamped without us. So we gathered together and tried to break out. But we only got as far as the broad field in front of the hill, and a cemetery. There we were shot at from all sides. I saw the first of us fall, and others raising their hands in surrender, but together with some others I ran into a nearby semi-ruined house. When the firing became fiercer and fiercer, the rest threw their rifles out of the windows as a sign that they were surrendering. Somehow a devil got into me, and I crawled up to the attic, found a sheet of iron, and hid under it. The firing stopped and the British entered the house, shouting for 'the fucking Germans' (shouting was the general thing during the war). I lay quite still and felt the lice running up and down my spine. When it was dark I tried to escape but only got as far as the already mentioned cemetery, because there was heavy traffic on the road I had to cross. So I crept back, searched the ruined house, and lay down in a room under the roof. Unfortunately, I couldn't find anything to eat or drink. The next day I was able to watch the advance of the British tanks and artillery from the window in the roof as they moved into the Reichswald Forest.

Because I was hungry and thirsty, filthy and covered with lice, it was clear to me that the next night I should either have to succeed in breaking out or have to surrender. So I crossed the cemetery again, and also the road, found myself between abandoned tanks, and moved once more in the direction of the front. On a woodland path I met some British soldiers, threw myself into a hedge, and lost my glasses. Then I ceased to care. I stumbled on through the wood and through British communication lines, where they were all asleep in their tents. I drank snow water out of puddles and finally reached a state of complete exhaustion. While I was looking for a hiding place in a more densely wooded part of the forest, an English soldier suddenly jumped up in front of me. 'I surrender,' I called, as clearly as I could. But he thought I was one of his mates who was playing the fool, and he called some of the others. They came, and we talked. They didn't shoot me, and, more than that, the next morning their lieutenant gave me a mess tin of baked beans. It was the first food I had tasted for days, and I have loved baked beans ever since. Then I was taken to the assembly point where the prisoners were herded together. There some of the British were waiting with DDT sprays in order first of all to free the prisoners from the frightful lice. The poison, sprayed under one's clothes, worked immediately. The lice crawled out at one's neck and sleeves, and in a short time I was free of them.

With this the war was for me at an end. I had survived the anti-aircraft unit, the labour service, and the German army, but now I was a POW, a prisoner of war. It was 15 February 1945.

Partly relieved and partly depressed, we moved into the huge POW camp 2226 in Zedelgem, near Ostend. We had escaped the mass deaths of the war, but for each of us who had escaped there were hundreds of others who had died. It was good to be still alive, but very difficult, in the presence of the dead, to go on living—to live differently—to begin afresh.

We had escaped the inferno, but now we were sitting behind barbed wire and had lost all our hopes. Some people became cynical; others fell ill. Many people were faced with nothing. East Prussia and Silesia were occupied by the Russians, and their inhabitants had fled or been expelled. The men who came from there no longer knew where they could go. They were homeless and saw no way out. Cold despair laid an iron ring round the heart and took away the air we needed to breathe. Each of us tried to conceal his bleeding heart behind an armour of untouchability and indifference. That was the inward imprisonment of the soul which was added to the outward captivity.

My spiritual sustenance had been Goethe's poems, which I had often recited to myself when I was on sentry duty at night. They had awakened the emotions of the boy, but now, locked into the dark huts with 200 other prisoners, they had nothing more to say to me. My dream of mathematics and physics was lost to me too. What was the point of it all? Then there were those sleepless nights when the tormenting memories rose up, and I woke up soaked in sweat—when the faces of the dead appeared and looked at me with their quenched eyes. It was a long time before I found a degree of healing for those memories. In those nights one was alone and, like Jacob at the Brook Jabbok, exposed to the sinister powers and destructive forces of darkness. The one with whom I was struggling, and the one who was struggling with me, only became clear to me later. In the middle of the war, one was driven from one thing to another and had no time to reflect. But in the prisoner of war camp there was nothing to do. One was exposed without any defence to what one had experienced and suffered, and had to 'come to terms with it', if that is, or can be, the proper phrase to describe this mental and spiritual torment.

The Belgian prisoner of war camp was frightful. We sat and slept on three-tier bunks on the bare wood. In the evenings the huge huts were locked, and two buckets were pushed in. Then all too frequently the Nazi terrorism began. Among the prisoners there were Hitler Youth leaders and members of the SS who beat up anyone who threw doubt on 'final victory', or made critical remarks about Hitler and the Nazi party, or didn't believe in the 'wonder weapon' that was soon going to save us. I can still hear the screams of their victims echoing through the huts. The engineer from Augsburg, an older man, with whom I shared a bunk in the second storey, held me down, because he knew my feelings. I got to the point when I wanted to give up. My boils spread over my whole body and I did nothing about it, until that engineer forcibly dragged me to the medical orderlies, and they sent me immediately to a hospital in Ostend. There I was able to have a bath, got fresh underclothes, slept in a proper bed, and was sent back healed two weeks later. I still have the scars to keep me from forgetting that time.

The end of the war on 8 May 1945 meant the end of the Nazi nightmare. But the Red Cross declared that since there was no longer a German state, they were no longer responsible for us. Our rations were then drastically cut, and the English porridge in the mornings, which we had gradually got used to, was watered down. Occasionally a few people were taken out to work. I remember a sunny May day. We were pushing a goods truck, and suddenly I stood in front of a blossoming cherry tree. I almost fainted with the joy of it. After a long period of blindness without any interest, I saw colours again and sensed life in myself once more. Life began to blossom afresh. In the summer of 1945, consignments of prisoners occasionally went home, but I was not among them. I joined a choir, tried to sing the second part (or at least pretended to do so), and learnt to appreciate a lot of German folk songs which earlier on I should have rather despised. I heard music again and was no longer deaf. I can't remember any other activities in that camp. Most of the prisoners led a bored existence from one day to the next, and waited.

In August 1945 my name was called, and I was assigned to a transport. We were taken to a landing craft in Ostend and thought that now we were being taken to Bremerhafen or Hamburg. In the morning we were allowed to go on deck, and lo and behold, opening up in front of us we saw the Tower Bridge in London. In Hampton Park we were again searched for watches and valuables, and then travelled north for 24 hours, finding ourselves once more in a camp, this time on the Ayrshire coast of Scotland. During the years immediately following, Camp 22 in Kilmarnock was to be if not precisely my home at least the place where I stayed. Here only 20 of us shared a Nissen hut, and we had beds with straw palliasses, and an iron stove in the middle of the hut for heating. It was a well-equipped camp, with a sports ground, a prisoners' orchestra, a canteen, a chapel, a library, and so forth. There was also an attempt to set up some kind of instruction. We often sat in a circle round the Catholic professor of philosophy Meunier, and tried out sequences of ideas with Aristotle and Aquinas.

As a way of getting out of the camp, I volunteered for every kind of work that was called for. I was especially successful as an electrician in a NAAFI camp. I only had to follow a skilled workman and move electric light cables or mend electric irons. In the camp I had a friend who stored away tins from damaged boxes. In the mornings I fetched corned beef and tinned sardines from him and ate them in a lavatory. So I began to regain my strength. I went along as carpenter to Dumfries House and cleaned a parquet floor with glass fragments. I dug out coal from a mine, too, and stood in the dust of a cement factory. After a time, the people in charge probably saw through me, and I was assigned to a working group for New Cumnock. Behind a mining village, we dug trenches and laid the sewage pipes for a new housing estate. The ground was slightly frozen, and it was hard work. Another group laid and asphalted the roads. Because we were all always hungry, every day I had to persuade our Scottish and Irish overseers to buy us bread. This led to my later being made interpreter for the group. I no longer needed to work and soon became the middleman between some prisoners in the camp who were making toys, and the Scottish families who wanted to do them a good turn and buy what they made. So I made friendly contact with the Scottish families. I became a favourite with a family by the name of Steele. They called me Goerrie. When one day I appeared with a running nose, because I had no handkerchief, Mrs Steele came with a brand-new packet of handkerchiefs and gave them to me. She also sent uncensored letters for me to Hamburg. I corresponded with Mother Steele for a long time. The Scottish overseers and their families were the first who came to meet us, their former enemies, with a hospitality that profoundly shamed us. We heard no reproaches, we were not blamed, we experienced a simple and warm common humanity which made it possible for us to live with the past of our own people, without repressing it and without growing callous. True, we had numbers on our backs and prisoners' patches on our trousers, but we felt accepted as people. This humanity in far-off Scotland made human beings of us once more. We were able to laugh again.

In March 1945 my mother was officially told that I was 'missing', which usually meant 'dead'. It was only in August that someone came to see her and told her that he had seen me in the Belgian prisoner of war camp. I think it was in September 1945 that we were allowed for the first time to send home a postcard of 25 words. Then I, too, got my first letter, and knew that my family had survived the end of the war and that my father had been taken prisoner by the French. We were far apart, but at least we had news of each other.

In September 1945 we were confronted in the camp with pictures of the Belsen and Buchenwald concentration camps. They were pinned up in the huts, with laconic commentaries. Some people thought it was just propaganda. Others set the gruesome piles of dead bodies over against the destruction of German cities. But slowly and inexorably the truth seeped into our consciousness, and we saw ourselves through the eyes of the Nazi victims. Was this what we had fought for? Was my generation the last of many to have been driven to death so that the concentration camp murderers could go on killing and so that Hitler could live for a few months longer? Some people were so appalled that they didn't want to go back to that murderous Germany. Later they stayed on in England. For me, every patriotic feeling for Germany—'holy Fatherland'—collapsed and died. It was only when my father's Jewish friend Fritz Valentin returned to Hamburg from his English exile at the end of 1945—he was president of the regional court, a convinced Christian, and later founder of the Protestant Academy in Hamburg—that my father in his French captivity and I in my English one felt in duty bound to return to this land of contradictions, where cities such as Weimar are linked with the names of Goethe—and Buchenwald. Depression over the wartime destruction and a captivity with no end in sight was compounded by a feeling of profound shame at having to share in shouldering the disgrace of one's own people. That really choked one, and the weight of it has never left me to the present day.

For me, two experiences raised me from depression to a new hope in life: the friendly encounter with those Scottish working men and their families, and a Bible. One day a well-meaning army chaplain came to our camp and after a brief address distributed Bibles. Some of us would certainly rather have had a few cigarettes. I read the book in the evenings without much understanding until I came upon the psalms of lament in the Old Testament. Psalm 39 caught my attention particularly:

> I am dumb and must eat up my suffering within myself.
> My life is as nothing before thee [Luther's version].
> Hear my prayer, O Lord, and give ear to my cry.
> Hold not thou thy peace at my tears,
> for I am a stranger with thee, and a sojourner, as all my fathers were.

That was an echo from my own soul, and it called that soul to God. I didn't experience any sudden illumination, but I came back to these words every evening. Then I read Mark's Gospel as a whole and came to the story of the passion; when I heard Jesus' death cry, 'My God, why have you forsaken me?' I felt growing within me the conviction: this is someone who understands you completely, who is with you in your cry to God and has felt the same forsakenness you are living in now. I began to understand the assailed, forsaken Christ because I knew that he understood me. The divine brother in need, the companion on the way, who goes with you through this 'valley of the shadow of death', the fellow-sufferer who carries you, with your suffering. I summoned up the courage to live again, and I was slowly but surely seized by a great hope for the resurrection into God's 'wide space where there is no more cramping'. This perception of Christ did not come all of a sudden and overnight, either, but it became more and more important for me, and I read the story of the passion again and again, for preference in the Gospel of Mark.

This early companionship with Jesus, the brother in suffering and the companion on the road to the land of freedom, has never left me ever since, and I became more and more assured of it. I have never decided for Christ once and for all, as is often demanded of us. I have decided again and again in specific terms for the discipleship of Christ when situations were serious and it was necessary. But right down to the present day, after almost 60 years, I am certain that then, in 1945, and there, in the Scottish prisoner of war camp, in the dark pit of my soul, Jesus sought me and found me. 'He came to seek that which was lost,' and so he came to me when I was lost.

There is a medieval picture which shows Christ descending into hell and opening the gate for someone who points to himself as if he were saying, 'And are you coming to me?' That is how I have always felt. Jesus' God-forsakenness on the cross showed me where God is present—where he was in my experiences of death, and where he is going to be in whatever comes. Whenever I read the Bible again with the searching eyes of the God-forsaken prisoner I was, I am always assured of its divine truth.

In the spring of 1946 I realized that for me the captivity was going to last longer than I had thought. Anyone who could somehow or other prove, through whatever kind of scars, that he was unable to work was repatriated. I once tried it myself, giving myself palpitations through an immoderate amount of coffee, but I had no success. I was too young and too capable of working, and I was probably intended to stay on. After my experiences with the friendly Scottish people, and with the consolation of the Bible, to be released was also not so important for me as for some of the others. So I applied to be sent to an educational camp in which 'baby prisoners' could repeat their messed-up Abitur, the final school-leaving examination, which was required for the university. This possibility really did exist in the British camp culture. I passed an English language test, and on 25 June 1946, guarded by a soldier with a rifle, I was put on the train and travelled in a special compartment through sunny and oh-so-peaceful central England to Camp 174 in Cuckney, near Mansfield in Nottinghamshire. Romantically situated in the park belonging to the Duke of Portland, it was an educational camp, intended to train teachers and Protestant pastors for post-war Germany, and it was set up by the British YMCA and financed by the American businessman John Barwick. Norton Camp was England's generous gift to German prisoners of war.

At the entrance I was greeted by some high-ranking German army chaplains, the like of whom I had never seen at the front and never knew existed. But I was soon assigned to the Abitur course, which was run by German teachers among the prisoners, and was recognized by the Hamburg school authorities. The camp was divided into two: on the left were students training to be teachers, on the right the theology students, and in the middle those whose aim was the Abitur. The Nissen huts stood under tall oak trees and were grouped round a hill on which the camp chapel stood. The parade ground was beyond the sports ground, and so were the taller Nissen huts used for lectures and teaching and for meals. Outside the camp was the YMCA central office responsible for the mental and spiritual welfare of all the camps in Great Britain.

For us, Norton Camp was a kind of enclosed monastic existence, 'excluded from time and world', as my friend Gerhard Noller wrote in his farewell letter.[1] The day began at 6.30 a.m. with a bugle reveille and ended at 10.30 p.m., when the lights were put out. All at once we had time, plenty of time, and stood, completely intellectually famished as we were, in front of a wonderful library put together by the YMCA. At that time I read everything I could lay hands on—Rilke's poems and the novels of Thomas Mann and Hermann Hesse, mathematics and philosophy, and any amount of theology, and that literally from morning to night. For me everything was fabulously new, the theology especially. The YMCA also printed books as part of their prisoners' aid programme, and I still possess A. Nygren's *Eros und Agape* and Dietrich Bonhoeffer's *Nachfolge* (*The Cost of Discipleship*). My first theological book was Reinhard Niebuhr's *The Nature and Destiny of Man*, which impressed me deeply although I hardly understood it. Intellectual worlds that had been forbidden to us now opened up. We read emigré literature, as well as the new English and American novels.

At the end of 1946 I passed the supplementary Abitur examination and now counted as a student. I listened to lectures on the educational side as well as in the camp's theological school, and in 1947 I decided not to become a teacher like my forefathers, but a pastor. I became the first 'black sheep' in my 'Enlightened' Hamburg family. The curriculum was extensive, but then, we wanted to listen to everything. I learnt Hebrew under Dr Dammann and Gerhard Noller. Gerhard Friedrich, later professor of New Testament in Erlangen, introduced us to his field. Anders Nygren from Uppsala stayed in the camp for two weeks and taught systematic theology. Professor Soe from Copenhagen gave us an introduction to Christian ethics. Fritz Blanke from Zurich expounded selected chapters of church history. Werner Milch, later Germanist in Marburg, offered a fascinating survey of twentieth-century literature. Matthew Black came from Scotland, Karl Ludwig Schmidt from Basle—and so on. Norton Camp was also a 'show' camp, and so John Mott, Willem Visser't Hooft, and Martin Niemöller, among others, visited us and talked to us.

Not least among my memories are the moving sermons of the camp chaplains Rudolf Halver and Wilhelm Burckert. They were the first sermons of my life, and I could still repeat some of them today. In my mind's eye I can still see the long procession of prisoners on the way to Cuckney's village church, or to the Methodist church where the minister was Frank Baker, whom I later met again at Duke University, Durham, North Carolina.

At night we sometimes crawled through a hole in the fence in order to fetch wood from the Duke of Portland's park for the iron stove that stood in the middle of the hut. How much time we had for night-time talks in the glow of the stove, long after the lights had been put out! I have never again lived so intensive an intellectual life as I did in Norton Camp. We received what we had not deserved, and lived from a spiritual abundance we had not expected.

In the camp, I often walked along the fence in the evening and looked up to the chapel on the hill. I felt I could echo Rilke's *Stundenbuch*: 'I circle round God, the age-old tower ...' I was still searching, but I sensed that God was drawing me and that I should not be seeking him unless he had already found me. On 15 August 1946 I wrote to my family, 'I end most days in a curious way. In our camp there is a hill covered with huge old trees. It is really the centre of camp life, for there is a little chapel on it where we meet for evening prayers, so as to end the day with a hymn and collect our thoughts for new life ... Perhaps we ought to see this whole imprisonment as a great church-going ...' We loved this little church. It cast a unique spell over us. But when I told my father that I had decided to become a theologian, he reacted oddly: he wrote that I should 'not forget to pass on the family'. He evidently thought that his effete son wanted to become a Catholic and monk. But I never had any tendencies towards celibacy. Later, after his initial scepticism, my father accompanied my career with interest and sympathy, and after his death left me his 'religious testament' in which he rendered me an account of what he could believe and what not. It has accompanied me ever since.

A special event which completely turned my life upside down was the first international SCM conference after the war, which was held in Swanwick, Derbyshire, in the summer of 1947. A group of POWs were invited to attend, I being one of them. We came still wearing our wartime uniforms, and we came in fear and trembling. What were we to say about the wartime horrors and the mass murders in the concentration camps? But we were welcomed as brothers in Christ and could eat and drink, pray and sing together with young Christians who had come from all over the world, even from Australia and New Zealand. To be accepted like that was for us a wonderful experience. Students had come from Berlin too. Dorothee Schleicher, a niece of Dietrich Bonhoeffer, told us about the resistance against Hitler and talked about the ruined city. The one-armed Lord Henderson gave lectures, and all at once I perceived that the Christian faith is a great reconciling force, which sets standards even in the world of politics. 'In Christ there is no East or West …' We enjoyed singing the English and American hymns, because they gave us fresh courage.

Then a group of Dutch students came and said that they wished to speak to us officially. I was frightened at the prospect of meeting them, because after all I had been at the front in Holland, during the fighting for the bridge in Arnheim. The Dutch students told us that Christ was the bridge on which they were coming to meet us, and that without Christ they would not have been able to speak a word to us. They told us about the Gestapo terror in their country, about the killing of their Jewish friends, and about the destruction of their homes. But we, too, could step on this bridge which Christ had built from them to us, even if only hesitantly at first, could confess the guilt of our people and ask for reconciliation. At the end we all embraced. For me that was an hour of liberation. I could breathe freely again and felt like a human being once more, and I returned to the camp with new courage. The question of how long the captivity was going to last no longer bothered me.

In April 1948 I came home with the last but one transport from Norton Camp, travelling via Harwich, Hook of Holland, and Munsterlager; I was discharged on 19 April. I had spent more than five years in barracks, camps, dugouts, and bunkers, but I had experienced something that was to determine my whole life. For that reason this time is for me so important that I would not have missed a day of it.

I have often rediscovered my own little life history during those years in the great story of Jacob's struggle with the angel of God at the Brook Jabbok, the story told in Genesis 32.[2] What looked at the beginning like a grim fate became an undeserved blessing. It began in the darkness of war, and when I came to Norton Camp, for me the sun rose. We all came there with severely wounded souls, and when we went away, 'my soul was healed'. I suffered under 'the hidden face of God', which the Jews call *hester panim,* for that is also 'the dark night of the soul' that the mystics talk about. And

I sensed 'the light of God's countenance' when it became light in my life. I felt the warmth of his great love as my senses awoke and I could love life again. I experienced this turn from the hidden face of God to his shining countenance in the nearness of Jesus, the brother in need and the leader of resurrection into true life.

When we, the survivors, returned to England again in 1995 after 50 years—this time of our own free will—we saw the old places again. The huts had disappeared, but the great trees remained and nature had taken over what for us was once so precious. We thought of the people who at that time came to meet us with so much readiness for forgiveness and such hospitality. We shall never forget Pastor Birger Forell from Sweden and John Barwick from America. We have warm and lasting ties with the YMCA and the British Student Christian Movement, which organized that generous 'prisoners-of-war aid'. I closed my sermon on that occasion with Psalm 30, the psalm of thanksgiving:

> Thou hast turned for me my mourning into dancing;
> thou hast loosed my sackcloth and girded me with gladness,
> that my soul may praise thee and not be silent.
> O Lord my God, I will give thanks to thee for ever.

The camp's old commanding officer, Major Broughton, said the same thing, somewhat more dryly. 'I never heard before that prisoners returned of their own free will to the place where they were imprisoned, and thanked God for what they had experienced there.' But that was just what we did.

part II

APPRENTICESHIP

FOUR

THEOLOGY STUDENT IN GÖTTINGEN, 1948–52

In April 1948 I came home, but it was no longer the home I knew. The house had been damaged by a bomb in the autumn of 1944, and three of its seven rooms were occupied by a refugee family from East Prussia. My father had returned from his French imprisonment in 1946 and was again working as a teacher. My younger brother, Eckart, and my younger sister Elisabeth were growing up. However, in the evenings we camped in the four remaining rooms, two of us together, and I found a little working space at the stove. But I enjoyed the new freedom of movement and wandered around, one night even getting as far as the Baltic. I explored the spacious world of the mind, read Heidegger's *Sein und Zeit* (*Being and Time*), Greek tragedies, and the new American and French literature which the publisher Rowohlt was bringing out in newspaper format for only 1 Reichsmark.

In Hamburg there were theological lectures as a preliminary step to a faculty. Those interested met in the church hall of the Johanniskirche and attended lectures held by Hamburg's chief pastors in their own churches. Every two weeks Professor Karl Ludwig Schmidt came from Kiel and taught church history. It was an odd collection. Pastor Echternach was so Lutheran that he even considered Luther's translation of the Bible to be verbally inspired. Herntrich, who was a member of the Consistory, came only when he could spare the time from church politics, and was generally unprepared. A Dr Mülbe led the bunch, and wandered round with his dog; otherwise he knew nothing. Norton Camp had accustomed me to more quality.

However, there was one ray of light, and that was Pastor Hellmut Traub.[1] He was a radical Barthian and from 1932 onwards had studied the first two volumes of Barth's *Church Dogmatics* in Bonn under Barth himself. Later, in Berlin, with the Confessing Church, he stood up for people who were being persecuted, and suffered for it in a concentration camp. Traub preached in Volksdorf so 'vertically from above' that in his receptivity for the Word of God he always ended up in stammerings and pleadings, and seemed to me like an Alyosha Karamazov. He collected theology students round himself in his apartment, where I also got to know his admirable wife, Änne, one of the first generation of female theologians. Traub gave a seminar titled 'Sanctification in Luther, Calvin, and in Pietism' and studied the original texts with us. I enjoyed working with him. For the winter semester of 1948–49 he gave me an introduction to his friend Ernst Wolf in Göttingen, who helped me to a place there.

My main work in that first summer in freedom, however, was to prepare for the required examination in Greek. My classically educated father took me in hand with touching assiduity, and after a few months brought me to the point when I was able to pass the exam. In return, I was supposed to coach my brother in mathematics, in which I was less successful. In the autumn I worked for a small hourly wage for the electrical firm Philips. Then, at the end of October, I was at long last able to pack my case and my kit bag and move to Göttingen. My father impressed on me that he himself had only spent six semesters (i.e., three years) at the university and that he was therefore not prepared to grant me any more. He allowed me 100 Reichsmarks a month, which left him hardly anything for himself, since one of my sisters was beginning at the university at the same time.

In 1948 Göttingen was overflowing with refugees, with people who had been expelled from what was formerly East Germany, and with students, and the housing shortage was a constricting hindrance for everyone. For the first two weeks I found refuge in the superintendent's attic,[2] and then Ernst Wolf (at that time director of the seminary) allowed my friend Reinhardt Dobbert and me to spend the nights in a former cloakroom in the cellar of the seminary building. There we lay in the evenings on camp beds and—existentialists as we at that time wanted to be—wondered on which of the cloakroom hooks we should hang ourselves. In order to make my money last out, I confined myself to what was provided by the Hoover food plan. The sweet soup was available in the morning until 11.00 a.m. and in the afternoon from 3.00 onwards, and cost 30 pfennig. But as compensation, in the theological faculty a new world opened up for me. We had to pay tuition fees (10 Reichsmarks a lecture, 5 Reichsmarks a seminar), but I enrolled for as much as I could: four hours on Genesis with Gerhard von Rad; four hours on church history with Ernst Wolf; four hours on the Synoptic Gospels with Günter Bornkamm; and in addition two hours with Hans Joachim Iwand on Luther's early Latin writings, as well as with Ernst Wolf on the so-called Apologetic Fathers. Apart from that, I heard whatever was on offer. Nicolai Hartmann strutted about with a silver knobbed stick like a king, and held forth without notes. Helmut Plessner gave an introduction to his phenomenology. In public discussions in the university canteen, former officers disputed with Martin Niemöller; while there were passionate evening discussions in Ernst Wolf's home, it might be on infant baptism (which Barth had rejected) or the right to resistance and the use of violence, which a Dutch theologian maintained. In addition, the Deutsches Theater under Hilbert opened, and at 11.00 at night there were French and Italian films. So who cared about his rumbling stomach?

My first theological experience was Hans-Joachim Iwand.[3] No one else could so communicate theological passion through his whole person. In the winter of 1948/49 he presented to us the young Luther. There were still occasionally electricity cuts, so we came to the lectures with little home-made candles (called Hindenburg lights), while Iwand brought two candlesticks. Of course he was unable to read his manuscript, but he identified himself so closely with the young Luther that he seemed to us like a Luther *redivivus*, Luther revived. We had the impression that Luther must have been just such a hothead—no, that this was Luther himself. After the lecture Iwand was so carried away by the spirit of what had moved him that he could say in complete self-forgetfulness: 'Wasn't that splendid?' I attended all his lectures, sat in all his seminars, listened to his sermons, and soon became his 'disciple'. Inspired by him, a small group of us studied Luther's Heidelberg Disputation of 1518. Luther's theology of the cross, as it was embodied in Iwand, touched us profoundly, war-wounded as we were in soul and body. It was in his spirit that in 1972 I wrote *The Crucified*

God. Iwand's doctrine of justification went right to our hearts, godless and God-forsaken as we felt after our wartime experiences.

Iwand gathered together a group of students in his house, his wife made coffee, and we listened to his stories about the struggle of the Confessing Church in East Prussia, where he had headed the illegal preachers' seminary, as well as tales about the misery of people expelled from East Prussia, for whom he organized a 'house of helping hands' near Helmstedt. Then we went for walks with him, on the Hainberg or to Nikolausberg, and listened to his prophecies, which often began: 'I see the time coming …' And when in the evening we looked down on the little lights of Göttingen, he might say, 'There sit the people who put hard work in place of the spirit.'

Iwand's pet aversion was Friedrich Gogarten, who had switched over from dialectical theology to the conservative revolution and had distanced himself from the Confessing Church out of enmity towards Barth. Gogarten especially attracted to himself former officers and also, oddly enough, Dorothee Sölle. Gogarten liked the clever young student. He smoked pipes with her and gave her one as a farewell present. She was probably attracted by his liberalism, but he would have turned in his grave if he had known how she was later to develop. I attended Gogarten's class on homiletics in 1950–51 and put him down as a cynic. If Iwand and Gogarten held seminars at the same time, they passed each other without a word, or with a snort of indignation—and we 'disciples' of course did the same, or went one better. For Iwand, I wrote a paper on Kierkegaard's paradox and Luther's *Deus absconditus* which was so obscurely profound that he probably never read it right through, but after a year gave me a good mark for it.

Iwand was continually on his travels in the interests of politics and church politics. The point at issue was the legacy of the Confessing Church in the developing Evangelical church in Germany (EKD), as well as reconciliation with the peoples of Eastern Europe. His appearance on the scene in Prague and Moscow opened doors that untill then had been firmly closed. He himself was like a message of reconciliation in person, convincing and irresistible. Of course, his teaching suffered from these activities. Often only the first five or six lectures were well prepared, and brilliance did not always make up for lack of diligence. He invested his splendid theological achievement in his Göttingen sermon meditations, which were collected and published in 1963.[4] Even today they are a treasure trove of profound theological insights and pioneering vision. When his beloved wife died in 1950, it was good that he received an invitation to Bonn and could make a new beginning there in 1952. I personally owe Iwand a great deal. He must have put my name forward for a place in the Academische Burse (or hostel) in the summer of 1949, and he nominated me when Danish students invited Germans who were not Nazis to Copenhagen. Iwand also suggested Elisabeth Wendel in this connection, and that was how I first met her in Copenhagen.

Joachim Jeremias impressed us with the picture of 'the historical Jesus' which he painted for us in his lectures, with high spots when he let us hear 'the very voice of Jesus himself'. He was a faithful church elder in St Albani and took up the collection at the services there.

Günter Bornkamm lectured in the St Albani church hall. Highly educated, over and beyond his New Testament exegesis, he interpreted Matthew's Gospel with the help of Johann Sebastian Bach and confronted Jesus' God-forsakenness on the cross with Jean Paul's *Rede des toten Christus vom Weltgebäude herab, dass kein Gott sei* (Speech of the dead Christ from the cosmos, saying that there is no God).

I mention Jeremias and Bornkamm because neither close ties with the church nor a broader education are firm components of academic theology any more.

At the beginning of the summer of 1949, I slept on a sofa in the sitting room of a private house, but in July I was given a place in the Akademische Burse, or students' hostel. 'A room of one's own', a community of students, and an open and always stimulating atmosphere: in Göttingen that was paradise. Erich Boehringer, formerly a cultural attaché at the Athens embassy and otherwise an archaeologist, had started the Burse with great competence and flair, and even had it built out of natural stone. The square building with its inside court looked like a monastery, and so we liked to call Boehringer our 'Abbot', which he very much enjoyed. He was not just a disciple of Stefan George; he was the very figure of the young, front-line volunteer of the First World War, whom George had reverenced and celebrated in his poetry. Although Boehringer had a selection committee, he mainly chose for himself, because he wanted 'not average people, but interesting young personalities belonging to all faculties'. Among the first chosen were

Horst Ehmke, Heinrich Popitz, Hans-Paul Bahrdt, Günter Stratenwerth, Wilhelm Hennis, Theodor Fliedner, and Kurt Gottstein. There were as yet no women. We addressed each other formally as 'Mr', because we had all had enough of the forced camaraderie of army days. We felt that we were a kind of college of democracy, and an alternative to the student associations or fraternities, which were unfortunately coming to the fore again.[5] There was a debating society and a profusion of spontaneous discussions, summer and winter festivities, and a wine cellar where everyone wrote down what he took and there was never a deficit. We wrote our dissertations and, committing a breach of the peace, protested against the films of the Nazi producer Veit Harlan. When the old, and oldest, members of the Burse met there again in May 2003, I sensed how deeply they had put their impress on me between 1949 and 1952, and my love for the old walls reawakened.

In the autumn of 1949 came the invitation to Copenhagen sent by the Danish student society. Its head, Hans Thyssen, became our friend. It was an exceedingly generous approach to the German post-war generation. We came from Göttingen and Erlangen and were put up in private houses for four weeks. For me it was the first journey abroad after the war, and it proved to be decisive for the rest of my life: for in Elisabeth Wendel I found the love of my life. She was also studying theology in Göttingen, but we had never met. It began in the main station in Hamburg. We went up the steps, and I wondered whether I should carry her case. After I had taken two steps, I decided to do so and have never regretted it. In Copenhagen we were met by a fantastic sea of lights, with neon signs flashing the latest news in the town hall square. We had never seen anything like it in Germany's ruined, darkened cities, with their electricity cuts. I stayed with Copenhagen's cigarillo-smoking female chief of police. Every morning we met in the student house Varov next to the town hall and were fed with good milk and smørebrød. We eagerly discussed the war, war guilt, and resistance, and sang a lot as well. With the Danish students we cycled through the countryside; saw castles, old churches, huge parsonages, and breweries; and came to appreciate the placid, level-headed, occasionally somewhat stolid but always worldly-wise Danish way of life. The only Danish theologian we Germans had heard of was Kierkegaard. But the Danish theological students were without exception Grundtvig enthusiasts and thought little of our absurd hero of the paradox. Their hymnbook, their movement for the people's education, their national religion, and their national church all took their stamp from Grundtvig. When we saw the national flag, the Danebrog, standing behind the altar in the Grundtvigskirche, we were shocked and thought of German nationalist religion in the Kaiser's time and of the 'German Christians', who were no more to be seen once the war had ended. 'The Danes are still in a state of national innocence,' Heinrich Vogel explained to me later in Berlin. That was no longer true for us Germans, but for that very reason we were also unable to criticize the link between church and nation in Demark. For a week we were distributed among different schools for people's education, and there I learnt a little Danish so that I could get along.

There was a particular tram which Elisabeth and I always took together, and before we separated at the terminus we often bought ourselves chocolate-covered marshmallows, which were called 'negro kisses'; but beyond that, our shyness did not take us. My liking for her grew slowly but steadily. I was personally reserved and admired her political theology, which was radically democratic and pretty far left, envied her for her background in the Confessing Church, listened astonished to her Barthian shibboleth 'the immanent Trinity', in the light of which theologians were weighed and for the most part found wanting. Luckily I found grace in her eyes. She was working on a dissertation on a certain Hermann Friedrich Kohlbrügge, of whom I had never heard but who was a Barthian before Barth. So she was a doctoral student. We spent a pleasant and amusing return journey from Copenhagen in a compartment with Helga Meyer and Wolfgang Jakobeit, both folklorists studying with Peuckert in Göttingen. When we were back in Göttingen, Elisabeth and I met more and more frequently, either in my room in the Burse or in hers in the Theaterstrasse, which, however, could only be reached through the kitchen of the landlord and landlady. I once bought two coffee cups, which later seemed to us like the beginning of a shared home.

When the winter semester of 1949–50 began, I summoned up my courage and went first thing to Elisabeth's supervisor, Otto Weber. At the end of a lecture, on the square in front of the Albani church, I asked him whether he could give me a subject for a thesis. He looked at me briefly, because he hardly knew me, and said somewhat condescendingly, 'You might look at Moyse Amyrut.' I had never heard the name, but it turned out to be a piece of scholarly luck for me. I read up what the lexica had to say about this Huguenot theologian, who belonged to the theological school of Saumur, in the south of France, and who as a seventeenth-century Calvinist maintained a 'hypothetical universalism' in the doctrine of predestination. In the university library I found almost all his works, which had earlier been collected in Helmstedt University. In addition, I discovered his Saumur predecessor and teacher John Camero, a Scottish Federal theologian. After two weeks' intensive study, I had found an idea to spark off the thesis and went happily to Otto Weber. Having probably meanwhile enquired who I was, he accepted me and found my idea for the subject (which he had given me somewhat mischievously) very good. So I then became a doctoral student, too, in the same stable as Elisabeth. From that time on I attended all Weber's seminars. He advised against his lectures, because they were intended for the rank and file. Instead he invited us to weekly evening discussions in his house. We were permitted to remain until, at ten o'clock, he lit up his horrible black cheroots for the following day and laid them down in front of himself. That was the signal for us to leave.

Otto Weber (1902–66) was an expert teacher.[6] His *Grundlagen der Dogmatik* (1955, 1962)[7] is still a much-used textbook even today because he could present the unity of biblical and systematic theology in every dogmatic tenet. He was at the same time a compelling preacher in Göttingen's Reformed church. From him we learnt the unity in difference between pulpit and rostrum. He had made a name for himself through his introductions to the Bible and through his translation of Calvin's *Institutio*. To us young students he opened up the wealth of Dutch theology. In the summer of 1950 he discussed with us the *Fundamenten en Perspektieven van Belijden*, the new Confession of the Dutch Reformed Church, which he translated. Through him we heard about Abraham Kuyper, Arnold van Ruler, Hendrik Berkhof, Cornelis Heiko Miskotte, and the mysterious Oepke Noordmanns. He threw open to us the world of West European Reformed theology in Holland, France, and Scotland, together with its Swiss origins in Zurich and Geneva. It was he who awakened my early interest in the post-Reformation—and thus also pre-Enlightenment—epoch in theology, and for more than ten years my studies were devoted to this seventeenth-century era, which has been so little explored.

But there was a shadow on Weber's soul and a weight on his conscience. In 1933 he was in the National Socialist Ministry for the Churches, representing the Reformed churches, and was condemned by Karl Barth in his polemic *Theologische Existenz heute* alongside the German Christian theologians. During the Nazi period Weber sat on many committees representing the established Reformed churches and, to put it mildly, shunned the path taken by the Confessing Church. In 1934 he was invited to the chair for Reformed theology in Göttingen. Although he did not have to be 'de-Nazified' in 1945, but was able to participate immediately in the university's new beginning, the mistaken path he had followed during the Nazi period weighed on him greatly. At the church conference in Treysa, he must have made, Karl Barth personally an admission of guilt and must have received his absolution. But he evidently felt constrained to 'make reparation' by writing 'introductions' to the continually growing number of volumes of the *Church Dogmatics*, in order to promote the influence of Barth's theology.[8] Barth was not at all grateful, but called Weber's summaries contemptuously a 'Baedeker to the *Church Dogmatics*'. I well remember Otto Weber's pleasure and excitement when he was invited to Basle for Barth's birthday for the first time, in 1950. We often urged him to follow his *Grundlagen der Dogmatik* with a dogmatics of his own, but he could no longer summon up the courage and preferred to busy himself with establishing the university in Bremen. The first volume of his *Grundlagen* is still completely at the service of Barth, but in the second volume his own ideas also come to the fore. As a result, the great man in Basle thought very highly of the first volume, but not of the second. After the Barth worship, which I had experienced in the three-star constellation Iwand-Wolf-Weber, I thought there could be no more theology after Barth, because he had said everything and said it so well—just as in the nineteenth century it was said that there could be no more philosophy after Hegel. It was only in 1956 that I was freed from this error by the Dutch theologian Arnold van Ruler.

For Elisabeth and me, Otto Weber was not just a supervisor; he was a fatherly friend. He guided providence very effectively with regard to our further careers. He arranged for a position as curate in Westphalia, for an appointment to the Reformed preachers' seminary in Wuppertal, for my first and only pastorate in Bremen-Wasserhorst, and was behind an invitation to teach at the Church Seminary (Kirchliche Hochschule) in Wuppertal. He baptized our first child, Susanne, in Wasserhorst, was her godfather, and took pleasure in the shared life of his 'doctorate children'. He had envisaged that I should succeed him at Göttingen, but he died very suddenly in 1966 when I was already involved in negotiations with Tübingen, and when we would perhaps also have liked to stay in Bonn. A return to Göttingen would have meant returning within the shadow of my great master, and I should always have felt myself to be his incompetent student. This prospect weighed on me so much that I decided for Tübingen, where Ernst Käsemann had fought hard for me. But I have never been able to shake off a certain feeling of guilt at not having taken on the mantle of Otto Weber. He always remained my model, my friend, and my mentor, and whenever I come to a theological standstill, I read his *Grundlagen der Dogmatik*.

Elisabeth and I met more and more often and with more and more pleasure. We walked through the Hainberg, cycled through the countryside, attended seminars and lectures together, and went to films. Slowly my inward imprisonment, which I had hidden behind Kierkegaard's motto 'despairing yet consoled', dissolved. My soul expanded and I became lighthearted again. At the end of February 1950 we exchanged the first kiss and rejoiced in each other. The next morning I had to wake her by throwing snowballs at her window, since she proposed to go to Amsterdam in order to work in the Kohlbrügge archive there. In April 1950 I was then able to stay with my godmother, Elisabeth Spinner, in Horgen near Zurich so that I could read Amyraut writings I still did not know, which were in the Zurich central library. But I also used the time to explore Switzerland by bicycle, and one day even got as far as Lugano. In July 1950 we got engaged, and I travelled for the first time to Potsdam, to Elisabeth's mother, and to Friedland, to her sister Rose and her brother-in-law Gerhard Stappenbeck, who was pastor there. We began to make plans for our joint future in a pastorate in East Germany (the GDR). When I returned to Göttingen, my time was divided almost entirely between Elisabeth and Amyraut. During the next three semesters, my record of attendances at lectures and so forth became increasingly scanty, for I had to use the time for my dissertation; otherwise my doctorate would have come to nothing. My father kept strictly to the limits of his duty to support me.

Apart from Hans Joachim Iwand and Otto Weber, Ernst Wolf (1902–71) had become my most important teacher. His lectures on church and doctrinal history were worked out with scrupulous care and annotated in minute handwriting. They were not just brilliant; they were beautiful too. His quotations were always correct and his knowledge was immense. Wolf was the archetype of the almost universally learned German professor. But he was so self-critical that he himself only brought out two volumes of essays under the title *Peregrinatio,* as well as a book on the Barmen Theological Declaration, *Kirche zwischen Versuchung und Gnade* (Church between Temptation and Grace).[9] He smoked black cigars, drank strong coffee in the evenings, and often worked right through the night. A great deal of his time and energy was invested in theological politics. As early as 1934 he brought out the periodical *Evangelische Theologie*, the periodical of the Confessing Church, which was soon forbidden. He was the founder and president of the Gesellschaft für Evangelische Theologie, at whose annual meetings in 1940 in Alpirsbach Rudolf Bultmann delivered his famous lecture on demythologization.

After the war, Ernst Wolf took up both the periodical and the society again, and we students snatched the first numbers out of one another's hands, for who didn't want to read Iwand's protest 'Wider den Missbrauch des *pro me*' (Against the Missuse of the *pro me*) in the doctrine of justification, or the new Old Testament hermeneutics of the von Rad 'school'? With the publisher Chr. Kaiser Verlag, Wolf published the *Zeitschrift für Kirchenrecht*, the periodical *Verkündigung und Forschung*, research into the history of the struggle with and in the churches during the Third Reich, and a series of books and writings. The *Zeitschrift für Kirchengeschichte* and much else passed through his hands. Like Iwand, he counted as a 'Lutheran Barthian'. Karl Barth greatly admired his learning but was not sparing with critical remarks when Wolf declared the doctrine of justification to be the 'centre' of Reformation theology and not 'Jesus Christ himself' (as if that could be an antithesis!).

I came to Wolf's attention in my first Göttingen semester with a paper on Justin Martyr and his 'apologetic theology'. I sensed his influence like an invisible hand held over my career in Wuppertal, and probably in Bonn too. He published a summary of my work on Amyraut in the *Zeitschrift für Kirchengeschichte*, and my examination thesis on the mystic theology of Gerhard Tersteegen in *Evangelische Theologie*. In the 1950s he co-opted me to the working group of lawyers and theologians (the *Institutionenkommission*) in Heidelberg and published my essay on Bonhoeffer's doctrine of mandates as a special number in his series *Theologische Existenz heute*. He saw my *Theologie der Hoffnung* (1964; ET *Theology of Hope* 1966) as a counter-model on the part of Word of God theology to Pannenberg's

Theologie der Geschichte (1961; ET *Revelation as History*), which, in the context of church politics, he placed in proximity to the 'German theology' of a nationally coloured religious group in the Nazi era. That was unfair towards Pannenberg, but it helped the breakthrough of my theology of hope in West and in East Germany. When Ernst Wolf died in 1971, I took over responsibility for the periodical *Evangelische Theologie*, that being his wish, and later also for the *Gesellschaft für Evangelische Theologie*.

In 1951 I heard Rudolf Bultmann give his lecture 'Formen menschlicher Gemeinschaft' (Forms of Human Community, *Glauben und Verstehen* II, 262–73), in which he rejected social legislation because it deprived the rich of the virtue of giving and the poor of the virtue of gratitude. That put an end to my initial interest in his existential theology. In 1957 Götz Harbsmeier tried to gain Bultmann's support for our campaign 'Fight Atomic Death'. Bultmann refused, because for him faith was 'a private matter' and could have nothing to do with politics. But we had Karl Barth on our side.

The best-known theologian in Göttingen was at one time Emmanuel Hirsch, but of him I saw nothing. Emanuel Hirsch was not just a learned man; he was also 'a man of contradictions'. According to Otto Weber, who knew him very well, he would have liked to lay down his life for the Fatherland in 1914 in the onslaught of the German student regiments in the Langemark in Flanders. But when war broke out, short-sightedness kept him from being accepted as a volunteer. In compensation he liked to tell heroic tales of the First World War. Hirsch was a convinced Lutheran, yet for preference wrote novels about Huguenot refugees in the hilly region round the Weser. Philosophically he was a rationalist, yet possessed the gift of second sight. One morning when Weber met him on the street, he told him sadly that that very morning his son had been killed on the eastern front. Two weeks later a letter brought the confirmation. He was a 'German Christian' and an academic middleman for the Nazis. Otto Weber told us that in 1945, when the Americans marched in, he sat down at the piano and with his family sang the dearly loved national anthem as well as the (Nazi) 'Horst Wessel Song', and then proceeded to have himself prematurely pensioned off. When the 'denazification' then proved to be not as bad as he feared, he tried, for financial reasons, to exchange his pension for the more profitable status of professor emeritus. But the rector of the university, Rudolf Smend, was able to prevent this. It was only after Wolfgang Trillhaas abandoned the tradition of the Confessing Church in 1950 and was converted to liberal (or, as it was also called, 'modern') Christianity that Hirsch was again, through Trillhaas, sent theological students. These then spread his 'theology of Christianity' and tried to write down the Confessing Church as a mere episode in church history. They wanted to go on living as if it were still the nineteenth century, and as if two world wars, two revolutions, and a murderous dictatorship in Germany had also been mere episodes. In their own way, as it seems to me, they spread Hirsch's revenge on Karl Barth.

In September to October 1950 Elisabeth and I were invited to the summer school (Sommermøde) which the Danish student association held in Askov in Jutland, and there we got to know Knud Løgstrup and his German wife. At the end we sailed with a little ship from Arhus to Copenhagen through the Cattegut, a rough sea claiming its victims on the voyage. We were taken in by a dean who was living south of Copenhagen in a huge parsonage where he pursued his studies on the church fathers. We had meanwhile become so much at home in Denmark that later we always spent some time there during the holidays with our children, our favourite place being the island of Møn.

In Göttingen, things were becoming serious for Elisabeth. She handed in her dissertation on Kohlbrügge and prepared for her oral examination. In July 1951 she sat the first theological exam and two days later the oral, that being Otto Weber's idea. Having passed, she became the first *virgo doctissima.* I now counted as 'prince consort', as Walter Zimmerli complacently remarked, and that put me on my metal. In order to bridge the time between her final examination and mine, Elisabeth spent six months helping in the household of Ruth and Karl Lehner in their parsonage in Arisdorf, Switzerland. I handed in my dissertation in the autumn, and as I began to prepare for the exam I was appalled to realize the gaps in my theological education, especially in the exegetical subjects. I was totally ignorant of practical theology, too, because I disliked the people who taught it in Göttingen and thought their theology weak. I also became aware of the religious gaps going back to my childhood. I knew none of the catechisms, was not well versed in the Bible, and when Zimmerli asked me in the oral examination what the fifth commandment was, was unable to tell him. As a result I have been trying all my life to make these weaknesses good, and became an 'eternal student' of theology. A single semester's preparation was very little, especially since there were so many interesting diversions and I did not want to miss anything. In February 1952, following Weber's method, I first took the theological examination, immediately afterwards the oral, and was then completely finished. Even after two weeks I was still so exhausted that I went to sleep in the train, woke up in a siding in Basle, and even left my passport lying.

Although my Amyraut thesis was marked *summa cum laude*, orally I was so weak that I came off well with my overall mark of *magna cum laude* and happily sent off my telegrams. Then I struck my tents in Göttingen and prepared for the wedding. Elisabeth's family was not allowed to travel to the West from the GDR, and my father did not want to enter the 'eastern zone', so we got married on 17 March 1952 in a neutral country, first in the registrar's office in Basle and then in Arisdorf Church. Karl Lehner married us, his daughter Christeli scattered sweets for the village children instead of flowers, and Ruth Lehner gave us a wonderful wedding feast in the parsonage garden, for which my godmother, Elisabeth Spinner, and her son Wilfried also came from Zürich. For our honeymoon we travelled to Lugano by way of Lake Lucerne. Later, we went back there again and again at the end of the winter semester.

FIVE

PASTOR IN WASSERHORST, 1953–58

I was now in possession of a theological doctorate but had still found no home in the German church. And so our odyssey through the different regional churches in Germany began. I had no ties with the Lutheran church in Hamburg. Through Otto Weber I had come to love the Reformed tradition. So I followed Elisabeth into the United Church of Prussia. We wanted to work in Berlin-Brandenburg wherever we were most needed, and that was Oderbruch, which had been completely destroyed in the war. True, Probst Grüber had tried to dissuade Elisabeth from this plan during a visit to Basel, but nevertheless we first moved to West Berlin in order to apply for a permit to East Germany, the German Democratic Republic (the GDR). The church authorities subjected me to an oral examination, and Oberkirchenrat Kegel invited me afterwards to pea soup with wiener. He was satisfied with the examination and, while I was waiting, sent me to the Hubertus Hospital in Schlachtensee. Here the matron, Doris Müller, held the reins, and a converted Catholic priest provided the pastoral care. The very next day he sent me to the women's ward. I stood helplessly outside the door, armed with picture cards with texts in one of my pockets and magazines under my arm. I went into the ward and found 25 women in a huge room. Since my studies had left me completely unprepared for this situation, my pastoral care, apart from the offer of sympathy, left much to be desired. After one had preached, one was invited to the 'pastor's breakfast' of sandwiches with the matron and had to put up with her critical comments. Elisabeth gave religious instruction to the probationers. We had rooms in the hospital, were well looked after, and, full of curiosity, explored Berlin.

There we found a group called the 'Unterwegskreis' (Wayfarers) which we immediately joined. It was a church-critical circle of 'young brethren', illegal theologians from the Confessing Church, and there we met Renate and Eberhard Bethge, Helga and Rudolf Weckerling, Harald Poelchau, Wolf-Dieter Zimmermann and his eternally knitting wife, Franz von Hammerstein, Graf Lynar, and many others whom we found interesting. One day, at Harald Poelchau's suggestion, Emil Fuchs arrived. He was a religious socialist from Leipzig who wanted to enlist me as his assistant. But I could not get a permit for the GDR. However, the suburban train (the S-Bahn) still ran to Potsdam, in East Berlin, and Elisabeth's mother and aunt came repeatedly, bringing china, linen, and so forth, to start our household.

At that time I applied four times for a permit to move to the GDR, but all my applications were turned down, probably because I had been so long a prisoner of war in England, and the East German authorities were afraid of western spies. But providence had our good at heart. In the ruling conditions of the GDR, I should probably soon have got into trouble, or would have collapsed mentally and spiritually. When autumn came, Präses Scharf sent us back to the West, because there was no place for us in Berlin. After the war, the Protestant churches all over Germany were overflowing with clergy who had been expelled from East Prussia and Silesia.

The Westphalian church accepted me for training as curate, and I was sent to the back of beyond, to Erndtebrück in the district of Wittgenstein. I am describing this in some detail in order to give a picture of a curate's training (and lack of it) at that time.

After we had found the place with some difficulty on the map, we travelled through the night with our few possessions via Hamburg to Marburg, and from there with a local train via Laasphe to Erndtebrück. Our arrival was entirely too much for Superintendent Kressel, and he received us somewhat helplessly with the news that he had no apartment for us; he had only found two empty attic rooms, one in number 10, another in number 17. But since we didn't want to be separated, we decided for Number 17, in the house of a Frau Treude. Our young marriage began in wretched conditions. Our room could only be reached via a loft and had to be heated with an iron stove. We fetched water from the kitchen downstairs, and there was a lavatory downstairs in the stairwell. Because our room was so small, we spread out a three-piece mattress for Elisabeth, and for me two pieces, pushed up to the wall. We had one hot plate for cooking, so that we ate the potatoes first of all, and whatever else there was afterwards. When winter came, there were often snowdrifts on the floor of the loft. But we had each other and were happy, and did not feel the lack of comfort unduly.

In Bielefeld I had to pass another oral examination in front of an Oberkirchenrat Randenbourg, and then the superintendent gave me a confirmation class that was too much for him. It consisted of 50 wild boys, but I was not allowed to divide the class. So I prepared resolutely for a twice-weekly battle. Once I had twisted the arm of a notorious nuisance and thrown him out of the door, I won a certain degree of respect. The children liked to call their curate 'Fakir'. But after 50 years, this confirmation class remembered me and asked me to send them a greeting for their 'golden confirmation', which I was touched and pleased to do. I had a forest village to look after in addition, with services and Bible study. In winter the women telephoned and ordered herrings, margarine, sugar, salt, and much else. I packed all this into my rucksack, side by side with the Bible, and skied over the mountains to the village. According to the church records, I must also often have preached in Erndtebrück's large church, but I have no recollection of it. It evidently made no great impression on me.

The first question I was asked everywhere was whether I believed in the devil. The country round Wittgenstein was well known for its superstition, its poltergeists, its sects, and the pietist revival movement. Even in the seventeenth century it was terrorized by the sectarian group of the Butlarsche Rotte. During my time, buses came from Holland bringing people who wanted to see haunted houses. As well as the church with its large congregation there was a hall where those belonging to the revival movement met. When I answered the question about the devil by saying that the triune God is mentioned in the creed but not the devil, but that the creed is directed against the devil, the young curate met with general satisfaction.

Using a little typewriter, I prepared a copy of my Amyraut essay for press, but it was not after all printed in Neukirchen in the *Beiträge zur Geschichte und Lehre der Reformierten Kirche.* Only the already mentioned essay appeared in the *Zeitschrift für Kirchengeschichte.*[1]

Elisabeth and I celebrated our first Christmas together in 1952 in our attic. We decorated it with fir tree branches and were happy. For the Christmas service we skied to the forest village and were warmly welcomed by a teacher couple, who had come to this lonely place from the east. Elisabeth taught in the Erndterück vocational school and later in the fine country women's school in a nearby valley. I had a grant of 150 DM, but Elisabeth earned more and finally bought us a motorbike, a DKW 125, for 750 DM, which carried us to the end of our time in Wasserhorst in 1958. In Siegen we also bought two small armchairs and a triangular table: our first furniture. In Laasphe we met interesting discussion partners—the East Prussian pastor Fischer, from the Confessing Church, and a lively doctor working in the Berleburg hospital.

In January 1953 we then finally found a space where we could live, in the house of Fritz Wunderlich, a railway employee who also headed the revivalist congregation. He distributed revival tracts while working as a guard on the train, and led the Bible study in the community's hall. Elisabeth was allowed to come, but women were only permitted to ask questions. The answers were given solely by the 'brr-ethren'. Fritz Wunderlich and I spent a whole evening in discussion, and at the end he stood up and said, 'Let us say brr-other'. In April 1953 I took a funeral in the forest village. I thought I preached a good sermon on the text 'Who will roll away the stone for us from the door of the tomb?' But the village people afterwards complained to the superintendent: I had mentioned that the woman had died of tuberculosis. Tuberculosis was rife in the village and was hence a taboo.

In the spring we took many walks in the nearby Rothaar Mountains; but then our time there came to an end, for I was admitted to the Reformed Preachers' Seminary in Wuppertal-Elberfeld. On Ascension Day, in an outdoor service, I said goodbye to the first congregation in whose life I had officially shared a little.

In the Reformed Preachers' Seminary lived the tall Udo Smidt, who before 1933 had been secretary general of the Evangelische Jugend Deutschland (German Protestant Youth). There were ten of us candidates, all of us war veterans; for example, a Stuka pilot and an SS officer, as well as soldiers who had come through the war. Professors from the teacher training college and a few elderly clergy, all devoid of our experience, came to teach us practical theology; but after the morning metrical psalms, we preferred to play table tennis, with success: in the doubles, where I was partnered with my friend Johannes Kuhn (later a television pastor), we defeated the

Lutheran Preachers' Seminary. In the streets of Wuppertal we demonstrated with Johannes Rau[2] and Dieter Posser on behalf of Gustav Heinemann's[3] Gesamt-deutsche Volkspartei and 'All Germany', and against Adenauer's restoration policy. After the authorities had thought about it for a while, Elisabeth was allowed to move in with me. But she could only wash after we had hurried off to morning prayers, for there was only one washroom. In the little library I found the works of Johannes Coccejus, a Bremen federal theologian famous in the seventeenth century, and I generally buried myself in this quiet room. I cannot remember acquiring any other knowledge. Elisabeth gave religious instruction in vocational schools, and we occasionally heard good lectures in the 'Bund', a Wuppertal culture group. After six months we were glad that we had got through the time more or less respectably; but where were we to go now?

Advised by Otto Weber, in September 1953 Werner Brölsch, the youth pastor in Bremen, arrived and offered us a pastorate in Bremen-Wasserhorst, coupled with a position as student pastor at the teacher training college. Since we had no choice, we accepted. So I became village pastor in the hinterland of Bremen. For five years we lived in this community on the Wümme dyke, and it was here that our first two children were born. Whenever I thought of 'church' later, wherever I was, it was always this farming community that I saw in my mind's eye. After 48 years I went back again in 2001, so that I could say in a sermon, 'I thank my God in all my remembrance of you' (Phil. 1.3); and on this return visit I met many of my former confirmation candidates again.

At the beginning of October 1953, I drove over the dyke with a little truck, for we didn't have much except for books and the motorbike. Elisabeth came by train, because she was pregnant. At dawn, hundreds of toads crept over the dyke, and we halted respectfully. Then I arrived in the huge, empty parsonage, with its eight rooms. We could do no more than plant our two chairs and little table in front of an iron stove in the corner of one of the front rooms. And so we began. It was an uncanny house. In the cellar huge water rats ran about. They ate all the preserves, leaving only Elisabeth's somewhat unsuccessful raspberry jam, until I banned their entry once and for all with barbed wire. The kitchen and larder were a playground for numerous mice, which we could only get rid of with difficulty and then only for a time. In the huge attic bats hung from the rafters, and owls flew in and out. We had to hold our own among these not always savoury 'fellow creatures'. The house was surrounded by a huge overgrown garden, which was too much for us in the spring with sowing and planting, and in the autumn with its immense fertility. It was regularly flooded by the River Wümme, for the parsonage lay behind a dyke. The little twelfth-century Gothic marshland church stood on a hill, with the family churchyard round it. Opposite us was the single-class village school; its somewhat infrequent gymnastic classes took place in front of the parsonage. The community consisted of 60 farms in Wasserhorst, Wummsiede, and Niederblockland, the houses being strung out like a row of beads, eight miles long, along the Wümme dyke. There were about 500 yards between them—a wise way of avoiding quarrels.

Wasserhorst was from early on a Reformed community with what were at that time firm principles: on Sunday, either the older people went to church and the young ones looked after the cattle, or vice versa. One farmer, who did not come to church regularly, once asked me, 'Pastor, what would you prefer: should I sit on my muckheap and think of the church, or sit in church and think of my muckheap?' I advised him first to do the one, and next time the other. He found that good advice, for he did not particularly like sitting on his muckheap either. On the church pews the arms of the farmers indicated their traditional places, and it was not advisable to sit in one of them. The women sat on one side, the men on the other. The congregation as a whole went to communion twice a year, four communion services being held, on the two Sundays next to Good Friday and on the two next to the Day of Repentance (in November), and it was considered right and proper to be at peace with one's neighbours beforehand. If someone was involved in a quarrel, it was thought better for him or her not to come to communion. One day something happened which fell under church discipline. It was a case of drunken driving in Wasserhorst: a goose had been run over, there had been a disturbance of the peace, and someone had been hurt. I told my elders that I was doubtful whether I should give communion to the two people involved in the dispute. My elders took the matter up and talked to the two men about the forgiveness of wrongdoing, but they were stubborn. However, before the next congregational communion service came round, they thought better of their behaviour, came to the parsonage before the service, wept, and were reconciled; and we then went together to the church and celebrated the Lord's Supper with lighter hearts.

When someone died, the neighbours washed the body, gave the shroud, and read aloud Psalm 90 with the mourners. The body was laid out under the deceased person's own roof. Some commemorative words were spoken, and a long procession to the church was followed by the funeral service, which always included the hymn 'Jerusalem, du hoch-gebaute Stadt ...' (Jerusalem the golden ...). Only after that was the coffin carried round the church by the neighbours and then lowered into the grave. Together with the reception and meal in the deceased person's house, a funeral could easily last a whole day. But on the other hand there were not so many funerals during any one year.

There were two women's groups in the congregation. These met regularly every two weeks, and after cake and conversation the women wanted a story and then devotions. Their great annual trip took them as far as Hamburg. There was also a singing group for girls, with whom I visited everyone over 70. 'Goodness and mercy all my life shall surely follow me,' sang the girls, and then I gave a short address. There was no boys' group when I came, but I soon started one. The high spots of the year were of course Harvest Festival and the celebrations of the various groups, which the pastor was supposed to attend, the only one to which he was not invited being that of the bulls' insemination club.

With my doctorate, I at first felt a fool standing in the pulpit in front of this farming congregation. But earlier I had lived with workers and farmers in 'the hard school of life', and it was out of these experiences that I preached, not from my Göttingen lecture notes. This congregation taught me 'the shared theology of all believers', the theology of the people. Unless academic theology continually turns back to this theology of the people, it becomes abstract and irrelevant. For the fact is that theology is not just something for theological specialists; it is a task laid on the whole people of God, all congregations and every believer. I only got into difficulties when I used the same sermon for the student congregation in Bremen and the farmers in Wasserhorst. The farmers were not interested in questions about the meaning of life and were not going through any adolescent orientation crises. They trusted in God and loved the Ten Commandments. When my elders rolled their eyes, I knew that I had lost them. So they guided me and preached to me.

My own personal theology developed as I went from house to house and visited the sick. If things went well, on Monday I learnt the text for the following Sunday's sermon, took it with me as I visited the congregation, and then knew what I had to say in my sermon. Here a 'hermeneutical circle' developed, not the one between textual interpretation and one's own private interpretation, as in Bultmann, but the one between textual interpretation and the experience of a community of people, in their families, among their neighbours, and in their work. In conversations, in teaching, and in preaching I came to believe that this was a shared theology of believers and doubters, the downcast and the consoled.

Our first winter, 1953–54, was a dramatic one. One night we were wakened by the bright glare of a fire. The oldest, and very beautiful, farmhouse near us burnt down. Only the well was left. Then one evening we heard steps round the house. I picked up a hammer and went out of the door. It was a herd of cows which had gone wild and was trampling through the garden. Soon afterwards, during a spring tide, the Wümme burst its banks, and the parsonage was under water. But the dykes held—at least the Bremen ones, for they were somewhat higher than the dykes in Lower Saxony, on the other side of the river. The fire brigade, all volunteers, came and pumped out our cellar. My own modest contribution was to provide some crates of beer, which kept them all in good spirits. One evening I played cards with some neighbouring farmers—a German game called skat—and won one round after another. They thought there was something uncanny about it and admired me greatly. After that I never played skat again, so as not to tempt fate.

My work as pastor was quite exciting, for I had hardly any practice. Every Sunday I stood at the window, looked over to the church, and asked myself, Will they come or won't they? They did come, regularly, first of all the aged elder Harje Kropp with his snow-white hair and his green coat. The first Christmas, Elisabeth put on a nativity play with the children, which was received with delight. We also introduced a service on Christmas Eve, which there had never been before. On Christmas Day the girls' choir always sang, and the boys filled the church; on Boxing Day the men's choir sang, and the women filled the church. At Easter 1954 I came with my first confirmation candidates and blessed them with a shaking hand (as some of them remember even today), for I was at least as nervous as they were. Then I invited the boys to the house and waited one evening: Would they come or not? For a long time everything was quiet, and then they arrived, with the loud roar of their motorbikes, and the young people filled the church hall. The spell was broken. They had accepted me, and we became part of the village community.

As long as I was a hungry curate, with a small salary, the farmers often came to the door bringing something, if a beast had been slaughtered on their farm. This stopped with a bang once I was ordained and became a salaried pastor. I was ordained in Aurich in 1954 by the Reformed regional superintendent Herrenbrück, two of my elders accompanying me there. The Bremen Protestant church was in a curious position where the Confessions were concerned: it appealed to the confessional writings of the Reformation but did not say which, and at the same time in §1 it guaranteed 'the freedom of every individual congregation in matters of faith, doctrine and conscience'. Consequently, every pastor could choose what he wanted to believe. When I appealed to the Barmen Theological Declaration, the church commission disclaimed competence. So I became 'Reformed'. The chairman of the Bremen church commission installed me, blessed me, and gave me an envelope. I expected a Bible text, but what it contained was my salary statement. That was the true Hanseatic style—not religious but practical.

In the Reformed church it was usual to make annual house visits. I got to know all the families, and had their names and house numbers off by heart. But once I had paid a visit during the forenoon and found only the housewife in the kitchen, it became clear to me that nothing could be done during the morning. I could divide up my days, spending the mornings on my theological work, the afternoons on teaching, and the evenings on visiting. I had to prepare for the second theological exam with a paper on the mystic theology of Gerhard Tersteegens, and Otto Weber passed on to me a goodly number of articles for the *Evangelisches Kirchenlexikon*, which he was editing, so I had plenty to do.

In February 1954 we had a great grief. For some inexplicable reason our first child died at birth. We had looked forward to it with so much love, and its vigorous movements in the womb had made it so much of a living person between us. We walked through Bremen as if distraught. When I told the congregation during the service, we were overwhelmed with a wealth of warm sympathy; it was as if we belonged to the family. Elisabeth then prepared her dissertation for print, and in that way worked off her grief. She was soon pregnant again, and after less than a year, once more in February, Susanne was born, a strong, healthy, and chubby child.

We were immensely happy, a proper family. A year and three quarters later, shortly after Christmas 1956, Anne-Ruth was added to us, strong, healthy, and very pretty. The lonely parsonage was filled with life, and our hearts were warm.

In the spring of 1956 a fresh wind blew through the village, a ray of light in foggy Wasserhorst. The single-class school was taken over by a teacher couple from Berlin. Richard Köhler was an excellent teacher and a much-loved teller of stories. Tamen Köhler came from the Internationaler Sozialistischer Kampfbund (the International Socialist Task Force) and was trying to find her way from socialist atheism to Christian faith. Elisabeth and I soon made friends with them both. Tamen was unable to come to terms with the traditional church, but she loved theological discussions, and when the Telephone Samaritans group was started in Bremen, she at once offered her services. She then came with the questions of people who were seeking help, and sought answers. My successor Wilhelm Gröttrup baptized her. She took over the music in the congregational groups and later joined the movement 'Christians for Socialism'. We kept in touch with them both during their career, and they with us.

At that time about 30 to 40 members belonging to the student congregation in Bremen met one evening a week during the semesters, spent weekends in Haus Hügel in Bremen-Nord, and went on holiday retreats lasting about two weeks either on the North Sea island of Langeoog or at Adlerspoint, near St Johann in Tirol. We also met for Sunday morning worship and for Bible study in various Bremen church halls. The era of nineteenth-century liberalism, as well as the Nazi period, meant that the Bible had become almost unknown in Bremen, and interest in it was great, especially in the Old Testament. Through his personal conviction and his boundless capacity for sympathy, Pastor Karl Kampffmeier of the Liebfrauenkirche, a pastor from the Confessing Church in Silesia, inspired many students to study theology; some of them had first to be baptized before they began. In the ten years after the war, there were as many as 25 and more of these students. Werner Brölsch's lively youth work brought a fresh, reviving wind through this city, which was otherwise religiously so stagnant. The student congregation drew life from the renewal and also contributed to it. Wasserhorst was 15 miles outside Bremen, and it was not always easy for me to get to the city in winter by motorbike. But in summer the students liked to walk out to the Wasserhorst church and to make themselves at home in the huge parsonage garden.

I went to the Adlerspoint mountain hut above St Johann only once, and never again. Elisabeth came with me, more or less willingly. It was a large house in a wonderful position high in the Alps, but to reach it one had to climb for two hours on skis equipped with skins. In February 1956 when we arrived at the top, everything was bathed in sunshine. A couple called Hövelmann took over the practical side of things, so that I was only responsible for the 'spiritual' part. I seem to remember that on this mountain we took as our subject the Sermon on the Mount. One day I led a group down the mountain on an expedition to Zell am See. On our return, when we were nearly at the top, we were overtaken by a terrible snowstorm. It was pitch black; we couldn't see anything and completely lost our bearings. The wind tore the skins off some of the skis, so that their owners could not go any farther. We cowered together, thinking we might perhaps have to dig ourselves into the snow, when suddenly a student loomed up out of the darkness, coming from the hut, which was not too far away, and saved us. I was depressed at having so failed in my responsibility, and the female students thought of our child in Bremen. For me that was the end of my skiing: never again!

Werner Brölsch had just had a house for the Protestant youth of Bremen built on the North Sea island of Langeoog ('Haus Meedland') to which the student congregation went every year at the beginning of October. I also enlisted my friend Johannes Kuhn, at that time pastor in Bremerhaven, for we complemented each other very well.[4] We always invited some students from the GDR, and in 1956 and 1957 a group of theology students from the Language Seminary in East Berlin came as well. Among them I got to know my later Tübingen colleagues Eberhard Jüngel and Hans-Jürgen Hermisson; and Wallmann, later a church historian, was also among them. We sang with the cantor Gebhard Kaiser, played volleyball, walked along the shore, jumped into the cold water, and held theological and other lectures. Jüngel's first lecture was devoted to what was at that time a German hit: 'A man mustn't always be handsome …' It all needed a good deal of preparation every year, but I always had the feeling that it had been worth it. In Langeoog I still felt young enough to jump on a horse and to gallop along the shore. Unfortunately, the brute was incalculable and threw me. I limped away with a swollen ankle—and for me that was the end of the riding I had so much loved in earlier days. One must renounce the things of one's youth gracefully, said Elisabeth. I didn't find it difficult.

During my time in the student congregation in Bremen, two experiences made a profound impression on me: two students committed suicide. The one—Gottfried—was found dead on the bank of the Weser with a rope in his hand. His heart had stopped before he had laid hands on himself. The reason remained a mystery. He had been a cheerful student. For his funeral I found this saying from the book of Job: 'You too he allured out of distress into a broad place where there is no more cramping' (36.16), a verse that has accompanied me ever since. The other, Ivo, suffered from a deep depression which none of us had recognized. He visited us in Wasserhorst in order to take leave of us, although nothing was said. He always lived very quietly for himself, but always came to every holiday retreat in Langeoog. I have never forgotten either of them, although I can no longer remember the names of many others.

Through lecturers at the teacher training college, such as Lily Simon, who always came with a large dog, and Ilse Strecker, who later also worked in the Gesellschaft für Evangelische Theologie, I came into contact with people belonging to the Internationaler Sozialistischer Kampfbund. Bremen was ruled by the SPD, and the SPD was ruled by the ISK, as its inner circle. The people who belonged had, of course, all left the church and declared themselves to be atheists; but after the second glass of wine they always became theological and talked to me about God. This was not the banal consumers' atheism of today; what moved them was the old protest atheism of Ivan Karamazov. Although I remembered Heinrich Böll's bon mot—'I don't like these atheists; they are always talking about God'—as a theologian I felt at home in this group and didn't find it difficult to talk about God to these people who were godless or rebelling against God.

My theological development as a pastor in Wasserhorst initially ran in the peaceful groove of historical studies. Since I was quite contented with Karl Barth and the critical potential of the Confessing Church, I continued my research into theological history between the Reformation and the early Enlightenment. I wrote something about the Huguenot philosopher Petrus Ramus, who was murdered in 1572 in Paris in the St Bartholomew's Day massacre, but whose textbooks were known far and wide throughout Europe.[5] Otto Weber intended me to present him with a post-doctoral thesis in Göttingen, and suggested as subject Christoph Pezel and Bremen's transition to Calvinism.[6] Pezel was a pupil of Melanchthon's and was attacked by the Gnesio-Lutherans as a 'crypto-Calvinist'. He found a refuge in Bremen, where in 1595 he wrote the *Consensus Bremensis* as the Confession of what was later known as the German Reformed tradition. His predecessors at the Bremen grammar school, the illustrious Albert Rizäus Hardenberg and Johannes Molanus, were his theological precursors,[7] and they were more influenced by Dutch and Zurich theology than by Wittenberg. In the Bremen archives I found much material that was new to me, in Detmold I discovered Pezel's papers, and in Dr Jessen I found an interested archivist who helped me. When a city church in Bremerhaven was looking for a pastor, Elisabeth and I seriously considered going there.

I found the way back to contemporary theology in 1956 through my encounter with the Dutch theologian Arnold van Ruler of Utrecht. I met him at a conference of Reformed theologians in East Frisia. He maintained a 'theology of the apostolate' and a theology of Exodus and the kingdom of God.[8] He began his lecture by saying, 'I smell a rose, and smell the kingdom of God.' I had never heard anything like that before, and it was hardly something that would have occurred to Karl Barth. Van Ruler convinced me that Barth had not after all already said everything and, moreover, that he would not have said very well everything that theology has to say today. He put me on the track of the forward hope in eschatology for the kingdom of God and his righteousness on this earth. These were visions which I had also found in Christoph Blumhardt and Leonhard Ragaz. When I wrote my *Theology of Hope* in that spirit and published it in 1964, van Ruler wrote to me that we two were now 'like two hands on a single belly'—a nice Dutch metaphor for friendship! Later we drifted somewhat apart, because he wanted to preserve the state in the kingdom of God, but not the church as God's emergency measure, whereas my negative experiences with the state made me turn rather to the reverse idea: in the kingdom of God I had no wish to see 'any authority and power' any more, and knew that I had Paul on my side (1 Cor. 15.24). Van Ruler looked for 'Christ taking form in the world' and with this idea roused us young theologians out of the stagnation of the post-war era.

At the end of 1956 I finished my work 'Christoph Pezel und der Calvinismus in Bremen' and sent it to Otto Weber. He was satisfied with it and submitted it to the Göttingen faculty as a post-doctoral thesis

(Habilitation). After an examination before Göttingen's great men, the thesis was accepted, and I was 'habilitated' on 27 February 1957 by Joachim Jeremias (who was dean at the time) and was given the official permission to teach (the *venia legendi*). This meant that I had academic work in addition to my work with the congregation and the students in Bremen. On 8 May 1957 I took the train to Gottingen, early enough for me to hold my first lecture at 10.15, ten minutes after the train's arrival. In the afternoon a seminar followed. In the evenings I went home or spent the night in the Burse. I had these teaching commitments every two weeks. The stress was sweetened because every time I treated myself to breakfast in the train. In the winter semester of 1957–58, I continued my lectures on the history of Reformed theology and took as the subject for my seminar, after Luther's Heidelberg disputation, the Confession of the Dutch Reformed Church, *Fundamenten en Perspektieven van Belijden*, which was new at the time. The number who attended was of course small, but not so small that we could only form a quorum with the addition of the Holy Spirit—*tres faciunt collegium* (three form a quorum).

In September 1957 came my last holiday retreat with the students on Langeoog. This time we had invited 25 students from the GDR, the language seminary in East Berlin being well represented under the leadership of the matron 'Miss' Uhl, who came from Bremen. The morning Bible study was devoted to the story of the Exodus according to the book of Exodus, chapter 2. My diary shows that in the evenings there was an extensive cultural programme, from Brecht and Benn on ideal and reality, messianism, law and morality, and finally Martin Buber.

In January 1958 I heard from the Church Seminary (Kirchliche Hochschule) in Wuppertal that they had a vacancy. On 15 January I held two probationary lectures there and was soon accepted, with the invitation: 'You can lecture on what you like.' When I told my farmers that I had received this 'call' to Wuppertal, one of them said, 'Well, Pastor, if you can better yourself …' Fortunately, I quickly found a highly suitable successor in Wilhelm Gröttrup. He himself came from a farm in East Frisia and was by origin Reformed. Many farewell visits followed, some people pouring out their hearts for the first time because they knew that we were leaving. On 14 April we packed, and on 16 April the furniture van arrived in Wuppertal. Hans Walter Wolff was rector, and he had arranged everything splendidly.

A semi-detached house was ready for us, with central heating, refrigerator, and all the urban amenities that we had lacked in Wasserhorst.

For me, a decisive question was what I should teach, and what direction my theological interests should take. I well remember sitting in the market square of Finale Ligure while we were on holiday and putting the choice before Elisabeth: either to offer lectures on Zwingli and his theology (a historical and effortless subject) or to lecture on the history of hope for the kingdom of God. That would be a bridge to systematic theology but would be for me completely virgin territory. Encouraged by Elisabeth, I took up the challenge and threw myself into 'the kingdom of God', not knowing that this theme—the future—would keep me on the move for the rest of my life.

part III

Beginnings

SIX

THE CHURCH SEMINARY IN WUPPERTAL, 1958–64

Theology at the Charge of the Church

Because the Nazis had brought the theological faculties 'into line' and had dismissed opposing theologians such as Paul Tillich and Karl Barth, in 1935 the Confessing Church established two church seminaries of its own in Berlin and Wuppertal in order to be able to train future clergy in an independent institution. Both seminaries were closed by the Gestapo the day they opened. Nevertheless, studies were carried on illegally in private houses. At the end of the war, both seminaries were reopened in order to make it possible to study theology both at state universities and in independent faculties.[1] I still think this double strategy was a wise one, for one never knows from which quarter the freedom of theology may be threatened.

In the spring of 1958 I was invited to Wuppertal at the same time as Rudolf Bohren. Bohren was a student of Eduard Thurneysen's and was a wonderful preacher. He became the head (Ephorus) of the seminary. We soon became good friends and each entered into the joys and sorrows of the other's family and professional life. In Wuppertal Georg Eichholz already held the chair for New Testament, and Hans Walter Wolff was professor of Old Testament, both of them high-ranking scholars. Eichholz was an aesthete through and through. He loved good literature, spoke a polished German, and saw the world through the lens of his camera, which he took with him on his afternoon walks on the 'holy mountain' where the seminary was situated, next to the house belonging to the the Rhenish Mission. It is to Eichholz that we owe the book of photographs entitled

Das Gesicht des Theologen.[2] Hans Walter Wolff lived with his large family in Barmen and was not merely a fabulous scholar but also a great encourager of students plagued by doubts and a consoler of weary colleagues. Erwin Mühlhaupt taught church history. He could always be heard even before he loomed into view, for his voice filled the whole house. A passionate German nationalist, he occasionally made life difficult for me, but as a person he impressed me by the enthusiasm with which he threw himself into playing football against the students. Hermann Schlingensiepen was already very ill, so that one saw little of him. When the teaching staff came to be rejuvenated, Wolfgang Nauck was the first to be appointed. He came from the New Testament stable of Otto Michel in Tübingen. Unfortunately, he died very young.

It is a point worth remembering that in Wuppertal there were professors who were at the same time pastors of their parishes, and never considered exchanging their congregations for the seminary. One of these was Wilhelm Niesel, who was admired as the former 'iron Wilhelm' in the conflict between church and state. He combined his congregational work with his teaching at the seminary and with worldwide activity in the World Alliance of Reformed Churches, of which he was for many years president.[3] Other pastors were Otto Bückmann, of the Dutch Reformed congregation, who taught Hebrew and knew the Old Testament by heart, and Harmannus Obendiek. Joachim Beckmann, president of the synod of the Evangelical Church in the Rhineland, came over from its headquarters in Düsseldorf to teach ecumenical and practical theology. Oskar Hammelsbeck, who had established the neighbouring teacher training college on the same 'mountain', came and enjoyed reading stories from his private treasury. I knew Walter Klaas only during the last two years of his life. Arnold Falckenroth, Beckmann's son-in-law, looked after the students; Gottfried Gurland was manager; and Frau von Friesen acted as matron and looked after everyone. We were not just a community of teachers and pupils, but also to some extent a community in a wider sense. The professors held morning prayers every day, and we ate together in the 'Bauch von Paris' (Belly of Paris), a large room in the cellar of the mission house. During the first years I was there, we went out into the country with the students to hold evening meetings in the local congregations—a way of enabling the students to get enough potatoes. There was a student *collegium tabacum*, to which it was an honour to be invited. On the football field the students liked to attack the professors, though generally in vain. Each of us was rector for a year and was installed with a torchlight procession; my turn came round in 1959–60. Every semester finished with a party. The seminars were small, between 10 and 20 students, the lectures also kept within bounds, everything was clearly arranged, and everyone knew everyone else. For me it was a good way of beginning.

The church authorities gave me Dr Klaus Bockmühl to be my assistant. He had a doctorate from Basel, but was an adherent of Frank Buchman's moral rearmament. He alienated me somewhat because he used to intimidate the students who visited us so that they ate very little and hardly dared to say anything. Later he became pastor in Düren, then went to Basel to the Krischona Mission seminary, and finally to Regent College, Vancouver, where I visited him in 1989 shortly before his death. Of the students, Hans-Ulrich Kirchhoff was close, both work-wise and as a friend of the family. Gerhard Martin joined him and became a lifelong friend. He was still in doubt whether to become a poet or a theologian, and finally became both, as lecturer at the Evangelical Academy in Arnoldshain and professor of practical theology in Marburg.

Cultural Life in Wuppertal

For us as family, Wuppertal opened up a new world. It was an industrial city and not beautiful, but it was honest. Its overhead railway is unique and runs for nine miles or so over the River Wupper from Vohwinkel to Oberbarmen. The hilly landscape was full of beauties which we gradually discovered. Robert Koch Platz, where we lived, was elegantly laid out, with semi-detached houses. It was off the main road and was not only quiet but also safe for our children. Susanne and Anne-Ruth found friends to play with and friendly neighbours whom they liked. Behind the house there was a garden with trees, and in front was another with rhododendron bushes. We soon felt at home.

On 6 September 1959 our third daughter was born. Rudolf Bohren baptized her in the tower of the theological seminary, giving her the biblical name of Esther and allowing a degree of royal splendour to fall on our child.

In Wuppertal there were churches galore, and it was the Reformed church which we liked best to attend. In addition, there were about 200 different pietistic sects, as was common among the middle and lower industrial classes. Different though these sects were, they were united through one musical instrument: the harmonium! There was a wealth of inviting cultural activities. 'Der Bund' was headed by the Balt Dr Leeb and brought some astonishing people to the city, from Gottfried Benn to Ruth Fischer, from Carl Schmitt to Ernst Bloch. After the lectures we were able to sit together in a pub, and that was the best of all. Later on, when I was travelling about myself, I never tried to escape from this kind of meeting, for I knew my own lecture but was curious about my listeners' questions. In 1961 I was a guest in 'Der Bund' myself, speaking about 'The Hidden Human Being'.

For three years I belonged to the Rotary Club and went to dinner every Monday with friends from industry and trade, afterwards listening to a brief lecture. They already had Pastor Fiffi Specht for 'theology en detail', but they recruited me for 'theology en gros'. The participants—though all of them men—were undoubtedly interesting people. In many of them the old, bold entrepreneurial spirit was still alive. If they saw a chance to do good, they were there. If they were able to start up a new business, they were of course on the spot too. What drove these men was not so much a striving for profit as the entrepreneurial pleasure in creative action linked with a gambler's pleasure in risk. Once a year there was a meeting 'with ladies'. I gave a lecture at one of the regional meetings on Rotary's four basic values. After we moved to Bonn, I went to the meetings once or twice, but then it became too much for me. I never became a 'Rotarian'.

Elisabeth and I formed a critical circle of friends with Johannes Harden, a Mennonite from the Volga who was professor at the teacher training college;[4] Johannes Rau,[5] at that time SPD member of the North Rhine Westphalian parliament; and Jürgen Schroer, who came from youth work in the Rhenish church. We met repeatedly, criticized the restoration policy in state and church, made catty remarks about Adenauer and Dibelius, told stories, and drank vodka.

Work on My Own Theology

For me, work on the Sunday sermon now gave way to work for four hours of lectures every week. I remembered what Ernst Käsemann used to say: 'For every hour's lecture, ten hours of preparation! Every sentence must be precisely weighed up!' So I began in the middle of the vacations and wrote and wrote and wrote, so as to have a good stock in hand at the beginning of the semester, for during the semester there were always many things that prevented one from working on a lecture. But once the semester had begun, I felt like a hare hunted by hounds. My lead over my listeners quickly shrank; by the end of the semester they had caught up with me, and I sank back exhausted. This drama regularly repeated itself in the initial years, until I had so much work in hand that I could occasionally repeat a lecture. Once one had given a lecture three or four times, with this intensive preparation the next book was ready.

That brings me to the history of lecturing in German universities: Kant still fell back on philosophical textbooks, reading them aloud and then commenting on them; but from the time of Fichte and Hegel onwards, what the lecturer presented was what he intended to publish himself in the near future. Professors 'read' their future works in advance and made the lecture a run-up for their future printed works. It was only in America that I found the old way of lecturing again. It saves a great deal of trouble and time, but is also somewhat unproductive!

In my first two semesters in Wuppertal, I lectured on what I had discovered about 'The History of Hope for the Kingdom of God'. In the summer of 1959 I gave what later came to be my lecture hit, 'A Comparison between the Theology of the Reformers (Luther—Zwingli—Calvin)'. Here I could develop and give expression to my historical interests and at the same time build a bridge to contemporary systematic theology. I also lectured on patristic Christology and the theology of the Reformed and the Lutheran confessional writings, finally arriving at the present with 'Introduction to Present-Day Theology' and 'The Beginnings of Dialectical Theology'. In 1963–64 I then took as subject my 'theology of hope'. I gave these lectures in Wuppertal and simultaneously in Bonn, and they were the only ones I have ever given where the audience was bigger at the end than at the beginning. But with this I overstepped the boundaries of my teaching assignment in Wuppertal: Wilhelm Niesel admonished me, saying that here Reformed theology was his field and that I should confine myself to theological history. However, at this point the admonition was no longer necessary, because I already had the invitation to Bonn in my pocket. Niesel nevertheless remained well disposed to me, even if I seemed to him to be not genuinely cut out of Reformed cloth.

As well as lectures, I held theological seminars and philosophy classes. In these I could more quickly free myself from the spell of historical studies and could enter into contemporary discussions. From 1959 onwards I held theological seminars on Bonhoeffer's theology and ethics, and philosophy classes on Feuerbach, Marx, and Bloch. In 1961 we read Karl Marx's early writings and made a joint expedition to Amsterdam because the papers of Marx and Engels are deposited in the Institute for Social History there. We wanted to find out, just for our own amusement, whether Marx's 'total human being', who 'hunts in the morning, fishes in the afternoon, and breeds cattle in the evening' because he is not tied down to a profession, in fact 'also criticized the food' or only 'criticized after he had eaten' (Marx, *Frühschriften*, ed. S. Landshut, 1953, 361). We found the original with a handwritten correction, probably made by Engels, which permits both readings. This expedition to Amsterdam was organized by Hans-Ulrich Kirchhoff and was enthusiastically undertaken. In the Bloch seminar, in our shared journey of discovery through his work, we became disciples or apostles of his hope. In seminars on the beginnings of dialectical theology, we set out to search for forgotten essays and articles written in the early 1920s, a search in which the students were successful. That was the beginning of the two volumes about these 'beginnings', which Ernst Wolf brought out in the *Theologische Bücherei* published by Kaiser Verlag.[6] In the philosophy class I finally dealt with contributions to philosophical anthropology made by Landmann, Gehlen, Plessner, Buytendijk, Buber, and Bloch, which I was supposed to review for the periodical *Verkündigung und Forschung*.[7]

Because the secluded seminary on Wuppertal's 'holy mountain' had no constricting tradition of its own, it offered me the unique chance to find myself and to begin something of my own. In Göttingen, as a former pupil, I should always have stood in the shadow, or in the light, of my revered and wonderful masters. I should at best have been able to contribute modest footnotes to their brilliant works. I should always have had to struggle for their recognition and try to win their esteem. But in Wuppertal there was neither the light nor the shadow of tradition. We had to make our own little lights shine and bravely cast our own shadows. Consequently, we pursued our own theology, quite untrammelled, perhaps even recklessly, and arrived at something new.

When I began in Wuppertal in 1958, I still had to complete the extensive research programme on the history of Reformed theology in the sixteenth and seventeenth centuries that I had begun in Wasserhorst. Otto Weber was editing *Das Evangelische Kirchenlexikon*, and he passed on to me numerous articles on Reformed theologians from Amyraut to Theodor Undereyck. In addition, I was approached on behalf of the third edition of *Religion in Geschichte und Gegenwart* and wrote a number of brief articles for it on theologians from Amesius to Gisbert Voet. In 1958, as a coda to my work on Pezel, I published an essay on the theology of history maintained by the federal theologian Johann Coccejus,[8] and in 1960 an article on Jacob Brocard, as precursor of Johann Coccejus's kingdom of God theology.[9] Both articles went through the hands of Ernst Wolf. I also wanted to write a fuller account of the Huguenot philosopher Petrus Ramus, because his textbooks (in which he did not follow Aristotle as was usual) were so widely disseminated. They can be found in Hungary as well as Harvard. I was even given a small grant by the government of North Rhine Westphalia so that I could pursue the necessary research in the British Museum. But there I immediately found Walter F. Ong's two volumes on Ramus, which already unearthed everything that I meant to look for; so I gave up. That, too, is the common lot of researchers.

Inwardly my thoughts turned to the fundamental idea underlying the predestination doctrine of Calvin and the Calvinists. It seemed to me that there the point was not the dualistic notion of separating humanity into the elect and the damned, the good and the evil, in order to put oneself on the right side; the heart of the doctrine was the concept of the perseverance of believers in temptation and persecutions: 'He who endures to the end shall be saved.' From Otto Weber I had also learnt the mutual efficacy of 'the faithfulness of God and the continuity of human existence'.[10] In 1959 I edited for the 450th anniversary of Calvin's birth *Calvinstudien 1959*, with interesting contributions from Dutch theology, for example, an article 'Calvin and Music'. The subject of my own essay was 'Election and the Perseverance of Believers according to Calvin'.[11] After more than 40 years, my former Tübingen colleague Heiko Obermann, later in Arizona, praised my insight: 'Calvin's doctrine of election will remain open for misunderstanding as long as people do not realize that it serves to express the faithfulness of God and the perseverence of faith'; and in this connection he mentioned my *Theology of Hope*.[12] In 1961 I then took leave of the history of theology with my first independent book, *Prädestination und Perseveranz, Geschichte und Bedeutung der reformierten Lehre 'de perseverantia sanctorum'*[13] (Predestination and Perseverance: The History and Meaning of the Reformed Doctrine of 'the Perseverance of the Saints'). The introduction brings out my theological interest in this question at that time. To leave historical studies behind was a wrench, but then the theological challenges of the present were so much more interesting.

In June 1958 Ernst Wolf had already co-opted me for the commission 'Recht und Institution' (Law and Institution), which met in the Forschungsstelle der Evangelischen Kirche (FEST) in Heidelberg and which was ruled by Hans Dombois and Georg Picht. I had to present a paper on the doctrine of mandates in Bonhoeffer's ethics. This was so well received that Ernst Wolf published it in expanded form in 1959 in the series Theologische Existenz, which he edited.[14] It later appeared in English,[15] Korean, and Japanese. I ended with the critical comment: 'But are these "structures" of reality constructions which constrain the living flow of the divine history?' and this might be seen to indicate my early departure from Bonhoeffer's theology. In 1960 I tried once more to arrive at an understanding and wrote an article titled 'The Reality of the World and God's Concrete Commandment'. Eberhard Bethge included it in his series Mündige Welt, volume 3,[16] but he was never in entire agreement with my view of Bonhoeffer. This finally came out once more when in 1995 I spoke about Klaus and Dietrich Bonhoeffer in the context of a series of lectures about members of the resistance who had studied in Tübingen.[17] The eschatological consideration of history had drawn me away from Bonhoeffer's incarnational thinking. Clarke Chapman later wrote an appreciation of my Bonhoeffer interpretation.[18]

At that time I put forward my own, post-Barthian ideas in a lecture titled 'The Congregation in the Horizon of the Lordship of Christ. New Perspectives in Protestant Theology'. This lecture was published separately in expanded form in 1959.[19] Here, with Bonhoeffer's 'new wordliness' and Blumhardt's hope, I was on the move towards new horizons, away from the Barthian 'centre of theology'. Looking back, I find much already touched on here that continued to occupy me, and which later slowly took on form.

Meeting with Ernst Bloch

My meeting with Ernst Bloch was for me the most important event during my time in Wuppertal. Dr Leeb had invited him to the 'Bund' on 8 May 1961. After his lecture Bloch and his wife sat with Elisabeth and, me in an Elberfeld pub. Carola Bloch ordered scampi, which seemed to us very bourgeois. Ernst

Bloch had a cold but smoked his horrible weed in spite of it. Because he had talked very positively about religion, I asked him, 'But you are an atheist aren't you, Herr Bloch?' to which he shot back at me, with a twinkle in his eyes, 'I am an atheist for God's sake.' That took my breath away and later robbed me of my sleep, until I realized that a Jewish philosopher is bound to observe the Old Testament prohibition of images even in his thinking about God. But when I went on to ask him whether he was a Marxist, he replied, 'Why? After all, I have built Marxism into my system.' And then I knew that he would not remain for long in what was then the GDR.[20]

A year before, I had discovered *Das Prinzip Hoffnung*[21] in the linen-bound GDR edition and was fascinated.[22] I read it in 1960 while I was on holiday, and the beauty of the Swiss mountains passed me by unnoticed, while in addition I bored Elisabeth on our walks with the fruits of my reading. The whole book is shot through and through by 'the eschatological conscience that came into the world through the Bible' (German ed. 240). Bloch is the only German philosopher for centuries who quotes the Bible extensively and knowledgeably, and in his own way proves himself to be a good theologian of what he calls 'the religion of the Exodus and the kingdom'. Talking about the forward-thrusting hope, he writes, 'All Christians know it in their own way from the Exodus and the messianic parts of the Bible, be it with a sleeping conscience or profoundly touched' (German ed. 17). In 1960 I by no means had the impression that we are aware of this biblical message or that this forward hope is something in which we can find ourselves. So I set out to search for a theology of hope. I had no wish to follow Bloch or to fall heir to him, let alone to 'baptize' him. What I was looking for was a theological parallel act to his atheistic principle of hope on the basis of the promissory history of the old covenant and the resurrection history of the new.

In many daytime (and even more night-time) discussions, I later discovered the sources from which Bloch drew. If one touched on his Judaism, he would often turn surly. He had no wish to be pushed into this corner, out of which he had long since emerged. 'Marx yes—Rothschild no,' he would then say. Gershom Scholem reported that in Switzerland during the First World War, Bloch began with a theory about Jewish and Christian messianism and later saw 'Judaism' as the biblical salt which is nothing by itself but has to be added to the soup of the world to give it savour. Bloch was a Jewish universalist.

When midnight drew near (and conversations with Bloch nearly always lasted until midnight), he regularly began to talk about his first wife, Else von Stritzki. It was then as if she appeared and was present to him. I was acutely conscious of this in Jyvaskyla, Finland, where I accompanied him in 1966. For him she was a 'true early Christian' and a 'Marian figure'. It was together with her that he wrote his first book, *Geist der Utopie* (1918, 1923).[23] The tender *Gedenkbuch*, which could appear only posthumously in the last Surhkamp volume of his writings, is written in her memory. In 1921 he had inscribed on her tombstone the words in Revelation 3.5, which commemorate those who overcome, and on his writing desk under her picture stood the saying from Isaiah 35.10: 'And everlasting joy shall be upon their heads.' It was from Else von Stritzki that Bloch took his eschatologically revolutionary Christianity with, for the present, the exodus motif and, for the future, the explosive apocalyptic saying: 'Behold, I make all things new' (Rev. 21.5).[24]

In 1960 I wrote a review on *The Principle of Hope* in the form of an essay, 'Messianism and Marxism: Introductory Comments on Ernst Bloch's Book *The Principle of Hope*'.[25] With the title I wished to indicate the inner tension in Bloch's philosophy. My final question was, 'Did Messianism vanquish Marxism in Bloch, or was Marxism the victor? This question remains open, but in the disputes of the present the fate of our time will probably be decided by its answer.' As I followed Bloch's path further, it became clear to me that central for him was a messianic philosophy which lived from Jewish and Christian roots, and that he only used Marxism as a temporally conditioned analysis of the world. Bloch thought in an idiosyncratic 'Jewish-Christian' force field, and he was entirely aware of the fact.

After his move to the west in 1961, he published—as a visiting card, so to speak—his book *Naturrecht und menschliche Würde*,[26] and again I wrote a similar critical accompanying review.[27] Here I advised him to complement the social utopias for 'the weary and heavy-laden' and human rights for 'the humiliated and insulted' by developing hopes of resurrection for the dying and the dead, so as to give hope to those whom 'death has swallowed up'. Only when 'death is swallowed up in victory' does 'the principle of hope' arrive at its goal. He never took this up. And that was for me a further reason for developing a 'theology' of hope.

The next step was my essay of 1963 in *Evangelische Theologie* titled 'The Principle of Hope and the Christian Assurance'. The subtitle was 'A conversation with Ernst Bloch'; and this conversation really did take place on 23 May 1963, in the smoky atmosphere of the pub Zom Kiess in Tübingen. I included the article as an appendix in the third German edition of the *Theology of Hope* because few readers knew it from the periodical.

From 28 to 30 September 1961, Ernst Wolf invited the editors and friends of the periodical *Evangelische Theologie* to his summer house on the Walchensee. He saddled me with one of the main lectures, and I worked for weeks on the subject 'Exegesis and the Eschatology of History',[28] for I was convinced that the key to hermeneutics for the Old and New Testaments is not to be found in an imaginary 'centre of Scripture' but in 'the future of Scripture', that is to say in eschatology. The promissory history of the Old Testament and the gospel history of the New point beyond themselves to the coming kingdom of God, and belong together in this common reference to the future in which 'the Scripture is fulfilled'. But I also wanted to work up the principles of historical study that were available to me. In order to impress the masters who were also my teachers, such as Ernst Wolf, Ernst Käsemann, Hans Walter Wolff, Walter Kreck, and others of that generation, I used many superfluous specialist terms and chose complex rather than simple sentences. The night before I was due to give the lecture, I could hardly sleep and remained up for a long time, while Elisabeth slept peacefully. But then I was very well received, and the lecture was discussed in favourable terms. That was my entry into contemporary theology. Fundamentally speaking, this somewhat overloaded essay contains the main part of my *Theology of Hope*, which appeared three years later.

Rudolf Bohren had driven us to the Walchensee. He also gave a lecture there. But when he dared to make a few especially original remarks about Bultmann, Ernst Käsemann interrupted him in a fury and shouted, 'Herr Bohren, if you go on like that, I shall immediately leave the room. It is intolerable.' Since Käsemann's rages were not unknown, no one dared to calm him down and to speak a good word for the unlucky Bohren, myself, unfortunately, included. After the conference we were driven back to Wuppertal by a visibly unnerved Rudolf Bohren.

SEVEN

PUBLIC THEOLOGY

My time in Wuppertal was also the time in which I began to get involved outside theology, first in a German-Polish society concerned with reconciliation between the two peoples, and with recognition of the Oder-Neisse line (as frontier), and then in the ecumenical movement for the renewal and uniting of the churches. In addition, I occasionally took part in medical congresses and made the voice of theology heard in that world. And finally, Ernst Wolf drew me into the editorial circles of the various periodicals and book series brought out by the publisher Christian Kaiser, Munich.

The German-Polish Society

Through Johannes Harder, the Mennonite from the Volga whom I have already mentioned, I became a member of the committee of the German-Polish Society, which was based in Düsseldorf, and became co-editor of the *Deutsch-polnische Hefte.* As a native of Hamburg, I had no links with the German east and the Polish west. But politically I did not want to go on talking generally and only critically; I wanted to become involved in concrete terms too. The driving force behind the society was Paul Wolff, a former combatant in the Spanish civil war. The society and the periodical were of course subsidized by the Polish government. But they offered a unique opportunity to enter into conversation with Polish intellectuals and to break through the wall of silence built up by painful memories. One was to some degree compromised, but it was in a good cause, and necessary. At any rate, Heinrich Grüber and Karl Rhode were also active in the society, as well as Johannes Harder. A few years later, in 1965, the East Memorandum of the Evangelical Church in Germany appeared, calling for reconciliation with Poland. It finally inspired the Catholic Church in Germany as well to come to an agreement with the Catholic Church in Poland. Willy Brandt said later that without the East Memorandum of the Evangelical Church (EKD), he would have found his new eastern policy towards the Eastern bloc more difficult, if not impossible.

I undertook my first journey to Poland together with the committee of this society from 8 to 18 October 1962. We went by train and stopped over in East Berlin, where I visited Jüngel and Hermisson in the language seminary. The Berlin Wall had been erected on 13 August 1961. When we arrived in Warsaw in the morning, we were greeted especially warmly by the Polish 'comrades' because we did not come from 'the first walled workers' state'. At that time Warsaw had just been rebuilt, after it had twice been destroyed during the war, and cultural life was once more flourishing. The government was certainly communist, but the people were still Catholic. So most members of the Party and the functionaries were Catholic, too, and had their children baptized and went to communion. The churches everywhere were packed, and the bishops were greatly respected. There was no popular atheism as there was in East Germany (the GDR). Whereas the GDR was a surveillance state, the Poles spoke freely and cheekily, laughed at the party leaders, and liked to make nasty remarks about the Russians. The philosopher Adam Schaff invited us to his apartment, where the nameplate on the door was Schaffowi, 'the two Schaffs'. In his anthropology Schaff went beyond Marx, which the Party did not much care for. Later he lived in Vienna. In the Palace of Culture, Stalin's hideous present to the Poles, we visited Professor Stepanski, whom I already knew from a visit to us. We went to the Yiddish theatre with Madame Kaminsky, saw the Korczak house, and stood moved in front of the Ghetto monument. In the Ghetto museum we saw paintings of the last Ghetto fighters. They were represented in a victor's pose, like Germanic warriors, a particularly painful detail.

Then we travelled to Gdansk (Danzig) and had to view the harbour and the shipyards. Here one could hear the Marxist utopia with one's own ears: 'This black wall isn't black; it's white, because we shall paint it white tomorrow.' In line with this way of thinking, the harbour and shipyards were presented to us in the world dimensions they were going to reach in the future. Twenty-five years later the Lenin yard had to be closed because it could not survive against competition from the Far East. Its fictitiousness was the rock on which Marxist 'realism' perished. The governments were given more and more of the success reports they wanted, until the house of cards collapsed.

The most deeply emotional experience was to walk through the Maidaneck concentration and death camp, near Lublin. The plank beds in the barracks were the last resting places of starving and tormented men, women, and children. Behind glass lay the little shoes of the murdered Jewish children, and hair that had been cut off from the gassed women. We saw the pits in which more than 10,000 people had been shot on a single day. At the time I wanted to sink into the ground for shame, and would have suffocated in the presence of the mass murder, if on one of the roads through the camp I had not suddenly had a vision. I looked into the world of the resurrection and saw all these dead men, women, and children coming towards me. Since then I have known that God's history with Auschwitz and Maidanek has not been broken off, but that it goes further with the victims and with the perpetrators. Without hope for the 'new earth in which righteousness dwells' (2 Peter 3.13), this earth, which has suffered Treblinka and Maidanek, would be unendurable.

I worked in the German-Polish society and on its publications until the autumn of 1968, and felt confirmed by the political development. But when Polish troops then marched into Czechoslovakia side by side with the Russians and the National People's Army of the GDR in order to suppress Alexander Dubček's 'socialism with a human face', I resigned from the society in protest and had no more to do with the German-Polish pamphlets.

The Ecumenical Movement: Faith and Order

I first became involved in the ecumenical movement at the fourth Faith and Order conference in Montreal, which took place from 12 to 26 July 1963.[1] I believe that Oberkirchenrat Hanfried Krüger, whom we knew from Langeoog, had proposed me. At all events, I already took part in a preparatory conference in the Evangelical Academy in Arnoldshain in April 1963, and was given my homework for the conference in Canada. I then remained a member of Faith and Order for 20 years, resigning in 1983.

For us as a family the conference was dramatic. Elisabeth was six months pregnant; I travelled to Montreal with a bad conscience and returned with a worse one. But fortunately everything had remained peaceful. Friederike was born on 15 October 1963. But that was the way things continued to go for me with ecumenical conferences. I could not really get away and never had the time. The conferences always took place in the American semester vacations, so they interrupted the semester work in Germany and put paid to many a semester project. To this was added the extended absence, often in countries from which it was impossible to telephone. I always got to the conferences some days too late and left early, in order to save time.

But for me personally the ecumenical encounters with theologians from other denominations and from the Third World were very important. My theological horizon was enormously expanded. German theology was largely wrapped up in its own, admittedly very long and rich tradition, and seminars are only concerned with Augustine, Aquinas, Luther, Kant, and Schleiermacher, as well as Barth and Bultmann, to name only a few; but now my theology developed in an ever wider ecumenical field. Close links with contextual theologies of the Third World, especially liberation theology, developed. I began to do theology for 'the whole of Christendom on earth', no longer only for our own church and our own country. Unfortunately, I could move only a few colleagues to turn their attention not solely to the Fathers of our own past, but to the brothers and sisters of the worldwide fellowship as well.

In Montreal, Friedrich-Wilhelm Kantzenbach and I were the youngest of the German participants, and Katzenbach—later professor of church history in Saarbrücken—was both versatile and stimulating. We met the old guard of the ecumenical movement: Visser't Hooft, Oliver Tomkins, James McCord, Roger Mehl, Hendrik Berkhof, and others, as well as Orthodox and oriental theologians, in all the splendour of their rich apparel. Here I also got to know my later friend Frederick Herzog of Duke University. The younger guard consisted of Lukas Vischer and Nikos Nissiotis, Visser't Hooft's right and left hands.

The conference was full of surprises. At one point I suggested we could take as a basis our consensus over the patristic dogmas, but an Ethiopian protested that his church had never accepted the Chalcedonian definition and would never do so. When we proposed making our common Bible the foundation, Ernst Käsemann provoked the assembly with his thesis that the canon guaranteed not the unity of the churches but rather their multiplicity; their unity has to be understood only eschatologically.[2] When in a group session we lamented the division of the churches, the Orthodox theologian Nissiotis maintained that the body of Christ was not divided at all; in Christ we are all already 'one' (John 17.21). With the general theme 'Scripture and Tradition', we took a good step forward, since we started from the *traditio Dei*, God's self-communication and self-giving, and only then moved on to the ramifications of the historical traditions—which means, conversely, that the ecumenical unity of the many churches is not effected by way of bi-lateral or multi-lateral negotiations but rather when every church traces its own tradition back to its foundations, and in those foundations finds the *traditio Dei*, which is common to all. 'The closer we come to Christ, the closer we come to each other,' we said later.[3] Yet this advice to return *ad fontes*, though theologically correct, naturally often means that in one's own church one swims against the tide. And that was not clear to everyone.

The ecumenical movement began with the aim of promoting 'the unity and renewal of the churches'. In the first years of my involvement, renewal out of their divine origin was still at the centre of our efforts and declarations. But then conservative churchmen pushed 'unity' into the foreground, and in the end most people sank back exhausted into the peace of a 'reconciled difference'. The conservative programme of 'reconciled difference' promoted by the Lutheran World Federation became the sleeping pill of the ecumenical movement. We all stay as we are and are nice to each other. No more new sounds were heard from Geneva later.

From conference to conference Faith and Order had splendid study programmes, on which excellent theologians from all over the world worked. At the outset I was most enthusiastic about what emerged theologically in these studies in the ecumenical world format. The studies were always accepted and their praises sung at the next full assembly. But then the new study arrived, and the old one disappeared.[4] As time went on I saw through the method. The way was supposed to be the goal, because no goal outside it could be reached. Ecumenical co-operation was the main point, irrespective of what one worked on. And for that reason these studies have long since been forgotten. Which is a pity.

When I came to realize this, I suggested a theologically relevant project to Lukas Vischer: a specialist group from Faith and Order should try to find a solution to the *filioque* problem in the doctrine of the Trinity. After all, the insertion in the Nicene-Constantinapolitan Creed stating that the Holy Spirit proceeds not solely from the Father but 'also from the Son' (that is, *filioque*) was the dogmatic reason for the split between the Orthodox Eastern Church and the Roman Catholic Western Church in 1043. In 1978 we were finally able to begin: we, that is to say a group of Protestant, Roman Catholic, Old Catholic, Anglican, and Orthodox theologians, met in Schloss Klingenthal in Alsace. The Goethe Institute, not the churches, helped financially. The participants were excellently conversant with the material, the Orthodox theologian Dumitru Staniloae being a great help. In 1979 we met in Klingenthal once more, and I believe with the help of Michael Welker we were able to solve the problem: If the Holy Spirit proceeds from the Father, the Son is presupposed as being always already present with the Father. The insertion 'and from the Son' is therefore superfluous. It is moreover detrimental, because it makes the Holy Spirit definitively the Third Person of the Trinity, so that a Spirit Christology, such as we find in the Synoptic Gospels, is inconceivable. But the relationship between Son and Spirit, like the relationship between Word and Spirit, is a reciprocal relationship, not a one-way street. We sent out declarations to all the churches belonging to the World Council of Churches, with the recommendation that the *filioque* be omitted from the creed so that we could have a common creed in East and West.[5] In 1982 the Vatican also held a symposium on pneumatology at which Yves Congar strongly advised the omission of the *filioque*, using similar arguments to those we had used. In the Sunday Mass, the Pope then recited the Nicene Creed in Greek—without the *filioque*.[6]

I think the Klingenthal conferences were the high spot of my ecumenical efforts. And I am still convinced today that specific theological work does more for ecumenical understanding and the renewal of the churches than those general studies. Two of my best doctoral students, Geiko Müller-Fahrenholz and Hans-Georg Link, worked in the Geneva office of Faith and Order during this time and came back convinced ecumenists. I owe a great deal to my ongoing conversation with them. The outcome of my ecumenical participation, as I willingly confess, is this: my origin is Reformed—my future is ecumenical!

Theology for the Medical Profession

In the autumn of 1963 I received a surprising invitation to give the special lecture at the 31st Congress of the medical association in Regensburg; so on 10 October I was solemnly led by the Lord Mayor into the Reichssaal of the town hall, where I spoke about 'Theology in the World of the Modern Sciences'[7] and took part, as far as I was able, in this medical congress. This awakened my interest in a theology for the medical profession. The theological faculties in the universities and colleges were designed to train pastors and teachers of religious studies. I thought that this alignment was a limitation: theology is a task for the whole people of God; every Christian is a theologian! So I was always pleased when students from other faculties also came to my lectures and took part in the discussion. This happened especially if one was talking about so-called border sectors—theology and philosophy, theology and science, theology and culture, and so forth. When I discovered how interested non-theologians were in ethics, I purposely offered seminars on 'Ethical Problems in Medicine', and often there were more medical students present than theologians. We dealt with questions about the beginning and the end of life, health and sickness, and handicapped life. The medical students explicitly challenged the theologians to talk theologically and to say what was to be said in the theological dimensions of these problems regarding life and death—and in doing so they often disconcerted and confused the theology students.

After that remarkable beginning in Regensburg, I attended all the medical congresses to which I was invited. When I accepted a chair in Bonn in 1964, I found an ally and a good friend in Franz Böckle, the Catholic professor for ethics. We often attended medical congresses together and always found that we really talked the same language. The high spot was the Hoffmann-La Roche Symposium. Following a preliminary conference in Geneva, this took place in Basel from 31 August until 3 September under the title 'The Challenge of Life: Bio-medical Progress and Human Values'.[8] The chairman was Lord Todd, and the best biogenetic and biomedical experts in the international scientific world were there, including Jeanne Hersch and Margaret Mead, René König and Talcott Parsons. The symposium spared no expense. Franz Böckle was present, and Elisabeth came too. There was a 'ladies' programme, as it was then called, and many cultural events, which I could not profit from because I was too much concentrated on the lectures, especially of course on my own, which I went on trying to improve until the last minute, having a considerable respect for the illustrious assembly. I talked about 'The Influence of Human Beings and Society on Biomedical Progress' and tried to find a medically relevant concept of human life.[9] I was well received by the assembled experts and in my concluding remarks gave the conference a piece of advice for dealing with scientific results, so that all should be not merely 'healthy and wealthy' but also 'wise'.

I tried to go on thinking along the lines of these two lectures in Regensburg and Basel, and two special aspects emerged: on the one hand, to develop out of the mutual influence of theology and science a doctrine of wisdom that comprehends them both,[10] and on the other, to take up the problems of the disabled.[11]

On 29 and 30 November 1973, the Deutsche Gesellschaft für Sozialmedizin invited me to Nuremberg, to their annual conference. I was supposed to talk about 'The Rehabilitation of the Disabled in a Segregation Society'.[12] There were many disabled people present in their wheelchairs. Since I am not engaged in social work and am not a doctor, I did not feel particularly competent, but I remembered the fate of my brother Hartwig and accepted the assignment. The point under discussion was not just the wretched situation of the disabled, socially excluded as they are, but also the poverty-stricken attitude to life of the non-disabled who exclude them. 'It is not we who are your problem—it is you who are ours,' one often hears said in homes for the disabled. A humane society must be a society of the disabled and the non-disabled. That is why Article 3 of the German constitution, the Basic Law, has the addendum: 'No one must be disadvantaged because of his disablement.' The disabled are not a burden, nor are they a threat to the non-disabled; they are an enrichment for human society. But modern neo-liberal social policies again make the situation for the disabled more difficult.

The community of Christ is a community in the friendship of Jesus. The person who lives in his friendship also discovers Jesus' friends his brothers and sisters, the people whom he calls blessed. If we look at his example, we see that these people include the sick, the excluded, and the disabled. Jesus liked being with them, and they sought him out. He embraces them with his friendship, and they are as close to him as he is to them. Consequently, disabled people belong in the worship of the congregation. Church congregations become communities when they themselves accept their disabled members, as far as they can. Diaconal service begins in one's own family, neighbourhood, and congregation, not just in special homes and institutions. In my book *The Church in the Power of the Spirit* (1975; ET 1977), I stressed the community of the disabled and the non-disabled very strongly and declared it to be a mark of the true church. A theology of the disabled was afterwards taken up by many people and further developed.[13]

I pressed with great enthusiasm into this sector of the sciences, medicine, and the theological consideration of human disablement; but I came to realize more and more strongly that I lacked the necessary specialist knowledge and that it was now impossible for me to acquire it. Luckily I met gifted students who had qualified in more than one faculty and who were ready to address themselves to the tasks involved. In England and America I worked with highly qualified scientists such as John Polkinghorne, Arthur Peacocke, and Ian Barbour, to name only a few, people who in the middle of their lives had studied theology, and some of whom had even become Anglican priests.[14] They were interested in theology for scientific reasons and came together with theologians who were interested in the sciences for theological ones. The co-operation in the Center for Theological Inquiry in Princeton was satisfying and fruitful. But there are still very few scientists who expect to profit scientifically from theology, and unfortunately hardly any theologians who read scientific books in order to discover the traces of God in 'the book of nature' too. It was a long time before I put aside my Barthian fear of 'natural theology' and realized that it was a task for Christian theology. To discover the 'traces of God' in nature does not indeed save us, but it does make us wise, as tradition says; for we discover in the memory of nature a wisdom of existence and life which mirrors the wisdom of God, and for human civilization it is wise to co-operate with nature and to become integrated in it, instead of exploiting and hence destroying it in the interests of human domination.

The Publisher Christian Kaiser

In 1962 and 1963 I had edited early texts of Karl Barth, Heinrich Barth, Emil Brunner and Rudolf Bultmann, Friedrich Gogarten, and Eduard Thurneysen under the title *Anfänge Dialektischer Theologie*.[15] Ernst Wolf was evidently impressed and invited me to the annual editors' conference of the publisher Christian Kaiser in Munich. When I arrived, he immediately put into my hands the systematic theology section of the periodical *Verkündigung und Forschung*. I edited this section until Wolf's death in 1971, and myself wrote two reports on the relevant literature: one in 1962 on recent work on the philosophical anthropology of the 'openness of the human being to the world', and another in 1966 on 'problems of recent Protestant eschatology'. I had to organize the other numbers and to call in the articles that had been commissioned. Ernst Wolf also took me to the editors' conferences of the periodical *Evangelische Theologie*. He had the uncomfortable habit of distributing at about ten o'clock at night manuscripts that had come in. We had to read them during the night in order to give him our opinion the next morning. After his death I took over editorship of the periodical for some years, and then again later. We tried to carry on the periodical in his spirit with varying editors, but also went through violent conflicts and tumults set off by the student protests of 1968, by Helmut Gollwitzer's anti-capitalism, and later by contributions from the quarter of feminist theology. All the same, the periodical is still in existence and has one of the largest circulations among theological journals in Germany.

The publishers, Christian Kaiser, under the management of Fritz Bissinger, also discussed their own theological publications with the editorial group round Ernst Wolf—for example, the complete Bonhoeffer edition, and editions of the works of Hans-Joachim Iwand and Helmut Gollwitzer, as well as the *Theologische Bücherei. Neudrucke und Berichte aus dem 20. Jahrhundert*. In addition to this specialist theological literature, I gladly addressed myself to theology for the general reader and published contributions for young people for Johannes Rau in the Wuppertal Jugenddienst-Verlag. I also contributed to a series called Bekennen und Bekenntnis. By the end of my time at the Wuppertal seminary, I therefore had additional activities in plenty. That was partly due to the fact that out of pure pleasure over my recognition I was unable to say no. So a double life began, with the normal work in the faculty and the many extra activities outside; and sometimes the second swallowed up more time and energy than the first.

From Wuppertal to Bonn

For our last two years in Wuppertal, we moved into a very large and comfortable apartment in the seminary itself. We lived above the library, with a view of Wuppertal and within earshot of the overhead railway. Here I no longer had to bother about the heating; but instead the students were in and out of the apartment.

Now the members of the faculty changed as well. Wolfhart Pannenberg came in 1958 and was invited to Mainz in 1961. Our meetings were always marked by vigorous theological discussions, and a discussion with

Wolfhart Panenberg made one occasionally forget time and place. We were once on the way from Wuppertal to Bonn, met at the station, and peripatetically began our theological dispute. An hour later we were surprised that the train hadn't arrived, and applied indignantly to the guard. He told us forbearingly that our train had gone through half an hour before. After a tedious journey and with some difficulty, we arrived at the conference in Bonn, which after our interesting discussion seemed a rather dull affair. We did not lose sight of each other. In December 2003 I gave the celebratory lecture for his seventy-fifth birthday, he returned the pleasure in Tübingen in April 2006 for my eightieth, and we assured each other again of our 'old ties'.[16] Klaus Koch, the Old Testament scholar, was only briefly in Wuppertal and then went to Hamburg. His place was taken by Robert Bach, who remained until his retirement. In 1961 Hans-Walter Wolff, the soul of the seminary community, also left us and went to Mainz. In 1963 my friend Wolf-Dieter Marsch came to Wuppertal from the Evangelical Academy in Berlin to teach social ethics. He fitted splendidly into our group round Johannes Harder. He published the periodical *Pastoraltheologie*, had a pleasant way with the students, and was a stalwart friend. He later took over the Institute for Social Ethics in Münster, and unfortunately died young as the result of a car accident. We remained in contact with his wife.

In 1961 I was invited to a chair in Vienna. We went there in May and were charmed and flattered with a great deal of hand kissing and 'gracious lady', in the Viennese style. Unfortunately, a professor's salary in Austria was considerably less than the salary in Wuppertal, so we should not have been able to participate much in Vienna's cultural life; and in the end we didn't want to inflict this on our children. So I sadly refused. As compensation, in Wuppertal we were somewhat freer. We were not afraid to ask students and assistants to look after the children for a few hours, and we explored the further surroundings of Wuppertal. We went to Amsterdam, Brussels, and Paris. We came to feel at home in the Protestant church in the Rhineland and got to know other colleges, congregations, and many interesting people.

During this time Elisabeth was busy with Fontane's journeyings through Brandenburg, her home country, and with his novels. She discovered the quiet, restrained, and often barely hinted at theological dimensions in his work, and wrote a little book called 'Hope beyond Faith and Scepticism: Fontane and the World of the Bourgeoisie',[17] which Christian Kaiser published in 1964. In a letter written from hospital, Karl Barth wrote on 17 November 1964, 'Tell your wife that I have read her account of Fontane with interest. In spite of my well-known reservations towards the "North German lowland plains", I am a great admirer of this noble Prussian, and pick up his novels again and again' (*Briefe 1961–68*, 277). During our first years in Bonn, Elisabeth wrote another piece of 'literary earthing of theology' titled 'The Flood and the Ark: Biblical Motifs in Wilhelm Raabe',[18] which appeared in 1967. Raabe was her father's favourite author. This theological dimension of literature was quite new to me, and I profited greatly from this different kind of theology. It expanded my horizon. Four eyes simply do see more than one's own two.

My diary shows that in 1963 I received more and more invitations to lecture at other universities. In May I was in Tübingen for the first time, in June in Heidelberg and in Mainz. At first I thought that it was my theology that was in demand, but it soon emerged that it was rather that the faculties wanted to see whether I was a possible candidate for a chair. But the faculty in Bonn had already invited me in April 1963 to take up the chair for systematic and social ethics, after Arthur Rich (who was teaching in Zurich) had refused. So in May negotiations in Düsseldorf began. It was difficult to find a house for a family with several children, for Bonn was the capital of the Federal Republic and full of civil servants. In the end, an apartment was found for us in Bonn-Endenich. It consisted of six not very large rooms on the ground floor and two attics. After a moving farewell from the seminary on 24 February, we moved to Bonn at the beginning of October. Our children liked it there very much, for in the quarter where we lived there were about 50 children of their own age. Elisabeth found the narrow apartment oppressive, although she found the city of Bonn delightful. I had to shovel coal again for the heating, and in the end make room for the growing children by moving two storeys up into the small, unheatable attics. We much admired the huge and excellently equipped studies of my celibate Catholic colleagues! Otherwise, Bonn between the Poppelsdorf Schloss and the bank of the Rhine was an elegant city. The university was accommodated in the city Schloss, on the border of the court garden, and was one of the most beautiful buildings in Germany. The city centre was easily reached by bus, and there I found a well-filled lecture room, with a view of the park and the bank of the Rhine.

The faculty was occupied by the older generation of my own teachers who eyed the newcomer mistrustfully as an upstart. My colleagues in systematic theology were Walter Kreck and Gerhard Gloege. Kreck, also a radical Barthian, was much concerned to set up delimiting fences, so as to keep his doctrine pure. He was concerned everywhere with 'the fundamental questions'—almost all his books have this title—and with the proper dogmatic course, so that the locomotive 'theology' should remain on the proper track.[19] He evidently viewed me as a rival, because more students came to me than to him. But politically his attitude towards Adenauer's restoration policy was as critical as my own. Later he regretted that he had not seen me as more of an ally. I missed such an alliance, too, for I valued his radicalism. Gerhard Gloege, the well-known Lutheran theologian, was older. He came to the west from Jena in the GDR and had the large-mindedness of a grand seigneur. He was friendly towards me and thought highly of my *Theology of Hope*. We very much enjoyed his hospitality and that of his wife. The other members of the faculty were all excellent specialists in their respective fields, but they were not a community of the kind we had had in Wuppertal.

I did not find the transition from the service of the church to the status of civil servant easy.[20] Of course I took the oath[21] to respect the Basic Law, or constitution, of democratic Germany; but then I had also been made familiar with the other Germany, the German empire. Nevertheless, today I defend the right to exist of theological faculties in the universities against the laisizing tendencies of secular states. 'Theology at the charge of the church' is good and valuable, but theology at the charge of the kingdom of God goes further than that and reaches beyond the bounds of the church out into the world, into politics, society, culture—and also into the universities, the home of the humanities and sciences.

The chair in Bonn was equipped with a position for an assistant and several student auxiliary posts. My first assistant was Dr Karl-Adolf Bauer, who had done his doctorate under Ernst Käsemann. In Bonn I could also take on doctoral students. Among the first were Gerhard Marcel Martin, Reiner Strunk, Konrad Stock, Geiko Müller-Fahrenholz, Hans-Georg Link, Wilfried Schedler, Helmut Haasis, and Michael Welker. I lost sight of some of them later, but with most of them I retained ties of friendship, because for a while we had gone along the road of living and thinking together. The student auxiliaries were important, not only for their own scholarly work and their group work with students in the seminar: somewhat to my shame, I have to confess that we also misused them as babysitters for our four daughters. But our children loved them.

part IV

Theology of Hope

EIGHT

THE THEOLOGY OF HOPE, 1964

Genesis and Intention

In 1963 I began to sum up my various 'beginnings' during my time at the Church Seminary in Wuppertal. I have already described these 'beginnings' and their results, so here I need only touch on them. My researches into the history of Reformed theology culminated in my book on the perseverance of believers 'until the end' (*usque ad finem*); in the faithfulness of God the Father, in the advocacy of Christ, and in the power of the Holy Spirit, their faith is preserved in persecutions and temptations. That chimed in with my modest beginnings of a post-Barthian kingdom-of-God theology, to which I was helped by Christoph Blumhardt and Dietrich Bonhoeffer. It found its biblical foundation in the Old Testament theology of promise, which Gerhard von Rad expounded, and the post-Bultmann apocalyptic with which Ernst Käsemann had moved Christ's parousia and the early Christian 'Maranatha, come, Lord Jesus' into the main thrust of the New Testament. The Dutch theology of the apostolate had made clear to me the missionary anticipation of the future of God's kingdom in the world. And, of course, for me the challenge of Ernst Bloch's *Principle of Hope* could not be evaded.

These separate threads in my 'beginnings' came together as if it were a tapestry I was beginning to weave. I suddenly recognized connections where I had previously seen none, and for many months for my family and other people around me, I was abstracted and as if no longer present. The people close to me suffered accordingly. It was like a kind of possession.

In the summer of 1964 my rather illegible manuscript was finished. Trembling, I took it to the post and sent it off with my heart in my mouth. It then made its own way. In October 1964 the book was published by Christian Kaiser, which had also published Barth's commentary on Romans in 1922. I mention that only because some people (for example, Michael Welker) have compared the impact of the *Theology of Hope* with the impression made by that epochal book. Elisabeth seems to have sensed this more than I did: she put the book on the sideboard and lit two candles in front of it. For our children it looked like an altar. But I was tormented by worry about the book's reception.

In the Kairos of Its Time

According to a Latin saying, 'books also have their own destiny.' And that is what happened with the *Theology of Hope*. It was originally written for internal discussions in the group connected with the periodical *Evangelische Theologie*. But things turned out differently. The book 'took', as one says. It freed Christians from doubt and awakened hope in non-Christians. Within two years it went through six editions and was translated into English, Dutch, Italian, French, and Japanese.[1] Other translations were added later. The book made its own history. I had difficulty keeping up with its progress myself, and with the lectures I was asked to give everywhere, in West and East Germany, in Western and Eastern European countries, and finally incessantly in America.

The *Theology of Hope* was published in English translation in 1967, and in the United States (where we spent 1967–68 at Duke University, North Carolina) its impact was explosive. On 11 December 1967 *Newsweek* opened with a long article titled 'The Theology of Hope'. The account was theologically competent and precise, and found the grounds for the hope of Christians in the promissory history of the Old Testament and in the resurrection history of the New. Then the confrères and allies were named: Wolfhart Pannenberg, Johann Baptist Metz, and the philosophical patriarch of the 'hope movement', Ernst Bloch. On 23 March 1968 an article appeared on the first page of the *New York Times* headed '"God Is Dead" Doctrine Losing Ground to "Theology of Hope"'. The author was Edward Fiske, who had also studied theology in Princeton. On the morning of that day my students called to Elisabeth, who was sitting in the car, 'You've made it!' Harvey Cox and Langdon Gilkey had given favourable opinions. On 5 May 1968 the *Los Angeles Times* brought a good article headed 'Theology of Hope Faces Tomorrow', with a picture showing people streaming out of the church onto the street in order to stand up for social justice. That was the path from the theology of hope to political theology during those years.

In January 1968 the stir the book had made in America also came to the notice of the German newsmagazine *Der Spiegel*. The three-column article put Dürer's picture of the resurrection side by side with my own portrait, with the caption 'Resurrection of Christ, Resurrection Theology: Iron in Anaemic Christian Blood. Moltmann: Children of Protest': 'Moltmann preaches a revolutionary society-changing Christianity—he says Christianity as it originally was—and in doing so he offers Christians and churches a theology which empowers and fires active, indeed aggressive, disputes with the political world around.' The *Gemeinschaftsgruss*, the organ of the pietistic Württemberg 'Bruderbund', commented similarly in October 1965 and welcomed this 'combative theology' (6–13). *Der Spiegel* also used 'the first selection of voices from the world-wide Moltmann discussion', which Wolf-Dieter Marsch had just published (1967) as *Diskussion über die 'Theologie der Hoffnung'*. A year later, on 26 December 1969, *Time Magazine* followed with an article titled 'Changing Theologies for a Changing World', mentioning Pannenberg and myself, Sam Keen, and Harvey Cox. The author was Mayo Mohs. In his article he also drew on the first of my books to be published only in America, *Religion, Revolution, and the Future* (New York, 1969), which I had dedicated to Martin Luther King.

Theological and other periodicals, Protestant and Catholic, pietist and Freemason, German and international, brought reviews, half of which were favourable, half critical—half enthusiastic, half disapproving. I had become 'internationalized', but in the process also thoroughly controversial.

In 1964 the *Theology of Hope* evidently met its kairos. The subject was, so to speak, in the air, in the church and in public life. In the Second Vatican Council, the Roman Catholic Church opened itself for the paradigm of the modern world. In the United States, the civil rights movement reached its climax with Martin Luther King in the struggle against racism and for the liberation of the oppressed black population. In Czechoslovakia, 'socialism with a human face' emerged under Alexander Dubček, a democratization of the Stalinist dictatorship, while in Latin America, after the successful 1959 revolution in Cuba, a Christian revolutionary spirit was abroad. But in West Germany, the spirit of Adenauer's security policy reigned supreme, and with it general stagnation: 'No experiments: vote CDU!' proclaimed the famous, later notorious, placard. That fitted in very well with the existentialist preoccupation with the alienations and anxieties of the individual soul, and with the general pessimism about the world which followed the German hybris dominant in the Second World War. It was only in the 1960s that there began to be a detachment from the (Nazi) past as it came to be consciously addressed, and a start into another future with Willy Brandt's 'Risk more democracy!'

Common to all these new beginnings was hope: with the power of hope one could let go of the old and begin something new. At that time 'the knowledge that there can be change' counted as 'the reasonableness of hope'. We sought out changes for the better because we expected the good. At that time there was always more in the new beginnings than could be achieved: a surplus of the power of hope and an added value of expectations. We linked the forward-looking hope in history with eschatological expectations, which went beyond historical possibilities and human powers. Martin Luther King expressed this better than anyone else in his vision for the civil rights movement, which he proclaimed in Washington on 28 August 1963:

> I have a dream that one day this nation will rise up and live out the true meaning of its creed: We hold these truths to be self-evident that all men are created equal … I have the dream that one day every valley shall be exalted, every hill and mountain shall be made low … and that the glory of the Lord shall be revealed and all flesh shall see it together.

In saying this he set the democratic ideal of the equality of all human beings, which necessarily leads to the liberation of the oppressed, in the perspective of the promise of the coming kingdom of God and his righteousness and justice for all, a promise expressed in the prophetic vision of Isaiah 40.3–5.[2]

Key Concepts

My intention with the *Theology of Hope* was to give back to Christianity its authentic hope for the world. In doing so I took up critically Ernst Bloch's hopes for 'a world without God' so as to link them with 'the God of hope' (Rom. 15.13) of Jewish and Christian traditions.

I believe that three key concepts are essential for every Christian theology of hope:

1. the concept of *the divine promise*,
2. the concept of *the raising of the crucified Christ* as God's promise for the world,
3. an understanding of human history as *the mission of the kingdom of God*.

1. At that time, following Gerhard von Rad, I read the Old Testament as the tradition history of God's inexhaustible promise to Israel for the future of the whole world. Eschatology is not based on predictions and prophesyings, trend analyses and extrapolations; it is based on God's promises.[3] What is the difference? In a prediction someone talks about future happenings that he himself will not bring about. That is why ever since the Delphic oracle such predictions have always been so ambiguous that they can confirm everything that actually happens. But in a promise, God pledges himself to do what he has said and guarantees it with his faithfulness; and that is unequivocal. The fundamental divine promises in the Old Testament are the promises of a covenant made to Noah, to Abraham, to Israel, to the Messiah: 'I will be your God and you shall be my people.' That is a self-determination on God's part, and Israel's election to be God's people. In this covenant promise the promising God himself is present. He promises this people his faithfulness, and since faithfulness is the essential nature of his divinity, so the promise and what is promised in it are one and the same, namely the presence of God.

God's promise throws open the future: in the *Theology of Hope* I strongly stressed this character of God's promise because it is only this side of the promise which wakens the power to leave behind everything that one has and is, and—like Abraham and Sarah (Genesis 12) and like Israel in Egypt—to risk the exodus into the unknown and to trust solely the star of promise. Whether we start out from our home country like Abraham, or out of an alien land, like Israel, the name the New Testament gives to the courage we need is faith: 'the assurance of things hoped for, the conviction of things not seen' (Heb. 11.1).

In an early criticism, a theologian in what was then the GDR, Christoph Hinz, wrote to me very pertinently in 1967: 'Don't forget the fire and the cloud in the Exodus!'[4] He was right. If we don't just look from the word of promise into God's promised future but also turn our gaze in the reverse direction, from this future into the present, we discover more than just the divine word of promise. From 1972 onwards, for this I took up the Jewish idea of the Shekinah. Part of the covenant promise to Israel is the promise of indwelling: 'I will dwell in the midst of the Israelites, says the Lord' (Exod. 29.45). The Eternal One comes down and shares Israel's fate in order to lead his people to freedom. As the Exodus Shekinah, God goes before his people in 'the pillar of cloud by day and the pillar of fire by night' and talks to Moses as to a friend 'face-to-face'. As the exile Shekinah, God is in the Torah, in the obedience, and in the Sh'ma Israel prayer.[5] God becomes the companion on the way and the fellow-sufferer of his people in the exile of this world, in order with them to come to the kingdom of his glory. The Shekinah *here* is the promise of glory *there*, and it is much more than just a word: it is a divine presence that fills even life in the misery of exile with happiness. I believe that the presence of God in Christ and in the Holy Spirit according to the testimony of the New Testament is *Christian Shekinah theology*: God's incarnate promise and the presence of the coming God in the Spirit.

2. 'For all the promises of God find their Yes in him' writes Paul in 2 Corinthians 1.20. For me that affirmation was the reason for interpreting the resurrection of Jesus from the dead as God's final and universal promise of the new creation of all things. This divine 'Yes and Amen' is the unconditioned and unconditional endorsement of the promise of his coming presence, as well as its universal implementation, which crosses all the frontiers. God enacted his promise. This fulfilment of the promise initially touches only Jesus, but God raised him 'from the dead' so that he might be 'the first fruits of all who have fallen asleep' and the leader of life for the universe.[6] With that, this fulfilment of the promise becomes universal—for the living and the dead and for the whole sighing creation. Without the coming kingdom of God's glory and the eternal life of the future world, God's raising of Jesus has no significance, but without his raising, the hope of Christians has no Christian foundation either. The christological centre

of theology must have an eschatological horizon: so I said to Karl Barth; and, as I said to Ernst Bloch, if they are not to remain uncertain and nameless, all eschatological horizons must be founded on the remembrance of the raising of the crucified Christ. 'Christian eschatology doesn't talk about the future as such ... but about Jesus Christ and *his* future' (cf. *Theology of Hope*, Introduction, 17).

After the *Theology of Hope*, eschatology in the light of Jesus' resurrection became more and more important to me, because it separates eschatology from the optimism of the modern faith in progress, which is especially prevalent in the United States. For if God has raised the persecuted, forsaken, assailed Jesus, who was executed by the power-holders of this world, then he brings future to the persecuted, forsaken, and damned of this earth. Christ's resurrection is the promise of a new future for godless and God-forsaken people, and not least for the dead. It was during an international Theology of Hope conference of 500 theologians at Duke University at the beginning of April 1968[7] that Martin Luther King was shot in Memphis (on 6 April); and it was then that I came to arrive at the idea that my next book should be on the theology of the cross. So I moved from the resurrection and the *Theology of Hope,* which had occupied me in 1964, to the cross, and to the book *The Crucified God* (1972). Without the *memoria passionis Christi*—the memory of Christ's passion—there is no Christian *meditatio vitae futurae*—no Christian meditation on a future life; and conversely, without hope for the coming of Christ, the remembrance of Christ loses its power.

Hope does not only give the power to break out of oppression, like Israel, and to seek the promised land of liberty. Hope also alienates people from their native land, their friendships and their homes, and makes them ready to let these go and to seek something new. By this I mean that hope for an alternative future brings us into contradiction with the existing present and puts us against the people who cling to it. The contradiction to existing reality into which the Christian hope brings believers is nothing other than the contradiction out of which this hope itself was born: the contradiction between the world of the resurrection and the world in the shadow of the cross. If we had before our eyes only what we see, then we should come to terms with things as they simply are, either cheerfully or unwillingly. The fact that we don't come to terms with them—that between us and the existing reality there is no harmony, either friendly or resigned—is the unquenchable spark of hope for the fullness of life, for righteousness and justice on the new earth, and for the kingdom of God. That keeps us unreconciled, restless and open for God's great day.

3. Against the horizon of the resurrection of the crucified Christ, life in history becomes a charge, a mission. The promise opens our eyes for the potentialities of history and the goals which we are intended to reach. It is only against the eschatological horizon of hope that the world appears to us as history. But history is not just full of everything possible, good and bad; for this future is not the vacant 'where to?' of possible changes. The *promissio*, the promise which God's future opens up to us, gives rise to the *missio*, the mission into history, so that this future can be anticipated in the context of the possibilities open to us. There are historical conditions in the world which are in contradiction to the kingdom of God and his righteousness. These must be contradicted so that they are changed. That is why Erich Fried wrote, 'The person who wants the world to remain as it is, doesn't want it to remain.' 'Another world is possible,' says the ATTAC organization today. There are conditions that are in correspondence with the coming kingdom of God. These must be promoted. As Zwingli and Calvin already said, human justice and righteousness ought to correspond to the divine justice and righteousness. Karl Barth also sought for 'correspondences' of this kind in culture, economics, and politics, and called them 'parables' of the coming kingdom.[8] But if the kingdom of God is in the process of its 'coming', correspondences of this kind are then temporal beginnings of that coming and forms of its arrival in this time. So at its 1968 assembly in Uppsala, at the peak of the new Christian and secular beginnings of the 1960s, the World Council of Churches made this appeal:

> We hear the cries of those who long for peace. The hungry and the exploited cry out for justice. The despised and disadvantaged demand their human dignity. Millions are seeking for the meaning of their lives. We ask you, trusting in God's renewing power, to join in this anticipation of God's kingdom, and already to allow today something to appear of the new creation which Christ will complete on his day.[9]

Practical forms of these anticipations were suggested:

1. Freedom and trust in the era of the Vietnam war.

2. Justice in view of the increasing gap between the poor and the rich.
3. Orientation towards the shared life of human beings and nature.
4. Even the ecumenical services were set in this perspective: 'We are glad that with our worship we can now already anticipate the time in which God himself will renew all human beings and all things.'

Because the eschatological kingdom of God is the future of history, it transcends all its historical beginnings. For that very reason it becomes the power of the future in history, and the source of these beginnings. We are living in Advent and are preparing the way for the Coming One.

At that time I welcomed the declarations of the Uppsala assembly as an ecumenical fulfilment of what I had in mind with the *Theology of Hope*.

The foundation of hope is not utopia and the exploration of unknown future possibilities; it is the new beginning and the beginning of the new, here and now, today: *incipit vita nova*—a new life is beginning. That is why the archetypal image of hope is not the far-off future; it is the birth of life. It is not for nothing that the First Epistle of Peter uses the phrase 'born again to a living hope'. With birth, a new life comes into the world. That is a reason for hope. With rebirth, a life that has become old becomes young again. That is a reason for still greater hope. And in the end what begins is eternal life. And that is the ultimate foundation for hope. So when I published my new book about hope in 2003, I called it *In the End—the Beginning*; for this book is mainly centred on the individual hopes of our existence, and I was recalling T. S. Eliot's poem which concludes, 'In my end is my beginning.' It is only the birth of new life that generates the powers and energies which enable us to trust the future of this life and to enter into the project of its future.

Personal Reactions

There were a great many reactions to the *Theology of Hope*, both public and personal. Here I am picking out a few that for me are important:

1. In 1961 Wolfhart Pannenberg and the group round him, with Rolf and Trutz Rendtorf, Ulrich Wilckens, and Dietrich Rössler, had published a new theological outline with the provocative title *Revelation as History*.

Here, with an eschatological view of 'universal history' indebted to Hegel, and a theological interpretation of 'the language of facts' as 'God's indirect revelation', Pannenberg introduced the horizon of world history into the theological discussion. This was supposed to put an end to the existentialist narrowing-down to the historicity of human existence (Bultmann) and the kerygmatic confinement to the divine history 'vertically from above' (Barth). With the concept of God's promise as the power that drives forward history, I had not departed so far from Barth, and initially understood Pannenberg's outline as a finalistic metaphysics of history.

It was in this light that I then criticized it in the *Theology of Hope*. Pannenberg, however, felt not so much wounded as taken over, and in 1967 he wrote, 'Moltmann's renewal of the eschatological theme converges very largely with my ideas. That admittedly comes out more implicitly in Moltmann's formulation of his own position than in his dispute with me.' This then also applied to his contribution to the Bloch Festschrift of 1965, *Der Gott der Hoffnung* (The God of Hope). Here I admittedly felt rather taken over by him and wrote, 'I agree largely with his remarks in this essay. If these are supposed to be the real meaning of his earlier theses in *Revelation as History*, some of my critical comments in the *Theology of Hope* fall to the ground. But if the "God of Hope" is supposed to be a step forward compared with *Revelation as History*, that would suggest a degree of self-criticism.' Pannenberg was my colleague at the Wuppertal Seminary from 1959 to 1961 and our theological discussions occasionally escalated into sharp disputes. We were not unknown to each other, and we had exchanged theological ideas. Consequently, in periodicals and newspapers we were later often made jointly responsible for the new eschatological orientation of Protestant theology. But whether in spite of that we were still worlds apart is a question that may be left to the judgement of keen-eyed doctoral students.

I was linked with Pannenberg over the years through our similar approach in the eschatology of history and a parallel development of Trinitarian thinking. We both, each in his own way, tried to do theology in the light of Christ's resurrection. But although my idea of promise and his idea of anticipation show theoretical correspondences, the practical consequences we drew in politics could unfortunately be completely contrary to each other. In 1969, along with the 'left-wing' intellectuals Adorno, Bloch, Jens, and Augstein in Frankfurt, we both protested against the

Emergency Decrees, because we believed that they were a restriction of the young German democracy. But when in 1981, in the peace movement, we protested against rearmament, wanting to change 'swords into ploughshares' so as to 'anticipate' Christ's kingdom of peace, Pannenberg was by no means prepared to allow this to count as an 'anticipation' of the Coming One. At that time Hans Walter Wolff opposed him in his Isaiah interpretation, giving sound exegetical reasons. But Pannenberg considered Ronald Reagan to be the greatest of American presidents because he forced the Soviet Union to rearm to an extent disastrous for its economy. Whereas he knew that I was on the side of the Latin American liberation theologians, he fought vigorously against them in Faith and Order and joined forces with conservative Republicans in the United States, such as Peter Berger, Richard Neuhaus, and Michael Nowak, with the aim of silencing liberation theology. Since then we have preferred to talk about problems of the immanent Trinity rather than about politics. Nevertheless, in a strange way our 'old ties' have remained at a deeper level.

2. In the philosophical field, Eugen Rosenstock-Huessey printed a harsh comment on the *Theology of Hope* in his ERH *Mitteilungen*. That pained me, because I thought very highly of his *Geschichte der europäischen Revolutionen* and believed that I had learnt a great deal from him. And perhaps his target was really Bloch rather than me. In compensation Paul Ricoeur wrote a wonderful essay titled 'Freedom in the Light of Hope'.[10] 'I was deeply impressed, indeed quite fascinated, by the eschatological interpretation of the Christian kerygma which Jürgen Moltmann puts forward in his book on the *Theology of Hope*.'[11] Ricoeur for his part convinced me about the 'logic of undeserved overflow' in Pauline theology, implicit in the phrase 'how much more' with which Paul extols the overmastering power of grace over against sin, and Christ's resurrection over against his death on the cross.

The Spanish philosopher Pedro Lain Entralgo took up my theology of hope with touching enthusiasm. In 1966 he published a first assessment in Paris, in *L'attente et espérance*, and in 1978 a larger *Anthropologia de la Esperanza* followed in Barcelona. In 1978 he also published a 'carta a Jürgen Moltmann' in *Mundo nuestro* and assured me of his friendship. I met him in Tübingen at Professor Togar's house and also in Madrid, and was impressed by his open-mindedness and his greatness of heart.

3. In 1966, on the occasion of Bloch's eightieth birthday, I first met the Catholic theologian and Rahner pupil Johann Baptist Metz. Metz belonged

to the context of Rahner's 'turn to anthropology'. 'The attempt to read and understand the whole of theology as anthropology is an important achievement. Yet this "anthropologically turned" theology remains in danger of excluding the world and excluding history as long as it is not understood as being at root eschatology. For the world appears as history only against the eschatological horizon of hope.'[12] That put Metz on the side of my theology of hope, and in return drew me on to the side of his 'political theology': 'Every eschatological theology must become a political theology, in the form of a theology that is socially critical.'[13] I willingly let myself be drawn on to this side, where I already felt at home. Here we worked a great deal together over a long period, and discovered the links with Latin American liberation theology.

The great men of modern Catholic theology, Karl Rahner and Hans Urs von Balthasar, were soon alerted to the book. But in 1967 Karl Rahner took up the theology of hope only as a heading; he did not address the book's content.[14] In his own contribution he treated hope as one of the three supernatural theological virtues, following Aquinas's model. He did not perceive the new eschatological determination of hope, nor the new active, resisting, and transforming eschatology which his pupil Johann Baptist Metz immediately perceived and integrated into his political theology, and which, following Gustavo Gutiérrez, all liberation theologians in Latin America took over. If only he had at least taken account not only of the sainted Thomas but also of Joachim of Fiore and the Joachimite tradition! If it is set side by side with faith and love as a supernatural theological virtue, all hope's passion for the future is transmuted into an unworldly making-present of eternity in the virtues of individual existence. I was unable to recognize any 'theology of the future' here.

Hans Urs von Balthasar reacted very similarly to my *Theology of Hope*: he wanted to see the Christian hope transcendentally but not messianically.[15] Only Johann Baptist Metz succeeded in finding a Catholic harmonization between the other-worldly and the forward-looking hope.[16] In the truth of the gospel, the two are in no way alternatives; they strengthen each other mutually: for if there is no hope for eternal life, contrary to death, why should I invest my efforts on behalf of better times in the future for life here? And on the other hand, how can I hope for the world beyond this one if the future of life here is a matter of indifference? With Christ, eternal, fulfilled life has already come into this world. Unforgettable is the absurd scene in Nicaragua when Pope John Paul II exhorted the priests who had been committed to the Sandinista revolution to abandon the politics of liberation and once more to prepare the people for the eternal life beyond. Shaking his finger at him, he admonished Ernesto Cardenal, the priest and poet of the revolution, who was kneeling before him and who was the minister for culture.

4. Numerous Dutch theologians also reacted to my *Theology of Hope*. The first to notice and draw attention to it was Johan Marie de Jong, in Driebergen. He rightly set it within the general, and especially German, theological situation by asking, 'What comes after Barth?' and found that there was in general an 'away from Barth' movement. He called my theses that Christ's resurrection is 'the dawn and promise' and that the coming kingdom of God is 'the ultimate perspective' the correct 'markers'. Hendrik Berkhof found the book 'illuminating, enriching and inspiring' in the theological confusions of the time, but over against my orientation towards the future stressed 'the time already fulfilled in Christ': 'Isn't the Holy Spirit also a small part of the fulfilment?' That reminds me of the indignant question asked by a student during those years in Bonn: 'But isn't there anything to enjoy in your theology?' An entirely justifiable question! Harminus Martinus Kuitert 'placed' me 'in the context of German-language theology as a whole', finding the surmounting of existential theology and the adherence to Word of God theology good, but like Berkhof wishing to see more attention paid to life already fulfilled here and now. He saw the *Theology of Hope* in continuity with my earlier book about the perseverance of believers. Arnold van Ruler wrote a charming letter in which, quoting a Dutch saying, he said that we were now 'like two hands on a single belly'.

5. Karl Barth read the *Theology of Hope* together with Eduard Thurneysen immediately after its publication. On 8 November 1964 he wrote to an old friend that he found it 'very simulating and exciting, because the young author makes a vigorous attempt to cope better with the eschatological aspect of the gospel than the old man in Basel did in his Romans commentary and his *CD*. I read him with a completely open mind, but hesitate to follow him because this new systematization, though much can be said in its favour, is almost too good to be true' (*Briefe* 1961–64, 273). To me personally he wrote more critically, so that the young theologian wouldn't get a swelled head: 'To put it somewhat brutally: isn't your *Theology of Hope* just a baptized version of Herr Bloch's *Principle of Hope*?'

I suspect that he had in fact never read a word of Bloch's, so the admission that follows is more important: 'You know that I also once had it in mind to strike out in this direction, but that I then decided not to touch it' (*Briefe*, 276). It was only later that I followed up this hint of Barth's about his youthful decision and came upon his love for Christoph Blumhardt, whom he had visited in Bad Boll in 1915. In his *Protestant Theology in the Nineteenth Century* (1947; ET 1972), he called Blumhardt a 'theologian of hope' (German ed., 590), and his first commentary on Romans of 1919 is still full of Blumhardt's spirit of hope. In 1919, in an essay on Friedrich Naumannn and Christoph Blumhardt in *The Beginnings of Dialectic Theology* (1962; ET 1968; German ed. vol. 1, 37–49), he assigned Naumann to 'the past' and Blumhardt to 'the future' and extolled Blumhardt's hope: 'Hope for the visible intervention of God's sovereignty over the world, hope for deliverance from yesterday's condition of the world, hope for the whole of humanity, hope in God for the physical side of life ... Blumhardt will remain alive because his concern was the victory of the future over the past' (German ed., 49). Can a theology be made out of this? In 1920 Barth still had in mind a radically eschatological theology: 'A theology which wanted to dare to be eschatology would not just be a new theology; it would also be a new Christianity, indeed something essentially new, itself already part of the "Last Things", towering above the Reformation and all "religious" movements' (*Die Theologie und die Kirche*, 1928, 25; cf. ET *Theology and Church*, 1962).

Barth presumably 'decided not to touch it' because in the end, like Franz Overbeck, he viewed such an eschatological theology as too radical, and because, on the other hand, Blumhardt was still very much imprisoned in the nineteenth century's faith in progress. In 1922 Barth's second commentary on Romans appeared, and lo and behold: Blumhardt has now been replaced by Kierkegaard, and the time-eternity paradox has superseded the dynamic dialectic of past-future. Blumhardt's dynamic forward-looking hope has fallen victim to the enveloping mantle of eternity in the moment of time, and Blumhardt's importunate expectation of Christ's future has been replaced by the contentedness of faith in the eternally bounteous God. Eternity is now supposed to encompass time from all sides—pre-temporally—con-temporally—post-temporally—but it is no longer to have any particular ties with the future of the God 'who will come'. My *Theology of Hope* had reminded Barth of this key turning point in his theological development in 1920–21. Hence this contradictory reaction.

6. Finally, simply for amusement, let me take the report which a certain Horst Dohle from the Government Office for Church Questions in the GDR drew up in 1966 for the censorship office of the East German Authority for State Security. He was paid a fee of 300 DM for his success in preventing the *Theology of Hope* from being reprinted in the socialist German state. His review of the book itself is good, because it is quite objective. But he then follows it with the 'Marxist-Leninist assessment' required of him. He writes, 'A distribution of the book in the GDR would encourage a Christian attitude which, in contrast to the socialist reality, looks for this reality to be surmounted in the future, and is orientated towards a future Christian society. In the process,' he says, 'Moltmann proceeds in the most scandalous way from Marxist-Leninist ideas,' which he 'presses into service for the Christian model of the future' (168). 'He interprets so much Marx into Hegel that he can enter into a dispute with Marxism without ever naming it ... He even goes so far as to take over parts of the materialist or Marxist criticism of religion, and theologizes them' (169). 'He demands of the Christian, as the substance of his Christianity, opposition to every social reality. Under socialist conditions, this does not amount to a co-development; it means non-conformity at all costs' (170). 'But,' says Dohle, 'every reflection about the future of the church in socialism must take the socialist society as starting point, not the Church.' With this criticism, the censor turns down a reprint of the *Theology of Hope*, although he points out that his objections cannot unfortunately exclude the possibility that 'at conventions and in the training of theological students a half-baked Moltmann will be propagated. That would be worse than anything' (171).

After the last Christian-Marxist conference in Marienbad in 1968, the censorship office decided that 'works written by the West German theologian Jürgen Moltmann are in the future to be put on the index of prohibited books' (171); the relevant customs authorities were also to be informed. In fact, I was not allowed to lecture at all in East Germany between 1967 and 1977, and my name was eliminated from all church publications. Later an acquaintance found a denunciation of me in the archives of the State Security Service, in which I was described as a 'convergence theorist, an anarchist and a CIA agent'. The denunciator was a state-supporting GDR theologian. After German reunification, Horst Dohle, the author of the review quoted, wrote to me that the prohibition of *Theology of Hope* had in any case proved useless, since the book was already on the shelves of every second parsonage. When, later, I was able to travel to East Germany again, a pastor showed me his copy. A friend had sent it to him through the post, page by page, and he had then had the pages rebound.

What was to some extent the peak of the theology of hope wave in Europe reached me in 1971. At the end of August, I had a telephone call from the secretary of the Editrice Queriniana in Brescia, which had published my *Teologia della Speranza* in 1970, in the translation by Aldo Comba, a Waldensian theologian. She rang to say that for my book I was to receive the island of Elba's literature prize. She summoned me to Pisa on 10 September 1971; there a car would be waiting, and at Piombino the ferry would bring me to Elba, where the reception committee would await me. Without having any written confirmation in my hand, I flew off and found everything just as she had described it. On Elba the friends of Editrice Queriniana—Rosino Gibellini; Dino Pezzetta, the translator; Mariangela, the secretary; and Abbot Giordano Cabra—were also waiting. They accompanied me to Marciana Marina, where in the evening I was solemnly presented on the marketplace with the 'Premio Internazionale di Letterature "Isola D'Elba" 1971', together with a little Etruscan statue, and in addition 1 million Lire (at that time about 5,500 DM). As thanks I was only able to utter a single Italian sentence: 'Mille grazie, molto onorato.' On the way back to Pisa we sang Bersaglieri songs and then sat together over glasses of good wine. In the evening I found reports in all Italy's daily papers. Ever since that time I have been warmly associated with 'the Holy Family of Nazareth', that being the congregation which publishes the Editrice Queriniana in Brescia.

Resurrection image that accompanied *Der Spiegel* article.

'Der Spiegel': Children of Protest

I have already mentioned the article which appeared in *Der Spiegel* on 22 January 1968 (no. 4). Because this shows an awareness of the theology of hope and of the reactions to it which is still noted today, I am ending the present chapter with the text of the article.

Moltmann: Children of Protest

In the last three years the book of a young German theologian has soared to the top of the world's theological literature: the *Theology of Hope*, written by the 41-year-old professor Moltmann, at present teaching in Tübingen.

Moltmann's book has hitherto run through six German editions, and has been translated into five languages, Dutch, English, Italian, Japanese and also French.

Moltmann has been lauded in the USA as 'the herald of a new Protestantism' (thus theology professor Frederick Herzog). Universities in Czechoslovkia, Holland, the USA and the GDR have called on him for lectures. There is hardly a high-ranking theological periodical anywhere in the world, whether Protestant or Catholic, which has not given a rundown of Moltmann's theology.

The probable reason for the book's unusual success is its revolutionary content.

Here Moltmann preaches a revolutionary society-changing Christianity—he says Christianity as it originally was—and in doing so he offers Christians and churches a theology which empowers and fires active, indeed aggressive, disputes with the political world around.

Christians, Moltmann exhorts his fellow-believers, 'should no longer carry the train of reality but should go ahead with the torch'.

The first selection of voices from the worldwide Moltmann discussion has just appeared, a collection of comments by 12 theologians, Protestant and Catholic, West and East German, Czechoslovakian and Dutch—its title: *Diskussion über die 'Theologie der Hoffnung'*.

The Dutch theologian Johan Marie de Jong comes close to a summing up of the twelve viewpoints: in the face of the theologies current at the present time, which had certainly not 'injected iron into meanwhile anaemic Christian blood', Moltmann's book performs excellent service by showing 'the ultimate perspective' of Christianity: 'the coming kingdom of God'.

In a 'Postscript' to the collection, Moltmann has now infused iron—even more iron than in the *Theology of Hope*. A powerful shot of Marcuse, Adorno and Dutschke vocabulary lends explosive contemporary force to the in any case rebellious 'hope' theology.

Like these neo-Marxist prophets and agitators, in his Postscript Moltmann pillories present-day society as 'repressive'.

Like them, he demands 'intolerance of the powers and spokesmen of the status quo'.

Like them, he recommends 'demonstrating' for the oppressed, so that a 'humane society' can emerge.

Christians, he thinks, should 'join the protesters and become "children of protest"'.

The Marxist undertone which was already evident in the *Theology of Hope* is not fortuitous. Moltmann's philosophical idol is a Marxist: the 80-year-old Ernst Bloch, like Moltmann a professor in Tübingen.

Bloch's famous work *The Principle of Hope* has obviously stood sponsor to Moltmann's *Theology of Hope*.

Consequently even Moltmann's Wuppertal colleague, Professor Wolf-Dieter Marsch, calls the theology 'Eine kleine Bloch Musik'.

Unlike Karl Marx, who wrote down religions wholesale as 'the opium of the people', in *The Principle of Hope* Bloch described Communism as the fulfilment of Old Testament religiosity: 'Where Lenin is, there is Jerusalem.'

Bloch saw ancient Judaism as progressive because it wanted to change this world, just as Communism claims it wants to do today.

Picking up Bloch's view of Judaism—but not going on to agree with him otherwise—Moltmann would like to see Christianity as the universal continuation and heightening of the world-changing Jewish religion: as a movement with a 'mobilizing, revolutionizing and critical influence' on the world around.

The central Christian event is for Moltmann the bodily resurrection at Easter of the founder of this religion, on the third day after his crucifixion on Golgotha—just as his disciples testified.

Moltmann attaches so much importance to the resurrection because it meant the radical breach of the status quo, the wretched condition of the world per se: 'In the raising of the crucified Christ, the frontiers on which all human hopes founder have been breached, and there faith can and must expand into hope.'

The hope which Moltmann claims has been conferred by Christ's bodily resurrection has to be understood in quite earthly terms.

Moltmann's eschatology—the doctrine of the Last Things—aims at the kingdom of God in this world. Just as Christ is risen, one day all human beings will rise: 'In this hope the soul does not soar out of the veil of tears into an imaginary heaven of the blessed; nor does it cut itself free from the earth.'

The extent to which this is meant politically is shown by Moltmann's dispute with the worldly, ideological 'utopias' of modern times—by which he evidently primarily means Communism, and Karl Marx's hope for a 'classless society'.

Moltmann believes that the Christian hope, which is directed 'towards the new creation of all things through the God of Christ's resurrection', will 'destroy' the 'presumption' of such utopias, Even if they were to be realized, the Christian hope would still not allow itself 'to be reconciled with existence as it is'.

There is a surprising reason for Moltmann's threat that a Christianity of hope will 'destroy' the utopias: for him they are not revolutionary enough.

Inherent in them are 'the seeds of resignation which will show themselves at latest in the ideological terrorism of the utopias, through which hope for reconciliation with existence as it is will turn into an extorted reconciliation'. Here Moltmann is alluding to Stalinism and the police states which are still the rule in Communist countries today.

But on the other hand Moltmann offers the utopias (i.e., again practically speaking Communism) a Christian alliance: For in spite of all, inherent in their 'presumption is still more true hope than there is in sceptical realism, and also more truth'.

Consequently, the 'directional thrusts' which proceed from the utopias should according to Moltmann, 'be taken up by the Christian hope and carried further'.

Moltmann's 'kleine Bloch Musik' has at least brought about a revolution in theology itself. For twenty long years, observed the Munich Catholic theologian Professor Heinrich Fries, the teachings of the great 'demythologizer' Rudolf Bultmann had held the stage of Protestant theology. Moltmann has now endangered Bultmann's dominance.

Bultmann demythologized Christian eschatology too. He viewed the New Testament accounts of the resurrection, the Last Judgement, the kingdom of God, a new heaven and a new earth as legends which the modern man or woman could not be expected to accept.

Over against this, Moltmann, 'the herald of a new Protestantism', now insists that 'Christianity stands and falls with the reality of God's raising of Jesus from the dead.' Christian faith is always 'faith in the resurrection'.

Whereas on the one hand modern Marxist thinkers, such as the East German Robert Havemann, the Jewish West German Ernst Bloch, the French Roger Garaudy, and the Polish Leszek Kolkowski, have recently become more and more theological, modern Christian theologians, on the other hand, are increasingly tending towards revolutionary ambitions.

Last year in Marienbad—where at a conference of the Paulus Society (*Spiegel* 20/67) theologizing Marxists and revolutionary Christians held the stage—Moltmann then also drew up a new kind of political world map.

He described an intellectual and political front which cuts across the 'Iron Curtain' and the ideological frontier of the Cold War.

Today in both world camps, Communist and Western alike, there are 'non-conformists': there 'critical, humanistic' Marxists, here 'critical, heretical' Christians.

These 'non-conformists in all the camps' should—thus Moltmann—'recognize each other in order perhaps to unite' and to combat the 'conservatives'—there, the Stalinist Marxists, here the Christians of the established churches.

Other German theologians, not only Moltmann, have raised the banner of Christian revolutionary hope—for example the young (39-year-old) Mainz professor Wolfhart Pannenberg.

In his last book (*Grundfragen systematischer Theologie*[17]) he declared God to be 'the power of the future' per se. 'That means the power of contradiction against the present.'

Similar ideas have been propagated for a long time in the Catholic camp by the professors Karl Rahner (63) and Johannes Baptist Metz (39), who goes so far as not even to exclude 'violence' as an instrument of Christian love.

'If Christian love,' he crows, 'mobilizes itself socially as the unconditional will for justice and freedom for other people, then under certain circumstance this very love can itself require revolutionary violence.'

The new revolutionary theologies have often been suspected of fraternization with the Marxists. And it is certainly true that Moltmann's 'theology of hope' is inconceivable without the directional thrusts of Marxism.

Nevertheless, in the essay collection *Diskussion über die 'Theologie der Hoffnung'*, the East German theologian Christoph Hinz (39) from Merseburg has now pointed out that Moltmann's 'theology of contradiction' looks very different in the Marxist environment of the German Democratic Republic from the way it looks in Moltmann's context, i.e., in the Federal Republic.

He claims that Bloch's 'say No' to social reality and the mere 'contradiction' which Moltmann recommends in the West does not help the Christian community in the GDR, which then swings between a 'tendency towards assimilation' and 'hard and fast, pathological protest'.

For that reason the Christian must not live solely in contradiction to the world, but must also rejoice over it—in Paul's words 'But thanks be to God'.

It would in fact be worth asking whether a theology of hope which, though it is certainly schooled in the Marxist example, is also rebellious in principal (Moltmann calls Christian hope a 'malcontent in its thinking') gives Ulbricht, the father of the GDR, any more pleasure than conservative Lutheran Christianity, which from the beginning has been committed to praise of the powers that be.

Moreover, in one respect Moltmann's *Theology of Hope* is at a disadvantage compared with Communism. Although it talks so much about 'future' and 'Christian mission', it has no concrete idea about the future kingdom of God. Moltmann's colleague Marsch observes: 'One would have liked to know more precisely *to what* Christianity is now really sent, and what for, and how it proposes to proceed.'

Moltmann's response to criticism of this kind: 'What isn't yet, can still be.'

NINE

THE CHRISTIAN-MARXIST DIALOGUE

In the era of the Cold War, an Iron Curtain did not only divide East from West Europe; it also ran ideologically through the heads of men and women and evoked friend-enemy thinking in East and West alike. State socialism in the East claimed Marxism for its ideology, while the 'free West', presenting itself as 'the Christian West', for its ideology needed Christianity. In this way Christianity was once more led into a strange Constantinian captivity. Anyone in the East who was a confessed Christian was suspected of being a Western spy; anyone in the West who wanted to be a Communist was banned from his profession. In West and East alike, it was difficult to be in opposition without facing suspicions of this kind.

In the 1960s fronts began to weaken for the first time. In Czechoslovakia Franz Kafka was rediscovered, and under the Prague philosophers—cautiously and at first hesitantly—a new Marxist humanism emerged. Here Milan Machovec must be remembered above all, for he succeeded in convincing his party that there was a point in dialogue, instead of the familiar condemnations and persecutions of those who thought differently. When Alexander Dubček then proclaimed the new 'socialism with a human face', a freer atmosphere came into being in Prague. New humanist tones could be heard on Marxist lips in Yugoslavia too.

In the West, Italian Marxists followed Gramsci along new paths, and after the beginning of the Second Vatican Council, they sought for contacts with Catholic theologians who were enthusiastic about reform. In France, Roger Garaudy, the 'chief ideologist' of the Communist Party there, initiated a similar development. In West Germany, the Forschungsstelle der Evangelischen Kirche (FEST) in Heidelberg had long had a commission on

Marxism which, under the direction of the philosopher Ludwig Landgrebe and the political scientist Iring Fetscher, brought out a whole series of thorough (but unfortunately exclusively academic) studies on Marx and Hegel, Lenin and Marx, and so on, for the knowledgeable and the initiated.[1] I took part in their meetings twice. But it was the Catholic Paulus Gesellschaft to which we owe the real break-through to the famous Christian-Marxist dialogue or, to be more precise, its head, Erich Kellner, who financed these dialogues with money from a private legacy which he had received.

The first conference of the Paulus Gesellschaft took place in 1965 in Salzburg, the second in 1966 in Herrenchiemsee (near Munich), and the third and last Christian-Marxist conference in 1967 in Marienbad in socialist Czechoslovakia. Today it is almost impossible to imagine the reverberations. These three conferences were intellectual happenings whose repercussions were worldwide, extending from Washington to Moscow and from Rome to Geneva. 'It is really the first great international conversation between Christianity and Marxism,' wrote Roger Garaudy, and even Cardinal Ottaviani acknowledged, 'The scholars and theologians who are taking part in this dialogue are persons of proved intellectual quality, intelligence and wisdom; their position is exemplary.'

At the conference in Salzburg in 1965, more than 250 professors and other university teachers from European universities met together.[2] Karl Rahner and Roger Garaudy were undoubtedly the dominating minds, but Gustav Wetter, Caesare Luporini, Gilbert Murray, and Johann Baptist Metz also played a determining part in the discussions 'The Future of Humanity' and 'Tomorrow's Society'. Garaudy later published his contribution in France under the typical title 'De l'Anathème au Dialogue' (1966). It appeared in German together with the lectures of Rahner and Metz under the joint title *Der Dialog oder ändert sich das Verhältnis zwischen Katholizismus und Marxismus?*[3] (The Dialogue, or Is the Relationship between Catholicism and Marxism Changing?).

Unfortunately, I did not attend the first and second conference, but when I turn to the lectures now, I can clearly recognize traces of my *Theology of Hope* in the texts of Rahner and Garaudy, Dantine and Metz. The Christian-Marxist discussion gradually concentrated on the theme 'Future': Hope or utopia? Absolute future and the future of dialectic-historical progress? In his spirited contribution, Karl Rahner maintained that 'Christianity is the religion of future. It sees itself and can be seen only in the light of the future which it knows is coming as absolute to meet the individual and humanity as a whole.'[4] In his own way Roger Garaudy assented, 'This future thrown open to the infinite is the only transcendence which we atheists acknowledge.'[5] In his criticism of the present, Garaudy demanded that Christians should 'distinguish the opium from the leaven, faith from ideology, the Constantinian element from the apostolic one, and the existential demand from its alienation', and, with Lenin, he warned Christians 'not to forget the democratic revolutionary spirit in primitive Christianity' once its cult becomes the state religion.[6] The Christian theologians, for their part, made the Marxist philosophers dissatisfied with Stalinism, which was also called 'socialism as it really exists', and wakened in them a restless desire for more freedom and a different future for humanity. Metz and Girardi touched the nerve of the original Marxist spirit of opposition, even towards its own 'successes' as they were called. While others condemned Christian Constantinianism, they criticized 'socialism from above' and socialism '*for* the people' instead of the original socialism *of* the people. 'In the warm current of hope' (as Bloch had called the true Christian, and the original Marxist, hope), people belonging to the hostile camps of the politically severed world came very close to each other.

To look at the list of participants in the Salzburg and Herrenchiemsee conferences is to be struck by the fact that no one belonging to the countries of what was then the Eastern bloc participated. The inception of the Christian-Marxist dialogue was a Western affair, apart from two philosophers from Zagreb and Belgrade. If one tries to evaluate these Christian-Marxist dialogues, their limitations also quickly become evident. It was a free exchange of ideas between philosophers and theologians, scholars and publicists, but it was not a negotiation between official representatives of the church and the party. Conference dialogues are always better and more enjoyable than the laborious work of convincing one's own set and the colleagues who have not taken part in the dialogue. That is general experience. But it does not detract from the value and profit for the participants of the free communication at such conferences, outside the confines of the power game.

Marienbad 1967

At the peak of the 'Prague Spring',[7] the noteworthy, and last, Christian-Marxist conference then took place from 17 to 30 April 1967 in Marienbad in Czechoslovakia. It was the first, and unfortunately also the only, conference of this kind to be held in a socialist country in Eastern Europe. Erich Kellner had succeeded in convincing Erika Kadlecova, professor from the Czech Academy of Sciences in Prague, that such an encounter across the frontiers could be useful. I assume that Milan Machovec also played a vigorous part. Machovec and Erika Kadlecova took a considerable political risk and had to pay the price in 1968. As well as the phalanx of the Czech reform Marxists Machovec, Prucha, Kalivoda, and Gardavsky, other philosophers and scholars from the Eastern bloc had also been invited. I remember people from Romania, Bulgaria, the GDR, and Hungary. Neither Marxists nor Orthodox Christians came from the Soviet Union. The Czech theologians were also perforce absent; only Joseph Hrdmadka had been permitted to attend. It was a kind of closed circle. The most important encounter was between the Czech philosophers, the well-known West European Marxists such as Garaudy and Luporini, and the Western Catholic theologians. I was the only Protestant voice in the midst of the theologians Metz, Girardi, Fries, Kaufmann, and Kellner. Of the participants from West Germany, I can recall Richard von Weizsäcker, the later president of the Federal Republic; Alexander Schwan, the Berlin political scientist, who died young; Iring Fetscher; Peter Glotz, the Social Democratic politician who had a special interest in education and culture; Wolf-Dieter Marsch, the Protestant moral philsopher from Münster; Martin Honecker, my successor in Bonn; and Gottfried Mahrenholz, later a judge at the constitutional court in Karlsruhe. Participants from the GDR were Günter Wirtz, a CDU publicist; and Hanfried Müller, a conformist state theologian from the Humboldt University in Berlin.

Elisabeth and I travelled to Marienbad by train via Nuremberg and Eger. During the journey we were joined by Martin Honecker. The train stopped for a long time at the frontier, and in the carriage ahead of us we saw the French participants already gathered round Roger Garaudy. In Marienbad we were lodged in a beautiful old spa hotel, so that we could also enjoy the waters and eat the famous Karlshad Oblaten, or wafers. During the conference someone drove us through the gloomy forests to a castle belonging to Prince Metternich. When Hrodmadka then also went round kissing the hands of the ladies present, we felt that something of the splendour of the old Austrian-Hungarian monarchy was still alive beneath the surface of proletarian socialism. The conference itself had its highlights, when the Marxists joined us in seeking a transcendence that was not alienating, and we strove together for an immanence of liberty. We met, so to speak, between transcendence above and immanence below. The young Prague philosopher Milan Prucha surprised us with an encouragement to transcendence: 'For a long time we Marxists were concerned to criticize the Christian striving for transcendence, and to curb it. Should our task not rather be to encourage it to still greater radicalism in its striving for transcendence?'

But the conference also had its lows, for example, when Kellner cut the time of a Romanian philosopher so much that out of anxiety she spoke so quickly that no one could understand her, let alone translate. Or when, after a Hungarian Marxist had extolled his world too ideologically, Kellner shouted at him and asked him about the closed-down monasteries and the imprisoned nuns in his country. At the end, Ludwig Kaufmann from Basel presented Erika Kadlecova with the biggest bunch of flowers of her life, a Jesuit to a Marxist, as he proudly added. In this exclusive society I myself ventured to give a lecture titled 'The Revolution of Freedom', and talked about the revolutionary history of Christian liberty in Europe, from the papal revolution against the Christian emperor in the Middle Ages down to Reformed freedom of belief, and modern religious liberty.[8] Christians and Marxists ought to view the vista of an all-embracing 'realm of freedom' within a shared vision for the future, for which co-operation, not confrontation, is worthwhile. I then evidently even cried, 'Nonconformists in all countries unite!' an appeal which was specially held against me in Moscow. Machovec and Gardavsky, Garaudy and Luporini welcomed it, but the GDR theologians felt they were under attack and reported me. They also felt despised by the reform Marxists in Prague and denounced them to the State Security Service.

There was a memorable evening discussion in private between the Czechs and us West Germans. When I asked Milan Prucha whether Müller from Berlin could take part (I knew him from student days in Göttingen), he shot back at me curtly, 'If he comes, we won't utter a word.' So on that evening it was a closed circle of reform Marxists and reform theologians. Richard von Weizsäcker, Gottfried Mahrenholz, and Hans Schaefer, a doctor from Heidelberg, were also present. And the Marxists broke their silence, told of earlier repressions, the pressure Soviet Russia was bringing to bear against Dubček's new idea, and the hopeful beginnings of a democratization of socialism and the liberation of culture in their own country.

For me that was the highlight of the conference. The trust between people broke through the ideologically ordered mistrust.

I think it was that evening which for me opened up a new perspective. If they democratize their socialism, and we socialize Western Europe's democracies, then with a democratic socialism there, and a social democracy here, we ought to come so close to one another that we would put an end to the East-West conflict in Europe and would be able to open the Iron Curtain. The two systems would converge, and liberty, as in the West, and equality, as in the East, would unite and harmonize in the spirit of fraternity, as the French Revolution had promised. But with this idea I was committing the worst sin possible in the eyes of the GDR ideologists: I became a 'convergence theorist'. In August 1968, when the troops of the Warsaw Pact marched into Czechoslovakia in order to end 'socialism with a human face', I was 'confuted', as even years later a Moscow periodical noted with satisfaction. But tanks are not an argument; they are mindless.

When, after almost 40 years, I look back at the Christian-Marxist dialogue and especially at Roger Garaudy's contributions, I recognize how much my theology of hope was alive in it and was radicalized by it. In this new beginning, away from Stalinism on the one hand, and away from Constantinianism on the other, there emerged a shared revolutionary belief in an alternative future for humanity. I have already mentioned how vigorously Karl Rahner introduced 'Christianity as religion of future' into the first conference. Garaudy, a highly educated, universal French scholar who was unable to put up with the die-hard blockheads in his Communist Party for long, picked up this orientation and stressed the future to us 'as an appeal, as a demand …' For him, Rahner's absolute future was 'a permanent future: God is always in the process of coming.'[9] 'At the beginning of every revolutionary activity stands an act of faith: the certainty that the world can be changed, that the human being has the power to create something new, and that we are personally responsible for this change.'[10] But what he thus claimed for 'revolutionary activity' applies to all activity in history. Garaudy drew me, too, into this historical future orientation in the direction of the possible, and in the possible the new, and in 1972 wrote, 'In his *Theology of Hope* Jürgen Moltmann responded to this Marxist appeal: experience would have no foundation if it were not anchored in faith, in faith in the resurrection. To have faith means to hope, that is, to perceive the possibilities beyond what is immediately existing.'[11]

Johann Baptist Metz then succeeded in combining the view of the future as a challenge with hope for the future as promise. Over against Garaudy, he stressed the presence of the future as God's promise, while over against the Christian tradition he demanded with my *Theology of Hope*, 'Christian eschatology must see itself as a productive and combative eschatology.' The world is not a waiting room where we can sit about bored until the door to God's consulting room opens.[12] But as a productive, combative hope, faith must also preserve a 'negative theology' of the future in order to respect it as God's future and not to distort it with our own wishful thinking and projections. 'And Abraham went out not knowing where he was to go' (Heb. 11.8).[13]

But although we were heart and soul at one in the field of creative eschatology, we nevertheless often discussed the meaning of this negative theology of hope. Metz always wanted to know how I knew everything I said about the kingdom of God and the new creation of all things; I wanted to know why he was content to know so little, although he could quite well know more. Between us it was always a friendly back and forth of questions.

To Roger Garaudy I owe the ethical understanding of hope as postulate, as a call to creative action in the sphere of the historically possible. And I communicated to him an understanding of hope as promise, so that the demand made by the future may go hand in hand with new powers, in order that the demand can be met. In the living hope, the gift and the task—in German, *Gabe* and *Aufgabe*—are two sides of the same coin. I was much touched when I read in Garaudy's autobiographical account of 1975: 'How much gratitude I owe you … Jürgen Moltmann, for having shown me that faith is hope.'[14]

The conference in Marienbad ended on Sunday, 30 April 1967. Together with our friend Wolf-Dieter Marsch and his wife, we travelled to Prague, called on Jan Lochman of the Comenius faculty, whom I had already visited in January 1967, and admired the 'golden city' in spring, the Charles Bridge, the Hradshin, the Jewish cemetery, and the market in the old city. Prague seemed to us like the throbbing heart of divided Europe. The conference seemed to have opened up new horizons for theology and socialism, for a new Europe, and a more peaceful and just world. This hopeful enthusiasm carried me through my new beginning in Tübingen in the summer semester of 1967, and the year I spent as visiting professor in America. At that time I gave numerous lectures on 'the Christian-Marxist dialogue'.[15] In America it was greeted as a new beginning in old Europe and as a reinforcement of America's own civil rights movement with its preliminary in the social gospel.

When we returned to Germany in 1968, the student revolts were in full swing. I shall be talking about my second beginning in Tübingen in 1968 later. In July 1968 the 'forward hope' won over the conference of the World Council of Churches in Uppsala, with its motto 'Behold, I make all things new.' Unfortunately, I was unable to take part because I had already agreed to attend the World Student Christian Federation Conference in Turku, Finland. There, at the end of July, things were extremely noisy: the 'theology of revolution' had its moment, and I made my own contribution to it as well.[16]

Then, at the end of August, came the terrible and sobering collapse of the hopes for a new world which had fired us in the Christian-Marxist dialogue: with a majority of one, the politburo in Moscow decided to put an end to the Prague Spring. The Warsaw Pact troops marched into Czechoslovakia, among them, to its shame, the army of the GDR, so that Germans now occupied the country for a second time. In Prague there were moving scenes of protest and resistance. I sat for days glued to the radio, and suffered with the resisters. For weeks I was as if paralysed and incapable of working. I had not expected this collapse. I have been told that at that time I said, 'Now the lights are going out in Prague for 20 years.' The darkness lasted for exactly 21.

In Prague, in 1970 a great purge of the party and the university began, in which the reform Marxists (now called dissidents) were removed from their positions. Milan Machovec was one of the main sufferers. Milan Prucha was able to escape to France in time. Viteslav Gardavski, who as officer taught at a military academy, was interrogated and tortured until he collapsed with a heart attack. Joseph Hrodmadka, who had returned to Prague from his American exile after the war, and who as theologian had stood up for socialism of the Eastern type at the Prague peace conference, was so embittered that he sent back his Order of Lenin to Moscow. He died soon after, broken-hearted. His theology students, who belonged to what they called the 'new orientation', were dismissed from their parishes under state pressure and had to scrape along with difficulty in unskilled jobs. Jakub Trojan was the pastor who took the funeral service for Jan Pallach, the student who burned himself to death in protest on Wenceslas Square and who from that time was revered by the people as a martyr. His funeral was attended by thousands of sympathizing mourners. Things went hard for Trojan. He had to work as a labourer in a warehouse and dared not let it be known that he had any contacts with the West. My brother-in-law and sister-in-law lived in Potsdam and were able to travel to Prague, and through them we were able to help Trojan a little now and again. When I published his book *Entfremdung und Nachfolge* (Alienation and Discipleship) in the series of Kaiser Traktate, he knew that we in the West had not forgotten him.

Moscow's long arm reached out even in the West: Roger Garaudy was isolated in his party and was expelled from it in 1970, although it had been his political and spiritual home for 36 years.[17] His opponents now had the upper hand, and the party collapsed slowly but surely into political insignificance. For Garaudy that was also in some sense a liberation. In the books he published after 1970, he pursued an early dialogue between cultures and developed 'the project hope' for humanity—an anticipatory alternative to the capitalist globalization of our own day.

What has happened to the leading minds of that time? Because their fate affected me deeply, I shall describe some of them briefly.

Milan Machovec

I first met Machovec in 1966 at a Christian-Marxist dialogue in Hamburg, a clever young philosopher, who was able to disseminate more tolerance as a Marxist than the theologian at his side. The Hamburg participants were grateful to him and were not put off by his Marxism. When I visited him in January 1967 in the philosophical faculty in Prague, he was just the same: intelligent, versatile, and very friendly. He declared frankly, 'For my political struggle I read Karl Marx's *Capital*, but when I am dying I shall read the psalms in the Bible and sing hymns.' In the autumn of 1968 he was deprived of his professorship and consequently of his whole income. He then gave private Latin lessons, but when that became known, it was forbidden. Then he played the organ in a Catholic church, until the priest was obliged to tell him that unfortunately this could no longer continue either. As a citizen he was isolated by the party and the State Security Service, and economically reduced to nothing. In 1978 he visited me briefly in a Prague hotel but had to leave again almost immediately because the visit had been forbidden. And during these years of humiliation he always bravely continued to say, 'I am a Marxist,' which was as much as to say, 'And you are not.' In his keen intellect he was no doubt a Marxist, but in his heart he remained a good Catholic Christian.[18]

In 1997 we met again in Marienbad, with Erika Kadlecova. Dorothee Sölle and Fulbert Steffensky joined us, and we remembered the great days of the dialogue. For Machovec's seventy-fifth birthday on 23 August 2000, Elisabeth and I travelled to Prague, and together with Horst Pöhlmann and his wife took him out to dinner, which, as a lonely bachelor, he much enjoyed. Otherwise no one visited him. He was as if forgotten, and yet he had once moved the world a little. Horst Pöhlmann, Protestant professor in Osanbrück, looked after him with touching solicitude. For 20 years we paid into the 'Sonnenblume' to support Machovec, and Pöhlmann always found a way of getting the money to him by some subversive means. Machovec died in 2002.

Viteslav Gardavsky

I had the impression that Gardavsky was a highly sensitive man with a poetic vein, and personally he was very modest. His book *God Is Not Yet Dead*[19] attracted great attention among people who thought that all Marxists were atheists. It appeared in German and English translation just at the time when in America the so-called God is dead theology was at its zenith, and it was discussed in all the periodicals. Gardavski later wrote some very fine biblical reflections on Jacob and the patriarchs. In the summer of 1968 the rebellious students in Tübingen finally discovered Karl Marx, and in February 1969 I invited Gardavski to give a lecture. However, instead of the orthodox ideology, he disseminated critical scepticism, and the students consequently attacked him; but he only looked at them sadly and said, 'Just come and visit us, and see for yourselves.' I never understood why he had become an officer in the Czech army and taught at a military academy. He became a victim of the re-Stalinization of the CSSR.

Roger Garaudy

It is 6 February 1970. The hall of the nineteenth Congress of the French Communist Party is hung with red hessian. After three days Garaudy is reluctantly allowed to speak: 'My final words are followed by a deadly silence. My body feels like lead. When I take my place again among those 2,000 comrades, most of whom were yesterday still my friends, and not one of whom dares to take my part today, I feel that I am sinking into a deep well. At the end of the session I am shunned like a leper.' Garaudy had been a member of the Communist Party for 36 years. For 24 years he was a member of the central committee for 12 years he belonged to the politburo. For the party he had been imprisoned during the war in the internment camp in Algeria. It must have been like the farewell to all that life had meant. But intellectually Garaudy had always been above the party ideology. His dissertation on Hegel, 'Dieu est mort', became a classic. He was as much at home in theological ideas as in Western philosophy. He was famous for having said, 'Marxism would be the poorer if it ceased to know St Augustine, St Teresa of Avila, or Pascal.' The 'religion of the future' and the 'theology of hope' which were disseminated in the Christian-Marxist dialogues offered him a way to be both a Marxist and a Christian. And so in 1975 he closed his autobiographical account with this confession:

> Live according to the principle of being: love.
> The cross has taught me love's renunciations.
> The resurrection the overcomings.
> I am a Christian.[20]

He then threw himself with great enthusiasm into the dialogue of the civilizations and travelled the world.[21] In the course of these travels, after the 'Abrahamic tradition', 'Marx and transcendence', he came upon 'the message of Islam: transcendence and community', and discovered the necessary dialogue with the Islamic world long before immigration had put this on the agenda of theologians and philosophers in Western Europe. He is even said to have been converted to Islam. I met him again in October 1989 in Barcelona, where we were staying in the same hotel. He was now married to a Palestinian. She was very beautiful, but approached me with piercing eyes and asked immediately, 'Do you know the Koran?' When I answered somewhat too casually that I did, she exhorted me to immerse myself thoroughly in the Word of God. Garaudy himself explained his Islam to me by saying that when he journeyed to Mecca he always had Marx's *Capital* in one pocket and the Bible in the other. I doubt whether the Wahabi there had much pleasure in this firebrand. He gave me his 'philosophical testament', *Biographie du Xxème Siècle*, which had appeared in 1985, with a personally moving dedication.

Roger Garaudy often impressed me, and I learnt a great deal from him. He was a scholar capable of great enthusiasm, who could enthuse other people with his deep feeling and his clear-cut conceptual clarity. Without him there would have been no Christian-Marxist dialogue. With the dialogue of civilizations, he opened up new ways for a globalization of humanity's hopes.[22] If Samuel Huntington had known him, he would not perhaps have written his *Clash of Civilizations*. In Cordoba, if one crosses the great stone bridge, one comes upon an ancient fortified tower, the Torre de la Calahorra. In it Garaudy presented the 'Paradies von el Andalus' in the Museo de las Tres Culturas. There Maimonides, Averroes, and King Alfonso are deep in interreligious dialogue. If one switches on the audio guide, one can hear a lecture by Roger Garaudy. In this tower he tried to present his project for the encounter of the civilizations and religions in a permanent exhibition. One should not fail to visit him there.

Two other important participants in the Marienbad conference were the Salesian Father Julio Girardi and the Reformed theologian George Casalis. Girardi was a leading figure in the Christian-Marxist dialogue in Italy, Casalis in France. I met them both again later in Nicaragua. They had joined the Sandinista revolution against the murderous Somoza dictatorship. In the Sandinista movement a joint Christian-Marxist front did in fact develop. It was as radically Christian along the lines of liberation theology as it was humanistically Marxist in Garaudy's sense.[23]

TEN

MY AMERICAN DREAM

'America' is a new creation, a discovery of the modern mind, formed out of unnumbered human dreams.[1] Down to the present day, it is the dream of immigrants: first from old Europe, then from venerable Asia, finally from young Mexico and Latin America. They are all bound together by the 'American dream'. That dream makes the USA the unique central land of the peoples. 'America' grew up out of the dream of the English Pilgrim Fathers, the dream of the kingdom of God in the wilderness, and the divine covenant of a free people 'conceived in liberty and self-government'. From the very beginning 'America' became the 'New World', with all the biblical and messianic overtones which, highly stylized, echo in the phrase. This dream first became a reality with the American Declaration of Independence of 1786. With the American constitution, the dream of liberty, equality, and the happiness of all human beings was meant to determine this first modern nation: 'We hold these truths to be self-evident that all men are created equal, that they are endowed by their creator with certain unalienable rights, that among these are Life, Liberty and the Pursuit of Happiness.' Ever since, all American presidents in their inaugural addresses have invoked 'a new belief in the old dream', as Jimmy Carter finely put it in 1976. This makes of the American constitution a mission to the world, and that mission becomes the fate of the nation, but it is also an invitation to the oppressed, the persecuted, and lovers of freedom from all nations, as the Statue of Liberty in New York proclaims. 'America' presents itself as a land of hope for all peoples, hope for a new community of humanity. Through immigrants from all over the world, America has become an experiment made by humanity as a whole. The

Soviet experiment of 1917 was meant to create out of many nations the 'new Soviet human being'; in 1989 that experiment failed. The American experiment of all humanity has not failed yet, but it has not as yet succeeded either.

What was it that fascinated me so much about this dream 'America' that from 1967 to 1968 we with our whole family accepted an American invitation to Duke University, in Durham, North Carolina, and expected of our children more than we had thought?

For me it was 'the call of freedom'. I had spent my life in cramped circumstances, in barracks and prisoner of war camps, and then in the depressing conditions of ruined post-war Germany. I dreamt of freedom in the wide-open spaces of America and even today, although I no longer smoke, can still understand the fascination of the Marlboro cigarette advertisements. When in preparation for his novel *Travel with Charley* John Steinbeck set off with dog and trailer to rediscover America, he saw in the eyes of his neighbour something that he was to see again everywhere: the ardent wish to strike tents and go away from every 'Here' simply somewhere or other. People talked about going on their travels free and untrammelled, not just in the direction of somewhere, but away from everywhere. That is freedom in the boundless spaces of America: 'Westward ho!' I had the same feeling, and whenever I am in America I again sense the invitation of these wide spaces, this freedom of movement in open country.

Then it was also the right to happiness, which after the German tragedies and our post-war pessimism seemed like the promise of a new innocence. Through Ernst Bloch we were, of course, already 'in love with success' and no longer only heroically in love with failure, like Heidegger.

Like other German academics, I of course also learnt to value the American culture of appreciation. In Germany at that time, at the end of a colleague's lecture, one first of all said only something critical or derogatory, in order to put him down and to elevate oneself. Later one might perhaps admit that it wasn't, after all, completely bad. In America, after lectures and sermons one heard only hymns of praise—'Best sermon I ever heard in my life,' and 'Brilliant, magnificent,' and the like—and received standing ovations. It was only later that critical comments would occasionally be offered. But first of all one was encouraged, so that one could gain self-confidence. Even if one didn't take this too seriously, something always rubbed off, and it did one good.

In order to get from Tübingen in Swabia to Durham in North Carolina, Elisabeth and I went via Paris, in order to say goodbye to old Europe, and we spent two wonderful days between the Louvre and the Jardin du Luxembourg, which our children so loved. On Saturday, 26 August 1967, in Le Havre, we embarked in the 'France' for New York. Somehow we gained access to the first-class deck and enjoyed the deck chairs and the first-class service. Then it got rougher. Friederike, aged three, became ill, and the other children were seasick. In the end I sat down to breakfast alone, and greatly relished it. After six days, we sailed at dawn under the Verazzano Bridge into the Hudson River and, under heavy cloud, docked in still-dark Manhattan. It was not an overpowering sight. But beside us we heard two old ladies who were standing at the railing sigh, full of emotion. 'Home, sweet home.' We stayed in New York for two days. In the evening Elisabeth and I sat under the charming Prometheus statue in the Rockefeller Center and asked ourselves, Shall we make it? We visited the Empire State Building and Battery Park and thought, This is America. But that wasn't even half the truth.

On 2 September our aircraft landed in Durham, North Carolina, between extensive forests of long-leaf pine trees. Elisabeth put her finger on it with her shocked comment: 'So this is our mission station.' At the airport Fred Herzog and his wife, Kristin, met us. He had long before engineered my visiting professorship via Georg Eichholz, and I knew his name through volume II/2 of Barth's *Church Dogmatics*, for he had had the honour of reading the proofs and of being immortalized in the foreword. Unfortunately he said to our seven-year-old Esther, 'And tomorrow school begins,' at which she turned an embittered face to him and did not say another word.

We rented our house, 1108 Watts Street, from a music professor who had gone to Vienna for a year. It was a pretty house, under the omnipresent pine trees and with a cat in residence. A black maid helped us to keep the house in order. Behind the house was a small garden with a playground for the children. My way to the university was via the East Campus to a shuttle bus. Next morning I explored the neighbourhood and went into town on foot. Several drivers stopped and offered me a ride, because no one went on foot in Durham. Nor were there any 'sidewalks'. I wandered through the grounds of the cigarette factories and reached Main Street at Five Points. I tried to find the centre, but Main Street soon took me out of the town again. I then grasped the difference between an old German town, with its marketplace, town hall and church, and an American town with its Main Street.

In the other direction Watts Street led straight on, past numerous churches, a synagogue, and a Freemason temple, until one reached the North Gate shopping center. The Herzogs had taken a great deal of trouble to find suitable schools for our children, and we sent our representatives to all the suitable educational establishments, from the Roger Herr High School to St Luke's Kindergarten—of course with varying success. Soon our previous au pair girl Alison White from Ireland joined us, in order to help 'the kids' (as they were now called) with their English. Then my student assistant Douglas Meeks with his wife, Blair, turned up and took a touching amount of trouble to make us feel at home in this Southern culture. We became close friends with both of them, and our friendship has continued to the present day. My colleague Hans Hillerbrand helped me to find a second-hand Rambler, so that we were mobile.

At Duke Divinity School the dean, Bob Cushman, had given me three two-hour lectures weekly for undergraduates, and a two-hour seminar. I had to translate my first lectures into English, have them corrected by Doug Meeks, and then deliver them. Every beginning is hard, and this one was especially so. The students were not used to concentrated German lectures, where they were expected to take notes, and I wasn't used to students who chewed gum. I could note that I had caught their attention when they stopped chewing and their jaws dropped. Without Doug Meeks's help, my encounter with them would hardly have been a success. On 1 October I preached my first sermon in Duke Chapel, a neo-Gothic cathedral in the centre of the ivy-covered university, built in imitation of Oxford.

Duke University had been founded by the Duke brothers. They had made their fortunes in tobacco and now stood, or sat, with cigars in their hands, on the Methodist campus, cast in bronze. When we arrived in 1967, we had the impression that this was a pretty closed society. The only black person I met in the faculty was the janitor who collected the rubbish. Foreigners and Catholics also felt that they were outsiders. Roland Murphy came at the same time as myself. He was a six-foot-tall Catholic of Irish extraction who belonged to a religious order and taught Old Testament. We often compared notes and laughed over our first impressions.

The Divinity School was a Methodist foundation. The normal course lasted for no longer than three years because it had been preceded by four years at college. This did not leave much space for Hebrew and Greek and systematic theology. Much more important were the practical subjects, such as 'how to run a church' and 'heart-warming' extemporary preaching. As Waldo Beach explained to me, the graduates were divided into Bible boys and Thought boys. Female students were still rare. It took me some time before the Thought boys also brought their Bibles to my seminar. Systematic theology was rather the philosophy of religion and biblical interpretation, generally historical exegesis; the hermeneutical bridge over Lessing's 'horrid wide ditch' of history was missing. Most of the students came from good white families, but some of them were student pastors as well as students; and on the weekends they were already busy in their congregations. There was very little interest in the faculty in the European discussions about 'demythologization', 'the secular world', 'political theology', Karl Barth and Dietrich Bonhoeffer, and so forth. Instead, 'hobbies' played an important part. Someone invited me to play golf; another wanted to play poker with me. At first Duke University seemed to me like a country club university. But appearances were deceptive.

In the little country town of Durham, whites and blacks lived strictly segregated in different districts. A first wave of the civil rights movement had just shaken up North Carolina. Some members of the faculty had been involved in public protests against racism and racial segregation and had been taken to court. Our friend Fred Herzog made this struggle his personal concern and the subject of his theology. He was the author of a first 'liberation theology' in the form of an interpretation of the Gospel of John.[2] Whenever he and we had time, he drove us through the countryside, where we saw the burnt crosses of the Ku Klux Klan in front of integrated churches. We visited black sharecroppers in their miserable huts in the woods, and sat with him at the bedsides of disabled blacks. Fred Herzog's theology had always been diaconal and hence praxis-orientated. He had written about Oberlin and August Hermann Francke. In the civil rights movement he had found his American home—or, perhaps better, his front line.[3] In the faculty there were people who fought at his side, but for some he was still an oddity. And since it was he who had brought us to Durham and looked after us there, we also remained a little strange for many people.

Our children learnt English through television especially. There were very exciting children's series, about the dog Lassie, the bear Uncle Ben, and the scout Daniel Boone. Elisabeth followed the news (it was the time of the Vietnam War) and listened to Walter Cronkite, who always ended his show with the words, 'And that's the way it is.' As our time in Durham drew to an end, she wrote to him and as a fan was sent a signed photograph. We read the *Durham Morning Herald,* a local paper, but found no German news in it—if at all, then on page 4 or 5, and at most about the Oktoberfest in Munich. Instead, we were kept up to date about the farmers' problems with maize and tobacco, the football matches of Duke's Bue Devils, and other sporting events. We enjoyed driving north to Carr Lake, where we could swim and picnic. We were generally alone there, because Americans preferred their own hygienic swimming pools. The landscape, with its wide plains, had a look of East Europe. There were hardly any villages, but many scattered houses and barns instead. Apart from the tedious pine trees I have already mentioned, and the fields of maize and tobacco, there was not much to see. And we did occasionally ask ourselves, Why are we here? The Meeks, who quickly became our friends, took us with them to football games. We admired the pretty cheerleaders but could hardly understand the rules of this rough fight of one man against another. The Meeks also took us to a wonderful evening with the political gospel singer Pete Seeger, with whom we enthusiastically sang, 'We shall overcome …' At the end of our time in Durham, we drove with them to Clifton Forge, Virginia (where Blair's parents lived), using the wonderful Blue Ridge Parkway. Dogwood and redbud bloomed in the woods, and we found the American spring as beautiful as the Indian summer in autumn, when the leaves turn.

At the end of October 1967 I undertook my first lecture tour. On 28 October I spoke about 'The Category Novum in Christian Theology' in the John XXIII Institute of the Saint Xavier College in Chicago. The conference, at which Rabbi Borowitz and the Revd Crossan also spoke, had the fine theme 'The Future as the Presence of Shared Hope.'[4] This began the series of my 'Hope' conferences in the USA. On 30 October I gave the Ingersoll Lecture in Harvard on 'Resurrection as Hope' and, in talking about the anthropological consequences, discussed Norman O. Brown's famous book, *Life against Death: The Psychological Meaning of History* (1959). That brought lively assent from Harvey Cox and was the beginning of a friendship between us. On 1 November I was in Chicago again, and repeated this lecture at the University of Chicago Divinity School. Afterwards I had a stimulating discussion on 'promise' and 'providence' with Langdon Gilkey, who at that time still looked like a smart Yankee professor. We got on very well, for we had had similar experiences when we were young. During the war Langdon had been in a Japanese internment camp in China and had written a moving book about it, *The Shantung Compound*.[5] Later I invited him to Tübingen, but by then, in spite of his age, he had turned into a hippie and wore his scanty hair long.

At the beginning of December I flew with Elisabeth to New York. In Union Theological Seminary we met Letty Russell, and she introduced us to her partner, Hans Hockendijk, whom I already knew from Holland and the ecumenical movement. On Sunday we accompanied them to East Harlem, to the Ascension Church, and for the first time experienced the emotional worship of a black congregation. On Monday, 11 December, we were then in Yale University, where I talked about the Christian-Marxist dialogue. At that time the university's noble guesthouse was still barred to blacks and Jews. But the notice soon disappeared. In Yale Divinity School I met James Gustafson for the first time. We had a common pupil in Jürgen Hilke. At first, Gustavson was very receptive of my ideas, but then he tried to persecute me, which he hardly succeeded in doing, because his pursuit always came somewhat too late.

With Douglas Meeks's help, I published my 1968 lectures with Scribner in New York under the title *Religion, Revolution and the Future*, dedicating the book to the memory of Martin Luther King. That was, so to speak, my visiting card for America. 'Although Jürgen Moltmann's theology of hope is radically open to encounter with the many dynamic currents in the contemporary secular world, it is just as radically rooted in Christ and his resurrection': thus the jacket blurb. This double radicalism in Christian identity and secular relevance was apparently attractive for many Americans, who were fed up with secularism on the one hand and fundamentalism on the other.

Let me come back to our family life in Durham. Variety is the spice of life, as Elisabeth said. If the children are all right, everyone is all right. We had the impression that the kindergarten presented no problems for Friederike. She liked playing with the other children and didn't bother about English, which she found particularly difficult to understand when it was a question of clearing up. Esther was at first put at the back of the class and was allowed to occupy herself with drawing and painting. Then, when she became a Brownie, she began to mix with her class and made friends. She also looked charming in her Brownie uniform. Susanne and Anne-Ruth were put among American girls who were already complete adolescents, used lipstick, shaved their legs, and so forth; and they felt looked down on and laughed at. By the time we left, of course, they looked just the same as the rest, with their long hair. But whereas Anne-Ruth made many friends, Susanne suffered so much from that closed society of American girls where she was not accepted that she has never been back to America since. For her birthday in February 1968, Doug and Blair invited her to dinner in the Rebel Room, with a jazz concert. There she was for once 'completely in'.

From 23 to 26 November, over the long Thanksgiving weekend, we went to Washington with the children. We viewed the Capitol, the White House, and the various memorials and were much impressed by the centre of this world power with its classical style. But what our children remember most vividly are the games of tag in the lifts in our hotel.

Then it was Christmastime in this foreign land, and a low in our general mood. So we got hold of a proper fir tree (not a pine) and German-style candles, although open flames were forbidden. The Herzogs had comic American bubble lights on their tree. For the children we bought a large doll's house in plantation style, with a flag of the Southern states. We learned the happy American Christmas carols about Santa Claus, 'Joy to the World', 'Away in a Manger', and 'The Twelve Days of Christmas'. But Elisabeth's heart was set on the meditative Paul Gerhardt hymns. So we went to a Lutheran church and sang them. We were also invited to Christmas dinner there. But after Christmas we were still feeling depressed, so we decided to do something, and over New Year drove to Williamsburg, the pre-revolutionary colonial town, which is so reminiscent of old Europe. After the fireworks on New Year's Eve, the new year began, and for me the lowest point of our American adventure was past. I was full of hope and wanted to make use of the rest of our time in America. Luckily, in order to give me some free time, the dean only gave me a small teaching load, with two hours of lectures and a two-hour seminar for graduate students. That galvanized me and I accepted many invitations.

On 11 January 1968 I was in Atlanta for the first time. The Candler School of Theology and Emory University were later to be my second American home. Manfred Hoffmann, a Methodist Church historian from Germany, took me up Stone Mountain, which I later came to love so much. We went up in the cable car. He pointed down into the depths, for he was still in his existentialist phase, but I pointed up to the mountaintop and convinced him of the momentum of hope. We also arrived at the top. When I began my lecture on the Christian-Marxist dialogue with a reference to Gardavsky's book *God Is Not Yet Dead*, Tom Altizer laughed aloud. He was the father of the American 'God is dead' theology and understood this revolutionary message from the atheistic world of the Soviet imperium very well. On 21 January the American Society of Christian Ethics met in Kansas City in the St Paul's School of Theology. I lectured on 'Freedom in Christian and Marxist Perspective'. Charles West, a Barthian from Princeton, was chairman. On 23 January I gave the same lecture in the Chicago Theological Seminary, was then in the Garrett School of Theology in Evanston, dared to take part in a TV discussion on 24 January, was invited to dinner by a family called Crawley, on 25 January was in the MacCormick Presbyterian Theological Seminary and on the 26th in the Lutheran Theological Seminary in St Paul, Minnesota, where I held two lectures—and, out of a snowstorm in Minneapolis via rain in Chicago, arrived back happily in sunny Durham on 27 January.

On 17 February we set out on my next lecture tour, this time to California. In Claremont I stayed with the well-known New Testament scholar James Robinson. In the theological seminary, which was situated on the edge of the desert, I met the most important of the process theologians, John Cobb Jr, with whom I have remained on friendly terms throughout many years. He entered into many of my own concerns, for example, political theology and the ecological doctrine of creation, while I participated sympathetically in his Christian-Buddhist dialogues. On 19 February I was supposed to speak in Santa Barbara, but there was thick fog over Los Angeles and I was unable to fly. Elisabeth had gone ahead. I followed her by bus and gave my lecture after two hours' delay. The audience had waited with loyal patience. In Santa Barbara we met Lois and Walter Capps, to whom we later often returned, and always with pleasure. Santa Barbara always seemed to me like a paradise in the 'American dream'. But we had soon to go on to Berkeley, where my old acquaintance Charles McCoy was waiting for us at the Pacific School of Religion. He had once visited me in Bonn, where we talked about Coccejus and seventeenth-century federal theology, from which he derived the political federalism in the American constitution. In the meantime, the English translation of the *Theology of Hope* had made its way, so I gave three Earl Lectures on the theme 'Elements of Hope: Toward a Theology of the New'. With Charles and his wife, Margie, we viewed the wonders of San Francisco, with Chinatown and Fisherman's Wharf, took the cable car, and walked through Muir Wood under the age-old redwood trees.

On 23 February we flew to Salt Lake City, visited the Mormon Hall, and the next day caught a train to Denver, Colorado. That was my most profound insight into America: the endless spaces of the Wild West, seven hours long only rolling hills and nothing else, nothing at all, except Fort Laramie, familiar to us from Karl May's books. The whole of the German Federal Republic could have been hidden here, and hardly anyone would have noticed. In Denver we visited the memorial to the terrible Buffalo Bill on Lookout Mountain and then flew via Chicago back to Durham, to our children. We had seen a different face of America.

On Thursday, 7 March, in Princeton I met the great Jim McCord, president of the Presbyterian Seminary and of the World Alliance of Reformed Churches and of many other institutions. He was interested in me and opened many doors for me all over the world. On 25 and 26 March I spread the theology of hope at Union Theological Seminary. More than 600 people pushed into the chapel, standing in the aisles and against the walls, for two days previously the article I have already mentioned had appeared in the *New York Times*.

From 1 to 3 April Walter Capps arranged a Centennial Symposium of the University of California in Santa Barbara, with the title 'The Future of Hope'. As well as myself, Harvey Cox, Johann Baptist Metz, and Emil Fackenheim took part. We had already flown to Santa Barbara via Atlanta on 28 March with all four children and spent a few days at the beach. A young priest took our children to Disneyland, south of Los Angeles. At the conference everything was bathed in hope and future. I was especially impressed by Emil Fackenheim, who interpreted hope as divinely enjoined: 'The Commandment to Hope'. Walter Capps speedily created what he believed was a coherent 'hope movement' and set about 'Mapping the Hope Movement'.[6] Ernst Bloch was present by way of a translated article called 'Man as Possibility'. It was a great time!

On 4 April we were back in Durham, because the conference on 'The Theology of Hope and the New Tasks of Theology' was beginning at Duke University, drawing participants from all over the country. Everyone of note was there, from Harvey Cox to John Macquarrie, from James Robinson to Langdon Gilkey, and there were about 500 other participants.[7] That was the highlight and also the end of my time as visiting professor at Duke University. Dean Cushman had arranged this conference, and Fred Herzog had organized it. I felt greatly honoured. And then, on the very first day, it happened: in the evening I was sitting on the platform with Professor Van Harvey, and we were just disputing about the English concept 'history' and the mysterious and untranslatable German concept *Geschichte*, when Harvey Cox rushed into the great lecture hall and shouted, 'Martin King has been shot.' The non-violent leader of the black civil rights movement, the prophet of the true American dream of 1963, had been shot in Memphis at 6.30 p.m. by a white man. Cox had just heard it on the radio. The conference continued for another day. But then television showed pictures of the demonstrations by the black population, and burning cities all over the country. The conference was broken off, and everyone tried to get home as soon as possible. The barometer of the times stood at storm. And a curfew was imposed on Durham.

That was a turning point at Duke University. That same night the somewhat sleepy, or at least tranquil, university woke up. About 400 students, men and women, spontaneously started a vigil and sat in the university quad for six days and nights in wind and rain and mourned for Martin Luther King. Finally, black students from a nearby college came and passed through the rows of our students and joined them. Then we all took hands and sang, 'We shall overcome ...' With that the ice was broken in Durham too. The civil rights movement poured like a stream of living water over the country and made black and white, men and women, poor and rich, ready for a new humane society, which would recognize that 'all men are created equal.' This America fulfilled my 'American dream'. These days in Duke University, when I saw this true America face-to-face, are for me unforgettable.

When we came to America, we were immediately asked everywhere, 'How do you like America?' There was a great desire for recognition in this nation, which still felt young. My first spontaneous answers were always very positive. I found the upper side which I could see really splendid. But then Fred Herzog showed us America's downside, in the wretchedness of the black Americans, whose grandparents had still been slaves on the cotton plantations of North Carolina. With their suffering, I began to suffer, too, from the violence, the injustice, and the contempt of the whites. I disliked America, to put it mildly. I found it repulsive. But then when I stood in the quad hand in hand with the white and black students and sang the song of the civil rights movement, I began to love America. And that is how things have stayed. The subject of my first lecture after my return to Tübingen on 22 April, held in the main hall of the university, was accordingly this 'new America'.

After a harmonious farewell evening with the faculty and a very stimulating farewell evening with the students from my seminar, we struck our tents and started on our journey home. I flew ahead, in order to lecture in Princeton at the next big theological conference on 'The Future as New Paradigm of Transcendence'. Jim McCord had given me the subject. Then I met Elisabeth and the children in Battery Park in Manhattan. We said goodbye to the Statue of Liberty and on 20 April arrived back in Stuttgart.

I have often asked myself why my *Theology of Hope* found so great an echo and was so enthusiastically received in the United States. If I read the newspaper commentaries of 1968 today, it seems to me that at that time, without knowing it, I touched the nerve of the American attitude to life: the turning away from tradition and the turn to the future, the discovery of apparently unlimited possibilities, and the enterprising pleasure in the creative moulding of the new. When, on the pattern of Israel's Exodus, I discovered 'the God before us' and 'the God who goes ahead of us', I did not yet know the 'Battle Hymn of the Republic': 'My eyes have seen the glory of the coming of the Lord ...' and 'Our God is marching on.' Nor did I as yet know the refrain 'When the saints come marching in'. My stress on the creative power of hope and the eschatology of God's coming kingdom as promise and demand apparently struck a chord in the American soul, with its feeling for the possible and its pleasure in experiment. I found 'the vision and the courage to reinvent America', as President Bill Clinton put it in 1993, incomparable. Who would ever arrive at the idea of 'reinventing' France or Florence? My stress on the forward orientation of the resurrection hope fitted in with the 'puritanical march forward'. The social and political horizon of the praxis of hope fitted the earlier social gospel movement, too, as well as the new movement for civil rights. The *National Observer* wrote, 'A new and significant basis for a theology that is both Biblical and secular.' *Newsweek* pronounced, 'Moltmann may well be the herald of a new Protestantism battling for the transformation of culture.' 'Christian hope of final redemption is in fact an imperative for the restructuring of the orders of human life today. Hope is not merely the assurance of the believing Christians, but a pressing vocation, one that comfortable Christianity has often ignored and shunned.' *Christianity Today* described me as 'one to disrupt the status quo'. In 1968 the archdiocese of New York based its new catechism on the *Theology of Hope. The New York Book Review* awarded a prize for the best limerick of 1968: 'German theological breakthrough: God found in future:

> In Das Wort we have found God again;
> Not in space, but in time does he reign.
> Barth's "God on High",
> Tillich's "Depth of my I"
> Now exist in a future domain.'

In 1968 the United States was profoundly unsettled by the sorry and untenable Vietnam War. I can remember two Americans at the conference in Turku. One of them said, 'I don't come from the USA; I come from Newark'; the other said, 'I don't come from the USA either; I come from Portland.' The protest marches in American cities grew steadily, until on 4 May 1970 the National Guard shot four students at Kent State University, Ohio. Through the simultaneous civil rights movement, the country, especially in the South, was in the process of a social and cultural revolution. Self-doubt penetrated far into the church congregations and into theology. In this situation the call to new hope acted like a deliverance and encouragement, especially because it came from outside.

But this call to new hope first reached the already mentioned upper side of America especially, and was seen as reinforcing the general and official optimism of a world in rapid progress.[8] It could also be viewed as a reinforcement of the old American visions of making the world a happier place: of Christianizing the world, of civilizing the world, of saving the world for democracy, and however the messianic justifications for the new American empire run. I myself also came across high-flown notions of this kind in New England and in Washington, and I felt oppressed by this insensitive missionary zeal.

But I was also interested in America's downside, which Fred Herzog had showed me in North Carolina, and which my friend Jim Cone of Union Theological Seminary, New York, impressively depicted for me in his books about black theology and black power. The Afro-American contribution to American culture and American life cannot be overlooked, but it is seldom sufficiently appreciated. The racism under which the blacks chafe, and the capitalism under which the poor and the people 'who haven't made it' suffer, belong together to this downside of America. Martin Luther King wanted to follow up the march of the blacks to Washington by a march of the poor as well. In Atlanta I later got to know an open-door community which Murphy Davis and Ed Loring established.[9] It gathers together people who are black or poor, unemployed or homeless, whom no one wants to see and who are supposed to be driven out of Atlanta. As prison chaplain, Murphy regularly visits prisoners in the death cells. Whenever I visit Emory University in Atlanta, I visit this open-door community too.

The reasons that bring me to this downside in the USA are not just social; they are theological as well. The theology of hope is based on the resurrection of the poor, assailed, forsaken, and executed Christ, and he therefore brings hope where otherwise there is little to hope for—to the poor, the assailed, the forsaken, and the imprisoned. What I have come to know about the downside of society—and not just in the United States—convinced me at that time that another theological book was needed.[10] *The Crucified God* (1972; ET 1974) was intended to present the other side of the *Theology of Hope*. With this book, I believe, I also appealed to the suffering of people living on *the upper side* of society, a suffering suppressed by the official optimism and faith in progress; for these people by no means always feel like 'keeping smiling' as they are told to do.

Even after these experiences of America as it really is, America has remained for me so fascinating that I have accepted every invitation, and whenever possible have flown over for lectures and conferences. Apart from the churches and theologies, I have always been interested in American 'civil religion', as Robert Bellah called the political philosophy of the USA in 1967. With its messianic overtones, the public ideology of the United States is typically modern and a secular product of the millenarian branch of the Christian hope. But because this messianic certainty of a better future always goes hand in hand with an apocalyptic dualism in the final struggle between God and Satan, Christ and Antichrist, good and evil, these religious politics are by no means merely a blessing. 'God bless America' is often heard on the lips of American presidents. But whether God blesses America will become apparent when it emerges whether America is a blessing for the peoples of the world, or their burden and curse; for one is blessed only in order to be a blessing oneself.

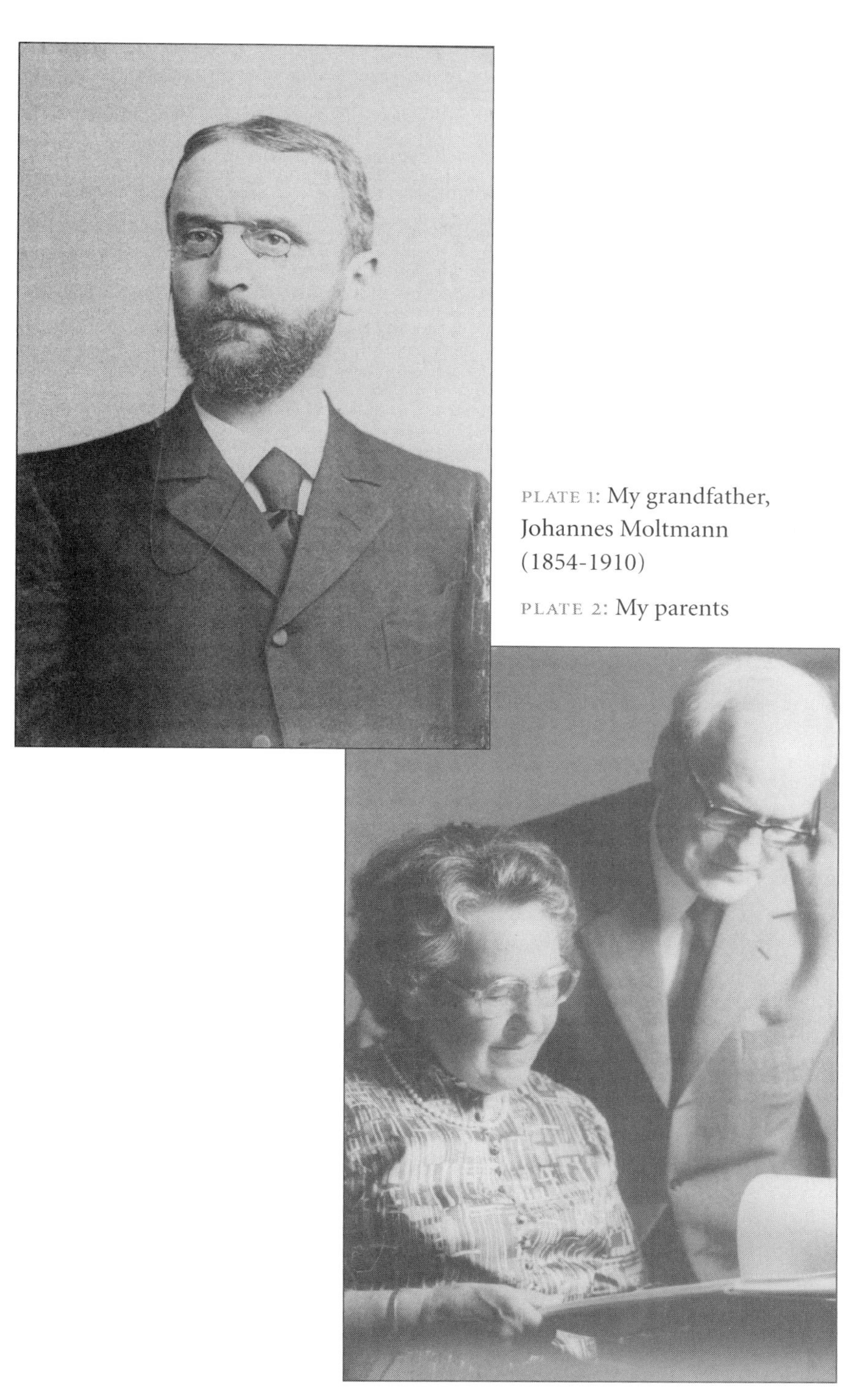

PLATE 1: My grandfather, Johannes Moltmann (1854-1910)

PLATE 2: My parents

PLATE 3: With my sisters and brother

PLATE 4: The first day at school, 1932

PLATE 5: With my mother

PLATE 6 (TOP): Air force auxiliary, 1943–. Myself third from left; next to me Gerhard Schopper, the friend killed at my side during 'Operation Gomorrah'

PLATE 7: Karl Barth and Ernst Wolf at the meetings of the Gesellschaft für Evangelische Theologie in Bielefeld, 1953

PLATE 8: Hans Joachim Iwand, 1952

PLATE 9: My doctoral supervisor, Otto Weber, 1952

PLATE 10: Wedding in Arisdorf, Switzerland

PLATE 11: The church in Wasserhorst

PLATE 12: Confirmation class in Wasserhorst with myself as pastor, 1954

PLATE 13: At the Church Seminary in Wuppertal

PLATE 14 (TOP LEFT): Hans Walter Wolff

PLATE 15 (TOP RIGHT): Rudolf Bohren, colleague and friend in Wuppertal

PLATE 16: With Gerhard Gloege

PLATE 17: Farewell to New York, 1968

PLATE 18: Elisabeth Moltmann-Wendel, 1970

PLATE 19 (TOP): Ecumenical World Youth Conference in Turku, Finland, July 1968

PLATE 20: With Wilhelm Niesel at the General Assembly of the World Alliance of Reformed Churches in Nairobi, 1971

PLATE 21: With Archbishop Knox at the World Eucharistic Congress in Melbourne, February 1973

PLATE 22: A visit to Union Theological Seminary, New York City, in the early 1970s, photographed with James Cone, visiting professors Dorothee Soelle and Gustavo Gutiérrez, and doctoral student Christopher Morse.

PLATE 23 (TOP): Discussion with Professor Kitamori about 'the pain of God', Tokyo, 1973

PLATE 24: Kyoto, 1973

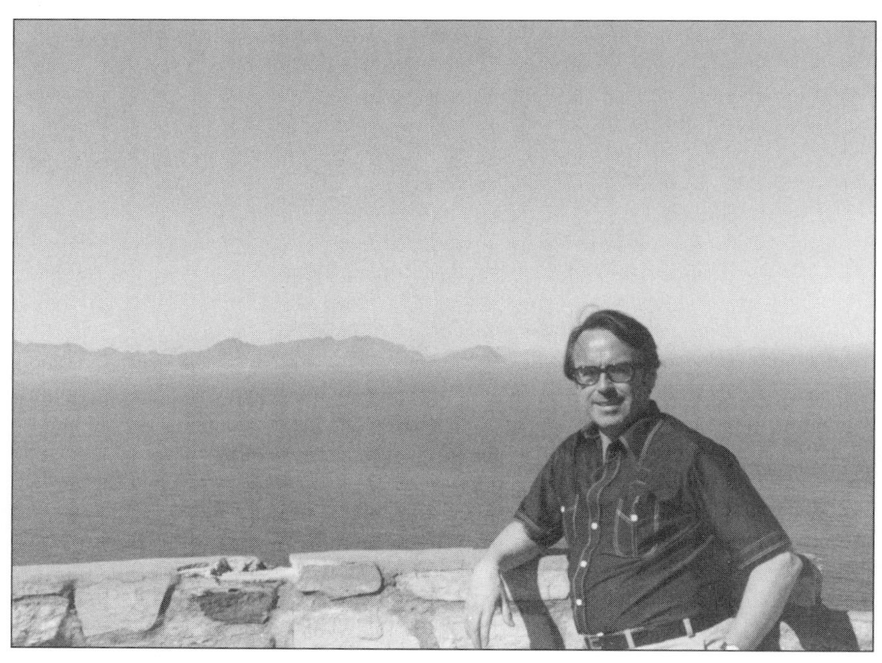

PLATE 25: At the Cape of Good Hope, April 1978

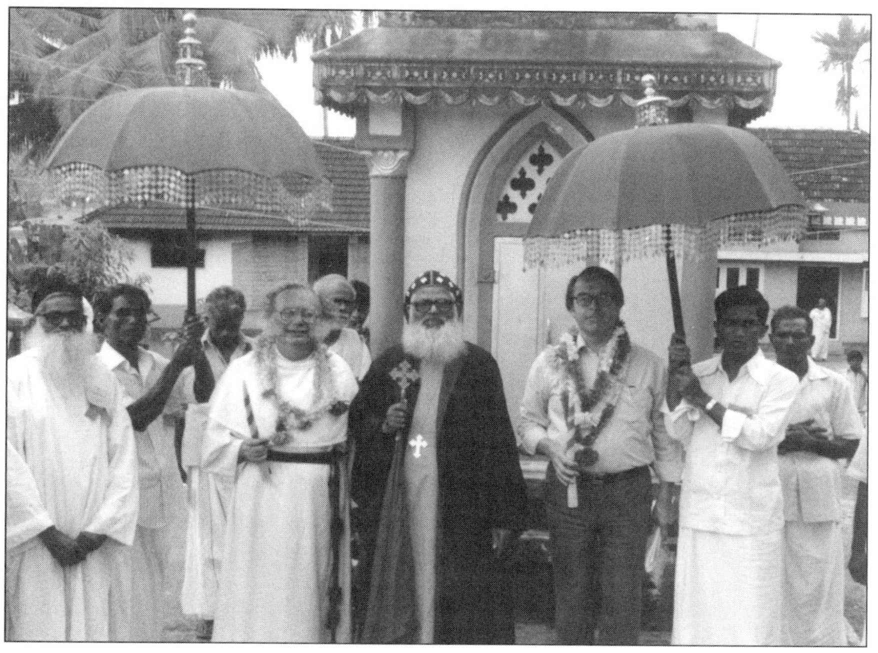

PLATE 26: With Metropolitan Mar Osthathios at a missionary festival in Kerala, India, September 1978

PLATE 27: Audience with Pope Paul VI, March 1972

PLATE 28: Meeting with Pope John Paul II at the Congresso Teologico Internazionale di Pneumatologia, March 1982

PLATE 29: With Emil Fackenheim in Bangor, Maine, December 1983

PLATE 30: In the Christian Academy House, Seoul, Korea, 1984

part V

Political Theology

ELEVEN

A FIRST BEGINNING IN TÜBINGEN, 1967

I am giving the troubled years from 1968 to 1972 in Tübingen the heading 'Political Theology'. This was certainly not the only field in which I was involved during these years, but it was nonetheless at the centre of the dispute with the protesting students, and in those years political theology was the theme of my lecture tours and conference addresses.

We had two beginnings in Tübingen, in 1967 before our journey to America and in 1968 after we came back. The first beginning was peaceful and purely academic, the second turbulent from the start. I shall try to describe these experiences, starting from the personal ones and passing on to the outward circumstances of life during that time.

In 1967, while I was in Bonn, I received an invitation to the chair for systematic theology in the Protestant theological faculty of the Eberhard-Karls University, Tübingen. I was first on the list of candidates. The previous year had faced us with a question of conscience. Our teacher Otto Weber had died suddenly, and his chair for Reformed theology in Göttingen was therefore vacant. In Bonn we had an opportunity to build a house on the other side of the Rhine. Elisabeth had already drawn up exact plans. Where ought we to go? I was not drawn to Göttingen. Moreover, for the Reformed brethren I was not Reformed enough—at least I had not the blessing of coming from a Reformed family. Then there was Ernst Käsemann. He had pushed foward the invitation to Tübingen, and he now came and appealed to my heart in prophetic tones, and to my conscience with threatening apocalyptic warnings. In the end it was probably the offer of a large flat in Tübingen that turned the scales, as a way of finally escaping from the unhappy situation in Bonn, although Elisabeth found it difficult to say goodbye to her plans for the house. With the help of my research assistant Winterberg and our friend Hans-Ulrich Kirchhoff, we packed up and on a cold day in March drove south. As we drove in darkness through the Schönbuch to Tübingen, we felt that, like Snow White, we were travelling over 'the seven mountains' to 'the seven dwarfs'. We then arrived in the land of the Swabians. Our Rhenish furniture-removers came back from their meal and said they had been given 'chopped-up noodles' to eat: these were the famous Swabian 'spätzle'.

Hausserstrasse 43 was a large house in Bauhaus style, with a wide balcony and a glorious view. But the flat was above the Institute for Mission and Ecumenical Studies, and we had a good climb to get to it. But each child had her own room and we had plenty of space.

The chair was well equipped with two posts for assistants, research assistants, and a secretary. I also brought with me more than 15 doctoral students and soon began work with them. For me, the seminar for graduate students was important, not just academically (because there I could try out my ideas for the first time), but personally too. If one has gone along a stretch of the road together and has worked together on something, friendships often develop which endure after the doctorate has become a thing of the past. Later I invited my former doctoral students to Tübingen for two days every year, not in order to found a 'school', but so as to share in their careers and their work. We always had a report from one of them, one year from those involved in academic theology and the next year from someone engaged in practical work, and we remained in contact.

The venerable faculty still kept up its fine old academic customs: On Sunday between 11.00 and 12.00 one received a first visit, which never lasted longer than 15 minutes, and this visit was then returned. Unfortunately, this custom died out in the generation after me, so that people no longer know each other, family to family. Gowns were still worn on academic occasions. These disappeared without a trace in the cellars of the new main lecture hall in 1968, when cheeky students maintained that under the gowns 'they could smell the fug of 1,000 years'. The theological faculty had a good reputation and attracted students from abroad. Without daring to characterize my great colleagues of those former days, I shall not suppress my personal impressions completely.

In systematic theology, Gerhard Ebeling was the star. He was also the editor of the *Zeitschrift für Theologie und Kirche* and tried to combine Luther's doctrine of faith with the truths of historical-critical research. His lectures were prepared with scrupulous care, but left no room for students' questions, either during the lectures or afterwards. After 1968, when the students did begin to ask questions, this made him so unhappy that he went to Zurich, where in the Hermeneutical Institute things were still as they should be. His eloquent sermons in the Stiftskirche (which was always full on these occasions) were real events. The second systematic theologian was Hermann Diem, a Barthian with a love for Kierkegaard. As a pastor in the Confessing Church in the Third Reich, he had only come late to the faculty and to academic work. When he was rector from 1966 to 1967, he put in hand the critical appraisal of the university's National Socialist past. He willingly explained his liking for Württemberg wine by the fact that he was a cooper's son. It was because Diem retired that I was invited to the chair.

For New Testament studies there were the brilliant Otto Michel and Ernst Käsemann. They always took up a contrary position to each other, the one having Pietist inclinations, the other a rigorous love of truth. Michel was a historian of rank. His interpretation of the Epistle to the Hebrews could be relied on.[1]

Käsemann and his wife became close friends. Their daughter Elisabeth went to Argentina in order to put into practice what her father had talked about and, after having been cruelly tortured, was shot by the military junta in 1977. Astonishingly enough, her body was released. I had to take the funeral, and Käsemann had impressed on me, 'The sermon: no more than 10 sentences!' In his lectures and seminars Käsemann continued the struggle of the Confessing Church, which he had carried on in Gelsenkirchen with a congregation of miners. Unfortunately, during the war he had acquired a sergeant-major's voice, which was not to the liking of every student. The maxim of his life was the old pirate saying: 'the friend of God and the enemy of the whole world'. For truth's sake, he broke off old friendships, first with Bultmann, then with Fuchs, then with Ebeling, finally, alas, with me, too, because he did not like my dialogue with Judaism. But our ways already began to drift apart a little when I replaced his 'new obedience' in faith by 'liberty in the breadth of the Holy Spirit'. His interpretations of the Epistle to the Hebrews (written in prison) and of the Epistle to the Romans—his great work—were always theological.[2] As a result he roused the criticism of historical scholars in the English-speaking world, who sought for an answer to 'the new question about Paul'. As a Christian, Käsemann felt himself to be a 'partisan' in a country occupied by foreign forces. He had a powerful theology of the cross, but he had problems with Christ's resurrection. He was buried with the text of Isaiah 26.13: 'O LORD our God, other lords besides thee have ruled over us, but thy name alone we acknowledge.' And that characterizes his theology of resistance in the Babylonian captivity of Christianity in this world, in its alienation from God.

The Dutch Heiko Oberman was a rising star in the heavens of church history, and from Harvard he brought to Tübingen the wind of a wider world. His Institute for Late Medieval and Reformation History flourished, for with his journalistic gifts he was well able to communicate effectively his eminent historical researches. Where the apartheid regime in South Africa was concerned, he was too conservative for my taste, but he and his wife kept an open and hospitable house, and with both of them one could carry on a controversial discussion without their taking offence. Oberman also finally brought the spirit of the West European Reformation to Lutheran Tübingen and brightened the deliberate ignorance one occasionally came across.[3] His wife's health required a dry desert climate, so an invitation to Tucson, Arizona, was timely. There Heiko had to give courses in history to undergraduates, 'From Stone Age to Renaissance' or 'From Plato to Nato', as he derisively put it. But he took it on. I visited them later when I was in Tucson to give a lecture. Heiko Oberman died two years ago. He knew he was dying and wrote a moving farewell letter to his friends, among whom he included us too.

In the autumn of 1970 Eberhard Jüngel came to Tübingen from Zurich in Gerhard Ebeling's place. I had fought for him, against the wishes of Werner Jetter, who did not want him because Jüngel, like his master Karl Barth, had called infant baptism in question. Jetter wanted Ratschow from Marburg, whom I did not want. But I got my way. I knew Jüngel from my student recreational retreats on Langeoog, to which he came with other students from the language college in East Berlin. My pleasure in his coming was somewhat dimmed later, because we were so similar theologically that we perhaps felt that we were rivals The formality between colleagues in the faculty which was then the custom often provided the distance needed if one was to avoid stepping on the other's toes. But we probably did not always make things easy for each other. So my pleasure in our friendship in our later years is all the greater, a friendship in which Hans Küng also shares.

Among colleagues of the same age as myself, I appreciated Hartmut Gese's Old Testament learning, even though he was otherwise high church in his thinking. The liberal theologian Dietrich Rössler held the chair for practical theology. Theologically, he and I were worlds apart, but personally we got on well, and our two families went on outings together. Early on, he gave a check to our new theological beginnings by declaring us to be 'positional theologians', while considering himself to be a 'critical theologian' who was above all positions.[4] I might of course mention others, too, such as Werner Jetter, Eltester, Galling, and Steinbach, but I shall content myself with those I have named.

On an earlier visit to Tübingen, the student pastor Aichelin had offered me the bait of interdisciplinary discussions, especially with scientists. I also came with great expectations, since for many years I had taken part in similar discussions in Heidelberg in the FEST. Unfortunately, after 1968 the number of students in our faculty grew in a few years from 600 to over 2,000, so that seminars overflowed and examinations were endless. Consequently, I had neither the time nor the energy for these discussions.

But from 1961, on the fringe of the university, lived my revered Ernst Bloch, with his wife, Carola. To his surprise, more and more theologians came to him and sought the 'warm Red' of his hope. In 1968 he published his book on the religion of Exodus and the kingdom, which he called *Atheismus im Christentum*.[5] In the prologue we find the words: 'Only an atheist can be a good Christian, only a Christian can be a good atheist.' The first statement is his own, the second mine. He gladly accepted my 'offering', as he called it, and expected from me a book about 'Christianity in atheism'. His book contains a splendid but wilful interpretation of Job—Job as a Hebrew rebel against God—and ends by marrying two texts: 'To be radical means grasping things at their roots. The root of all things is the human being', said Karl Marx. And: 'It does not yet appear what we shall be. But we know that when it appears, we shall be like him (i.e., God) for we shall see him as he is' (1 John 3.2). That was nothing less than a crafty eschatological annulment of atheistic humanism.

As well as Ernst Bloch I found Walter Jens, who had brought Bloch to Tübingen, and also the philosopher Walter Schulz, who always filled several lecture rooms simultaneously with his lectures. There was also the liberal Österbergkreis which had been established in opposition to the conservative group Für Forschung und Lehre (For Research and Doctrine). In 1969 I stood in Tübingen's marketplace together with Dietrich Geyer, the expert for Eastern Europe, and spoke against the emergency decrees. We enjoyed meetings with the political scientist Klaus von Beyme, while together with the lawyer Jürgen Baumann we theologians also threw ourselves into support for a revision of the law on abortion (§218 of the Civil Law Book) and drew up a report.[6]

In the Catholic theological faculty I very soon formed lasting friendships with Norbert Greinacher and Hans Küng. In Küng's ecumenical institute we arranged a joint seminar with twelve Catholic, twelve Protestant, and six American theologians on christological questions. Küng and I took over the theological study group of the two faculties from Hermann Diem and Ernst Käsemann and headed it for 25 years. It had its highlights—when, for example, Herbert Haag delivered his 'Farewell to the Devil' and Ernst Bloch, whom I had invited, protested vigorously that a-theism was not followed by a-Satanism; or when Hans Küng put forward his doubts about the dogma of infallibility, and Ernst Käsemann claimed to be deeply disappointed 'because this very afternoon I wrote two infallible statements'. While he was still in favour, Küng arranged via Cardinal Willebrand for Elisabeth and me to have a special audience with Pope Paul VI in Rome. We were impressed.

Later Küng co-opted me to the editorial committee of the reform Catholic periodical *Concilium*. Year for year we published our ecumenical numbers and worked excellently together without any problems. In the editorial conferences I got to know the splendid Catholic breadth and learnt to move freely in it. As far as Rome was concerned, I was occasionally the only one who had no problems with the Congregation for the Doctrine of the Faith! When Küng's Catholic permission to teach (*missio canonica*) was withdrawn in 1979 and he had to leave the theological faculty, my colleague Eberhard Jüngel and I came out on his side publicly and very vigorously. The outcome was the so-called Tübingen solution: Küng, together with the ecumenical institute, was placed directly under the president of the university; that is to say, he remained a university theologian, even if

Rome was no longer prepared to view him as a Catholic one. Together with Walter Kasper and Eberhard Jüngel, we had formed the 'meeting of systematic theologians', to which Elisabeth of course also belonged. When, after Rome's affair with Küng, Walter Kasper disappeared, only four of us were left. We disputed and were reconciled. What had been a kind of professional organization grew into a circle of friends, in which mutual listening and mutual respect held the balance.

On 11 July 1967 I received an unexpected visit. A delegation of Swabian Pietists appeared, consisting of Pastor Grünzweig, Magister Brandenburg, Pastor Tlach, and the missions inspector Fritz Hubmer from Hülmen. They brought me the biggest bunch of flowers of my life, gave me Johann Albrecht Bengel's *Erklärte Offenbarung Johannis, oder vielmehr Jesu Christi* of 1724, and welcomed me into 'the company of those who are waiting for their Lord'. I was almost bereft of speech in this for me quite unaccustomed group, but was also delighted at receiving so much sympathy.

This meeting had of course its pre-history: I do not come from Württemberg and was hardly familiar with Swabian traditions, but in 1958 in Wuppertal, before I came to Ernst Bloch, Rudolf Bohren and the Mennonite Johannes Harder had drawn my attention to Christoph Blumhardt. Bohren was interested in the healing miracles and the pastoral ministry in the Blumhardt movement, Harder in the religious-social hope for the kingdom of God.

When in 1965 I talked about the *Theology of Hope* in the Protestant Academy in Bad Boll for the first time, a little man sat quite literally at my feet and wrote everything down. It was Fritz Hubmer. He is the author of a long enthusiastic review of the book, published in October 1965 in the *Mitteilungsblatt des Gemeinschaftsverbandes Württembergischer Brüderbund: Gemeinschaftsgruss*. In the introduction he said, 'With this article we are fulfilling the promise we made in the last number to elucidate more fully the hopeful new beginning in German theology which is linked with the name of Professor Moltmann ... For we do not wish to see only the night-time shades of the End-time which interpenetrate Christianity, but would also greet the joyful signs that the many prayers for a new, biblically based beginning in theology have been graciously heard.' He found in me a 'combative theology!' and the much-desired alternative to Rudolf Bultmann: 'Whereas Prof. Bultmann stops at Christ's death and tomb, Prof. Moltmann begins there: Christian faith lives from the raising of the crucified Christ and reaches out towards the promises of Christ's universal future.'

Life in the presence of the Coming One was indeed a link between me and the Swabian Pietists, but what for me was alien was their stress on the salvation of the individual soul, and their quiescent eschatology, with its conservative political consequences. As early as 1959, in opposition to 'theology in the sphere of the consciousness' from Schleiermacher to Bultmann, I had invoked the two Blumhardts: 'Contrary to the solution "only be saved!" they put at the centre the Word: Seek first the kingdom of God and his righteousness and all these things shall be added unto you.' At that time I wanted to follow Leonhard Ragaz: 'From religion to the kingdom of God, from the church to the world, from concern about my own self to hope for the whole.' That was the way Christoph Blumhardt preached: 'Everyone goes about sighing and looking for something and does not know what it is. One would like to call to these people: Men, forget yourselves! Think of the things of God!'[7]

But in 1968, when I followed this path of Blumhardt's in critical solidarity with the Marxism of Roger Garaudy and Ernst Bloch and the obstreperous students, the Swabian Pietists shrank back from me and, disappointed, wrote in their circular letters, 'We thought that we had got a theologian in Tübingen who was waiting for the Second Coming of the Lord, and what we got was a Marxist.' When a journalist reported my lecture at the Eucharistic World Congress in Melbourne in 1973, in which I talked about the unity of the church and the unity of humanity in this divided world, I was actually defamed through false quotations, as if I had been taken in by the Antichrist. After clarifying conversations with Mr Tlach before the church authorities, the polemic against me disappeared; but the mistrust remained.

I myself have never, as far as I am aware, attacked the Swabian Pietists. But Bengel's salvation-history, dispensationalist reading of the Bible with the help of 'numbers as a key to the world'[8] was quite alien to my thinking: as Christoph Blumhardt said, 'Jesus is coming,' and not in 1836, as Bengel calculated, but now—now already, every new day. That was also my prayer. When John Wesley heard about Bengel's calculations, he said that he didn't want to wait so long. If the future of Christ is delegated to the calendar, we have to wait for it; but if we accept it in its hope, we become creatively active in order to fall into line with it and to prepare the way for it. In 1991, in my book *The Spirit of Life: A Universal Affirmation*, I took up Friedrich Ötinger's *Theologie ex idea vitae deducta*, written in 1765 to confute Descartes' mechanistic world view and La Mettrie's *L'homme machine* (Man a Machine), and I found even his millenarian eschatology 'Die güldene Zeit' (the golden age) as congenial as the pedagogical millenarianism of Johann Amos Comenius before him and the biblical millenarianism of Johann Tobias Beck later.[9] I was more concerned with this, admittedly somewhat speculative, side of Swabian Pietism than with the pietism of the devout soul, which probably goes back to Friedrich Hofacker in the nineteenth century.

When the Bengelhaus in Derendingen was established in opposition to the protesting students and the alleged atheism in the Protestant *Stift* in Tübingen, and Peter Beyerhaus, the most conservative member of our faculty, had the say there, I was against this split among the students. But when the first Bengelhaus students appeared in the peace movement with the placard 'live without armaments,' and had learnt from Taizé the unity of 'contemplation and struggle', I was quite reconciled to this house too.

I was greatly touched when the regional bishop Paul Dieterich honoured me on my seventy-fifth birthday in Bad Boll with the title of a 'Swabian Father': 'So they are, those who 34 years ago finally found their way to Württemberg like "wandering Arameans". He has become a true Swabian Father, even if a somewhat different one. That is the highest title which the Protestant church in Württemberg can confer. Please accept it! A Swabian Father who has also served the church of Württemberg faithfully by waking its traditions of resistance to new life. We thank you for opening up for generations the path to freedom and for teaching us to hope.' My love for Christoph Blumhardt deepened so much in these Tübingen years that in 1999 I acknowledged in Bad Boll that 'Christoph Blumhardt was a reason for my coming to Württemberg; and he is a reason for my staying in Tübingen. With the two Blumhardts I feel at home in the land of Swabia.'

Theologically, my beginnings in Tübingen were dominated by the development of the programme for a political theology. Johann Baptist Metz, professor of fundamental theology in Münster, had brought the designation into the public discussion, so as to break out of the narrows of bourgeois 'religion as a private affair' and the limitations of the personalist, existentialist, and transcendentalist theology of that time. Metz belonged to 'the anthropological turn' in Karl Rahner's theology, but he at once grasped the significance of the eschatological horizon of Christian theology. In his important essay of 1966, 'Kirche und Welt im eschatologischen Horizont' (Church and World in the Eschatological Horizon), he described the step he had taken in this direction as follows: 'The attempt to read and understand the whole of theology as anthropology is an important achievement in present theological work. But this "anthropologically turned" theology remains in danger of becoming devoid of the world and devoid of history unless it is understood as being first and foremost eschatology. For it is only in the eschatological horizon of hope that the world appears as history.'[10] For this he also cited the *Theology of Hope*. But for me a key sentence was the following: 'Every eschatological theology must become a political theology, as a theology critical of society.'[11] I gladly took up this directional thrust, because it corresponded very well with my own thinking; and so in those years there came to be a link between the theology of hope and political theology. Metz's intention was not, as some people feared, to politicize theology; his aim was a 'theology with its face turned towards the world', 'talk about God in our own time'. My concern was the prophetic Christian criticism of the idols of political religion and the arrogance of power; and hope for the victims.

As I have said, I first met Baptist Metz in 1966 at Ernst Bloch's eightieth birthday in Tübingen. The 'atheist for God's sake' brought about our ecumenical friendship. Later we were often apostrophized as 'theological twins'.[12] But we did not stop short at Bloch. At the deepest level, what led to the development of a political theology in those years was shock over the failure of the churches and the theologians in the face of the German crimes against humanity, symbolized by the name Auschwitz, a name that can never be blotted out. Why that appalling Christian silence? Had the bourgeois privatization of religion secularized the politics of our country so far that they fell into this abyss? Did conscious or unconscious anti-Semitism keep the Christians silent when the Jews were taken away? Was the misinterpreted Lutheran two-kingdoms doctrine responsible: 'Christ for the soul—Hitler for the people'? As can be seen from our publications, talk about God 'in our own time' became talk about God 'after Auschwitz'. For Metz, the consequence was the demand for a post-Enlightenment 'anamnetic culture' of 'dangerous remembrances' of suffering and the theodicy process of modern history.[13] For me, what followed was the turn to a political theology of the cross. This began in 1969 with an essay titled

'The Theological Criticism of Political Religion',[14] and found fullest expression in 1972 in the book *The Crucified God* (ET 1974).

The name political theology was not our invention, however. It had an unfortunate earlier history. In 1922 and 1934 Hitler's conservative Catholic, anti-Semitic, and anti-democratic constitutional lawyer Carl Schmitt made it the slogan for the political dictatorship for which he had a predilection.[15] 'That one is sovereign who can declare the state of emergency,' and the political state of emergency corresponds theologically to the miracle, he declared, in order to justify Hitler's enabling law, which, however, was the very opposite of a miracle, being in fact a catastrophe. He found a theological justification for dictatorship with a political doctrine of sin: 'Against absolute evil ... there is only dictatorship'—as if dictatorship were not itself absolutely evil! Whereas the anarchists cried with Bakunin, 'Neither God nor state,' Carl Schmitt, in the final apocalyptic struggle against these Antichrists, was 'for God and state'. The subject of his political theology was state power, not the church. But Metz and I were thinking of the church and the political responsibility of Christianity. That was why Metz later called his theology 'new political theology'.[16] But although these differences are easily recognizable, they did not unfortunately prevent confusion at that time.

With a lecture on the theological criticism of political religion, I travelled up and down the country and spread my views in Germany, Sweden, Italy, England, and North America. Metz and I brought out a series called *Gesellschaft und Theologie* (Society and Theology), in which we made available to German readers among other things James Cone's *Black Theology* (in 1971) and Gustavo Gutiérrez 's *Theology of Liberation* (in 1973), as well as Elisabeth Moltmann-Wendel's *Menschenrechte für die Frau* (1979). We very quickly came into lively contact with the liberation theology that was growing up in Latin America, with the rebellious black theology in the USA, and with the popular Minjung theology in Korea. We shared the forward hope of the new eschatology and political commitment to the liberation of the oppressed and the victims of institutionalized violence.

For Metz and myself these two factors have remained. What is a thing of the past, however, is the over-valuation of the political aspect as 'the total' (Carl Schmitt). The political and military East-West conflict ended in 1989, but its place was taken by the globalization of the economy and the total marketing of everything and every relationship. Whereas once politics deregulated the economy, today politics are regulated by the economy, for this has become trans-national, whereas politics are still persistently national. Theology 'with its face turned towards the world' must therefore also become an economic and ecological theology if it wishes to take on the forces of our time.

TWELVE

A SECOND BEGINNING IN TÜBINGEN

In the winter of 1967–68 the situation in Tübingen had already changed dramatically. In April 1968 I came without warning into the unrest of the student world. The external factors are quickly named: the Vietnam War evoked a growing anti–Vietnam War movement all over the world. In some places this turned into anti-Americanism: 'Ami go home!' On Good Friday 1968 Rudi Dutschke, the student leader and Bloch's friend, was shot in Berlin. May saw the beginning of the Paris revolts, in which students joined with trade unionists. In tranquil Tübingen, at first the changes appeared only in lecture rooms and seminars. Everything began quite reasonably, when students wanted to ask questions during the lectures. Some of my colleagues permitted this; others did not. Things got hotter when radical students asked other participants to discuss political questions instead of listening to the lectures. Some of my colleagues fought for their lectures with the help of porters and threats of the police; others—including myself—quickly took a vote, and lo and behold, most of those present wanted the lecture and not a political protest. Then came the sit-ins, taken over from the civil rights movement. These took place in front of the entrances to the new lecture hall, to which there was therefore no access. Colleagues who were prevented from entering objected, sometimes forcibly, so that in the end both professors and students felt physically under attack.

Then there was a flood of leaflets. At first, right-wing and reactionary professors were the objects of attack, and 'progressive' ones were unmolested. But then the radicals realized that the 'progressives', who knew their Marx but were not Marxists, were much the more dangerous. The result was an ominous leaflet attacking Ernst Käsemann and me. Our theology of the cross was criticized from an 'anti-authoritarian' perspective; the word sado-masochism being already used, before Dorothee Sölle came forward with this misinterpretation. The reproaches against the *Theology of Hope*, which had been made in the GDR, were warmed up. Moreover, Käsemann and I were both 'over 30' and for that reason alone no longer trustworthy. The author of the pamphlet was the child of a good family—his father was a professor of theology—and had been my research assistant in Bonn. He mutated from theologian into social worker and landed in the social services in Stuttgart instead of in a parish. His anti-authoritarian gesture always seemed to me to be in this case the result of a late adolescent attempt to free himself from his family.

Among the students, the Marxist-orientated scene soon split up into orthodox Stalinists and Maoist sectarians, Marxist-Leninist groups, hippies, and Trotskyists. I remember a group that enthusiastically supported Hodscha's Marxism in Albania. Some were very strictly ideological; others preferred to 'play' with drugs and commune experiments and caught up with Woodstock. In the student clubhouse there were trainings, held with authoritarian seriousness and an ultimate religious claim. One of my doctoral students became a 'Jacobin' and with his band struck up the Marseillaise on his trumpet at Hölderlin's grave in the old cemetery. Colleagues who had been in the same student fraternity as him prevented him from getting his doctorate (contrary to my vote), because they were afraid of being hanged from the lampposts in the Wilhelmstrasse by him and his comrades. Today he is a well-known Swabian writer. An older student, with a doctorate in law, attended my seminars. At first he was a follower of Bultmann, then of Moltmann, and finally of Mao. He could later be seen in the Zoo Hotel. One student with rich parents proved his left-wing affinities by standing under the window during faculty meetings and whistling the Marseillaise. Today he is engaged in teacher training. Once these left-wing students had caught up with their Marx reading and were no longer able to impress their professors with it, some of them went over to 'critical rationalism' and recommended us to read Karl Popper. Instead of Marxist criticism of religion, there was now rationalist criticism of theology.

During those years there were no university festivities and no student fêtes any more, because everyone was afraid of the people who turned up in tattered proletarian-look, shouting, 'And in Vietnam the people are dying.'

The students were surprised that no workers joined their demonstrations on Tübingen's streets against whatever it might be. But these people were at work at the time, because their families had to be fed. However, the old Tübingen families did not take amiss anything the students did, for they lived from the rents they paid for their rooms. I can remember an anti-war demonstration that was being planned. Then the news came that police had already taken up a position in Lustnau. Brave colleagues left the house, and the number of students who were prepared to protest also shrank noticeably. But then everything passed off peacefully.

What was the outcome of all this? Did the unrest produce any results?

Student generations come and go, so the climate of protest did not endure for long. The winners were the people in the institutions. The ministry of education in Stuttgart changed 'the system' in its own favour and curtailed the academic freedoms of students and professors. Some assistants tried to further their careers and applied for positions as university presidents. To prevent the students from getting foolish ideas again, the universities were in the long run reduced to schools: academic freedoms were driven out in favour of study courses, examination pressure was increased through intermediate exams, members of the Communist Party were forbidden to practise their profession, and general fear for their jobs kept the following student generations subdued.

In theology, concern with the atheism of Marx and Nietzsche, Freud and Bloch was superseded by the return of religiosity—preferably in the form of multi-religiosity. We had just acquired a taste for Bonhoeffer's 'religionless Christianity', were praising 'Jesus for atheists' with Machovec, or even wanted with Dorothee Sölle 'to believe atheistically in God'. And now, lo and behold, here came Hans Küng arm in arm with all the better world religions and began the inter-religious dialogue. Heinz Zahrnt wanted to drive out the revolution with religion. After the bitter disappointment at finding that conditions were strongly resistant to change through students, the 'new inwardness' came into being, organized in encounter groups. And the theologians withdrew from the public forum in order, with Schleiermacher, to engage in 'arousing devout states of feeling'. The '1968-ers' undoubtedly left many traces behind them and noticeably changed the cultural climate in the Federal Republic, but as far as the public climate of opinion in the '80s and '90s was concerned, '68 was no more than an episode.

Admittedly, the more conservative professors did not see things in this light. They had seen apocalyptic visions, and still cherish them down to the present day. Here I am thinking not only of my conservative colleagues Ulrich Wilckert and Peter Beyerhaus, but also of Joseph Ratzinger. In his reminiscences, he writes, 'The "signs of the time" which I had increasingly sensed in Münster became noticeably more dramatic ... Almost at a stroke, the philosophical "paradigm" on which students and some of their teachers based their thinking changed. Whereas up to then Bultmann's theology and Heidegger's philosophy had determined the framework of thinking, now the existentialist pattern broke down almost overnight, and was replaced by the Marxist one. Ernst Bloch was now teaching in Tübingen and belittled Heidegger as a petty bourgeois; in the Protestant theological faculty, Jürgen Moltmann was invited to a chair, almost at the same time as I came to Tübingen myself. In his fascinating book *Theology of Hope* he had conceived theology afresh and completely differently, in the light of Bloch. Existentialism crumbled away and in the whole university the Marxist revolution took fire and shook it to its foundations. Years before, one could have expected that the theological faculties would be a bulwark against the Marxist temptation. Now the opposite was the case: they became the real ideological centre.'[1]

At that time Ratzinger joined together with Wickert and Beyerhaus in Tübingen in order to resist the 'cruel face of this atheistic religiousness', in the face of which the denominational controversies seemed to him slight. But in the disputes with these students he then abandoned us and moved to Regensburg in order 'to pursue his theology in a less over-heated milieu'. I later mentioned to him how quickly the spectre whose terrible face he thought he could see at that time had disappeared. He was also a little embarrassed at having left his colleagues in Tübingen in the lurch; but for him the apocalyptic vision of the future of Christianity's 'little flock' in the great dangers of the world apparently remained. Ratzinger did not understand that for Bloch and me at that time it was not the Marxist idea but the messianic hope which became the real anti-existentialist alternative.

In this troubled Tübingen, my lectures on 'Die Kirche in der modernen Gesellschaft' (The Church in Modern Society) had to be given in the great hall, in which there were no desks for the students to write on. The room overflowed, although our faculty had no more than 600 students. It emerged that a third of those present were Catholics and that of these a third were Jesuits. I arranged tutorials to accompany the lectures. At the end I put forward my ideas for a 'political hermeneutics of the gospel. Existential history and world history'.[2] The students joked that now rifles were going to be distributed. When I told Ebeling this, he just looked at me thunderstruck.

I had to hold my seminar on political theology in one of the student dining rooms, where the acoustics were for many people very poor. The struggle with overflowing seminars was a considerable burden in the years that followed, because as teacher one inevitably faced defeat. If one worked with groups, the seminar as a whole was poor; if one worked with the whole seminar, only people in the first row talked. I got no help even from older university experts in teaching theory.

On 19 June 1968 I held my inaugural lecture 'Gott und Auferstehung. Auferstehungsglaube im Forum der Theodizeefrage'.[3] The main lecture hall was so full that the dean (Rössler) and I could hardly get into the room, and at the rostrum I had no room to move. Afterwards Carola Bloch came in great excitement and complained that I had dared to talk about God at all. She suffered under the theodicy question because her parents had been gassed in the Treblinka death camp. Ernst Müller, the venerable editor of the local paper, the *Schwäbisches Tagblatt,* stopped me afterwards in the street and read me an endless lecture, telling me how he would have dealt with the subject, and twisting off a button from my jacket in the process. But he did the same with everyone he could catch who had given an academic lecture.

In 1968 the university was an attraction for foreign students and professors, and the Protestant theology faculty especially. Since we ourselves still felt a little strange in Tübingen, we were glad to invite these visitors to open evenings in our house. This resulted in lasting friendships with the Australian Jesuit O'Collins, the Japanese Shin Kitagawa, the Irish Dick McKinney, the French Alain Blancy and Jean Pierre Thévenaz, and others. The Americans were particularly grateful, since many people showed them the cold shoulder because of the Vietnam War. I mention that only in order to show that it is not just great ideas that can have an effect, but little gestures too.

In October 1968 I had two different eucharistic experiences which made me think, and later put their stamp on my doctrine of the Lord's

Supper.[4] On 25 October I flew to London, where I met Paul Oestreicher, who was at that time working in the external office of the Church of England. He invited me to an anti-Vietnam demonstration that was to take place in the streets of London. A motley collection of Protestant and Catholic Christians, together with people from 'the highways and byways', met in the offices of the Catholic publisher Sheed & Ward, and with a celebration of the Lord's Supper, sitting on the floor, we prepared ourselves for the demonstration by agreeing to renounce violence; for in the previous demonstration many people had been hurt. Bread and wine passed from hand to hand in a small circle, and we felt the bodily presence of Jesus among us. The next morning we sprang through Fleet Street and Trafalgar Square, shouting, 'Ho Ho Chi Min.' It all passed off without any violence or obscenities, and everyone was happy.

Afterwards I gave lectures in Cambridge for Professor Nineham, and the old eccentric Donald McKinnon, and in Lincoln for Alan Webster, and then went on to Edinburgh. There the conservative Barthian Tom Torrance eyed me very critically; his colleague MacIntire was more congenial.

Finally, I preached in St Giles, John Knox's church. After the sermon, those who stayed behind were served the Lord's Supper on silver trays by servers clad in black. The participants sat separate from one another, scattered here and there in the great church. There was no sense of community, and I went out of the beautiful church depressed. Where does Jesus' feast belong? On the streets of the poor who follow Jesus, or in the church of the baptized, the confirmed and established? I decided for the feast that is open to all, and to which the weary and heavy-laden are invited. Baptism, on the other hand, should be reserved for believers. That certainly contradicts the practice of our mainline churches, but it is in conformity with Jesus according to the Synoptic Gospels. Jesus' Supper is not a church meal for people who belong to one's own denomination. It is the feast of the crucified Christ, whose hands are stretched out to everyone. In my view the Roman Catholic and Orthodox restrictions are un-christian. In the worship of every denomination, I go to the Supper of Jesus whenever I hear his inviting voice, and I have never and nowhere been turned away. The Eucharist is in Jesus' literal sense 'catholic', that is to say all-embracing, exclusive of no one but inclusive of all.

THIRTEEN

LECTURE TOURS WORLDWIDE, 1969–75

I should only be telling half the truth if I hid the fact that after my return from America I always enjoyed lecture tours. Invitations came from many countries in response to the *Theology of Hope*, and these gave me so much pleasure, and buoyed me up so much, that I was seldom able to say no. If I now leaf though my diaries of those years, they make me feel somewhat dizzy. I seem to myself like a rider on a frozen lake who looks back in horror at the crumbling ice he has ridden over. But I was young and curious, and always unable to resist temptations. I led a kind of double life.

In the spring of 1969 Elisabeth and I again flew to America for three weeks. I gave lectures at Duke University, in Richmond, Virginia, in Boston, and at the Goethe Institute in New York. Together with Robert Bellah and Paul Lehmann, I held a conference at the Wellesley women's college. In Richmond we were caught in a snowstorm, and there were several feet of snow in Boston. From 18 to 23 July I flew to Philadelphia for two lectures and gave an interview for *Time Magazine* in New York. From 4 to 7 December we were both in Lund as the guests of Gustav Wingren, and were honoured by the faculty with a festive candlelight dinner.

In April 1970 Elisabeth and I flew to a Middle East conference in Cairo, at the invitation of the German congregations and schools, and in three weeks visited Cairo, Luxor, Beirut, Teheran, Istanbul, Thessaloniki, and Athens. The last war with Israel had just ended, and there were few tourists in Egypt. So together with our friend Rudolf Weckerling, at that time pastor in Beirut, we were able to view Karnack and the Valley of the Kings, Aswan, the pyramids, and the Egyptian Museum, and admire them in peace. I was introduced to the Coptic Institute by Boutros Ghali, later General Secretary of the United Nations and a Coptic Christian. Elisabeth went on to Baalbeck from Beirut, whereas I flew to Teheran. She flew home from Constantinople, while I gave a lecture in the theological faculty in Athens on 'Cross and Trinity', my purpose being to bring together the Protestant theology of the cross and the Orthodox doctrine of the Trinity—a subject that has never ceased to occupy me ever since. Unfortunately, there was a sherry party afterwards instead of a discussion. I can still clearly remember my first morning in Athens: I opened the window, and there lay the Acropolis before in all the splendour of the Greek sun. Unforgettable!

From 16 to 31 August 1970 my first appearance as speaker at an ecumenical conference followed. The World Alliance of Reformed Churches (Presbyterian and Congregational) had invited me to give the main lecture at its general assembly in Nairobi in Kenya. The theme was 'God reconciles and makes free.' It was James McCord, the president, who had invited me—the German Reformed brethren had not been asked. But Wilhelm Niesel's annoyance quickly disappeared because he heartily agreed with what I said. I related liberation and reconciliation to divided cities such as Berlin and Belfast, divided countries such as Germany and Korea, and the divided world of that time, with its separate hostile camps.[1] This met with agreement but also evoked protests from people who were bound for political reasons to support these divisions. The Koreans, with Professor Pong Nang Park, immediately invited me to Korea; the Hungarians, with Bishop Toth, also invited me to their country; but the representatives of the South African Reformed churches defended their apartheid regime, and the Northern Irish Presbyterians did not like me either.

The impression made by an African city with its huge slums was overwhelming. I came into contact with Donna Haldane's group of social workers, and she took me to Mathare Valley, where countless people were living in corrugated-iron huts without water, drainage, and electricity. When I got back to Tübingen, I collected money to provide huts with sewing machines for the women. We flew for a church service to Kikuyu, and to Nakaru to the Flamingo Lake, and also viewed the beauties of the country in the East African Great Rift Valley.

From 18 to 25 October 1970 I was in North America again. I had been elected dean in Tübingen for one semester, so I had no lecture obligations. I began my American tour with five lectures at Knox College, Toronto, then flew to Kalamazoo to give the first Homer J. Armstrong Lectures.[2] Here the full church had to be evacuated at short notice because of a bomb threat, so I spoke in the nearby theatre. Later I was invited to give these lectures every ten years, and was finally given an honorary doctorate by the faculty. I then went on via Rochester to Kansas City (where I was regaled in the 'Golden Ox' with the biggest steak that I have ever been offered); then on to Santa Barbara, to Lois and Walter Capps; to Montgomery, Alabama, where Meeks had meanwhile cast anchor; and to the AAR meetings in New York, where I was at one with Jim Cone in asking the question: 'How can I sing the Lord's song in a strange land?'[3] The subjects of my lectures were now shifting from political theology to the theology of the cross, and from the theology of hope to 'the first liberated of creation'.[4]

The year 1971 was marked by conferences rather than by lectures. At the end of January (29.1–2.3) I attended a conference of Danish clergy in Roskilde and then gave guest lectures in Arhus and Copenhagen. My stay increased my love for Denmark.

In July I interrupted the semester (2–9.7) and flew to Kampala, Uganda, in order to speak to the ecumenical Theological Education Fund on 'Christian Theology and Its Problems Today'.[5] We also visited the tomb of the last king of Uganda and saw women dancing in front of it: for when ancestors are reverenced, the ancestors themselves are present. In the West we have forgotten the presence of Christ among those who have gone before us. Perhaps that is the reason why so few Germans come to terms with the long shadows over their Nazi forebears.

At the end of July (30.7–5.8) Marcel Martin and I, together with some students, travelled to Arhus in order to hold a celebratory conference on 'Kaerlighed og Fantasi' (Merriment and Fantasy). Marcel had just published his book *Wir wollen hier auf Erden schon ...* (We Want Already Here on Earth ...),[6] and I had just brought out *Die ersten Freigelassenen der Schöpfung*,[7] our common aim being to free ourselves from the moral pressure of the 1968 movement. The Danes co-operated enthusiastically. It was my first celebratory, not just learned, theology.

At the end of August (30.8—3.9) the 'Challenge of Life' Hoffmann-La Roche Conference, which I have already mentioned, took place in Basel.[8] Elisabeth was also present. We met 'living legends', such as Margaret Mead, Talcott Parson, Jeanne Hersch, René König, Lord Todd, and Josua Lederberg, and were very pleased that theology (represented by Franz Böckle and myself) was included in the discussion. That became more of a rarity later on.

In October (3.10–11.10) the 'hope boys', Pannenberg, Metz, and I, were invited to New York to discuss 'Hope and the Future of Man' with the 'process guys', such as John Cobb, Daniel Day Williams, and Schubert Ogden, and also with the 'Teilhardians', such as Phil Hefner and Joe Sittler. Each of us had to prepare responses to the lectures of the others. Schubert Ogden attacked me sharply, but his teacher and master Charles Hartshorne checked him and defended me. The discussions were hard but heartfelt, for our common concern was the one common truth. The conference was one of the last of its kind, before post-modern arbitrariness set in, and everyone was content with his own truth.[9]

In March 1972 (5–12.3) Elisabeth and I were in Rome. Marschall Bieberstein had invited me to the Goethe Institute, with which the Facoltà Valdese and the Germanicum then joined. We used the time to explore the 'eternal city'. We had just arrived in the Hotel Santa Chiara near the little elephant monument when we received news from Cardinal Willebrand that Pope Paul VI had invited us to a special audience. Hans Küng had set it on foot. So Elisabeth covered her head with a dark scarf, and I got hold of a copy of the Italian edition of the *Theology of Hope*. The photos show us emerging out of the darkness into the luminous aura of 'the representative', and him bowing affably to us. We had only a brief conversation. Then he gave Elisabeth a commemorative medallion and me an illustrated book about Peter. He asked us to pray for him and said he would pray for us and our children. Afterwards, deeply impressed, we sat in St Peter's. But when we got back to the hotel, we heard that in Tübingen Esther had been thrown from her horse and was hurt. Our Tübingen pastor consoled us by saying that it could have been worse. It was in fact not as bad as we at first feared. In the Goethe Institute I gave my first lecture on 'The Crucified God and Apathetic Man'.[10] The room was so crowded that Michael Marschall had some fears for the structure.

At the end of May we both flew to Warsaw, where I talked to the Christian Academy (the training place for all the non–Roman Catholic churches) on 'Reconciliation and Peace'.[11] We listened to Chopin in the Lowitz Park, went to a performance of the opera *Don Quixote*, and drove with Andrej Woitowicz to Thorn, where a Pastor Burchardt had dished up everything his kitchen could produce. We met with a touching hospitality everywhere in Poland. Unfortunately, I was unable to keep up the contact later. So much else intervened.

During September and October (24.9–9.10) we again travelled extensively through North America. We started in Montreal, then proceeded via St Louis and the jazz of the Mississippi river boats to the Ozarks, where we spent a short holiday. After that we stopped over in Columbus, Ohio, and here the gleam of feminist theology went straight to Elisabeth's heart. The impression was deepened still more through encounters in New York, Union Theological Seminary, Princeton, and Drew University. We spent a stimulating week in New York with Paul Lehmann and his wife, Daniel Day Williams, Jim Cone, Letty Russell, and Hans Hoekendijk.

FOURTEEN

WORLD MISSION ASSEMBLY IN BANGKOK, 1972–73

Salvation Today, the End or the Beginning of World Mission?' was the subject of the World Mission Assembly, which took place in Bangkok from 29 December 1972 until 9 January 1973. 'Salvation is hope in action,' said the general secretary, Philip Potter, about the subject, and he had therefore invited me.[1] I was supposed to work on Section II: Salvation and Social Justice.

The date could not have been more unfortunate—as was always the case for German professors with ecumenical conferences. December 28 was Anne-Ruth's birthday, and after 6 January the semester work began again. I travelled to Bangkok with a bad conscience two days late, and returned home three days before the conference ended. But, of course, Thailand made an overwhelming impression. It was tropically hot; it was only during the night, about 2 a.m., that a slight wind got up. Flowers and trees bloomed on every corner, and over 300 people had come from every continent. We were lodged in a conference centre in Swanganivas and slept in half-open huts together with lizards, mice, and other fellow creatures. Together with Lukas Vischer, we visited a nearby Buddhist monastery for 'inter-religious dialogue'. But the monks thought we were either silly or unenlightened, and only talked about the morality of the mediocrity. Strange and fascinating, the temples in Bangkok gazed upon us.

The assembly had dispensed with main lectures in order to lay more weight on the work in the separate groups. So at least one got to know a few people well. A 'Reflection Plenary' was then supposed to weave the groups together through the bond of meditation, singing, drama, and dance. My pupil, the Japanese artist Yoshi Nomura, tried to take part in a performance on 'Salvation and Art' and, since he was unable to swim, almost drowned in the ornamental lake. 'Anyone who wants to feel sorry for Europeans should see them dance,' was the African comment on the working group 'Salvation in Dance'. For many people who were there, Bangkok was an event, even a 'happening'—for me too.[2] In my group I found an Orthodox Father George from India and discovered that we agreed in our ideas about the perichoresis of the immanent divine Trinity, and about commitment on behalf of a classless and casteless society. Shortly afterwards he became Metropolitan Mar Osthathios of the Syrian Orthodox Church of Kerala, and he retained his friendship with me.[3] Rubem Alves from Brazil, who after me had written a *Theology of Human Hope* and counted as a liberation theologian; Samuel Amirtham from the theological seminary in Madurai, India; John Taylor, Bishop of Winchester—with all these and many others I came to be on close terms, and we remained in touch.

I had prepared myself thoroughly in Tübingen for Section II: Salvation and Social Justice. At the end, the section adopted my proposals for the final report and supplemented them in helpful ways.[4] We tried to find 'a comprehensive understanding of salvation' and withstood Western emphasis on the salvation of the individual. My Tübingen colleague, the mission theologian Peter Beyerhaus, tried to demolish the report, but in doing so only succeeded in putting it in the foreground of the conference, so that the Stuttgarter Zeitung wrote:

> The distant earthquake which the World Mission Conference in Bangkok has triggered off since the beginning of the year, has now made itself felt in the Federal Republic too. Most of the German guests—with a few spectacular exceptions—have returned from these days as people whose eyes have been opened to an understanding for an ecumenical movement which deduces more strongly than hitherto from the universality of the Christian message of salvation the task of working together to bring about social justice in the world.[5]

An American missionary showed the extent to which the Vietnam War influenced the situation and roused emotions, for he appealed to us to move the conference immediately from Thailand to Vietnam, so that we could act as human shields against the renewed bombardments by the US Air Force, which President Nixon had ordered. That was a real cry of despair from people who were suffering helplessly under the power of their own nation, and who were praying for community with the people who were also helplessly suffering under it. In Bangkok, indeed, there was a wonderful experience of community between Christians from the Third World and Christians from the First. There was no Western predominance, and no white setting-to-rights. 'It was the Africans above all, but also the Asiatics, who set the tone at the beginning, if not indeed the whole trend of the conference.' So Emilio Castro from Uruguay was right when he said, 'We are standing at the end of a missionary era, and at the same time at the beginning of the world mission,' a world mission in the sense of God's mission to the world. 'Salvation' was present at this conference in stories, songs, singing, and ideas about liberation from fear and from hatred, from violence and exploitation, from contempt and meaningless life. That was an unexpected and joyful experience which the conference brought us.

Here is the text of Section II, which many people judged to be 'the theology of the Bangkok conference':

Salvation and Social Justice in a Divided Humanity

1. The Mission of God

In the power of the Spirit Christ is sent from God, the Father, into this divided world 'to preach the Gospel to the poor, to heal the broken-hearted, to preach deliverance to the captives and recovering of sight to the blind, to set at liberty the oppressed, and to proclaim the year of God's favour'(Luke 4.18). Through Christ men and women are liberated and empowered with all their energies and possibilities to participate in his Messianic work. Through his death on the Cross and his resurrection from the dead hope of salvation becomes realistic and reality hopeful. He liberates from the prison of guilt. He takes the inevitability out of history. In him the Kingdom of God and of free people is at hand. Faith in Christ releases in man creative freedom for the salvation of the world. He who separates himself from the mission of God separates himself from salvation.

The salvation which Christ brought, and in which we participate, offers a comprehensive wholeness in this divided life. We understand salvation as newness of life—the unfolding of true humanity in the fullness of God (Col. 2.9). It is salvation of the soul and the body, of the individual and society, mankind and 'the groaning creation' (Rom. 8.19). As evil works both in personal life and in exploitative social structures which humiliate mankind, so God's justice manifests itself both in the justification of the sinner and in social and political justice. As guilt is both individual and corporate so God's liberating power changes both persons and structures. We have to overcome the dichotomies in our thinking between soul and body, person and society, human kind and creation. Therefore we see the struggles for economic justice, political freedom and cultural renewal as elements in the total liberation of the world through the mission of God. This liberation is finally fulfilled when 'death is swallowed up in victory' (1 Cor. 15.55). This comprehensive notion of salvation demands of the whole of the people of God a matching comprehensive approach to their participation in salvation.

2. Salvation and Liberation of Churches and Christians

Many Christians who for Christ's sake are involved in economic and political struggles against injustice and oppression ask themselves and the churches what it means today to be a Christian and a true church. Without the salvation of the churches from their captivity in the interests of dominating classes, races and nations, there can be no saving church. Without liberation of the churches and Christians from their complicity with structural injustice and violence, there can be no liberating church for mankind. Every church, all Christians face the question whether they serve Christ and His saving work alone, or at the same time also the powers of inhumanity. 'No man can serve two masters, God and Mammon' (Matt. 6.24). We must confess our misuse of the name of Christ by the accommodation of the churches to oppressive powers, by our self-interested apathy, lovelessness and fear. We are seeking the true community of Christ which works and suffers for his Kingdom. We seek the charismatic church which activates energies for salvation (1 Cor. 12). We seek the church which initiates actions for liberation and supports the work of other liberating groups without calculating self-interest. We seek a church which is the catalyst of God's saving work in the world, a church which is not merely the refuge of the saved but a community serving the world in the love of Christ.

3. Salvation in Four Dimensions

Within the comprehensive notion of salvation, we see the saving work in four social dimensions:

a. Salvation works in the struggle for economic justice against the exploitation of people by people.
b. Salvation works in the struggle for human dignity against political oppression of human beings by their fellow men.
c. Salvation works in the struggle for solidarity against the alienation of person from person.
d. Salvation works in the struggle of hope against despair in personal life.

In the process of salvation, we must relate these four dimensions to each other. There is no economic justice without political freedom, no political freedom without economic justice. There is no social justice without solidarity, no solidarity without social justice. There is no justice, no human dignity, no solidarity without hope, no hope without justice, dignity and solidarity. But there are historical priorities according to which salvation is anticipated in one dimension first, be it the personal, the political or the economic dimension. These points of entry differ from situation to situation in which we work and suffer. We should know that such anticipations are not the whole of salvation, and must keep in mind the other dimensions while we work. Forgetting this denies the wholeness of salvation. Nobody can do in any particular situation everything at the same time. There are various gifts and tasks, but there is one spirit and one goal. In this sense, it can be said, for example, that salvation is the peace of the people in Vietnam, independence in Angola, justice and reconciliation in Northern Ireland and release from the captivity of power in the North Atlantic community, or personal conversion in the release of a submerged society into hope, or of new life styles amidst corporate self-interest and lovelessness.

4. Means and Criteria of Saving Work

Speaking of salvation realistically, we cannot avoid the question of proper means. The means are different in the four dimensions referred to. We will produce no economic justice without participation in, and use of, economic power. We will win no political freedom without participation in, and discriminating use of, political power. We cannot overcome cultural alienation without the use of cultural influence. In this framework we discussed the physical use of liberating violence against oppressive violence. The Christian tradition is ambiguous on this question because it provides no justification of violence and no rejection of political power. Jesus' commandment to love one's enemy presupposes enmity. One should not become the enemy of one's enemy, but should liberate him from his enmity (Matt. 5.43–48). This commandment warns against the brutality of violence and reckless disregard of life. But in the cases of institutionalized violence, structural injustice and legalized immorality, love also involves the right of resistance and the duty 'to repress tyranny' (Scottish Confession) with responsible choice among the possibilities we have. One may then become guilty for love's sake, but can trust in the forgiveness of guilt. Realistic work for salvation proceeds through confrontation, but depends, everywhere and always, on reconciliation with God.[6]

FIFTEEN

WAYS TO THE FAR EAST, 1973 AND 1975

Australia, the Philippines, Japan

Four weeks later, the semester ended, I set out on a long journey through East Asia (10.2–10.3.1973). I took my first dip into the Asian world, for which Bangkok had given me a foretaste, and I was fascinated. The journey began with a short visit to Singapore, with two lectures and a sermon in Trinity Theological College on Mount Sofia. At that time the Chinese quarter was still in existence, with the houses into which the old people withdrew to die when their time had come. But otherwise the modern high-rise buildings were growing and obscured the old city. The Shangri-La Hotel surrounded me with Asiatic luxury.

An overnight flight then took me to Melbourne, to which our Jesuit friend Gerry O'Collins had invited me, to the World Eucharistic Congress. For the opening assembly, more than 3,000 people thronged into the town hall. I arrived together with Mother Teresa from Calcutta, who drew the masses. Cardinal Knox greeted us. It was the first Eucharistic Congress to lay its stress on ecumenical relations, and for that reason Tom Slansky and Lukas Vischer were there too. I talked about 'Peace in a Divided World'. Ruth Ihle wrote in our regional newspaper, the *Schwäbisches Tagblatt*, 'What Professor Moltmann tried to make clear to people in his lecture is already practised by Mother Teresa and the sisters belonging to her order: action in solidarity.' Later Cardinal Willebrands came and gave a rather sad lecture about 'The Ecumenical and the Non-Ecumenical'. Four hundred international theologians who were enthusiastic supporters of more ecumenical fellowship between Christians had met together for a theological seminar on 'Jesus and the Church'. I stayed in a Jesuit commune in which everything went well except for the cleaning; but that was the case in almost all communities of the kind. Gerry took me to see the kangaroos and koala bears in Healisville Sanctuary; and I also got to know his extensive family. Earlier generations had emigrated after the English had beheaded one of his Irish forebears a hundred years ago. From Melbourne I made a detour to Canberra in order to see my old New Zealand acquaintance Margaret, whom I had met as a POW at the SCM conference in Swanwick.

On 20 February I then flew on to my next stopping point, Manila. Here things began to be too much. At the airport two delegations from theological seminaries appeared simultaneously with two programmes, which were to keep me doubly on the go. I slept in the St Andrew's Theological Seminary and gave up to four lectures per day. It was hot and humid, and often I went to sleep in the car or on the pillion of the motor bike. Pedro Sevilla introduced me to Loyola Theological College; Carmencita showed me the old walled Spanish city; the Methodist Emy Nacpil took me to the Union Theological Seminary and drove me to the glorious Taal Lake, a crater lake containing an island that itself contains a crater lake; and Ciriaco Lagunzad invited me to his brother's nightclub. Out in the country I admired the tranquil water buffalos in the rice fields and came to understand the 'water buffalo theology' of the Japanese theologian Koyama. As far as lectures went, my greatest 'hits' were 'Freedom in the Light of Hope' and 'Jesus and the Church', the second subject being for many of my listeners more revolutionary than the first.[1] More or less in a state of exhaustion, I flew on to Tokyo on 23 February.

In Tokyo Professor Tokuzen met me and took me to the Lutheran seminary. He rolled out a mat and left me to sleep on it. I tried. The next morning, at a conference with the famous Professor Kazoh Kitamori, whose book *Theology of the Pain of God* had just been translated into German,[2] I presented my 'crucified God'. Unfortunately, I only had an English manuscript with me, and Tokuzen only understood German; so I translated back into German, sentence for sentence, and he translated into Japanese. Then a long public discussion with Kitamori began. At the end he drew his diagram about 'the pain of God' on the backboard, and I drew my diagram of the 'Trinitarian theology of the cross'. From this it became clear that he was prepared to let pain touch God only externally, whereas for me it goes through God's very heart. The outcome was a memorable dialogue that was to be the subject of discussion among Japanese theologians for a long time. After our hard work, we withdrew to an opulent faculty dinner. I was full of admiration for Japanese courtesy: the younger person must always continue to bow until the older person straightens up, and that can take a long time when both are about the same age!

On Sunday, 25 February, I preached for my friend Shin Kitagawa in the little Nazarene church in Yokohama, as I always did later, too, whenever I came to Japan. Then I stood for a long time meditating in front of the famous Kamakura Buddha, who with inwardly turned eyes has gazed over the sea for more than a thousand years. The same evening I took the express train to Kyoto, to the Protestant academy. Masao Takenaka, a theologian deeply versed in the arts, showed me the beauties of the temples and tea houses and took me to Mount Hiei and to glorious Nara. We went to the Noh theatre and the Kabuki theatre and saw the Shinto shrines in the Heian, 'the centre of the world'. At the beginning of March I drove back to Tokyo with Takenaka. There I gave another three lectures and three seminars, and with the whole crowd visited a Zen Buddhist monastery above Yokohama. It was cold, and I was frozen through. We tried to meditate in front of a white wall until the Zen master hit each of us between the shoulders. What I experienced was not enlightenment but only the chattering of my teeth.

At that time the Japanese Protestant church was deeply divided between the young people, who wanted to follow in the steps of Jesus personally and politically, and the older people, who were content with the belief in Christ held by the church.[3] The practical point at issue was whether there should be a Christian pavilion at an industrial fair in Yokohama. What has Jesus got to do with Mammon? asked some. We have to show Christian presence, said the others. The conflicts in Kyodan were so bitter that for years there was no joint synod. Pastor Nakajima, the general secretary of Kyodan, suffered greatly. As a farewell present he gave me a woodcut by Watanabe showing Jesus carrying his cross. It has hung in my study ever since.

It had actually been planned that I should spend a week in Korea, but I was worn out, had circulation problems, and cancelled my engagements. We flew home via Anchorage. In Stuttgart Elisabeth met me, along with Esther and Friederike. I had got through and brought back with me 'treasures from the East'.

Korea—Land of Hope, Land of Tears

I should now like to take a leap over two years in order to talk about the journey to Korea which I was then finally able to catch up with. But in 1973 we were faced with a difficulty which I must first briefly mention. I received three invitations simultaneously: one to the Charles Hodge Professorship in Princeton, one to the Charles A. Briggs Professorship at Union Theological Seminary in New York, and a third to the chair for systematic theology in Hamburg. In addition, Philip Potter wanted to have me in Geneva as his deputy. It was nice to see all these possibilities spread out in front of one, but the result of all our considerations and reflections was that it was too late. I was 47 years old, the children were at school in Tübingen, Elisabeth had conceived the idea for her new work on feminist theology, and a move—let alone to America—would have cost us years. My Hamburg father advised me against Hamburg. James Cone wanted to hear me as a prophet from outside, rather than to see me as part of the American scene. So in the end we said no to everything and stayed in Tübingen. It was a compensation when in 1973 Duke University conferred on me my first honorary doctorate, and when Hans Küng and I were chosen by editors of American church periodicals as 'living giants' of contemporary theology. They even called me 'the most dominant theological presence of our time'.

An invitation to the Urban Industrial Mission conference in Tokyo from 13 to 15 March 1975 at last also gave me the opportunity to visit Korea beforehand. I took with me the lecture 'Hope in the Struggle of the People',[4] and was put up in the Yonsei University guest house. First I visited Hankuk Theological Seminary, where Pong Nang Park and Ahn Byung-Mu were waiting for me. It was the seminary of the resisting Presbyterian Church of Korea. Then there was a tour round all the more notable theological institutions. As soon as a taxi brought me back to the guest house, the next one was already waiting. I also met there the founder of Minjung theology, Suh Nam Dong, who unfortunately died soon afterwards. I preached in Seoul and Daejeon and with some colleagues climbed high up a mountain slope through a slum to a Shaman temple. We attended a moving remembrance ceremony for the dead. The priestess personified the dead father and comforted the weeping family. My Korean friends had at first hesitated whether to take me to this 'heathen temple', but afterwards thought about ways in which Christianity could absorb the ancient Korean traditions. Does conversion mean that people have to give up the ancestor cult, or can its rituals and content be given a Christian form? With David Suh I got to know the developing Korean Minjung theology, and from a Professor Bum Yun I heard about a 'yellow theology', a Korean cultural theology. When I got back, I wrote about my experiences in the *Evangelische Kommentare*.[5] Here is my account:

A journey to South Korea cries out for a report. It is one of the most exciting countries in Asia, in both the good and the bad sense, and yet in Europe it is more or less unknown. The lectures that I gave in March in universities and seminaries, and the service I held in the churches of Seoul and Daejeon, were massively overcrowded, not just with Christians but with non-Christians too. At the same time the KCIA, the South Korean secret police, were continually on my trail. Rectors and professors, pastors and students were questioned about me, and interrogated, sometimes for hours, by telephone or directly by agents. That seems to be typical of this country today: on the one hand, an unheard-of missionary vitality among Christians, and on the other, the growing dictatorship of the state president, Park, who is suppressing democratic rights and duties. Both must be described, for in many ways they interact.

Today Korea is experiencing a missionary movement without parallel. More than 10 percent of the population of 33 millions are Christians. The Presbyterian Church, which was founded at the beginning of the century, doubles its numbers every ten years and now has 3 million members. The Presbyterian Theological Seminary in Seoul had two students when it was started in 1905; now it has about 900 and is one of the biggest in the world. Most of the churches have long been independent financially and in personnel. From the beginning they have seen themselves as a missionary church in Korea, and not as dependencis of Western churches. Billy Graham's mass evangelizations therefore fell on fruitful ground, and more than 3 million people gathered on the plaza near the Seoul airport from 30 May to 3 June 1973. There are evangelistic strategies 'to win Korea for Christ' in this generation, so as to go out from what would then be this first Christian country in Asia to missionize the whole of the continent. In spite of Billy Graham, this is not a 'Western idea'. It is the object of Korean Christians for Korea. When Christianity came to Korea, the Japanese came, too, only a little later. After 1905 the Japanese occupying power wanted to eradicate the Korean language and to 'Japanologize' Korean culture. During the era of Japanese oppression, the young Christian church put itself on the side of the people. In Seoul, in the Pagoda Park, stands the monument commemorating the revolt against the Japanese of 1919, in which lay Christians were prominently involved. Consequently, white people are not hated in Korea, and Christianity does not count as a religion of white people, as it does, for example, in China and Japan.

The missionary initiative of the Christian church in Korea is accompanied by a quite unusual prayer movement. During the evangelizations, most of the churches in Seoul were full to overflowing every morning with people who had come to pray. There are prayer services at sunrise on the hills all over the country. Last winter the Catholic cathedral of Seoul and the square in which it stands were full every morning with people who had come to pray for Christians who were in prison. The passion of prayer can be sensed everywhere, in churches, seminaries, and private houses. It is a power which convinces the people, and a liberating force of resistance against the political mistrust.

'In Korea there is no political freedom'; that can be heard and seen everywhere. When I left Seoul on 13 March, the last free newspaper, *Dong-A*, had been brought under government control, under dramatic circumstances—dismissals, hunger strikes, popular protests, and mass arrests. *Dong-A*, 'the voice of Asia', had lost all its advertisements the previous year, under government pressure. Afterwards private people had supported the paper with advertisements incorporating poems and epigrams. In that way the paper was able to survive with the people's help. That is now at an end. The next day the well-known Christian writer Kim Chi Ha was re-arrested, after he and some others had been released from prison on 17 February. He had stood up for freedom of the press in Korea.

For the people, the political development in Korea is depressing, and for the 'free world' it is shameful. General Park came to power through a military putsch on 16 May 1961. He abolished the old constitution and dissolved the national assembly. The 'Supreme Council for National Reconstruction' forbade all political activity except its own. Since the 'Constitution of Renewal' of 1974, a third of the parliament has been nominated by the president, a third is appointed by his party, and a third can come from the officially recognized opposition party, whose loyalty towards the president is presupposed. The 'United Representative Council of the People' has 2,300 members, and every member's personal loyalty to the president is scrutinized. Ever since 1971, the schools, universities, and seminaries have been under government control. In 1973 the Law for the Control of Freedom of Speech and Freedom of the Press was passed, one of its measures being that all publications are censored. Religious institutions must be registered with the Ministry of Education and Information. The government requires a strict separation between religion and politics. No one is persecuted solely because of his 'religion' (see the mass evangelization), but because of political and social activity *springing from* religion, hundreds of students, professors, and pastors were sentenced and imprisoned during the past year. Two women students were condemned to 17 years' imprisonment because they had organized relief for the families of political prisoners. On 29 June 1973, shortly after Billy Graham's campaign, Pastor Park Hyung Kyn, who works for the Industrial Mission in the slums of Seoul, was arrested, together with 14 members of his staff, and was convicted. The Catholic bishop of Pusan had a similar experience.

The most recent news from Korea is alarming:

On 9 April eight people who had been condemned to death for inciting student protests were executed; the general secretary of the National Christian Council, Pastor Kim (Kwan-Suk), and Pastors Park (Hyong-Kyn) and Cho (Seung-Hyak) were arrested, because they allegedly used donations from the German Evangelisches Hilfswerk to support the families of political prisoners. Universities, including the well-known Hankuk Theological Seminary, were closed. The National Christian Council, the Presbyterian Church, and the Catholic Church of Korea have protested unanimously and strongly against arrests, torture, and the suppression of the churches through illegal terror.

The ideology with which the government justifies such measures involves 1. anti-Communism and 2. the need to push forward the country's economic development. The government evidently decides who is a 'Communist'. Whoever is not unconditionally in favour of the president is viewed as an enemy of the state and as an accomplice of North Korea. The people affected make it obvious that democrats and politically responsible Christians belong to this category. Many of them have studied in the United States and are really simply maintaining the democratic ideals and institutions they got to know there. They are depressed by America's support for the Korean government and consider—surely rightly—that American foreign policy is a betrayal of American democracy.

But no society can be built up, or 'renewed', with the ideology of anti-Communism. On the contrary, the abolition of democratic institutions and rights which are thereby justified must rather be viewed as the best preparation for Communism. And in fact fears are secretly expressed among the Korean people that this president—a former pupil of a Japanese military academy and an ex-Communist—wants to unite the country with North Korea under Communist rule. After the terrors of the Korean War, in South Korea the alleged 'Communist danger' is minimal. The government's ideology cannot be justified by the opposition in its own country.

The other justification of the dictatorship says that human rights and democracy are *Western* ideas, and hence cannot provide a basis for an *Asiatic* government. What is Asiatic is rather a mild and if necessary strict political hierarchy. But the Koreans are asking whether they are not a people with human rights. It is high time for the German Federal Republic to review its relations with the government in South Korea. In the wake of the growth of public opinion about Korean conditions, the Senate in Washington cut its military help for South Korea last year and pushed for the release of political prisoners—successfully. On 17 February 1975 most of them were released. But their sentences were not cancelled. The people who have been released have no civil rights and can neither attend a university nor teach. What can the German Federal Republic do to help restore democracy and the observance of human rights in South Korea? Probably only international pressure can ease the situation for the Korean people and avert the dreaded transition from a military dictatorship to a Communist one.

For many Christians in Korea, missionary initiatives and political resistance belong together. Together they constitute the *full* Christian witness. Reports say that last winter an imprisoned theology student from the Presbyterian seminary baptized 32 other prisoners in the prison itself. Some of the students I spoke to in Hankuk Seminary still had shaven heads and in some cases the scars of torture on their fingers; but they said, 'We went to prison like frightened mice and came out like tigers. There we experienced the presence of God.' When they came out on 17 February, they frankly talked both about their treatment and about their experience of God. The behaviour of imprisoned Christians and public evangelization together constitute the missionary power of Christian faith in Korea. That was also already the case under Japanese occupation, for 50 long years. Anyone who overlooks the witness emanating from the prisons in Korea sees only half the truth. Clergy who have mission at heart, and who were involved in the mass evangelisations, regret that Billy Graham said not a word in public on behalf of the imprisoned, in spite of earnest recommendations. Of course, he wanted to make use of the freedom to testify to the gospel, and for this he also required the help of the government and the army. But to suppress the suffering of imprisoned Christians does not help the evangelization of Korea. For this suffering is itself in its credibility one of the most important factors in the mission. Just because in South Korea there is the liberty to proclaim the gospel so publicly, this proclamation will also thrust towards social justice and the democratic freedom of the Korean people. It would otherwise not be the proclamation of the *whole* gospel, as it is witnessed to today in the prisons and from the prisons.

In Korea one is continually reminded of the experiences of the Confessing Church during the dictatorship in Germany. At that time the Confessing Church stood up for the whole of Christianity in the world, and in the same way the church in Korea stands up today for the churches throughout the world. A worldwide fellowship with the Christians in Korea is necessary. Their witness is our witness, their suffering is our suffering, and their experiences are our experiences. If there can be any protection on earth for Christians in Korea, it can only be through the swift publication in other countries of their history. On the other hand, Korean experiences with the gospel in mission and in the prisons are an encouragement for churches in other countries. Ecumenical publicity for what is going on in Korea at the same time brings us the gospel as it is lived and experienced there. Korea must no longer remain a closed book for Europe.

Later I visited Korea again and again—seven times in all up to now. I find the country and people, the churches and seminaries wonderful. Many Koreans have also come to Tübingen to study under me. Eight of them have done their doctorates, most of them now being highly regarded professors in Korea. My books have always immediately been translated into Korean, often before being translated into any other language. In 1984 I published the relevant texts on Minjung theology in German.[6]

Why have I undertaken lecture tours so often and so willingly in far-off countries? When I retired in 1994, the dean (it was Eberhard Jüngel) said, 'I must first stress that Jürgen Moltmann exists in this faculty as a citizen of the world … One not infrequently hears Tübingen students singing sadly, "My teacher is over the ocean …" But you remained faithful to Tübingen and always came back again to the Neckar, bringing with you a breath from the wider world. That undoubtedly had a galvanizing effect on the worthy Tübingen attitude towards theology … Down to the present day you have led a theological existence *urbi et orbi* …' That was very kindly meant; but I was not just *drawn to* the wider world; I was also occasionally *drawn away* from Tübingen. 'The best place in Tübingen is the airport,' I said from time to time. The reason was not that Tübingen was too confined, for the university was certainly not provincial. The reason was probably in part that I didn't want to commit myself entirely to reality as it exists but always wanted to gain detachment and stand above things. Then it was easier for me to perform my everyday duties, and I had no need to take every irritation too much to heart. Gershom Scholem once wrote that it was the weakness of the messianic idea not to commit itself entirely to reality, but to linger in the anticipatory and provisional, and to remain suspended in the possible.[7] Whether he is right where exilic Judaism is concerned, I am unable to judge; but I have certainly noticed 'weaknesses' of this kind in Ernst Bloch and in my own thinking and doing. So my journeys, with their expense of time and energy, were a sign not only of my strength but also of this 'weakness'.

part VI

In the Sign of the Cross to New Trinitarian Thinking

SIXTEEN

THE CRUCIFIED GOD, 1972

Motives

The Crucified God was first published in 1972 (ET 1974), and in his foreword to the twelfth English edition, Richard Bauckham wrote that it was 'indubitably one of the theological classics of the second half of the twentieth century'. 'What marks it as a classic is that when one rereads it several decades later, themes which were innovatory in its time seem now rather familiar ... but also that it still shocks and surprises, enlightens and provokes, with its dialectical sharpness of expression ... It is a passionate book, written "so to speak with my lifeblood", as Moltmann said of it much later.'[1]

I don't know whether Richard Bauckham is right, but I do know that this book is part of my wrestling with God, my suffering under the dark side of God, his hidden face, *hester panim* as Jews say, the side shown in the godlessness of the perpetrators and the God-forsakenness of the victims of injustice and violence in human history.[2]

I had long been preoccupied with a theology of the cross, before the theology of hope. I had come to the Christian faith in God through fellowship with the assailed Jesus. At the beginning of my theological studies in Göttingen, the young Luther's *theologia crucis* was the first theological outline that I got to know at all, and I found it convincing.[3] But the traditional interpretation of sin, sacrifice, and grace did not reach into the depths of my experiences of death. I was still unliberated.

I have already told how, when I was 17, I experienced not just suffering but also annihilation: mass annihilation in the firestorm in Hamburg in

1943, in which more than 40,000 men, women, and children were burnt to death. I barely escaped the inferno, and without any apparent reason. That was not a 'normal' experience of suffering; these were the extreme and excessive burnings of hell. At that time the eclipse of God descended on my world, and the dark night of the soul took hold of my heart and destroyed my spirit. It was the unfathomable experience of annihilating nothingness. When I began to take the history of Jesus' crucifixion seriously in a personal sense, I had to read Golgotha, the darkness of Good Friday, and Jesus' dark night of the soul together with my own annihilating experience, and in this way I was able to find myself again in Jesus' history. Where was God that night? Was God present in the inferno of those burning nights I remembered, or was he untouched by them, in the heaven of a complacent blessedness? *Where is God?* That was my existential question, the question which took me to the theology of the cross. The possible theodicy question did not interest me.

The other experience was this: I belong to the generation of Germans who were contemporary with Auschwitz. We cannot look back in retrospect to this appalling crime with historical detachment. So we feel the weight of guilt differently from those who were born later, even if we were not actively involved at the time. I can remember one momentary encounter. In 1944 we were shipped to the front in cattle trucks. At the station in Kassel we met another train, and through the cracks in those other cattle trucks we saw pale faces looking out at us with huge eyes. We could see that these people were not wearing uniforms like us but were wearing the striped clothing of the concentration camps. What happened to them was a catastrophe brought about by my people. That catastrophe bears the name of that disgrace: Auschwitz. I can never forget the pictures of the starving and murdered people in Belsen which were shown us in our prisoner of war camp in 1945. I can never forget my walk through the concentration and death camp Maidanek, Lublin, in 1961, when I wanted to sink into the ground under the burden of shame and guilt. What was it: guilt, or sin, or radical evil, or something which cannot be comprehended through these traditional theological concepts? This dictatorship of the Nihil was for me so incomprehensible because the abyss of the mass annihilation is such a bottomless pit. What an apocalyptic eclipse of God lies over this godlessness of Treblinka, Maidanek, and Auschwitz! Is God himself—dead?

The annihilations which I witnessed in one or the other way extended not only to human beings, to victims and perpetrators; for me it reached into the depths of God himself. For me the question of God became the cry for justice uttered by the victims of those mass annihilations. It has been rightly said that my book *The Crucified God* is a Christian 'theology after Auschwitz'. But literally speaking it is a book about belief in God after the crucifixion of Christ. What we dare to say about God 'after Auschwitz' surely depends on what we can say about God after the event on Golgotha, and the way we talk about God when we hear the echo of Christ's death cry: 'My God, why have you forsaken me?' The whole book can be understood as an attempt to wrestle theologically with that death cry. There is something in it which links every theology of the cross with the apocalyptic expectation of the future: if Christ's suffering manifests God's own suffering, then that suffering cannot be infinite or endless. Pascal wrote, 'Until the end of the world Christ lies in his agony,' assuming a fixed end to the world at the end of Christ's agony. But could the reverse not be true: when Christ's sufferings from the annihilations in this world become unendurable for God, the end of this agonizing world will come?

When I was writing this book, a picture by Marc Chagall stood on my writing desk. It is called 'Crucifixion in Yellow' and shows the crucified Christ appearing in the world in an apocalyptic situation: people are sinking into the sea, people are fleeing, and running about homeless, the fire glows yellow from the background. And with the crucified Christ the angel with the trumpet from Revelation 14.6 also appears, showing the scroll of life, open. For a long time this picture was my companion, and was a symbol inviting me to theological thinking. In those years I often sat in the Martinskirche in Tübingen and meditated on Susanne Müller-Diefenbach's black crucifix. It drew me into the dark suffering of God.

Of course, I was not the first to set out on the path to this kind of theology of the cross. In the German tradition, there was the Kähler pupil Bernhard Steffen, whose book *Das Dogma vom Kreuz. Beitrag zu einer staurozentrischen Theologie* (The Dogma of the Cross. Contribution to a Staurocentric Theology) appeared in 1920. Earlier, in 1913, Adolf Schlatter had published his *Jesu Gottheit und das Kreuz* (The Divinity of Jesus and the Cross). In old age, Steffen was still able to experience the publication of my book, and wrote me a grateful letter for having rescued his own book from oblivion.

Karl Barth's doctrine of predestination in his *Church Dogmatics* II/2 is based on a theology of the cross, and it made a great impression on me. Eberhard Jüngel's programmatic essay of 1968 with the paradoxical title 'Vom Tod des lebendigen Gottes' (The Death of the Living God) pointed in the same direction. About the same time that Dietrich Bonhoeffer wrote about the 'suffering God' in his letters from prison, the Japanese theologian Kazoh Kitamori wrote his book *Theology of the Pain of God*. It emerged from my discussion with him in Tokyo that he knew that theologically he was indebted to Albrecht Ritschl, and that with 'the pain of God' he belonged spiritually within the Japanese Samurai tradition. It was only subsequently that I got to know other traditions in England, Spain, and Russia which pointed in the direction I had taken. I took account of these in my book *The Trinity and the Kingdom of God*, published in 1980.

Preliminary work for *The Crucified God* can already be found in the *Theology of Hope* of 1964. There, in a long excursus, I followed up 'God is dead' ideas from Jean Paul to Nietzsche by way of Hegel.[4] In the context of political theology, in 1970 I justified 'theological criticism of political religion' with a theology of the cross[5] which, as Carl Schmitt said, brought out 'the intensive political significance which is indestructibly subsumed in the worship of a God crucified in this way, a significance which resists sublimation into "the purely theological"'.[6] In 1989 I presented the book's fundamental ideas in a lecture held before the theological faculty in Basel under the title 'Gott im Kreuz Jesus' (God in the Cross of Jesus).[7] In these years my theological interest shifted from the resurrection of the crucified Christ, and the horizon of hope which that throws open, to the cross of the risen Christ and the spaces of remembrance of the experience of absolute death. *The Crucified God* was intended to be the other side of 'the God of hope'.

Some Fundamental Ideas

The real reversal in the theology of the cross is to be found in the question, What does Jesus' suffering and death mean for God himself, that is to say, for the God whom Jesus called 'Abba, dear Father'? The soteriological question, What does the death of Christ mean for the redemption of human beings? turns into the theological question about its meaning for God himself.

The first question which follows is whether Jesus' suffering and death on Golgotha touches God at all, or whether we have to think of God as being in his very essence incapable of suffering. *Is God capable of suffering?* This question was passionately discussed in British theology for a hundred years from about 1830 to 1930.[8] With the exception of Ernst Troeltsch, German theology did not so much as show awareness of the problem.

If we follow Greek philosophy as to what must appropriately (*theoprepes*) be thought about God, we have to exclude from the divine nature disunity, disparity, movement, and suffering. The divine nature is incapable of suffering—otherwise it would not be divine. The absolute subject of modern metaphysics is also incapable of suffering—otherwise it would not be absolute. It determines everything and is determined by no one. Impassible, immovable, self-sufficient, and a unity, the Deity confronts all the things and minds of this world which are moved, divided, suffering, and never self-sufficient. This is called the *apathy axiom*, which Aristotle formulates in book 12 of his *Metaphysics*.

If we turn to the Christian tradition, we find at its very heart the history of Christ's passion. The gospel proclaims to us the redemption of the world through Christ's suffering; the Eucharist communicates to us Christ's self-giving in the form of bread and wine. Wherever Christ's passion is made present in this way, faith in God for Christ's sake is awakened. We believe in the God of Jesus Christ because we perceive that in Christ God himself is present. But in what way? If the Deity cannot suffer, then we cannot perceive any revelation of God in the history of Christ's passion. Does God simply allow Christ to suffer on our behalf, as theological tradition prefers to say? Or does God himself suffer with us and for us in the suffering of Christ? Are the sufferings of Christ divine sufferings too? If they are, then they have a redeeming significance for us; if they are not, then they cannot take on any such significance.

The ability to identify God with the suffering Christ diminishes in the degree to which the Aristotelian apathy axiom dominates the Christian doctrine of God. But if God is incapable of suffering, the suffering of Christ can be viewed only as a human tragedy, and no redeeming power can be found in it. If we want to say both things, we end up in paradoxes, such as the title of Bertrand Brasnett's book, *The Suffering of the Impassible God* (1928). It is better for Christian theology to take leave of Aristotle's apathy axiom and to begin with the biblical axiom of the living God and to talk about the suffering of the passionate God. The God of Israel is a God of passionate love for his people, and of love for righteousness and justice in his creation.[9]

But why did the theology of the patristic church hold fast to the apathy axiom? Because God's essential impassibility distinguishes him from all beings who are delivered over to suffering, transience, and death. This argument knows only the alternative: either essentially incapable of suffering, or subjected to suffering. But there is a different form of suffering: the active suffering of love, in which one opens oneself in order to be touched and affected by the other, and so as to participate in what happens to him or her. If God were incapable of suffering in this sense, then he would also be incapable of love. God does not suffer out of deficiency of being; he suffers from the overflow of his creative and loving nature. In this respect God can suffer, is willing to suffer, and does suffer from the contradictions of his beloved world.

If we ask what the cross of Christ means for God himself, we discover the Trinitarian mystery of God. If Christ dies with a cry of God-forsakenness, then God the Father must have had a correspondingly deep experience of forsakenness by his beloved Son. But this cannot be the same pain. Jesus suffers his dying on the cross, but the Father suffers the death of the Son, for he has to survive it. We can make this clear to ourselves from our own experience: at the end of my life I experience my dying but not my death, for I shall not survive it on earth. But in the people I love, I experience death when they die, for I have to live with their death.[10] So Jesus experiences dying, and God, whom he calls 'Father', experiences his death. Here it becomes clear how deeply Christ's death reaches into the Godness of God, and in the depth of the Godhead is an event between the Father and the Son. Is what we see on Golgotha a fatherless Son on the cross, and a sonless Father in heaven? 'One of the Trinity suffered,' said the church father Cyril. This is loosely called the 'theopaschite formula', yet today it is generally accepted. But I would add: where 'one of the Trinity suffers', the others suffer, too, each in his own way. Seen in this way, Christ's death on the cross is an event within God before it takes on a salvific significance for the world.

It is the mystery within God of God's giving of himself for the redemption of the world. The pain of the Father and the suffering of the Son manifest a single movement of the triune God: the Father in his pain surrenders the Son (Rom. 8.32), and the Son surrenders himself (Gal. 2.20). The Greek word for 'forsake' is the same as the word for 'surrender': *paradidonai*. Through his self-surrender to annihilation on the cross, Jesus brings the light of fellowship with God into the abysses of annihilating God-forsakenness. That is the wonder of God's love, the God who gives himself in order to embrace those who have been given up. The Son of man who came to seek that which was lost must himself take their lostness on himself in order to find them. God 'gave him up' so that he might become the brother and redeemer of those who have been given up (Romans 1). Because this is my personal experience of God, I hold fast to it and am not open for reasoned criticism. In this matter I am entirely at one with Hans von Balthasar. Like him, I, too, have only radicalized the traditional Christian theology of the cross in such a way that it is capable of meeting the experiences of modern catastrophes.

There is a famous medieval image of the Trinity, the so-called mercy seat.[11] With an expression of deep pain, God the Father holds in his hand the crossbeam of the cross on which the dead Son is hanging, while the Holy Spirit in the form of a dove descends from the Father to the crucified Son. Here we see the cross pictorially at the centre of the triune God. What situation is pictured here? It is the breathtaking situation on Holy Saturday after the death of the Son on Good Friday and before he is raised from the dead. This is the mystic stillness between cross and resurrection.[12] There is also the picture in which God the Father holds the dead Son in his arms. That is called 'The Pain of God'. It is the exact counterpart to the Pietà, Mary with the dead Son on her knees. Johann Rist wrote a famous hymn, which Hegel quotes for his dialectic: 'O grosse Not, Gott selbst ist tot, am Kreuz ist er gestorben …' (O mighty dread, Godself is dead, he died upon the cross …); but it was a hymn for the Holy Saturday devotions. 'God is dead' theology abstracted it from the 'theology of the three days' and without this context isolated and falsified it.[13]

For me, the conclusion to be drawn from this was that a true theology of the cross must be a Trinitarian theology, and that conversely the doctrine of the Trinity becomes abstract and loses its relevance without the event of the cross. For me, it follows that we must sink ourselves deeply into 'the pain of God' in order to participate in the indescribable Easter jubilation of the whole creation in 'the joy of God'.

Academic theologies love formulas. So I have been reproached with theopaschitism, patripassianism, and the like. But because I was able to distinguish between the pain of the Father and the suffering of the Son, what comes into question would at most be a 'patricompassianism'. But if terms themselves have to be explained, they explain nothing.

What for me is more important are the consoling dimensions of the theology of the cross. 'Only the suffering God can help,' wrote Dietrich Bonhoeffer in his prison cell, and meant the crucified Christ.[14] His cross stands between the crosses of the victims of injustice and violence as a sign that God himself shares in our suffering, that he makes it his own and participates in our sorrow. There is an English hymn which brings this out:

> And when human hearts are breaking
> Under sorrow's iron rod,
> Then we find that self-same aching
> Deep within the heart of God.[15]

Why can we be sure of this? Because in the heart of God stands the cross of Christ.

In 1990 I received a letter from Robert McAfee Brown. He had just come back from San Salvador and sent this report. On 16 November 1989 government soldiers murdered with archaic brutality six Jesuit fathers in the Jesuit university UCA, as well as their housekeeper and her daughter. They wanted above all to silence the critical voice of Ignacio Ellacuría. Jon Sobrino was by chance abroad. 'When the murderers dragged some of the bodies back into the building, they pulled the dead Ramon Moreno into Jon Sobrino's room. They knocked against a bookcase and a book fell on the floor, and was soaked with the martyr's blood. When it was picked up next morning, it was found to be your *El Dios Crucificado*.' Two years later I myself made a pilgrimage to the graves of the martyrs and found my blood-soaked book there, behind glass, as a symbol of what had really happened there.

Criticism

IS GOD UNABLE TO SUFFER?

In his last interview Karl Rahner said, rather grumpily it seems to me, 'If I now wanted to counter-attack I should say that there is a modern trend—both in Hans Urs von Balthasar and Adrienne von Speyr, but also independently of them in Moltmann—which devises a theology of the death of God that seems to me basically speaking Gnostic. To put it somewhat crudely, it doesn't help me to get out of my own mess and my despair if God—again to put it crudely—is in just as bad a way as me ... But on the other hand it does help to comfort me that God, if and inasmuch as he enters into this situation himself making it his own, at least enters into it in a different way from me. For I am cemented into this beastliness from the very outset, whereas God—if the word has any meaning at all—is in a true and genuine and for me consolatory sense the *Deus impassibilis*, the *Deus immutabilis*, and so forth. And in Moltmann and others I seem to sense a theology of absolute paradox and patripassianism, perhaps even Schelling's projection of division, of duality, of Godlessness, of death in God himself. And here I would say first: what do we then know so exactly about God? ... And secondly I would ask: how can this serve me as consolation in the truest sense of the word?'[16]

I only came across these words of Rahner's after his death. So I tried to answer him in a posthumous letter, from which I will quote a few sentences: 'A *Deus impassibilis* is neither capable of love nor capable of feeling. For him, empathy is impossible. So it is not possible for him to console anyone either ... I cannot imagine the *Deus impassibilis* as a consoling God in the personal sense. He seems to me as cold and hard and without feeling as cement. But what most disturbs and horrifies me is what you say about yourself: "I am cemented into this beastliness from the very outset." That sounds bitter, segregated, isolated and incapable of movement ... like a life that is unloved and incapable of loving ... What right have we human beings to say that God is "incapable"? Are we not "cementing" God through the negations of negative theology? How can God, if he is cemented into his immovability and incapacity for suffering, be a comfort for a human being who feels that this is just what his existence is like as well? Then God really would be, as you put it, "in just as bad a way" as we are ourselves, and neither God nor human beings could find consolation in eternity.'[17]

My friend Johann Baptist Metz followed his teacher's argument and even added that God *musn't* suffer, because we have to keep the theodicy question open: if there is a God, why is there evil and suffering? At the end of the world it is not only God who will require of us an answer to the question why is there so much evil and suffering in the world; we shall require an answer from him too. I can entirely understand what I might call this Ivan Karamazov theology, but can there be a theology which is 'sensitive to theodicy and sensitive to suffering' such as he maintains if God cannot feel anything, and if the suffering of the world is a matter of indifference for him? Isn't there a christological acceptance of the theodicy question? And shouldn't the strength to live with this unanswerable question be found in fellowship with the crucified Christ?[18]

My Tübingen colleague and friend Hans Küng also wants to keep God out of the suffering of human beings, since for him God is the *Deus semper major*.[19] In the face of innocent and senseless suffering, all that remains for us human beings is a 'theology of silence'. When God sent out a fire to kill Aaron's sons, the Bible says tersely, 'And Aaron held his peace,' or perhaps better, 'Aaron was dumb.' It is easy for us to understand that, because many people have the same experience. But when they fall dumb and sink into silence, they are not reverencing the incomprehensible God by doing so; they are making life bitter for themselves. In this answer to suffering I cannot find any reference to Christ either. The human being is standing quite alone, over against God and his fate. In this confrontation we have to call silence heroic, and respect it; but it is comfortless. I cannot find any 'theology' in this silence.

A sadistic God?

Did God kill his own Son? The most severe attack on my theology of the cross came quite unexpectedly from Dorothee Sölle (at that time still more of a liberal theologian than a feminist) in her book *Leiden*,[20] which appeared in 1973, a year after *The Crucified God*. In my account of Christ's God-forsakenness on the cross, she saw signs of a 'theological sadism'. For me, Christ's God-forsakenness was the profoundest expression of his solidarity with forsaken men and women, but Dorothee read the story of the passion quite differently, which is to say morally, and rebelled indignantly against a 'sadistic God' who abandons his own Son to the Roman executioners. She even compared him with the concentration camp murderer

Heinrich Himmler. This perspective was for me so remote and alien that I had not even considered it, and had not covered myself against it. Dorothee sat in heaven, as it were, and criticized the God who in Christ became human 'even unto death on the cross', whereas I so to speak sat in hell, and awaited God's coming.

Unfortunately, this became something of a fixed theme in the criticism levelled at me. Whoever wanted to say something critical about me took it over from Dorothee Sölle.[21] I have consequently called talk about my 'sadistic God' a kind of 'migratory legend'. It appears in secondary literature on secondary literature. Apparently, critics no longer look back at what they criticize. Otherwise it could hardly have escaped them that stress on the difference in the suffering and pain of Jesus and of the God whom he called Abba, dear Father, is only the other side of the unity of the Father and the Son in their self-surrender, and hence the other side of the love of God from which 'nothing can separate us'. It is the precise opposite of cruelty and sadistic pleasure in torment.[22] One cannot well suppress this side of what I have written in order to criticize the other side. Anyone who cannot recognize in the God 'who did not spare his own Son but gave him up for us all' the love which surmounts every suffering, every eclipse of God, and even hell, and who sees only a 'sadistic God who makes us suffer'[23]—that person is on the way to abandoning the heart of the Christian assurance of faith; he has never sensed it or has never taken it seriously. What then do we find in the statement that 'he did not spare his own Son'? What then do we find in the statement that he 'did not count equality with God a thing to be grasped, but emptied himself ...' (Phil. 2.6f.)?

A few feminist theologians especially took sides with Dorothee Sölle in attacking me, and this certainly annoyed me, for my wife's sake.[24] The fact that they did not read what I wrote carefully enough is unfortunate but nothing special; the fact that they were unable to distinguish between victim and sacrifice, or between victim and self-sacrifice, is remarkable; but the fact that they identify Sölle's fiction of a God who kills his own Son with fathers who violate their own daughters is to depart from all reason. The victimization of daughters in a patriarchal society is atrocious, but it has nothing to do with the death of Christ on the Roman cross.

If I understand her last writings correctly, Dorothee Sölle came more and more to arrive at a perception of the God who is a co-sufferer in the pains and grief of the suffering people, so that fierce conflict of earlier years can probably be laid to rest.

But I did not only meet with criticism. None of my books has gone through so many editions as *The Crucified God*, and none has been so often translated. Just because, as I willingly admit, much in it is harshly formulated and overstated, it has not only aroused controversy but also acted as a stimulus to personal thinking. I very soon received powerful support from the Anglican theology of Kenneth Woolcombe and Richard Bauckham; I met with agreement in the ranks of liberation theology, with Jon Sobrino and Leonardo Boff and the Korean Minjung theology of Ahn Byung-Mu; and to my surprise I also won the assent of the wise teacher of Orthodox theology and spirituality in Romania, Professor Dumitru Staniloae, who found the pain of God subsumed in the concept of the merciful God. My links with Hans Urs von Balthasar were so many that his theology of the cross has been described as 'a Catholic pedant to Moltmann's ideas'.[25]

In the English-speaking world, something like a 'new orthodoxy of the suffering God' has developed which absorbs the earlier theopaschite tradition in Anglican theology.[26]

Countless dissertations have been written on the subject, and it has not been possible for me to reply to them. But I should like to refer not least to the fact that in his book *God as the Mystery of the World* (1977; ET 1983), my colleague Eberhard Jüngel has put forward an impressive theology of the crucified Christ, which is at once very close to mine and very far away. But to analyse that in detail must be left to future doctoral students.

SEVENTEEN

THEOLOGICAL EXPANSIONS OF THE HORIZON

It is not easy to look back and bring into some kind of order biographical details in a many-faceted and occasionally chaotic life. After all, it is seldom, and then only for short stretches of time, that one lives according to plan. Moreover, no one lives for himself alone. We are also lived through others and are influenced by things which we never desired. In the 1970s my theological thinking was expanded by new themes. Long journeys made me aware of the problems in Korea, South Africa, Latin America, and Romania, so that I was no longer able to write for German readers alone. At the same time I was brought down to my own earth by specific obligations. I took over the editorship of the periodical *Evangelische Theologie*, and then the chairmanship of the Gesellschaft für Evangelische Theologie, and, not least, we bought a house in Tübingen, ending our wanderings through a variety of rented accommodation. After all, even the people of God who wander in hope do not always have to dwell only in tents.

The Church in the Power of the Spirit 1975

In *The Crucified God* I interpreted the event on Golgotha as something that happened between Jesus, the Son of God, and the God whom he called his Father, and thereby came upon an approach to the Trinitarian mystery by way of the theology of the cross. This inevitably gave rise to the question, And where is the Holy Spirit? The Holy Spirit descended on Jesus when he was baptized by John, and it was in the power of this Spirit that he proclaimed the gospel, healed the sick, and shared with everyone the great fellowship of the table. Did Jesus 'breathe out' the Holy Spirit as he died on the cross, as we read in Luke: 'Into thy hands I commit my spirit'? Did the Spirit himself sigh in his death cry, as Luther thought? Or was God's silence on Golgotha also a taking back of the life-giving Spirit, which only manifested itself again in the raising of the dead Christ? However that may be, in a series of graduate seminars we enquired about the Holy Spirit, asked about the spirituality of Ignatius Loyola, and familiarized ourselves with the present-day theology of the Holy Spirit in Barth, Berkhof, Balthasar, Mühlen, and others.

Because I did not grow up in a church, the church was not for me a matter of course. As pastor, too, I tried to answer the questions, What is the church, and what is it there for? In Bonn in 1966 and in Tübingen in 1968 and 1972, I then lectured on the task, the form, and the future of the church. In the 1970s there was a powerful movement for reform in the German Protestant regional churches. Its aim was to get away from the pastoral church for looking after people, and to move towards a congregational church, a community. The aim was no longer to be a church *for* the people, but to become a church *of* the people. Men and women should no longer be looked on as 'attending' worship and as 'guests' at the Lord's Supper. They should be at home in the community of Christ. Our question was not as yet whether a congregational structure of this kind could exist at all in conjunction with binding participation in a regional church, with varying degrees of commitment, down to general non-commitment. That question arose only in the aftermath of disappointments. The Reformed church in Germany to which I belonged had always been a congregational church without a hierarchy. My teacher Otto Weber wrote a small but effective book called *Versammelte Gemeinde* (The Gathered Congregation).[1] On my journeys to Asia and Africa—where Christianity is non-European and non-Constantinian—I came across congregational churches as Christian minorities, as persecuted communities, and as congregations with a missionary thrust of a kind unknown to us in Germany.

The Church in the Power of the Spirit then grew out of these two concerns—a doctrine of the Holy Spirit and a reforming doctrine of the church. The book was published in 1975 (ET 1977). It fitted in well with the *Theology of Hope*, in which Easter was at the centre, and with *The Crucified God*, the centre of which is Good Friday; for now the point of departure was Pentecost. I occasionally presumptuously talked about the trilogy with which I began my systematic theology, but this sequence was not planned but only emerged fortuitously. I moved from one problem complex to the next, by way of the questions the first left open. That constituted my adventure in theological ideas. Hans Küng later reproached me, saying that my theological progress was a zig-zag through diverse themes.[2] Unlike him, since I came in 'from without the gates', the Catholic continuity of the *semper idem* had not been mine from birth. But 'God writes even on uneven lines,' as Lessing once said.

In the church it is always a matter of more than the church, so in this book I have presented it in the wider contexts of God's history with the world. It begins with the sending of Christ and the sending of the Holy Spirit into this world, and ends with the glorification of God the Father through the redeemed creation. If we set this in the Trinitarian history of God: the life-giving Spirit is sent into the world by the Father through the Son in order to redeem all who are subject to death; and in the joy of all the living, the Spirit glorifies the Father through the Son to all eternity. The church is to be found in these two divine movements, and in them acquires its assurance of God.

The church is *the community of Jesus Christ*. Here it was important for me to replace the traditional language of domination by the language of friendship. Anyone who lives in the community of Christ is not the servant of a master but is the brother or sister of Jesus, if we think in terms of the sonship or daughterhood of God, and Jesus' friend, if we think in terms of the closeness of his love. The event of the church is not defined; it is localized. The church is where Christ is. Christ is there wherever in his name the gospel is proclaimed, people are baptized, and his Supper is celebrated. That is the *manifest* church. But Christ is also in the place where the poor, the hungry, the sick, and the prisoners are to be found: 'As you did it to one of the least of these my brethren, you did it to me.' That is the *latent* church. In the manifest church, 'he who hears you hears me.' In the latent church, 'whoever visits them, visits me.' Here Christ sends—there Christ awaits, and the community of Christ stands between the Christ who sends it and the Christ who awaits it.

The church is the gathered community of God, gathered for the coming of his kingdom. In this respect, as well as Israel and in community with Israel, it upholds and sustains the hope of God in this world: it is *the messianic people of the coming kingdom*. This eschatological perspective had been lost in the established churches. But it is only that which frees Christianity from the compulsions of present-day society. Earlier, the church had either been equated with the kingdom of God, or had been detached from the kingdom of the next world, but more modern eschatological theology has been able to communicate both—present and future, anticipation and completion, beginning and goal—in such a way that the future of God's kingdom comes to bear in the present without ceasing to be future. For 'the church of the kingdom of God' I found Vatican II's declaration *De Ecclesia* helpful.

For me, what was especially important was of course to do justice to the title, and to present the activity of the divine Spirit in the church (chapters 5 and 6). I didn't want just to say the traditional things about preaching, baptism, the Lord's Supper, worship, congregational order, and the wealth of the charismatic gifts of all the members. I wanted to make new suggestions too. But with this I had probably undertaken too much. Hardly a single one of my suggestions was accepted. I thought, for example, of changing baptism and the Lord's Supper into a Lord's Supper for everyone and baptism for believers—whereas in Germany we have infant baptism for everyone, and 'allow' only the baptized and confirmed to partake of the Lord's Supper. But Jesus celebrated God's great banquet of friendship with everyone, even the people from the highways and byways, and, as far as I know, none of the apostles who participated in the Last Supper had been baptized except Jesus himself. But perhaps this suggestion was not very wise. Whether this was so or not in individual cases, my concern was *the church of the Holy Spirit* as the future of the churches as we know them.

In the ancient world, the church already took on a patriarchal form in the post-apostolic era once it acquired the 'monarchical episcopate': God the Father is represented by the bishop, as the father of his community. In the context of Rome's patriarchal religion, this developed into the hierarchical pyramid of the God-Father—the pope in Rome—every priest as the father of the children in his community. In the sixteenth century, in a contrary movement, the Reformers introduced *the christocentric principle.* Christ stands at the centre of the congregation as the first-born among many brothers and sisters. In fellowship with him they are free and equal. But in the church of the Spirit, the congregation is made up of different charismatically endowed people: there are many gifts but one Spirit. A plurality of powers and functions makes the spiritually endowed congregation a source of life for many people. It is only the church of the Spirit that fully opens up the Trinitarian mystery of God. It is only in the church of the Spirit that the church of the Father and of the Son will be completed. For that reason I interpret the 'signs of the times' in such a way that they point us to the church in the power of the Spirit.[3]

This book about the church has a whole series of themes instead of a central one, as is the case in the *Theology of Hope* or *The Crucified God*. Consequently, it was not so intensely discussed. It did not become controversial, although for some people it was too conservative and for others too progressive. My friend Rudolf Bohren thought it had been written from a raised 'hide' in the forest, high above the reality of all the different animals in the forest itself, because my point of departure was not the problems of my local congregation, but the various impressions of the church in other continents. But after all, my field is not 'practical theology', as is his; I am a speculative systematic theologian who tries to see the individual in the context of the whole. But for all that, some theses in the book had a lasting effect.

The Church of Which People?

In Germany the state church came to an end with the Weimar Constitution of 1919. In the self-understanding of the Protestant church, the idea of the state church was replaced by the image of the *Volkskirche*, the people's church. The church is there for the whole German people, and every member of the people should view it as his or her church. Here the term *Volk*, or people, was used in an ethnic sense and had a national colouring. Until 1945 the Deutsche Evangelische Kirche (German Protestant Church) was determined by its 'Germanness'. Here *Volk*, people, was not used in the democratic sense, as in the concept of 'popular sovereignty' invoked by Abraham Lincoln in Gettysburg, when he talked about 'government of the people, by the people, for the people'.

After 1945 the church gave itself a new name and called itself 'Evangelische Kirche in Deutschland' (the Protestant Church in Germany). Germany was supposed to be the place where 'the whole of Christendom here on earth' is present in the form of the Protestant church, but it was no longer to be the sign of a German Christendom. That was soundly ecumenical, but it left the notion of the 'people's church' untouched.

In the Catholic Church, the concept of the church as 'the body of Christ' reached its zenith in the 1943 encyclical *Mystici Corporis* of Pius XII; but then the idea of the church as 'the people of God' came to prevail, this being maintained in the Second Vatican Council. Here it is not the ethnic concept of people that is being transferred to the church, but the idea of the chosen people of Israel. Is this possible without rejecting Israel?

In the Greek New Testament we have three words for people: 1. *laos*, which is the people of God, Israel; 2. *ethne*, the Gentile peoples to whom the gospel is to be preached; and 3. *ochlos*, the poor, homeless people without the law, on whom Jesus has mercy. If we read the Gospel of Mark closely, as the Korean New Testament scholar Ahn Byung-Mu did in Heidelberg, we find that Jesus' closest relationships were with the *ochlos*; they are his family, he belongs to them, it was for their redemption that he came, they are 'the many' for whom he suffered death.[4] That Jesus was a Jew and belonged to God's people is a fact, but plays no formative part in the gospel. The gospel is directed to 'the peoples', as the command to missionize brings out—that is, to 'all people', as thesis 6 of the Barmen Theological Declaration of 1934 says. But if we want to discover the people of Jesus, we must look for the *ochlos*, the poor, marginalized, disabled, and excluded. That is not just a matter for diaconal service or charitable care; it is a matter of the friendship of Jesus. In fellowship with Jesus we also find the friends of Jesus, his people. So they have always belonged to the community of Christ wherever it may be. In all the peoples, these are his people, whom he called blessed because the kingdom of heaven belongs to them. Christians belong to this people for faith's sake. Solidarity with their sufferings and commitment to their liberation follows from this belief that Jesus is present in them. The Korean Minjung theology of Ahn Byung-Mu and Suh Nam Dong has unforgettably impressed on us Jesus' concept of people—*ochlos*.[5] In 1975 I made my debut in Korea with a lecture titled 'Hoffnung im Kampf des Volkes' (Hope in the Struggle of the People) and found allies in the two Minjung theologians.

When we talk about 'the people's church', we must think of Jesus' people and forget ethnic notions. And when we talk about 'the people of God', we must not think only of Israel, but first of all of the *ochlos* in all peoples, in Israel too.

Who Are the Disabled and Who Are the Disabling?

After the Hoffmann-La Roche conference of 1971, I received invitations to speak at medical congresses and gladly took advantage of this chance to develop a theology for people in the medical profession. Then in 1973 the Deutsche Gesellschaft für Sozialmedizin invited me to Munich for their annual meetings on 29 and 30 November and asked me to talk about 'The Rehabilitation of the Disabled'. I added to this title 'in a Segregation Society', and took up the challenge, remembering my brother Hartwig. He died in 1940 when the Nazi euthanasia programme was beginning, to which 10,000 disabled people fell victim.

For me this became a personal question: What meaning does a disability have, and how can the segregation of the disabled from the society of the non-disabled, the capable and the successful, be overcome? 'It is not we who are your problem—it is you that are ours': this cry of disabled people shows that there are not merely personal disabilities; there is the social disablement of the disabled in addition.[6] The sight of disabled people easily upsets the mental equilibrium of the non-disabled, and they shrink back. They do not see the disabled person but only the disability. The result is the 'leper syndrome', to use the phrase of scientific studies. People who are 'different' are not welcome, but are generally merely put up with; and that destroys their self-confidence. The fear of the non-disabled has to be overcome, for this makes them strive after a human image of performance, enjoyment, beauty, and power and makes them apathetic towards the sufferings of others. Once this fear is overcome, the depressions of the disabled can also be surmounted. Jesus established 'the kingdom of the Son of man' at the very place where that leper syndrome is dominant: he accepted the blind, the paralysed, and the mentally disabled and 'rehabilitated' them with God and human beings. In fellowship with him, Christians will seek the fellowship of the disabled, for these are Jesus' friends; and they will protest publicly against the social disablement of the disabled. The human rights of the disabled include the right to be listened to, the right to be adult, the right to love. It is only when the non-disabled cease to be a problem for the disabled that the problems of the disabled can also be solved. But today disabled embryos are often already singled out by way of prenatal diagnosis.

For me, these ideas were so important that I described the community of Jesus as a fellowship of the disabled and the non-disabled. Others later took up this idea and the corresponding practice, and carried it further.[7]

In 1981 I was invited to a great congress on disability in Nüremberg and talked to people who were personally affected, taking as my subject: 'Liberate yourselves—accept one another!'[8] It is not easy to arrive at self-acceptance and self-love if one is disabled. But in the experience of God's love one can also love what God loves: oneself. 'What is not assumed cannot be healed,' was a principle of patristic theology. In Jesus Christ, God has accepted the whole and true humanity and has made it part of his divine life—mortal humanity, too, and also disabled humanity. In this respect there is no reduced life and no disabled life either. Every life is in its own way part of the divine life and a reflection of God in the world. The moment we talk about 'disabilities' we are taking as our standard the perfect, the capable, and the beautiful. But that leads us astray. Isn't every disability an endowment of its own kind, too, and one which must be respected? In the community of Jesus, aren't 'disabilities' also 'charismata' of the Holy Spirit? When Paul talks about the gifts of the Spirit, he doesn't just name capabilities but the lack of them as well. Not just powers but also weaknesses (2 Cor. 4.7). 'Everyone as the Lord has called him' (1 Cor. 7.17): that also applies to a condition which others call disabled. This perception must lead to the building of a new fellowship of mutual recognition and varying interests among the 'disabled' and the 'non-disabled' in the community of Jesus.

When I later entered into discussion with representatives of the Pentecostal movement, they found this idea surprising, but it immediately convinced the people who had children with disabilities.[9] In 1994 I wrote the foreword to the biblical reflections of the Gemeinschaft Sant'Egidio, under the heading 'Jesus as Friend: With the Mentally Disabled on theP-path of the Gospel'.[10]

Ecumenism under the Cross

The ecumenical union and renewal of the church is something I always had very much at heart, and it was also one purpose of my book about the church. In the prisoner of war camps, the only important thing was whether one was a Christian or not, irrespective of the denomination.

The ecumenical fellowship of the separated churches does not go forward on the superficial levels of a comparison between doctrines and forms of organization; it only succeeds if every church turns to its foundation and probes the depths. That is why it was said at the conference in Lund in 1962: 'As we seek to come closer to Christ, we come closer to each other.' I took this a step further and said, 'Under the cross we all stand empty-handed. We have nothing to offer except the burden of our guilt and the emptiness of our hearts. We do not stand under the cross as Protestants, as Catholics, or as adherents to Orthodoxy. Here, rather, is where the godless are justified, enemies are reconciled, prisoners are set free, the poor are enriched, and the sad are filled with hope. We discover ourselves, therefore, under the cross both as children of the same freedom of Christ and as friends in the same fellowship of the Spirit.'[11]

I did not mean this only in the spiritual sense, but quite specifically, with reference to the fellowship of Christ's table, which some Christians call the Eucharist, others the Lord's Supper. 'The invitation to the Eucharistic meal is the inviting request of the dying Christ who was handing himself over for us all ... His welcoming hands open as wide above the Eucharistic meal as did his outstretched arms upon the cross ... I see no reason why any church should hold back the open hands of Christ which are outstretched toward all. I find no reason to refuse eucharistic fellowship to anyone who hears and responds to the invitation of the Crucified One.'[12] Once we sit together with Christ at his table, the dogmatic and canon-law differences can be solved, because then they have to be solved. On 16 October 1975 I put this forward at the Lateran University in Rome in the presence of Cardinal Willebrand, and during my lecture received spontaneous applause from my Catholic audience. The cardinal's later rejoinder was somewhat forced and laboured.

Later I maintained my view with more and more conviction. First comes the practice of the shared celebration of Christ's meal—then comes the theological theory and the discussion about the doctrine of the Lord's Supper. For in that meal we are celebrating the presence of Christ, not the correctness of our eucharistic theology. The place for ecumenical theological discussion is the table after the Supper, not beforehand outside the gates. In my view, to say that a shared eucharistic celebration should take place only when the goal of the ecumenical unification of the churches has taken place does not accord with Christ's invitation: people will die of hunger on the way. At that time I made it a rule for myself to go to Christ's Supper always and everywhere when I hear his words of institution and his invitation, irrespective of which church it is. But I expect the communion to be given in bread and wine, in accordance with Jesus' will and promise, and that it is given not only to the priests but equally to the laity too—that is, to the whole people of God. I consider the Catholic practice of separation un-christian. It is my ecumenical hope that with his invitation to his meal, Christ will prevail in all the churches so that divided Christendom may recognize its unity in him and surmount its divisions.

In the Friendship of Jesus

When I tried to find a new language to replace the traditional language of domination, I first of all came upon the language of community, the community of Christ, the community church, the community of men and women, and the community of solidarity in a society. The language of domination has only one direction, from above to below, as command and obedience, while the language in a community is aligned towards reciprocity—word and response, dialogue and assent. But the word *community* is still lacking in the warm tone of love. So I went over to *the language of friendship*. Friendship unites liking with esteem, love with respect. A friend is someone who likes you and someone you like to be with. A friend is always there, but can also leave you in peace. There is no need to make oneself sure of a friendship every day, because one has no need to worry about it. One can pour out one's heart to a friend, without having to keep up appearances. Friendship joins freedom with faithfulness and dependability.

Jesus is called 'friend' in two places in the New Testament. He is described as 'a friend of tax collectors and sinners' and then: 'Greater love has no man than this, that a man lay down his life for his friends. You are my friends' (John 15.13f.). The people who follow Jesus are no longer the servants of a master; now they are not even just the children of their Father in heaven any more; they are independent friends of Jesus and 'friends of God' in the Holy Spirit, just as Abraham, the father of faith, was called a friend of God (James 2.23). From this I concluded that the lordship of Christ means community with Christ, and the heart of this community with Christ is the friendship of Jesus; and this friendship of Jesus offers an 'open friendship' with other people. According to Aristotle, there can only be friendship between equals: 'Like draws to like'; so friendship is exclusive. But Jesus' friendship with the poor, sinners, and tax-collectors is inclusive: it draws in everyone and shuts no one out. His open friendship prepares the ground for a friendlier world.

These ideas in my book about the church, published in 1975, were taken up by a number of people and developed further, best by Elisabeth in her book *Wach auf, meine Freundin. Die Wiederkehr der Gottesfreundschaft.*[13]

The Beginning of an Ecological Doctrine of Creation

My early theological world was determined by historical categories: promise and hope, protest and exodus, movement and liberation. In the 1960s we tried to break out of the narrow confines of existentialist thinking and to participate in real human history. We also became influenced by the accelerating history of revolutions and repressions in the Third World, and the thrusts towards modernization in the First. It was at that time that Pannenberg's *Revelation as History*, Gutiérrez's *Theology of Liberation*, Metz's *Theology of the World*, and my *Theology of Hope* were written. It was only in 1972 that the Club of Rome's study *The Limits of Growth*, and the Western world's first oil crisis, made it clear to me that the future of human history is not 'a land of unlimited possibilities', but that if it is to serve enduring life and not universal death, it can only come about within the limits of the ecosystem of the planet Earth. 'History' as a term for reality as a whole must either be separated from 'nature', or nature must also be historicized. There is certainly a 'history of nature', too, as Carl-Friedrich von Weizsäcker showed, but it is identical neither with human history nor with the nature that is drawn into this history through the agency of human domination. If the progress of human history is to serve life and not death, we have to arrive at harmonizations between human culture and nature. I tried to find a new pattern, and came upon history in nature and nature in history, or: human history and the natural history of the earth in a common movement towards the common goal.

In 1973 I gave my first lecture on the doctrine of creation. I tried to find a concept of creation that would embrace both creation 'in the beginning' and 'the new creation' at the end. For with the word *creation* one instinctively thinks of a completed event and its outcome. So what occurs to examination candidates is always only the two creation accounts at the beginning of the Bible, but not the new creation in Christ and the new creation of all things at the end. During those years I took part in a working party, set up by the FEST (Forschungsstelle der Evangelischen Kirche) in Heidelberg and presided over by Ernst von Weizsäcker, on 'the theory of open systems'.[14] The biologist Helmut Wehrt showed me that the basic ideas of my *Theology of Hope* can also be applied to the understanding of the world of life which he was investigating.[15] That gave me the courage to depict creation theologically as an open system. I could integrate creation 'in the beginning' with the creations of the divine history—that is, its new beginnings—and with the completion of creation through its new creation by virtue of the indwelling of God. That was the beginning of the first outline which I put forward to the British Theological Society in Edinburgh on 9 April 1975, in the Festschrift for T. H. Torrance in 1976,[16] and then published in the book *Zukunft der Schöpfung* (*The Future of Creation*) in 1977.[17] This then took me into the ecology discussion. As a number of dissertations stressed, this was the beginning of 'the greening of Moltmann's theology'. In 1985 I then presented the result of my 'green' doctrine of creation in Edinburgh, in the Gifford Lectures. But I shall come back to that later.

The year 1972–73 was in fact not so much a turning point for my theology as a decisive widening of its horizon. In 1968 I experienced a catastrophe of my hopes; now in 1972 I saw virgin territory in what I may describe theologically as an eschatological doctrine of creation, with which I was able to expand the eschatology of human history by an eschatology of nature. Problems still remained open, however, because the future of human life cannot coincide with the future of the cosmos as Scripture and tradition assumed.[18]

The Search for a Theology of Mystical Experience

Some people have been surprised at finding me not only on the political paths of theology but also on the theological ways to mystical experience. But this is a long-standing interest. The second of all my publications had to do with mystical theology in Gerhard Tersteegen, the Reformed Protestant hymn writer from the Lower Rhine.[19] In Dietrich Bonhoeffer I had learnt that the 'true worldliness' of Christian existence must be accompanied by an 'arcane discipline', and 'the free political act' by constant prayer for perseverance. When during the student protests of 1968 in Tübingen I came across the first people who had been inspired by Taizé and knew that struggle should be accompanied by contemplation, I found that they, and myself with them, were on the right path.

In the summer semester of 1976, together with my assistant Michael Welker, I held a memorable seminar titled 'The Theology of Mystical Experience'. In this way I also wanted to bar the simple way from revolution to religion which at that time was being preached to the students. We read the relevant medieval mystical texts, as well as Thomas Merton and Ernesto Cardenal, and found that these theologies contain no special dogmatics but record the experiences of a road, a journey, a voyage of the soul.[20]

So as not merely to discuss theories but to arrive at practical experiences ourselves, we first went to Kloster Kirchberg, the Protestant Berneuchner community. We participated in two of their typical meditations in the monastery church. For some of the students, however, these were too simple-minded; they had brought their Indian meditation stools, thrown themselves into the meditative pose—and experienced very little. After this simple fare, we spent a weekend at the Catholic monastery in Neresheim, where a monk well known as an expert in meditation awaited us. First of all, however, we were confronted with a Bavarian gym teacher, who each time subjected us to three-quarters of an hour of eutonic exercises before we were allowed to meditate for fifteen minutes. This was work with the body, so that the soul might be relaxed and sent on its journey. I found the exercises quite pleasant and later repeated them in hotel rooms when I was on my travels; but mentally or spiritually, let alone meditatively, nothing came across. On Sunday morning we were then supposed to breakfast in silence and read the wishes of our neighbour from his eyes. We were glad when on the following Wednesday we could again turn to texts with rather more content.

In the end the seminar was after all something special, because it had no relevance for any examination but had nevertheless dealt with an important theological subject.

I myself tried to grasp what I had read and experienced in order to give one of the main lectures at the Meister Eckart congress in Erfurt in 1977. It was the first lecture I had been able to give in the GDR since 1968. I tried to understand the mystical journey to God of the soul, which has so pitifully miscarried, in the following way: action and meditation; meditation and contemplation; contemplation and mysticism; mysticism in martyrdom: the vision of 'the world in God'.[21] In political theology, Baptist Metz had always pointed to the tension between mysticism and politics in the discipleship of Christ.[22] I carried that over to 'the two cells': the monastery cell and the prison cell; after all, it was in the monastery in Ettal that Bonhoeffer prepared himself for the prison cell. The mystic is really the martyr of the soul, for he passes through 'the dark night of the soul' into the eternal light of God.

I discovered something else as well: Teresa's interior castle and Thomas Merton's mountain and many other descriptions of mystical journeys use the number seven: on the seventh level the soul finds its way to God, and it is in the seventh chamber of the soul that the mystical marriage takes place. This is nothing other than Israel's teaching about the Sabbath. The person who keeps the Sabbath, and who on the Sabbath experiences the union of the Shekinah with the Eternal One, is already at the place which the Christian mystics strive to attain through meditation and contemplation.[23]

A Theological Declaration on Human Rights 1977

In 1970 I gave the main lecture at the General Assembly of the World Alliance of Reformed Churches (Presbyterian and Congregational), my subject being 'God Reconciles and Liberates'. Afterwards the theological section decided that before the next General Assembly in 1977 there should be a study project on 'the theological basis of human rights and liberation theology'. Jan Lochman, the chairman of this section, and Richmond Smith, the secretary, gave me the task of preparing for the study with an orientation paper which would be sent to all the member churches. I gladly accepted this practical assignment, because I was no longer satisfied by the general speeches and discussions at ecumenical gatherings and was very willing to contribute something more permanent.[24]

As Heinz Eduard Tödt rightly pointed out, speaking for the Lutheran churches on the continent, in the Christian churches there was a 'profound aversion towards the modern movements for human rights'. But this was far from true of the Presbyterian churches in the English-speaking world. On the contrary, it is to them that we are indebted for the first enumeration of human and civil rights in England and in the USA.[25] I saw my function as being on the one hand to connect Christianity with the politics of universal human rights, and on the other hand to discover the theological perspectives of the declarations on these rights. 'The political and social directives of the churches take on their universal significance only in their relationship to human rights. For in relation to human rights the church becomes in duty bound to be a "church for others" or "church for the world".' I suggested that the study should proceed in three steps: '1. Christian theology is a theology of liberation, for it understands Christ as liberator in the comprehensive sense; 2. The theology of liberation is the theology of the human being, for every human being is destined to be the image of God; 3. The theology of liberation is the theology of the future, for the kingdom of the Son of man is the human future of human beings.'[26]

The response in the Reformed member churches was considerable and positive. Many suggestions came in from Korea to Canada, from South Africa to Sweden, and these were then sorted and grouped together in Geneva. The North Americans under the leadership of Professor Allen O. Miller produced particularly many papers and laid all their weight on the connection between human rights and liberation. President Jimmy Carter had just bound United States foreign policy to human rights, and by doing so had made things difficult for the military dictatorships in Latin America.

In 1976 a consultation was convened in London. It was the climax of the work on this worldwide study. As always in ecumenical circles, the person who suggested something was also entrusted, or saddled, with its implementation and completion. So I wrote a summary study for this consultation under the title 'The Justice of God and Human Rights'. Jan Lochman wrote that 'the London consultation gladly accepted Moltmann's study.'[27] But it also put forth critical questions and called on me to supplement the study in the light of 'the justification and renewal of human beings', which I then gladly did. The connection between 'justification' and 'justice' had been familiar to Reformed theology ever since Karl Barth.[28] The participants also resolved on 'some practical consequences' for the church in the differing world situations.[29] In 1977 this Theological Declaration on Human Rights was then accepted by the General Assembly of the World Alliance of Reformed Churches in St Andrews, Scotland, and was published.

In order to link what is specifically Christian with what is universally human, I said, 'It is precisely when Christianity fills its special "Christian task" that it serves the humanity of all human beings. Conversely, it fulfils its special "Christian task" to the extent to which it serves the humanity of all human beings. By proclaiming God's justifying grace, it proclaims the dignity of the human being. By practising the justice of grace, it practises a fundamental human right.'[30] My specific concern was to combine the declaration of individual human rights of 1948 with the covenants on human rights of 1966, and to find a balance between individual and social human rights.

The consultation of 1976 placed in the foreground as a further task 'the rights of future generations' and 'the rights of the earth'. We went on working on this after 1977 in a group of theologians and lawyers. Here the Genevan constitutional lawyer Peter Saladin was a great help. At the 22nd General Assembly of the World Alliance of Reformed Churches held in Seoul, Korea, we put forward the declaration 'Rights of Future Generations—Rights of Nature: Proposal for Enlarging the Universal Declaration of Human Rights'.[31] This declaration then became part of the discussion process in UNO which was carried on between the World Charter for Nature of 1982 and the Earth Charter of 1992.

Today human rights are no longer merely an ideal for the community of nations. They can be claimed before the international courts. On the grounds of severe infringements of human rights during the civil war in the Balkans, war criminals have been brought before the court in The Hague. The Chilean dictator Pinochet was taken into custody with an international warrant of arrest. Even if the USA still hangs back in pursuing infringements of human rights, in the long run it will not be able to refuse its co-operation. The UNO Earth Charter was in part implemented through the Kyoto Protocol, which Russia also ratified in 2004. Perhaps one day severe crimes against the natural world and the foundation of human life will also be indictable offences. For the General Assembly in Seoul in 1989, I again detailed my position on the indivisible unity of human rights and their integration in the rights of the earth and the community of its life.[32] Human rights certainly show the first contours of a worldwide human community, but the ecological obligations of the human race also point to the need to ensure a habitable earth and a humanity at home in the earth's organism.

More or less at the same time as the study programme of the World Alliance of Reformed Churches, the Lutheran World Federation was also working on a declaration on human rights. Heinz Eduard Tödt and Wolfgang Huber formulated the closing declaration.[33] It was clear that the two studies had much in common, but a difference in the theological method also became plain: whereas we related the justice of God directly to human rights, the Lutherans sought for an indirect mediation which would do justice to their doctrine of the two kingdoms. Martin Honecker wrote a critical comparison of the two studies.[34] At that time the Pontifical Commission *Justitia et Pax* also published a declaration on human rights.[35] In this way the voices of Christendom on universal human rights, which were in many respects very similar, became part of the worldwide discussion.

EIGHTEEN

ECUMENICAL EXPANSIONS OF THE HORIZON

I was fortunate enough to receive more and more invitations to lecture than I could accept all over the world. In this way I not only got to know the countries I visited in the way that a tourist does; I also got to know the people living there, their problems, their culture, and their beliefs. Consciously and unconsciously, they put their stamp on the context of my theological thinking and on me myself. Certainly in this way I became somewhat of a globe-trotter, a 'citizen of the world', as my colleagues in the Tübingen faculty mockingly said, but theologically I no longer worked only in the framework of our own tradition, and our own 'Fathers', but with the 'brothers and sisters' in the ecumenical present day as well. Moreover, I did not just draw American, African, and Asiatic theology into my horizon as far as I could; I also became present in these countries through translations of my books and essays. I have had excellent translators. So it came about that my books were also at once translated into eight to ten other languages, although some of my colleagues' books might have been more deserving of this wider distribution. Through the journeys I was able to take, I reached the world and the world reached me. But here I shall talk only about three extensive journeys during the second half of the 1970s, which took me to North America, Latin America, and South Africa.

Up and Down the United States 1976

On 1 August 1976 we set off for America for almost three months, taking two of our children, Esther (17) and Friederike (13). The particular reason is soon told. In the previous months so many invitations to lectures had accumulated, as well as the invitation to a visiting professorship at Princeton Presbyterian seminary, that it was worth accepting them at one go. In addition, the purchase of our house in Tübingen in October 1975 and its thorough renovation had put me in financial difficulties; so I had very prosaically to set off on a private fundraising tour. The two older children, Susanne and Anne-Ruth, looked after the house—or lived in it with their friends—while we set off on our long journey.

We began with a week's holiday in Boston. Faith and Joe Burgess had studied under Ernst Käsemann in Tübingen, and they invited us to stay in the home of their parents, Mr and Mrs Rohrbough. The house turned out to be a kind of castle. It was called 'Rockholm' and stood on cliffs high above the sea near Gloucester. It had many rooms and a separate apartment, and there we were able to spend a week. It was glorious. We sprang down the cliffs to bathe in the sea, and we visited the little coastal towns of New England and ate our first lobsters. In Boston we viewed the harbour, and Harvard, and the historic sites of the Revolution. For us it was an arrival in America like the arrival of the Pilgrim Fathers long ago, and of course it was a renewed meeting after nine years. Faith Burgess later became the president of a Lutheran seminar in Canada.

Thoroughly rested, we flew on to Colorado Springs. That was our first stop, in the Holy Cross Abbey in Canon City. I gave four lectures, the Catholic New Testament scholar Raymond Brown giving the others. In between times, we were shown the Wild West: the abandoned gold-mining town Victor (of which all that remained was a crossroads with a drug store between dilapidated huts) and the Red Canyon Park. Someone told our children stories about Buckskin Joe and showed us a Wild West rifle, with notches cut on the butt for the enemies the owner had shot. At night the transcontinental train thundered through the little town.

My first fee went on our next journey. We hired a car and in glorious sunshine drove south through the mountains and wide valleys, our goal being the Indian town of Taos, via Alamosa, and then Santa Fe, by way of the Rio Grande Bridge. Elisabeth had wanted to do this, probably because of the Karl May she had read in earlier days. The Plaza gave Santa Fe a fine European flair missing from other American cities. In the ruins of Rio Pecos, a student suddenly emerged from the bushes and greeted me as 'Professor Moltmann'. There was a YMCA camp nearby. We were invited to dinner and a discussion by a somewhat obscure 'messianic Christian brotherhood', led by a former theology lecturer from Los Angeles. He had something against Paul. The next day we explored the Indian country, saw the Los Alamos nuclear plant, drove through the bizarre rocky landscapes round Shiprock up to Farmington and down again through the Navaho country to Gallup. We visited Sky City and finally reached Albuquerque, again an old Spanish-Mexican town in the midst of the United States.

We then flew via Las Vegas to our second stop, Santa Barbara, and to our friends Lois and Walter Capps. We stayed in the Casa de Maria in Montecito with the much-loved Sister Bernadette, and enjoyed the beach and the water of the Pacific. Together with the children we visited Marine Land in Los Angeles; I preached in the Lutheran church, lectured in the Center of Democratic Studies, and, together with Elisabeth, spoke at the conference which Walter had organized with us and Professor Wiggins. On our last day we spent a very light-hearted evening at a restaurant above Santa Barbara, processing through the room, singing and dancing. Santa Barbara seemed to me like heaven on earth.

From Santa Barbara we moved on to San Francisco, again to friends, this time to Charles and Marjorie McCoy in the Pacific School of Theology. We showed the children Muir Wood, with the giant redwood trees, ate in Fisherman's Wharf, and travelled up and down San Francisco's streets in the cable car. In the mornings I tried to put the family in a good mood with fresh doughnuts, occasionally succeeding. However, Esther and Friederike also went off on their own and explored the city. I preached in the Stanford chapel and again gave my four standard lectures on hope, freedom, the passion for life, and a new lifestyle,[1] this time adding a special lecture titled 'My American Dream',[2] because it was jubilee year in the United States: the two hundredth anniversary of the Declaration of Independence.

In Seattle we lived in the art nouveau house of the Rt Revd Cabby Tennis. At night his huge dog came and sniffed us. On 6 September we celebrated Esther's birthday with a sail on Lake Washington, although unfortunately the wind died when we were in the middle of the lake. On that Sunday I preached, and after that and the pastoral conference during the next days, I was able to tell the family that now the costs of the journey for the four of us were covered.

By way of Chicago, we finally reached Princeton, the goal of our journey. We found an apartment waiting for us and registered Esther and Friederike in their schools, where they were able to choose such subjects as world history, speedball, creative cooking, and other practical arts.

We were warmly received and looked after with touching solicitude by Jim McCord, the generous and sovereign president, and his wife, Hazel. He was famous for the 'fatherly arm' he put round every student, male and female. His wife was the finest kind of 'Southern lady'. Colleagues such as Daniel Migliore and Charles West, Karlfried Fröhlich and his wife, and David Willis also looked after us. We drove through the surrounding countryside and took guided tours introducing us to the history of Princeton battlefield, George Washington Crossing, and the Delaware River Park. In Philadelphia we met Paul and Marion Lehmann of Union Theological Seminary and had an introduction to American history; and together with the children we went sightseeing in New York, which was only 40 minutes away from Princeton Junction.

In the week before the semester began, I travelled—indeed rushed—through the country. I was in Providence for the American Baptist convention, in Andover Newton as the guest of Gabriel Fackre, spoke at Boston University, and received an honorary DD at the Moravian Seminary in Bethlehem, Pennsylvania. At Union Theological Seminary I had a slight clash with Dorothee Sölle and a Latin American liberation theologian. I talked about 'Hope in the Struggle of the People', as I had already done in Korea, but Dorothee Sölle misinterpreted my term 'people = *ochlos* = *minjung*' in the racial sense, while the Chilean theologian found 'the proletariat' missing from what I said. However, together with Jim Cone, we afterwards celebrated Dorothee's birthday and got on very well with her and her husband, Fulbert, as well as with Eberhard Bethge, who was also present. We went with Jim Cone to see the Broadway musical *Bubbling Brown Sugar*, and enjoyed it.

In our last week but one, we went with the children on our travels again, this time to our old haunts in Durham, North Carolina, visiting our old friends Kristin and Fred Herzog, Tom Langford, and Bob Osborn. By way of Columbia, South Carolina, we arrived in St Louis, where we stayed with our friends Blair and Doug Meeks. Here Elisabeth gave a lecture. We supported 'Seminex', the Lutheran Concordia seminar of the Missouri Synod, which for the time being was for theological reasons 'in exile'. In the evenings we sat in the river boats again and listened to the Mississippi blues.

The weekend of 10 October saw the end of our time in Princeton. Dick Shaull and I discussed 'the theology of revolution', to which he had given the name in 1966, as well as liberation theology and the theology of hope.

Then came the farewell to the students in my seminar, and to the faculty, the latter in a most successful faculty meeting. Jim McCord took leave of us in a formal farewell ceremony. On 13 October 1976 we were back home again. We arrived in what had become literally 'our' home, for now I was able to pay off all my debts, since the dollar still stood at 1:4 DM.

On this journey through America I no longer felt controversial, affirmed or rejected, but accepted and appreciated in widely different quarters. That was a new experience, and perhaps already a sign of increasing age. At all events, I looked back somewhat nostalgically to 1974, when I had been invited to Union Theological Seminary in New York. After I had turned down the invitation, Dorothee Sölle accepted it. So all that was left to me was to write postcards to Käsemann, saying—as he had earlier written to me—'Five years younger, and I should have stayed in America.'

On this journey I noticed what had never struck me before: the rise and growth of the feminist movement in theology. In many places it overlaid commitment to black theology and the interest in liberation theology—certainly not rightly. At the Baptist Convention in Providence, there was a demonstration by and on behalf of women. The inclusion in my Trinitarian theology of 'the motherly ministry of the Holy Spirit', which Count Zinzendorff had preached in Bethlehem, Pennsylvania, in 1741, brought feminist theologians in their own way to Trinitarian thinking, and led to criticism of masculine, monarchical monotheism.[3] Elisabeth went down well in Santa Barbara, Princeton, and St Louis with her lectures on feminist theology, and was received with open arms at Union Theological Seminary, always the most progressive outpost of American theology.

Latin America 1977

For me, the United States journey took me to familiar ground and was a kind of homecoming. I understood the language and knew the people a little. Travelling through South America the following year was a different matter—a journey into what was unknown and strange. I knew no Spanish and was dependent on translators who either knew no English or didn't want to speak it. An ecumenical theologian on the staff in Geneva had encouraged me to take this journey. After my ill-fated letter to José Míguez Bonino (about which I shall be talking later), the idea was for me to see things with my own eyes. He had also arranged the finances by procuring me an invitation to give the Carnahan Lectures at the ISEDET (Instituto Superior Evangélico de Estudios Téologicos) in Buenos Aires, and there were additional lectures and seminars in Brazil, Mexico, and the Caribbean. In the end I was faced with a programme lasting five weeks.

There was another reason, too, for me to accept the invitation to Buenos Aires. At that time Argentine was ruled by a brutal military dictatorship. The daughter of my colleague Ernst Käsemann had gone to Buenos Aires as a social worker. In the spring of 1977 Elisabeth Käsemann suddenly 'disappeared'. A few weeks later it became clear that she had been tortured and murdered in a military barracks. Ernst Käsemann had tried everything, but in the end all he had achieved was the release of her body. She had been shot three times in the back. On 16 June 1977 I took her funeral in Tübingen. It was another 30 years before an international warrant of arrest was issued, the names of her murderers being known. While I was in Buenos Aires, I wanted to enquire into the exact circumstances of her death, and to talk to the German ambassador.

On 3 September 1977, after a meeting of the editorial board of the periodical *Evangelische Theologie*, I flew from Frankfurt to my first stopping-off point, which was intended to be Cuba. Unfortunately, the flight was delayed, so that I missed my connection in Madrid. I waited for two nights in an airport hotel but got no flight to Havana. I calmed myself down with mystical, eutonic exercises, then changed my arrangements and flew directly to Rio de Janeiro, where I was actually only expected two weeks later. However, the Theological Institute took me in, and Acir Goulart looked after me with touching solicitude. I bathed in the sea in Botafogo and at the Copacabana beach, and discovered here for the first time what I later saw everywhere: the signs of the Afro-Brazilian Macumba cult, which is also called Candomblé. On the beach Coca-Cola bottles with flowers inside them were buried. An old woman put down a toy car at the edge of the sea and prayed for her son until a wave carried the car off; he was probably a taxi driver. A wedding party came down to the water and, bowing deeply, threw flowers into the sea. The sea goddess demanded tribute—or was it Xango himself? I climbed the Corcovado to the Christ with his hands raised in blessing, and enjoyed the glorious views over the bays and the mountains. Down in Botafogo French Huguenots had once settled, until they were driven out by the Portuguese. Nevertheless, they left behind them the first Protestant creed in Latin America.

After two days, I flew on to Buenos Aires. The German professor Schröder met me, and in the ISEDET José Míguez Bonino embraced me. Then the time-consuming programme began: five seminar sessions during the two forenoons and five evening lectures.[4] An Italian Waldensian woman from the Tavola Valdese (a Waldensian settlement on the river) translated for me, and in the evening Beatrice Couch took over. I felt ashamed at never having learnt Spanish.

The first day I was there, I went to the German embassy. It was strictly guarded—it was only unclear whether the purpose was to prevent people from going out or from coming in. Kastl, the ambassador, was embarrassed by my questions about Elisabeth Käsemann. He had registered a protest by failing to appear at a football match between Argentine and Germany, only hardly anyone had noticed. Elisabeth Käsemann's friend, the American Diana Houston, with whom she had shared an apartment, had 'disappeared' at the same time. The American ambassador had at once intervened, had personally fetched her out of the military prison, and had taken her immediately to the airport. I talked to Diana Houston later, when she came to Tübingen. But the foreign office and Genscher, the foreign minister, had not apparently authorized the German ambassador to act similarly. At that time Germany was dominated by fear of the Baader-Meinhof terrorists, and Martin Schleyer, the president of the employers' federation, had been murdered. So there was probably no desire to protect people abroad when there was any suspicion of terrorism. But Elisabeth Käsemann was completely unsuspected of any such involvement. As her mother told me, she knew nothing about either firearms or explosives. She wanted to stand by the oppressed, in accordance with her father's radical teaching.

The Carnahan week from 12 to 17 September ended in a real Argentinian fiesta, with *assado*, barbecued meat. In the evening the Couches took me to a tango restaurant, where the singers yearned after 'Mamma mia', and at night we stood at the harbour where the immigrants from Spain and Italy had once gazed forlornly over the sea to their old home countries.

The next stop was the Lutheran seminar and high school in Sao Leopoldo, Brazil. In Porto Allegre a Catholic colleague from the Jesuit university met me and showed me the miracle-working tomb of a Catholic saint, then took me to the Lutherans. There I gave four lectures in three days and the first evening enjoyed a *churasco* on the Spiegelberg with the faculty. The situation of the Lutheran immigrants, especially the smallholders, was depressing. The Old Testament scholar Erhard Gerstenberger drove me round—to Novo Amburgo, where my cousin Hans-Joachim represented the Hamburg-South American line as consul before, during, and after the war; into the *Walachei* of the poor immigrants who had never made it; and into a Macumba hut, where people broke into trance and ecstasy in the Afro-Brazilian cult. The men had dressed in girls' clothes and spun round and round until they were dizzy and fell to the ground. We did the same when we were children, to make ourselves lose our balance, but it didn't occur to us that it was religious.

Walter Altmann was responsible for systematic theology. Some people assigned him to the liberation theologians, but he was in the main a Lutheran; and the Lutheran minority in Brazil needed a firm denominational identity in order to survive. Unfortunately, however, there was no missionary impact. It was only the evangelical Pentecostal churches that were first able to gain an entry to the Brazilian people. On one of our trips we visited an old German inn where there were pictures on the wall of the *Graf Spee*, which was scuttled in 1939 after being chased by British warships. Typical German dishes were served, and it all seemed to me very German in the style of an earlier age; for the inn went back to the era of the immigrants from Pomerania and other parts of North Germany.

I then flew to Sao Paulo, a nightmare of a megalopolis which had completely burst its bounds. I was taken through endless suburbs to Rudge Ramos and stayed for three days in the Methodist seminary. In addition, I visited Manuel de Mello, who had set on foot the 'Brazil for Christ' revival movement. On Sundays he gathered more than 20,000 people in a factory building, and he was under observation by the military dictatorship. An impressive personality. Less impressive was the liberation theologian who prayed, 'God, we thank thee for this unjust meal which we have received from thy bounty.'

During the weekend of 25 September, I was again in Rio, went to the famous beach once more, and finally gave a lecture at the Bennet Methodist Seminary. The lecture was a fiasco, for I talked without a manuscript but had an American translator who could never remember a single sentence and always asked to have it repeated just when I was thinking about the next one. I then flew on to Recife, where the Seminario Bautista de Norde was waiting for me. Manfredo Grellert was one of the first people to write a dissertation on my theology. I drove to the sea and to the partner city Oliva, with its old churches and monasteries in the colonial style. At an evening lecture I suddenly noticed a row of blond, blue-eyed boys and girls. They were Mennonites who had settled here. Dom Helder Camara received me for a long talk about human rights, a conversation which was reported in the newspapers the following day. In the Brazil of the military dictatorships, that was important.

It was not easy to get from Recife to Trinidad. Although the two are quite close, I had to go back to Rio in order to fly to the island via Caracas. As I ran through the Rio airport, I gazed longingly after a Lufthansa machine on its way to Frankfurt. It took me a whole night to get to Caracas. In Trinidad I first stayed with the Benedictines on Mount Benedict. I bathed in Maracas Bay, viewed the famous asphalt lake, and in the hotel during the evenings got to hear the steel bands which drum on discarded oil drums, the drummers with the shaggy hair of the Jamaican Rastafarians. It all seemed to me very exotic, especially since I hardly saw a white person anywhere in Trinidad. The conference to which I had been invited took place in San Fernando, which was situated behind endless sugar-cane plantations. I spoke six times and met interesting people, such as Idris Hamid, and also Sister Paula Andrews, with whom I still maintain a friendly correspondence today. But this Caribbean island was really too hot for me, and at every turn there were things that crawled, buzzed, and stung. I was glad when I could gather up the remains of my strength and fly to Mexico City, to the conference with liberation theologians.

The flight via Miami again lasted from seven o'clock in the morning until eight in the evening. In Mexico I was met by the curate of the German Protestant church, Harald Nehb, who had been a student of mine in Tübingen. He showed me Teotihuacan, with its giant pyramids, and the famous anthropological museum with its Mayan treasures.

For me it had been a long journey, but measured against the size of the continent, it was very brief. And I had found Latin America fascinating: this medley of peoples, this music and dance, this religious delirium, these glorious beaches and landscapes—and this abysmal misery in the barrios and slums. In Rio, we drove along a road on one side of which there was a guarded and well-tended golf course along the seashore for the rich, on the other side endless huts piled up one above the other on the mountain slope. In Buenos Aires a 'Third World priest' took me to a barrio in which refugees from Peru and Chile were sitting in self-built corrugated iron huts, waiting for a future that never came. It was here that I first heard the proverb, 'Hope is the last thing to die.' The rich upper classes had hidden themselves behind brutal military dictatorships and had sent their families abroad, and undoubtedly their money as well. Colonial rule and slavery had certainly been officially abolished, but both continue to exist so that the notion of a revolution springing from the people's right to resistance imposes itself on one's mind. I came back excited and angry: so much beauty and so much violence, so much fullness of life and so much premature death!

Conflict with Liberation Theologians in Mexico City 1977

This first love came to an end at a conference called 'Encounter of Theologies' which took place from 6 to 10 October 1977 in Mexico City. I arrived in Mexico already considerably exhausted after the four weeks' lecture tour through Argentine, Brazil, and Trinidad, and I found a phalanx of Latin American liberation theologians with strongly Marxist views awaiting me. As well as myself, they had invited, as representatives of what they liked to call 'the theology of the First World', Harvey Cox and David Griffin (the latter representing 'liberal' process theology), and not least my friend James Cone, representing 'black theology'. The liberation theology scene was headed by Hugo Assmann, the son of German immigrants to Brazil and a Catholic priest who had studied in Münster. He lauded the Communist parties as being the proper place for revolutionary theologians, probably because at that time they were not instigating rebellion in the South American military dictatorships; for since Lenin 'putchism' had been out of favour. After my lecture about the connection between individual and social human rights, the liberation theologians fell upon me, attacking me as a bourgeois theologian and an ideologist belonging to the US imperialism of Jimmy Carter. Here, in far-off Mexico, I suddenly heard the same vocabulary with which the state theologian in East Germany (the GDR) had tried to stigmatize my *Theology of Hope*. 'They want to crucify you, Jürgen,' Jim Cone whispered to me.

I was not entirely ignorant of the reason for this about-turn from the early hosannas for my theology of hope and the political theology of Metz and myself to this condemnation. In 1975 I had written an 'Open Letter to José Míguez Bonino' in which I had criticized the superficial 'seminary

Marxism' of the liberation theologians and their pupils, and their revolutionary rhetoric.[5] Many people interpreted this letter as a 'no' to liberation theology, whereas my intention had been to offer co-operation. Míguez Bonino himself also understood the letter as a rejection and was surprised when in the periodical *Concilium* he saw my name under an appeal on behalf of the theology of liberation, directed against Cardinal Ratzinger.

Probably, however, on my side an unconscious irritation had played a part. For in 1974 a group of left-wing theology students from Argentina and Brazil had visited us in Tübingen and, before the discussion had even begun, already declared to us that they wanted to have nothing more to do with European theology and philosophy, indeed with Europe in general; they had to free themselves from this imperialistic colonial mind-set. Barth, Bultmann, and Moltmann would no longer have anything to say to them, for Karl Marx had said, 'History is class conflict.' My ironic question whether, then, Karl Marx had been born in Buenos Aires or Rio de Janeiro, and not in Trier, they of course brushed aside as inadmissible. Marxism was to help the people in Latin America to stand on their own feet at long last. They were blind to the new dependencies into which they were thereby entering. And with that, the discussion in Tübingen was already at an end before it had begun.

In 1975 *incommunicado* was the new watchword of the Latin American liberation theologians at ecumenical conferences, to which they nevertheless liked to be invited. As far as I can remember, it was Hugo Assmann who pronounced this judgement at a conference in Geneva. I felt personally hurt by this termination of all forms of fellowship, for—like Metz—I had done much to win recognition for liberation theology in Europe and had incurred considerable criticism as a result, for example, from the Protestant publicist Heinz Zahrnt and the philosopher Hermann Lübbe.

Anyone who so much as looks at the index of names in his book sees at once that the first *Theology of Liberation* which Gustavo Gutiérrez wrote in 1972 is exclusively determined by European theology, and not least by my theology of the forward hope. It was only later that Gustavo began to drink 'from his own wells'.[6] But with Gustavo himself I was always on friendly terms wherever we met.

The indebtedness to European theology was no different in the case of Rubem Alves and José Míguez Bonino, and later with Leonardo Boff and

Jon Sobrino. In view of the harsh *incommunicado* declaration, this could certainly make one ask what, then, was really 'Latin American' about liberation theology in Latin America. It is only in the second generation that we find a recollection of pre-Columbian traditions, as well as of the Indian and black underground literature of the colonial era. Latin America is a brilliant continent, full of poetry and dance and of new original religious experiences, so it is quite capable of a theological tradition of its own. There was also an independent further development of Marxist criticism in the dependence theory of F. H. Cardos, later president of Brazil. But up to now there has been no liberation from the predominance of the America of the United States. The Monroe Doctrine 'America for the Americans' has not been abrogated. For that reason, realistic liberation theologians know that they are still 'in Babylon' and not yet on the road to the land of freedom. Rubem Alves understood his liberation theology as being a 'theology of captivity'.

The conference in Mexico City had its surprising climax on the last day. The black theologian James Cone went through the rows of the liberation theologians, looked each of them in the eye, and then suddenly said, 'As far as I know, there are more blacks living in Brazil than in the USA. But you liberation theologians are all whites. None of you is black or mulatto. Where are your black liberation theologians?' That shamed our Latin American partners. They were descendants of European immigrants, but not the descendants of black slaves. Who represented their liberation? The people at the bottom are still black and the people at the top white.

After we had somewhat recovered from this shock and had been made to realize that oppression through white racism had to be added to the oppression through the class society, the next shock followed, as it was logically bound to do: Dora Arce Valentin from Cuba, a strong woman and a person very much with a mind of her own, stood up, went through the rows not only of the liberation theologians but including us all, and began, 'As far as I know, more than half the human race is female. But among those of you here, whether you are liberation theologians, or black theologians, or theologians from the First World, there is not a single woman. And yet women are especially oppressed, sexually and in many other ways, and have been from time immemorial, through the patriarchy and in Latin America through your arrogant machismo. Where are the feminist liberation theologians?' There was a long silence. We all reflected and silently relativized the positions we had defended so obstinately against each other. So this conference, in which the Marxist liberation theologians intended to settle scores with the rest of the theological world, in the end turned into an eye-opener for us all. We saw the different but interrelated fronts where we have to fight for freedom and human dignity: capitalism—racism—sexism. In the end that brought us after all, after all our disputes, into profound community. We celebrated the close of the conference with a glorious Mexican fiesta, at which I even got Mrs Hübner to dance, in spite of her missionary inhibitions.

During the flight back to Tübingen from Mexico City, I was struck by an illuminating idea. In Mexico I had come to know a theology of *the liberation of the oppressed*. Mustn't there be a corresponding theology of *the liberation of the oppressors* if humanity is to be freed on both sides from the sin of oppression? The liberation of the oppressed is self-evident, at least for the oppressed; but the oppressors see no need of liberation for themselves. So 'the blind must receive their sight.' The scales must fall from their eyes. They must recognize themselves *with* the eyes of their victims, or better: *in* the eyes of their victims. The perpetrators always have only short memories, but the memories of the victims are long. In order to arrive at the truth, the perpetrators, and those who come after them, are dependent on their victims' memories of their suffering, and the memories of those who come after them. After my return to Germany I then wrote an essay on 'the liberation of the oppressors', which appeared in many languages.[7]

What became even more important for me was to conceive a new version of the doctrine of justification, in which the justification of the victims of sin comes before the justification of the slaves of sin. This would surmount the one-sided, perpetrator-orientated doctrine of repentance and justification held by the Latin-Western church. But up to now my victim-orientated doctrine of justification has met with little response.[8]

Through their vehement rejection, the Latin American liberation theologians really had 'crucified' me to some extent; and I was downcast. At that time I was staying in the house of the Lutheran theologian Roberto Hübner, on the campus of the non-Catholic seminary. And the next morning there was a knock on the door. The Cuban theologian Sergio Arce stood there and asked me if I would take his son Reinerio Arce Valentin with me to Tübingen, so that he could do a doctorate under me. (Reinerio was professor of psychology in Havana.) I was speechless. After that 'crucifixion' I had not expected such a proof of trust from a Latin American theologian. But the Cuban theologian was a liberation theologian 'after the liberation', and hence probably had a more sovereign stance. Reinerio did then come to Tübingen with his wife, Francis. Later Elisabeth and I visited them in Cuba. He took his doctorate in Tübingen with a thesis on the religious ideas of José Marti, the Cuban national hero, who had been killed in the struggle again the Spanish rulers. He is now rector of the theological seminary in Matanzas.

On the flight back to Tübingen something else became clear to me as well. I had come to know Latin American liberation theology, I knew the black theology of North America, and with Elisabeth I experienced the development of a feminist theology—and each time I sensed that I didn't belong, couldn't belong. I don't live in a Latin American slum, so for me personally no authentic liberation theology of the oppressed is possible. I am white, not black, so I cannot represent any authentic black theology. I am a man, not a woman, so my theology can never become an original feminist theology. So what is left for me? Am I to become a mere sympathizer and a hanger-on of these theological movements? Am I to pretend to be what I am not and deck myself with borrowed plumes, like some 'left-wing' men and women theologians in Germany? I have certainly promoted and defended these theological movements wherever I could, but have then turned again to my own job, resolving to devote my work to long-term theological problems.

In this way, to the surprise of some of my friends and some of my enemies, the series of 'systematic contributions to theology' developed, beginning with the doctrine of the Trinity in the concept of God. I think I expected that I should thereby acquire the odour of abstract and unpractical theological speculation, but the opposite proved to be the case: the Brazilian liberation theologian Leonardo Boff adopted my 'social doctrine of the Trinity' and linked it with the Latin American base community movement, whose motto at that time was 'The Holy Trinity is the best community.' My ecological doctrine of creation, *God in Creation*, which followed as the second volume in the series, expanded the liberation theology of oppressed and protesting human beings by the liberation of the groaning creation, and led to the incorporation of age-old symbols from the Indian animist religions.

I have accompanied Latin American liberation theology attentively ever since its beginnings, and as a member of the editorial committee of *Concilium*, I played a vigorous part in defending it against attacks from the Vatican. But the more I came to know the Latin American reality in Nicaragua, the more I began to have critical reservations. At first Nicaragua was for me a classic example of good contextual theology. It brought the Bible's liberation text into the context of the poverty and oppression in the slums of the mass cities of Latin America, and of the landless campesinos. It thought through the 'preferential option for the poor' in theology, which the Episcopal Conference in Medellín in 1968 had resolved upon, and translated it into practice. But of course at the time of this development the light of the successful socialist revolution in Cuba of 1959 was still shining for the most part. Revolutionary groups were springing up everywhere. Thirty years later, the socialist Eastern bloc collapsed and the military dictatorships disappeared from Latin America. Fidel Castro now seems like the last Caudillo. With that, the context has changed considerably. There is no longer any 'revolutionary situation'. So liberation must proceed from the people itself.

So that the people can invest their energies and make use of their chances, the general concept of 'the poor' has to be infused with real life; for the concept itself levels everything down to the same thing. And 'the poor' have no wish to be approached from the angle of *what they are lacking*; they want to be seen first and foremost from the angle of *what they are*. If we speak to them merely as 'the poor', then they are merely the victims of the rich and the powerful. But they are men or women, whites, blacks, or indios; they have families, language, understanding, and faith. It is only when they become aware of *who they are* that they can become the determining subjects of their own biographies. In some places the evangelical Pentecostal movement is more successful than the Catholic liberation theologians and base communities in making 'the poor' the determining subjects of their own experience of God and their own lives, not merely instructing them but also awakening them to life. The Latin American Pentecostal movement could become the true criticism and continuation of liberation theology. For there are points of contact, for example, the healing of the exploited and sick bodies of men and women. Services of healing have a liberating force. Without them, sociological situation analyses merely paralyse.

In Apartheid Country—South Africa 1978

The National Council of Churches, its secretary, the Swede Axel-Ivar Berglund, and Bishop Desmond Tutu (with whom I had led a Bible study group at the Assembly of the World Council of Churches in Nairobi) wanted to invite me to South Africa. The invitation arrived in 1976, so I applied for a visa, which was refused. Through the South African 'Christian League' I was denigrated—or ought I rather to say honoured?—as being a 'revolutionary theologian'. So I had to cancel my flights and instead flew to Madrid, in order to talk about 'Fe y derechos humanos'. But the refusal rankled nonetheless.

At the conference of the World Alliance of Reformed Churches in St Andrews in August 1977, at which our memorandum 'A Theological Declaration on Human Rights' was accepted, representatives of the white South African apartheid churches were also present, and I took this opportunity to deplore publicly the refusal to grant me a South African visa. One of these theologians at once came to me and assured me that he would immediately clarify this unpleasant matter. The next morning he promised me the visa. He was a member of the secret South African *Broederbond*, which pulled the strings behind the scenes everywhere in South Africa, and he was probably also in the employ of the South African secret service. In the circumstances, that suited me well enough. I planned the journey for March and April 1978, now received the visa without difficulty, and arrived in Johannesburg on 27 March. Desmond Tutu and his wife met me at the international airport. Because they were black, they were not allowed to enter the national airport from where I had to fly on to Cape Town. I felt deeply ashamed when, as a white man, I had to say goodbye to them at the barrier; but I felt that now I had arrived in the land of apartheid.

In Cape Town Daniel Louw met me. He had written a thesis in Tübingen on Heidegger and myself and was now teaching practical theology in the Stellenbosch faculty. He took me to the Muizenberg beach, where I saw the notice 'Net Blankes—White Persons Only'. Then of course I had to see the Cape of Good Hope. There, there was the notice 'Nie Blankes—Toilets Non Whites'. But the hills and bays which led to the Cape looked wonderful in the morning sun. Was this Cape also able to give hope once more to the separated and oppressed people there? On the other side, on Robben Island, South Africa's hope, Nelson Mandela, had been in prison for the last

15 years, condemned in his cell to silence, and yet through his unbroken faith still inspiring the struggle for the liberation of black and white from the apartheid system, with its contempt for human beings. In Cape Town University I met John de Gruchy, the theologian of resistance and Bonhoeffer admirer, and saw the statue of Cecil Rhodes, who had made the axis Calcutta—Cape Town—Cairo the dimension of the British Empire. I also met Theo Kotze, who was under house arrest. My special lecture was on 'the liberation of the oppressors' from racism, masculinism, and capitalism. 'He who does not love his brother whom he has seen, how can he love God whom he has not seen?' (1 John 4.20). That was very well understood and was applied to the South African situation. It was only 'the Christian League' that termed me a 'revolutionary in a theologian's doctoral gown', demanding that the university UNISA should render an account explaining why they had invited me and let me speak, and asking whether their aim was to prepare for a violent revolution in South Africa. So I was once again a properly controversial and disputed figure.

I met with most approval in the Federal Theological Seminary in Plessislear, in the trust of the family of the Revd Simon Gquabule, in whose house I stayed. Every evening they told me what they were not allowed to do and what they had been robbed of. I collapsed inwardly and like them felt as if I were in a huge concentration camp. On the other hand I met with icy rejection in the seminary of the white Reformed church in Potchefstrom. They explained to me later how as Boers they had first lost the war against the English, were now under pressure from the growing black population, and were going to be the losers a second time. They were very pessimistic but were not prepared to turn back, as their president de Klerk so bravely did later.

In Durban a black student met me at the airport and wanted to take me to dinner there. But naive as I was, I suggested eating in Pietermaritzburg. He said nothing, but when we went through the town in the evening, he told me that here he was forbidden to enter a restaurant. In Pretoria I stayed with Adrio König, who had been our guest in Tübingen. In general I met many South African theologians again whom I already knew from Tübingen. Holland had not allowed them in. In Johannesburg I talked to the German congregation, which was very conformist; hardly a single opponent of apartheid was to be found there. In the hotel lift I heard black women humming the song which black prisoners were accustomed to sing when, as again at that moment, they went to the gallows.

I also visited the Revd Beyers Naudé and his German wife, Ilse. He, too, was under house arrest and was only allowed to be with one person at a time in a single room in his house. So his wife went out. Outside were the police cars with the directional microphones. Beyers turned up the radio, so we could talk together more or less freely. For black theologians, the protest against the apartheid system was something to be combated within their own people, while protesting white theologians were made strangers and outlaws in their own country. That was hard. Later we conferred Tübingen University's Lukas Prize on Beyers Naudé and had him as our visitor. He died in 2004.

At the end something unexpected happened. I unconsciously became a marriage broker. A female Tübingen student, Renate Hoffmann, whom I knew from my seminar, had joined the Moravian Brethren in South Africa after her exam, and she wanted to talk to me while I was in Cape Town. So I waited for her with John de Gruchy and James Cochrane, and we then drove to Blawberg where we ate ice cream. Jim fell in love with her on the spot and paid for the most expensive ice of his life. A few months later Theo Kotze and I married the two of them in Waldenburg in Franconia, for Renate came from the Hohenlohe region. Ever since then I have counted as a mascot in their family. Jim teaches at the university in Cape Town, where they live with their four children.

In South Africa I had many good human encounters. But in the Federal Seminary I had learnt to see the apartheid system with the eyes of the blacks, and I found it so obnoxious that on my flight home I resolved never to go back until the system had disappeared. But after the 'turning point' in Europe in 1989, not only did the Russian Soviet system collapse; the South African apartheid system also quietly crumbled, without bloodshed—one of the 'signs and wonders' of political history, for which no one had dared to hope. The collapse was due in great part to the story of Nelson Mandela's suffering, and to his firm faith.

NINETEEN

IN MY OWN PLACE

The expansions of my ecumenical horizon which I have just described may give the impression that for most of the time, I was travelling and was all over the place, only not in Tübingen. But the impression is false. During these years I did my work in the theological faculty and university in Tübingen just as well as my colleagues.

'Home Worker' in a Family with Four Children

During the years when our children were growing up, I certainly travelled a great deal, but when I was in Tübingen I could be completely available, for I usually worked at home, was a 'home worker'. I had my study at home and lived the whole day in the midst of the family. I also had rooms and a part-time secretary in the faculty, and there I prepared for lectures and seminars, dictated letters, and read proofs; but I could only work creatively in the familiar surroundings of my books, notes, and papers, and that meant in my own home. My teachers in Göttingen had done the same, and to Elisabeth and myself it seemed a matter of course. It is only today that for the first time more and more younger colleagues have their studies in the university.

But when I think of all the different studies I have lived in, I feel somewhat dizzy. In the large parsonage in Wasserhorst, I had a formal 'office' at the front of the house. When the two of us moved in, this was also our living room, because we were only able to heat one stove. In the winter Elisabeth occasionally fetched frozen eggs from the kitchen to thaw them out here. It was in this room that I wrote my historical post-doctoral thesis between 1953 and 1957, as well as the many small articles which Otto Weber entrusted to me for the church lexicon he was compiling. It was here, too, that I wrote my Sunday sermons, looking over to the old Wasserhorst church. It was a large, high, official room, suited to the era when the pastor was a figure to be looked up to. Then we moved to Wuppertal, and the home worker settled into a dark room, only divided from the large, light sitting room by a curtain. Here I sat in the mornings, with the light on, and toiled over my first lectures.

Susanne was born in 1955, Anne-Ruth in 1956, Esther in 1959, and Friederike in 1963. Even in Wuppertal Elisabeth was already obliged to protect me from childish onslaughts and had to surround my study with an aura of untouchability. I was, and still am, endlessly grateful to her for doing so. Nevertheless, it didn't prevent any child at any time from fetching drawing paper from my store of typing paper. Moreover, our one telephone stood on my writing desk, and I had often to pass on calls until we acquired a second.

In 1961 we moved from the house in Robert Koch Platz into the seminary itself, and spatially speaking we arrived in paradise. We had a large apartment, with a room for each child and a long study for me, with a view of the city beneath the 'Heiliger Berg', and a sound-proof door. It was in these generous surroundings that I wrote my *Theology of Hope*. For a long time the work was split up between us in the traditional fashion: Elisabeth took over the kitchen and the children, while her homeworker attended to the income. Consequently, he never learnt to cook properly; he can only manage tea or coffee three times a day. At 6.00 in the evening I was called to help with the clearing up—building blocks in one tub, Legos in another, dolls in the doll's house, and so forth. Then the evening ceremony began. After they had been washed, we sat on the children's beds, and after the story—it might be a Grimm's fairy tale or an invented story about robbers—we sang their evening hymn with them. And then peace was supposed to reign. After eight o'clock they were not supposed to appear.

In 1964 we moved to Bonn. At that time Bonn was the capital of the Federal Republic, and housing was in short supply. We found a six-room apartment in a house with six families, a single-storey heating system fired from the cellar, and an unheatable attic under the roof. The homeworker sat in a room of only ten square metres, and the children slept in bunk beds. Then Susanne got too big, and I had to move out of my room to make room for her. So that my writing desk would fit into the attic, one edge had to be sawn off. I ran up and down stairs, between the furnace in the cellar, our living quarters on the ground floor, and the attic, and stayed slim. At that time I got to know and like my Catholic confrère Franz Böckle, and the splendid study of this celibate colleague made me green with envy.

The invitation to Tübingen in 1967 was sweetened for us by the offer of a very roomy apartment. We acquired eight rooms in a house in Bauhaus style, above the Institute for Mission in the Hausserstrasse, and an additional two rooms in the basement. It was a climb to reach the apartment, but we were still young and enjoyed our freedom of movement when we were there, the semi-circular balcony, and the view of the Österberg. Each child had a big room and could blossom and develop her own tastes. At first I had the largest room but then moved into a smaller one so as to give way to a sitting room. One problem was the growing mountain of books that had to be fitted in somewhere. Today bookcases fill every room in the house.

Of course, I couldn't simply and immediately switch off from whatever I was concerned with at the moment. So I was often absent-minded at table, which amused, or annoyed, the children, because I once again showed ignorance of their problems. When I occasionally arrived at a good suggestion, my fatherly reputation was again to some extent established. But it was Elisabeth who bore the whole burden of our four growing children, so that I could make good progress with the necessary, or perhaps less necessary, work. It was only when the children were over the worst that she returned to theological work; and feminist theology emerged.

On the children's birthdays the division of labour functioned particularly well. There was cocoa and cake from 3.00 to 4.00 p.m., which Elisabeth prepared. After that I took over the entertainment, first with a Punch and Judy show, then with games, and finally with the frightening 'murder' game in the dark. Then there was supper for the children, and the wild party broke up.

In order to stay in Tübingen, we of course looked for a house of our own with a garden which would be big enough for the whole family. In 1971 we were just about to buy one when the owner, a law colleague, suddenly raised his price by 50,000 DM. That was beyond us financially. Elisabeth was disappointed, and as compensation we bought a holiday house in the Beerenhalde settlement on the Swabian Alb, a 45 minute drive from Tübingen. Here we found a second centre for our lives in the region. The settlement was situated above Erpfingen near the older Sonnenmatte of the organization Schwaben International. Because of our children, other young couples came, too, so that our four children soon had company. As far as I can remember, we drove to Erpfingen every free weekend, shopped on the way in Melchingen, and took long walks through the woods and over the heights of the Alb (or alp). In the evenings the children took their milk cans and fetched milk from the farmers in the village, at night the owls screeched, and under our roof there was soon a large family of dormice, which we never got rid of.

In the summer we enjoyed joining in the festivities of Schwaben International. The dance round the Easter fire was always very romantic and exhausting. Up here Esther rode her Welsh mountain pony, which she had acquired from the compensation she received after an accident in Tübingen. She and her friends took day-long rides over the alp. I tried out the pony one day, but the brute immediately threw me. In winter there was a toboggan run for sledging. Elisabeth and I also tried cross-country skiing, but I was soon unable to keep up. Instead I liked to walk in all weathers, and brooded over my next lectures and books.

As Susanne and Anne-Ruth grew older, they preferred to meet friends in Tübingen and no longer went to the alp with us. The time came when Esther and Friederike no longer wanted to come with us either, and the hut was deserted. Now we only went there in the spring and autumn, to see that everything was in order. But in 1992 we celebrated Esther's wedding in Erpfingen. Since her husband is Catholic, they had an ecumenical wedding in the Protestant church in the village, and afterwards a reception in the community hall of the Sonnenmatte. Esther was the one of our children who had the closest ties with Erpfingen. But in the end we were relieved when in 1998 a Stuttgart couple bought the holiday house.

Meanwhile, in 1976, we had bought the house in the Biesingerstrasse. It had a large sloping garden, with old trees, and we always had plenty to do with renovation and maintenance.

The high spot of our family life was always the four weeks' summer holiday. Ever since our time in Wuppertal, we had spent them in Denmark, on the island of Møn. Elisabeth had found the place and the hut. We set out from Wuppertal, Bonn, or Tübingen and spent the night with my parents in Hamburg. The next day we took the car ferry from Travemünde to Gedser. For the children the great event was always the opening of the breakfast buffet. Then we drove over the Storestrømbrücke to Vordingborg, always stopping at a particular point so as to sing the children's favourite song: 'Winde wehn, Schiffe gehn weit ins ferns Land …' (Winds blow, ships go, far to a far-off land …). On Møn we had rented a holiday house in a marshy and wooded area, which was surrounded by moorland, and were often buzzed round by a myriad of midges. The house was small and cheap, and the sanitation was primitive, but we were always very happy there. We cycled to the beach, which sloped down gently and was good for children. Here I tried to teach the children to swim, but they preferred to build houses and gardens in the sand for the multitudinous ladybirds. In the evening we ate potatoes and *Hackebøf* with brown sauce in the Øestersøbad.

Once during the four weeks, Elisabeth and I each had 'a day off' and went separately to Copenhagen, sometimes even farther to Malmö and Lund, returning in the evening. During the long afternoons I turned to woodcarving. I had already begun at the Walchensee with a child's head, but in Møn I became fascinated by this minor creative art and worked with various knives. My chosen material was wood, which I simply found, and out of which I carved small figures. The result was not a work of art, but the unity between head and hand in creating form from the raw wood fascinated me greatly. Apart from cycling and swimming, wood-carving was my holiday recreation. I must admit that in the four holiday weeks I hardly read a book, let alone did any intellectual work. I pushed the theological problems on which I had been working into the subconscious, and left the possible solutions to the powers that are at work there. When I came home, the chapter of the next book generally went fairly smoothly and rapidly. One of the finest places on Møn is the eighteenth-century summer residence Liselund. We visited it regularly, one reason being that there was excellent cake to be had there. We then climbed down to the beach from Møn's *klint* (chalk cliffs like the ones on the opposite island of Rügen) and looked for fossils. I developed a good eye for fossilized sea urchins, and a number of them still stand on my bookcase.

But Møn's glories also came to an end. As the children grew older, one after the other wanted to go her own way. On the last occasion we were once again near Ebeltoft, near Arhus, in the holidays, and together with the Blochs visited Rudi Dutschke in his commune. But then Susanne already flew from Arhus to Northern Ireland, in order to look after children from Belfast in Corrymeela and to spread her wings.

Of course, my 'home work' did not compensate for my many absences on lecture tours. Sometimes these absences were even an additional burden on Elisabeth. I asked a great deal of her during those years and was grateful for the freedom that she gave me to pursue my theological 'missions'. I also missed out on something in the life we shared with the children. It was only when they were older, and the father became more of a friend, that I could, as compensation, catch up to some degree with what I had missed during their earlier years.

Everyday University Life in Tübingen

My weekly teaching commitments in Tübingen consisted of four hours of lectures, a two-hour seminar, consultation hours, and a two-hour seminar for graduate students. Added to this were the obligatory faculty meetings, commissions, university senate meetings, and, when one's turn came round, a year as dean. At that time we still restricted this term of office to a year so as to avoid any possible tyranny. From the beginning I always had about 15 to 20 graduates to supervise, and, with a few exceptions, they did well in their final exams. Five of them later became professors. After my visits to Seoul, I gladly accepted Korean students who wished to work for a doctorate. I felt a particular ecumenical obligation towards foreign graduates and gladly took them under my wing. I had only one condition. After I had supervised them and written my report, and after they had successfully passed their exam, I demanded a good 'doctor's feast', which no one then refused. I remained on terms of friendship with many of the people I supervised.

When I came to Tübingen in 1967, we had about 600 students in the faculty. Ten years later the number had doubled. After 20 years, we had more than 2,400 women and men students. The lectures were always overflowing, so one had to prepare very carefully. The seminars were bursting at the seams, so one had to try to find an appropriate teaching technique; but the colleagues whose subject it was also knew nothing about how to work with masses of students. If one divided the seminar into groups, the seminar as a whole was generally weak; if one tried to start a dialogue from the front, only the first few rows participated. At the end of these defeats one was then left at the end of the semester with more than 100 seminar papers. In addition, the number of examinations and dissertations set by the regional church increased, and these were also generally handed in at the end of the semester. It was not easy to do justice to it all.

During those years it was not the left-wing students who wanted to change the system; it was the bureaucrats in the ministry of education. They tormented the universities and faculties with continually new regulations which they termed 'reforms'. Every new dean in our faculty had to revise all the examination regulations yet again. With a total lack of imagination, the minsters of education were bent solely on an Americanization of the ancient German university, their aim being to satisfy the short-term interests of industry. So they turned students from academic citizens into attenders of vocational schools and made the university faculties into technical colleges. 'Freedom of research and teaching' was restricted through 'courses of study'. At that time universities throughout the country were forced to build up bureaucracies for themselves in order to counter the ministry of education and to defend their liberty, and we spent endless time and energy, and frittered away a great deal of public money, in meetings about the senseless regulations imposed on us. We could have worked better with the students if we had not been prevented by the ministry. During the whole of my time at the university, I did not encounter a single reasonable suggestion from that quarter that was worth considering from an academic standpoint. But the gentlemen were themselves not notably well qualified personally in their own academic fields.

Co-editor of the Periodical Evangelische Kommentare

After I had become somewhat better known through the *Theology of Hope*, Günther Heidtmann co-opted me to the editorial committee of the *Evangelische Kommentare*. This was a supra-regional compendium of Protestant church newspapers under the leadership of the Rhenish periodical *Kirche in der Zeit*, which Heidtmann had been in charge of for many years. It was intended to be something comparable to the Catholic *Herder-Korrespondenz*. Heidtmann had been an upright pastor of the Confessing Church in Potsdam. When after the war he came under pressure by the Russians, the church authorities moved him to West Berlin, and from there he then moved to the Rhineland. He was straightforward and vigorous, and I valued him greatly. My wife had met his wife in the youth group of the Confessing Church in Potsdam. In 1968, in the first number of the new *Evangelische Kommen-*

tare, he published my essay 'Die politische Hermeneutik des Evangeliums' (The Political Hermeneutics of the Gospel) and called it 'a break-through'.[1] Consequently, I could not well say no to a co-operation, which I in any case regarded as an honour. But it meant reading and assessing manuscripts and attending the annual editors' meetings. On the other hand, I thereby acquired a mouthpiece through which I could make my ideas on theology, the church, and society widely known. And the periodical also brought me somewhat closer to the so-called 'pulse of the times'.

Günther Heidtmann died early. After many misgivings, the somewhat crafty and intriguing Swabian Eberhard Stammler was appointed chief editor. But I still had Hans Norbert Janowski on the paper, and with his skilful help I was able to hold my ground against Stammler, the (right-wing) CDU member and military expert—he had been transferred to the parachutists in Italy in 1944 and felt himself to be competent in this field.

Co-editor of the Periodical Evangelische Theologie

On 11 September 1971 Ernst Wolf died, quite unexpectedly.[2] He had founded the periodical *Evangelische Theologie* in 1934 as the mouthpiece of the Confessing Church. In 1938 it was forbidden 'as a danger to public peace and security'. Wolf then re-founded it in 1946. When we were studying with him after the war in Göttingen, we bought every number separately, immediately after it came out. It was the central forum of the Protestant theology to which the Confessing Church, and with it the theology of Karl Barth, Rudolf Bultmann, Dietrich Bonhoeffer, and Gerhard von Rad, was committed. Ernst Wolf collected the contributions, edited them all himself, organized the theological conferences, and, until his death, published the periodical monthly. 'Ernst Wolf was present and sovereign in so many functions, leading, ordering, planning and reflecting, that he sometimes seemed to me like an Atlas who carried a firmament on his shoulders,' said Walter Fürst in his sermon at Ernst Wolf's funeral, and this was no exaggeration. 'With the same dependability with which he served the periodical's concern, he was available to all those who were joined with him in that concern.'[3] The work he got through was certainly immense. At eleven o'clock at night he drank some more black coffee, smoked another black cigar, and went on working. With his unbelievably tiny yet legible writing, he filled countless pages. During editorial conferences, in the evening he distributed manuscripts that had come in and expected us to give him well-founded opinions the next morning as to whether they should be accepted or rejected. Groaning and enthusiastic, we all went along with him.

Years previously, Ernst Wolf had co-opted me to the editorial committee. Nevertheless, it was a surprise to me when the other editors appointed me as his successor on 13 November 1971. In order to show both respect and distance, we formulated the imprint 'Responsible editor 1934–1971 Ernst Wolf', and underneath, 'Acting editor Jürgen Moltmann, Tübingen'.[4] I was able to persuade my colleagues that the periodical should now be given a new structure. From then on it was to appear every two months, with double the number of pages, and the contributions would be gathered together thematically and arranged in deliberate contrast to each other. New features were a 'Critical Forum' for the discussion of important new publications, and pointers to the theological dimensions of events in culture, politics, and church. This new form for *Evangelische Theologie* proved itself and still exists today.

It was a great help for me to have my graduate student Hans Georg Link on the editorial staff (he later became secretary in Faith and Order, Geneva, and then pastor for ecumenical relations in Cologne). We tried hard to produce issues on subjects of topical interest. But to plan issues of this kind is laborious. To look through the shower of lectures and essays that were sent in, and to print the best of them, was easy in comparison. Following the practice Ernst Wolf had established, we developed the editorial meetings into theological conferences. When we were no longer able to go to Josefstal in Bavaria, we went to Grafrath near Düsseldorf. In 1972 we published a number with the theme 'Hope and the Future of Humanity', with contributions by Wolfhart Pannenberg, John Cobb, Carl Braaten, Philip Hefner, Johann Baptist Metz, and myself, these being papers read at the conference in New York about which I have already talked. In 1973 my book *The Crucified God* provided the subject for one issue; in 1974 the topics were Christian-Jewish dialogue and black theology. After the World Mission Conference in Bangkok, I thought an up-to-date theology of mission was important, and this then became 1974/5.

Looking over the manuscripts, preparing the conferences, and discussing the theme numbers certainly took time, but in those years there was a positive flood of theological discussions and disputes. The editor of every periodical could draw on a wealth of material and could occasionally steer the excitement in a particular direction. In the 1970s theology was not, as it is today, pushed away into the inner sanctum of the church, and even there limited to the professional training of the clergy. Theology was in the public eye and was disputed from an atheistic, Marxist, secularist, or liberal standpoint. It was by no means left in peace as it is nowadays. Onerous though it might be, it was a pleasure to be a theologian. To read the numbers of *Evangelische Theologie* which came out during those years is to sense something of this.

In the editorial committee we had agreed that the editorship should change every three years. So in 1974 I passed this on to Gerhard Sauter, systematic theologian in Bonn. I was relieved and pleased that *Evangelische Theologie* continued after Ernst Wolf's death and that it had taken a leap forward. At this point I must also pay a tribute to Fritz Bissinger, the head of the publishing house Christian Kaiser. He was not only one of the periodical's supports; he also actively promoted it, because he had a personal interest in theology's concerns. For us at that time he was a publisher belonging to the old school, not a modern 'product manager'. In 1990 we honoured him with a symposium, to which the publishers invited us from 14 to 17 July in the study centre in Josefstal. Fritz Bissinger beamed, and we all sunned ourselves in what we had achieved. But only a few years later the Lempp family sold the publishing house to Gütersloh, that is, Bertelsmann. The periodical's publisher now appeared as Chr. Kaiser/Gütersloher Verlagshaus.

In 1988 I again took over the editorship of the periodical for four years. I now had rather more experience in dealing with authors and with manuscripts written by colleagues. That was often the most delicate part of an editor's work. But I was greatly helped by my last assistant, Carmen Krieg (later Carmen Rivuzumwami), so that I hardly had to trouble about the editorial work. When I retired in 1994, I lost all my assistants and would not have been able to carry on this work. In 1993 I passed the periodical on to Ulrich Luz, professor of New Testament in Bern, who did an excellent job.

In order to describe the inner relations of the editors of *Evangelische Theologie*, I must talk about a man who, after Ernst Wolf, became the secret *spiritus rector* of our periodical: Helmut Gollwitzer. His all-embracing human kindness and his youthful capacity for enthusiasm kept us together and at the same time drove us apart. The rebellious students of 1968 had divided the editorial committee of our periodical as they had the university faculties. Helmut Gollwitzer embraced their concerns as well and declared himself to be on their side. When their leader, Rudi Dutschke, was shot, dying later as a result, he took the funeral in the midst of the outcry of the protesting students; for Rudi was a sincere Christian. Gollwitzer accompanied the squatters into empty apartment houses. He expected a renewal of the universities with a democratic basis from everyone, from us too. He wrote splendid contributions for the periodical. But not everyone was able to go along with his generosity of heart. We lost some of the co-editors, who had misgivings.

Then at the beginning of the 1980s came the era of the peace movement. The discipleship of Jesus made of Helmut Gollwitzer an unremitting friend of peace and an opponent of rearmament. He had spent four years in Russian prison camps. In the periodical and in the Gesellschaft für Evangelische Theologie (the Society for Protestant Theology), we declared ourselves to be decisively against rearmament and unequivocally committed to the service of peace 'without weapons'—not simultaneously 'with weapons', too, as a Heidelberg declaration said, hoping to satisfy both sides through this complementary formulation. But who can make a decision in complementary terms? We wanted to live unequivocally 'without weapons'. During a conference, a violent controversy broke out between the kindly Helmut Gollwitzer and the charming Eduard Schweizer, who defended Helmut Schmidt as 'a Christian'—Schmidt, the federal chancellor, had just pushed through the NATO twin-track decision and had hence, because of the peace movement, lost his base in the Socialist Party (the SPD).

The person who was behind the criticism which Helmut Gollwitzer had to face in the periodical after 1968, and again after 1980, was an old Barthian friend of his, Helmut Traub, to whom, as I said earlier, I am indebted personally for good theology. Traub considered this politicization of the gospel to be a betrayal of Barth and of the periodical's tradition. Through Ernst Wolf's son, Uvo Andreas Wolf, he suggested that we ought to remove Ernst Wolf's name from the imprint and abandon the periodical's name. With this Traub caused considerable unrest among the editors, because no one really knew whom he had goaded on, and who had been taken in by him. However, we survived and kept faith with Helmut Gollwitzer until his death, as he did with us. For his eightieth birthday I wrote the following tribute:

On 29 December 1988 Helmut Gollwitzer will be 80 years old. In the name of all the co-editors and readers of *Evangelische Theologie* I should like to congratulate most sincerely the one who is now the oldest in our circle, and I do so with great gratitude and in friendship. But even as I say this, I stumble somewhat over my words, for it is almost impossible to realize that this always youthful mind and spirit is the 'oldest' among us. And indeed it is only in years that one is old, while God's Spirit renews from day to day. It makes one alert and present in mind, lets one experience life full of love and interest, and allows one to recognize and accept other people. These ideas come to me quite spontaneously when I think of Helmut Gollwitzer. For me, as for countless other men and women, theologians and non-theologians, he embodies this spirit. A brotherly theologian, who radiates friendship and spreads warmth.

Gollwitzer's name was known to the generation before me through his Dahlem sermons and biblical interpretations, which passed from hand to hand in the congregations of the Confessing Church. At that time he was the theological teacher of 'the young brethren'. To my generation he spoke from the heart through his book about his captivity '*Und führen, wohin du nicht willst* ...' [And carry thee whither thou wouldst not go ...]. Through this book he showed me personally how one can come to terms with those unfree years without bitterness. Ever since the 1950s, his name is to be found in the periodical and the Gesellchaft für Evangelische Theologie. Whether in the brotherhoods and in our campaign 'fight atomic death' (as the slogan then went), whether in the tension of EKD synods, whether in the Barth-Bultmann controversies—Helmut Gollwitzer was always present, combining in his own inimitable way decisiveness in his own standpoint with openness for others. For several generations of theologians he has exemplified the capacity for dialogue of a truly Protestant theology. It was he who inspired the Christian-Marxist and the Christian-Jewish dialogues. And, not least, Helmut Gollwitzer has carried the dialogue across the generations. He is one of the few who remained capable of sustaining dialogue across the generation divide of the 1968 era, when much younger people among us suddenly seemed to themselves very old. Helmut Gollwitzer has put his stamp on the periodical since the time of the Confessing Church down to the present day, spanning so many generations, and gives it his impress still. He belongs to this periodical as the periodical belongs to him, and we hope that in the future too he will be able to see it as 'flesh of his flesh and bone of his bones' and will continue to accompany it with encouraging and critical love.

The text for the 29 December 1988 is so splendidly appropriate for Helmut Gollwitzer, and for the thrust of the periodical too, that I should like to set our human greetings within this great hope for the God of Israel:

> In the latter days the LORD shall decide for many peoples;
> And they shall beat their swords into ploughshares,
> And their spears into pruning hooks (Isa. 2.4).[5]

Helmut Gollwitzer died on 19 October 1993. I represented *Evangelische Theologie* at his funeral on 20 October in Berlin-Dahlem, and later said in the Martin Niemöller House:

> I heard of Helmut Gollwitzer for the first time when I was studying with Ernst Wolf and Hans-Joachim Iwand in Göttingen, having returned from my prisoner of war camp in 1948. In the seminar we read his book *Coena Domini*, and for our personal edification his wonderful Luke interpretation *Die Freude Gottes* [The Joy of God], and together with our teachers, who were his friends, waited for his return home from the Russian prisoner of war camp. When at last he came, in 1949, he exceeded all our expectations. Whoever met him and looked into his shining eyes was infected by his enthusiasm and filled with the joy he radiated. His way through the prisoner of war camps—'and carry thee whither thou wouldst not go'—had not embittered him: on the contrary. He was a hope for theology in the Confessing Church, in the brotherhoods of the post-war era, and in the circle of the periodical and the Gesellschaft für Evangelische Theologie. He fulfilled, and much more than fulfilled, these hopes, and became a guiding light in the student and peace movement, a friend to whom everyone could turn and in whom so many put their trust.
>
> I then came to know him personally at the first theological conferences of this periodical (from 1961 onwards) in Ernst Wolf's summer house on the Walchensee, and he encouraged me to go ahead with my *Theology of Hope* although long-standing Barthians viewed me with a

degree of scepticism. He took part in all the conferences of this periodical, and inspired them through his broadminded capacity for dialogue. In 1981, at the height of the peace movement, he and I arranged a conference for the Gesellschaft für Evangelische Theologie in Arnoldshain. Hundreds applied, but we could only find room for 200. With his two-hour lecture on 'The Sermon on the Mount and the Doctrine of the Two Kingdoms' he kept us warm in the icy village church. On the periodical's editorial committee Gollwitzer did not just bring about peace; he also saw to it that the necessary dispute was not lacking. The editorial committee was tried to breaking-point in the 1970s over the Christian-Jewish question, with the controversial contributions by Friedrich-Wilhelm Marquardt and Günter Klein, over the debate about Karl Barth and socialism, and not least in the discussion about peace. Even those who did not agree with him will miss him. For me, as for so many others in the generations that succeeded him, he was a fatherly friend, a friend who never curried favour and who himself met enemy and friend with incomparable fearlessness. He spoke the truth to politicians and students, and maintained it authentically through his own commitment—and he was listened to. We miss Helmut Gollwitzer. He is with us still. [6]

On the Committee of Concilium

The Catholic periodical *Concilium* had long fascinated me. I admired it from the beginning. It was born out of the reform spirit of the Second Vatican Council, which took place from 1962 to 1965, and from the beginning the periodical was caught up in the tensions existing between Council and curia. The new Catholic theologians with whom we were in close interchange, such as Karl Rahner, Hans Küng, Johann Baptist Metz, Edward Schillebeeckx, Ives Congar, and others, were the founding fathers of *Concilium* in 1965.[7] The Dominican order in Nijmegen organized this international theological periodical, which always appeared simultaneously in seven languages—German, English, French, Italian, Dutch, Spanish, and Portuguese—and at its peak had 40,000 subscribers. That was unique. When had there ever been anything like it in the theological world?

At the beginning *Concilium* appeared 12 times a year, but later the number of issues had to be reduced. Today, in its fortieth year, it appears five times annually in seven languages. I was delighted when I was first invited in 1966 to write a contribution. The subject was 'Hope without Faith? Eschatological Humanism without God' and, as the title betrays, was a discussion with Ernst Bloch. After that I wrote more and more frequently for *Concilium*. The section on ecumenism was in the hands of Hans Küng and Walter Kasper, my Catholic colleagues in Tübingen. With them and with my Protestant colleague Eberhard Jüngel, my wife and I shared a systematic-theology and wining and dining table round.

In 1976 Walter Kasper resigned from *Concilium* in order to turn to other tasks in the Catholic hierarchy and the curia. As a result, in 1976 I was chosen in his place by the board of the periodical, in order to work on the ecumenical dimension together with Hans Küng. I of course accepted, and a whole new world opened up for me—Catholicism in all its breadth. But the costs were not inconsiderable. I took on new work in addition to all the rest. From 1977 to 1983 we produced an ecumenical number every year, from 1986 onwards one every two years. The last was published in 1996 by Karl-Josef Kuschel (Hans Küng's successor) and myself on 'The Pentecostal Movement as a Theological Challenge'. The editorial conferences took place year for year in the Pentecost week, generally in a monastery in Holland which had once been built for 200 monks and which now housed only ten; but we also met in Madrid, Bologna, Brescia, and Budapest. The work in groups and the discussion about the projected numbers were always followed by an evening surprise, an excursion to somewhere nearby, and an excellent dinner, for which the secular founder member, the businessman Antoine van den Boogaard, generously made himself responsible.

Through the collaboration on *Concilium,* I got to know Catholic reform theologians from many countries. I gratefully remember conversations with the French Claude Geffré, Jean-Pierre Jossua, and Christian Duquoc, with the Latin Americans Leonardo Boff, Gustavo Gutiérrez, and Jon Sobrino, and the North Americans David Tracy, Virgil Elizondo, Elisabeth Schüssler-Fiorenza, and Anne Carr. I think of the Spaniard Casiano Floristan, the Italians Giuseppe Ruggieri and Giuseppe Alberigo, the Englishman Nicholas Lash and the Irishman Sean Freyne, and many others, all of whom I cannot name here. Through *Concilium* I came as a Protestant theologian into Catholic seminaries and universities and was nowhere viewed as a stranger. The high spot of my collaboration was undoubtedly a visiting professorship at the famous Jesuit Università Gregoriana in Rome in the spring of 1987. I stayed in the Germanicum, walked daily past the Fontana Trevi to the Piazza della Pilotta, and felt very happy to be in Rome. The publishers from the different countries always attended the *Concilium* conferences, and Rosino Gibellini of the Editrice Queriniana and John Bowden of the SCM Press became my particular friends.

When one of the Catholic reform theologians again got into difficulties with the Congregation for the Doctrine of the Faith in Rome, we all suffered with him. Jacques Pohier lost his position and had to leave his order, and was compelled to make his way as a bank employee. Leonardo Boff suffered the same fate at the hands of his former teacher, Joseph Ratzinger. Edward Schillebeeckx was several times summoned to Rome. In 1979 Hans Küng lost the *missio canonica* in Tübingen and from then on no longer counted as a 'Catholic theologian'. But they were all kept on, remained on *Concilium*'s editorial committee, and worked until their time of membership was up. That made a great impression on me. I found it wonderfully 'catholic', even if not 'Roman', and could easily identify myself with this independent catholicism. In this sense *Concilium* made me 'catholic'. I became, so to speak, a Protestant Catholic, even if not a Roman one. In 1995 I received an honorary doctorate from the Catholic university of Louvain.

The co-operation with Hans Küng in Tübingen was effortless and always pleasurable. Other *Concilium* members were in Tübingen, too—Norbert Greinacher and Dietmar Mieth, and later Karl-Josef Kuschel. Work with them was also easy. The theological fronts had long ceased to run parallel to the confessional boundaries, but now cut across them, with 'fundamentalists' on the one side and 'modernists' on the other, to use a Protestant and a Catholic catchword, neither of them, it must be said, particularly informative.

In 1966 my time on the editorial committee of *Concilium* was up, and I said goodbye with a little word of gratitude:

> Farewell letters are not always merely painful. They are often also an opportunity for expressing one's thanks once and for all, and with special emphasis. I did not precisely know what I was taking on when, after Walter Kasper resigned, I took his place on the board, and together with Hans Küng became responsible for the section on ecumenism. Of course I had read *Concilium* before that, and had even written for it, but I did not

know what *Concilium* is, or its purpose. That was something I came to experience and discover during these many years, and I am deeply moved and grateful that I was permitted to have a part in it. I have always sensed increasingly that *Concilium* is not a finished institution. Every annual meeting was rather what in the ecumenical movement we call a 'conciliar process': a shared path, with the obligations of the Second Vatican Council behind us and with the catholic breadth of the kingdom of God ahead. Because of that, the so-called brainstorming at the annual meetings was always the most exciting part of them, and these brainstorming sessions provided me with a great deal of stimulus and many new perspectives.

But first I must mention the many years of harmonious and inspiring co-operation with my revered colleague and friend Hans Küng. From beginning to end we never had any differences of opinion about the projects which we set on foot, first for inter-Christian and later for inter-religious ecumenism. We were of one mind, 'one heart and soul'. The circumstance that we always quickly reached agreement is not a Tübingen miracle, but the fact that we almost never met with a refusal when we approached the various authors is truly a miracle to which I can only look back with astonishment. When I remember the series of our joint *Concilium* publications, in their many languages, I am in danger of believing in good Catholic fashion in the 'merit of good works', if not before God then at least before human beings. The transition from Hans Küng to Karl-Josef Kuschel took place without problems, without the creation of difficulties and without the struggle for status so often to be found in narrow Germany, especially in our university bodies. In short: the years when I was permitted to live with, think with and work with *Concilium* was for me a wonderful time.

I have no wish to hide the fact that *Concilium* also influenced me powerfully on—how does one put it?—the spiritual level. In *Concilium* I experienced the catholicity of the Church, not dogmatically and not hierachically either, but in human persons and in a human community. It was not in Rome, not in St Peter's Square, not even at an audience with the pope, that I experienced what the worldwide church is; it was in *Concilium*. The matter of course co-operation of theologians from Latin and North America, East and West Europe, Africa and England, and not least women and men, convinced me. At our annual meetings, what Martin Luther saw and sought was truly represented, 'the whole Christendom on earth'—in it beginnings and in part, as is usual among human beings, yet present, and in spirit very much alive, as our discussions showed. But another side is important for me too: without questions and without hesitation you have always allowed me as 'a Protestant' to participate in the shared Eucharist; and for that I should like to thank the *Concilium* fellowship with all my heart. I have always participated, for from the time of my early ecumenical beginnings I have made it a rule that wherever and whenever I hear the voice of Christ inviting me to his table fellowship, I come—in whatever church it may be.

The *Concilium* fellowship has also drawn me into the internal difficulties and conflicts of the Roman Catholic Church. At times it almost seemed as if I, as a Protestant, was the only person in *Concilium* who had no problems with the Vatican. But in sharing in your objective and often also highly personal sufferings at the hands of the curia, I began to love the Catholic Church. I am only speaking personally when I say that I came to have the impression that it is the worldwide community of the Catholic Church which manifestly sustains the curia, and not, conversely, the curia which guarantees the catholicity of the Church. Sometimes during our yearly meetings I was reminded of the image of a huge elephant which carries a saddle with the little howdah on his back. The people who are sitting on top of the elephant think they are riding it, but in fact it is the elephant who is carrying them, with boundless patience. My picture is not intended as an insult to anyone; but I love elephants. The curia, I believe, needs the Catholic people all over the world more than the people need the curia. That is not a subtle Protestant polemic directed against Rome; it is my personal option for 'the whole Christendom on earth'. And I have found it, not only in Geneva, but perhaps even more profoundly and with a more powerful motivation, in *Concilium*. For that I must as a Protestant theologian thank each one of you from the bottom of my heart, but even more the spirit of your conciliar fellowship. I have no hesitation in confessing that what I have found in *Concilium* was an especially powerful experience of 'the fellowship of the Holy Spirit'.

But so as not to end on so exalted a level, let me in closing extol *Concilium*'s table fellowship, which at the end of every annual meeting brought the heated participants together in peace and earthly enjoyment. For *Concilium* possesses not only spirit but taste too. Long live *Concilium*!

President of the Gesellschaft für Evangelische Theologie 1978 to 1994

The Gesellschaft für Evangelische Theologie (Society for Protestant Theology) is a foundation of the Confessing Church and dates back to 1940. According to its constitution, its purpose is 'to promote Protestant theology in accordance with the Reformation, and in the service of the Evangelical church. With this aim theologians and theologically interested lay members are joining together in a society for Protestant theology. The society arranges theological conferences and meetings of specialist groups.' Once again the moving force was Ernst Wolf. Theology was to become aware of its responsibility in the church, and the church was to become aware of its theological responsibility. In that era of dictatorship, culture and scholarship were to find in the church a free space for truth, and the church and theology were to lay hold of their prophetic task in public life.

It was at its first conference in Alpirsbach in 1941 that Rudolf Bultmann then gave his famous lecture 'The New Testament and Mythology'.[8] After the founding of the EKD (Evangelische Kirche in Deutschland) in 1945, the society became a reservoir for critical groups in church and society, for brotherhoods, seminars, working groups in church and theology, 'Solidarische Kirche' (Church in Solidarity), and others.

In 1953 the society organized a 'Theological Week' in Bielefeld. After six years, Barth came to Germany again for the first time and, following an introduction by Ernst Wolf, gave his important lecture 'The Gift of Freedom: Foundation of Protestant Ethics'.[9] The whole Reformed preaching seminary travelled from Wuppertal to Bielefeld, and we were all filled with enthusiasm. There must have been a thousand people present. Important theologians from the GDR, such as Johannes Hamel and Walter Feurich, were there, and I also remember a theologically well-versed theologian from Warsaw. The smouldering conflict between Barth and Bultmann had already flared up. Barth was therefore afraid of a 'parade' of non-Bultmannites rallying round me, and of Germany's 'demonic-angelic confusion', and he was sick of lecture tours in general. After he had returned to Basel exhausted, he cancelled a journey to America.[10] Instead, he now preferred to be invited 'to answer questions'. His Bielefeld lecture was of course a way of settling scores with Bultmann, and we saw it as such. The Barthian 'cohorts' grew tremendously, at least in the society.

After Ernst Wolf's death, Eberhard Hübner, professor of practical theology in Münster, took over the presidency of the society. The Westphalian superintendent (or regional bishop) Fritz Viering was treasurer. Lack of time prevented me from attending the society's meetings, so I was surprised when in 1978 Fritz Viering asked me to take over the presidency. I had really no desire to shoulder any further burdens, but my journeys all over the world had already become too much for Elisabeth. She wanted to 'earth' me and advised me to accept. So I took on this post, too, overtaxed myself, and for another 12 years organized the society's theological conferences and working parties. At that time we also had a working party in the GDR called Arbeitskreis Evangelische Theologie, which from 1961 onwards even met every year in a church hall in East Berlin. At least one member of our board went over regularly. Hannelore Hansch was, and is, the soul of the society. A theology pupil of Ernst Wolf's and an active member of the Confessing Church, she personifies the enduring presence in the society of its origins and the tradition that sustains it. She participated in every conference and often invited the board to her house near Karlsruhe. The society is greatly indebted to her for her wisdom and her confidence.

My first conference took place in the Church Seminary (Kirchliche Hochschule) in Wuppertal from 5 to 7 March 1979. The subject was 'The Right to Work', for against the background of the increasing unemployment in West Germany, which was beginning to make itself felt, we had established that while 7 out of 11 state (*Länder*) constitutions in the Federal Republic acknowledge a right to work (Bremen even has an obligation to work), the federal constitution, the Basic Law or *Grundgesetz*, makes no mention of this right. Yet all international contracts on human rights take into account Article 23 of the UNO Declaration of Human Rights of 1948, which states that 'everyone has a right to work.' I got Günter Brakelmann of the Ruhr University, Bochum, to give the main lecture, and Walter Zimmerli and Bertold Klappert to take over the Old and New Testament Bible study. We then passed, and published, a declaration on the right to work. The judge Dr Albert Stein oversaw the voting on each clause and proved to be a brilliant chairman for the purpose, again and again helping us to arrive at resolutions. Because of my connection with the publisher Chr. Kaiser, all the society's theological conferences were from now on published as Kaiser Traktate.[11]

Two years later, in 1981, there was great public excitement in the Federal Republic because of the Russian stationing of rockets in the GDR, and the NATO twin-track decision. Divided Germany was rearmed by the Great Powers until it became a powder barrel where the Third and, as we believed, final World War could be touched off at any time. A giant peace movement developed, strongly supported by Christian congregations and groups, with human chains stretching from Stuttgart to Ulm. In 1982, in its declaration 'The Acknowledgment of Jesus Christ and the Church's Responsibility for Peace', the executive board of the Alliance of Reformed Churches proclaimed the *status confessionis*. The EKD put itself on the side of the Heidelberg complementary formula 'Creating peace with and without weapons'. In Württemberg, the movement 'Live without Armaments' came into being. The society's board decided to prepare its own statement on peace and sent out invitations to a theological conference to be held in the Protestant Academy in Arnoldshain, the subject being 'Discipleship and the Sermon on the Mount'.[12]

We could not have foreseen it, but 1981 became the year of the Sermon on the Mount. Not only bishops and theologians but in the end the president of the Federal Republic, Carl Carstens, and the federal chancellor, Helmut Schmidt, also tried to arrive at its proper interpretation and application. The *Frankfurter Rundschau* newspaper printed the whole of the Sermon on the Mount on page 2. Never before had there been such a public and political 'Bible study' in Germany. It showed how dangerous Jesus' words could be for the one, and how liberating for the other. It also showed that the interpretation of the Bible is never only a matter for the church, and that theologians do not have a monopoly in the interpretation. Jesus addressed his Sermon on the Mount not only to his disciples but also to the people (*ochlos*), and down to the present day the people have understood him very well. But what we got to hear from the ruling politicians at that time was that a suspension of the Sermon on the Mount was necessary out of political responsibility—an echo of Bismarck's brusque statement that 'no country can be governed with the Sermon on the Mount.' But anyone who excludes the precepts of the Sermon on the Mount from certain parts of his life also loses the assurance of its Beatitudes.

In the society at that time we were looking for a new theological approach, beyond the Lutheran doctrine of the two kingdoms and the Reformed-Barthian doctrine of the kingship of Christ, and we found it in the concept and praxis of the undivided discipleship of Jesus. During the Reformation period, with the struggle against the Anabaptists, who had refused to do military service ever since the Schleitheim Confession of 1527, the theme had been suppressed; it was Dietrich Bonhoeffer who took it up again for the first time in 1937.[13] I invited Mennonite pastors to this conference too. Earlier fought against as a sect, they were now recognized as a traditional peace church.

The response to the invitation to the conference was immense. We could not accept even half the applications and had to hire other houses in addition to the Evangelische Akademie. The academy had no room big enough to seat everyone, so we had to move to the village church in Schmitten. It had no heating, but we were in any case packed together as closely as possible. Ulrich Luz spoke on 'The Sermon on the Mount in the Mirror of its Impact', and because he was in the process of writing his extensive commentary on Matthew, he needed two hours for his lecture. Then Helmut Gollwitzer came and talked about 'The Sermon on the Mount and the Doctrine of the Two Kingdoms'—again for two hours. The time for discussion was therefore cut excessively short, but instead conversations lasted far into the night. It was a happy moment when the older generation, coming from the years of the struggle between church and state, met the younger generation of the peace movement. The traditional 'evening with the church authorities' was in the hands of the president of the Hessian church, Helmut Hild. He also talked about the Sermon on the Mount. At that time we sensed that 'it is the validity of the Sermon on the Mount which will decide whether Christianity in our country becomes a *religion*, which no longer makes any demands and no longer consoles anyone, or whether there will be a revival of a *congregational community* which confesses Jesus and follows him alone and undividedly.'[14]

In August 1981 we then published the society's peace declaration, 'Spreading Peace'. We did not want just to say no to rearmament with weapons of mass destruction. We also wanted to invite people to a positive alternative commitment to peace:

Spreading Peace

Jesus Christ as he is testified to us in Holy Scripture and as he lives among us in the Holy Spirit is our peace (Eph. 2.14). In him the eternal God has reconciled the world to himself (2 Cor. 5.19). Through him he will redeem the world. Through the gospel he lets his peace be proclaimed among us (Eph. 6.15).

There is no sphere of our life in which we cannot be assured of the peace of God. There is no conflict in our life, either personal or political, which could ever be withdrawn from God's will for peace with human beings and his whole creation. There is no enemy, either personal or political, to whom God's will for peace does not apply. God's peace prevents us from having to secure ourselves against our enemies by making ourselves their enemies, by meeting their threats with counter-threats, and their terrors with intimidation. He rather destines us to love our enemies creatively, by understanding their sufferings, by thinking critically about our own position, and by trying in every way to mitigate their enmity and ours. Love of our enemy is an expression of the sovereign freedom of God's children, and has nothing to do with weakness and submission.

Modern weapons of mass destruction are not merely a source of deadly danger for humanity and all life on earth. They also threaten us with immeasurable guilt.

To include weapons of mass destruction in the threat and exertion of state power can only be a *de facto* denial of the will of the God who is gracious towards his creation and human beings. From a Christian standpoint such an action cannot be justified. Neutrality in this matter which we recognize as sin is irreconcilable with the confession of Jesus Christ (Declaration of the Bruderschaften of 1958).

If the use of weapons of mass destruction is a sin, then the possession of weapons of mass destruction for the purpose of threat and deterrence cannot, from a Christian standpoint, be justified either. Because this threat is only effective if one is also prepared to carry it out, the very threat with weapons of mass destruction must itself be viewed as sin.

With modern military weapons of mass destruction the limit of responsible political employment of the weapons of war and the threat of war has clearly been overstepped. Every warlike threat and dispute which reckons with possible escalation into a universal nuclear war is irresponsible. Today's peace through deterrence is also irresponsible.

The planned increase in nuclear armaments threatens us all even more than hitherto. We therefore urge immediate and binding disarmament conversations between the Great Powers. We are in favour of a European disarmament conference with the declared goal of establishing 3a zone free of weapons of mass destruction. We support a gradual disarmament in the sector of conventional arms, and the comprehensive build-up of co-operation in Europe and Asia, especially in the sphere of worldwide economic justice.

To minister to peace is the substance of life in the community of Jesus Christ: the church's institutions and organisations can do no more than support and lend form to this ministry of peace on the part of Christians. The ministry of peace which is alive in the congregations and must be promoted by the leaders of the churches should have the following emphases:

To learn to love our enemies. Friend-foe thinking prepares the ground for wars. Artificially built up pictures of the enemy exploit fears and evoke aggressions. Through psychological warfare people and nations are made to hold life cheap and are mobilized to kill. The commandment to love our enemies requires us to do away with these hostile images and to overcome the fears and aggressions to which they lead. Once fear of the enemy is made the counsellor of politics, peace is endangered, not only outwardly but inwardly as well. The loyalty of a country's people to the government they have chosen will then no longer be assured through the fulfilment of the mandate to rule but through the spread of fear, whether it be fear of the state's enemies, or whether it be fear of being considered such an enemy. The spread of psychological unrest and public mistrust are the consequences. Anyone who on the other hand disseminates peace will resist the exploitation and evocation of fears among our people.

To recognize the real dangers and collaborate in overcoming them. While the Great Powers revive and intensify their East-West conflict, they dispel from public awareness the much more dangerous North-South conflict, and the danger of ecological catastrophe. The new rearmament policy is pursued at the cost of aid for the Third World, and leads to its further exploitation. Today the poor are already paying for the arming of the rich. Today rearmament in East and West is already costing the lives of people in the Third World. Today time, intelligence and capital are already being wasted on weapons of mass destruction instead of being used to overcome hunger in the world. The Christian ministry of peace must therefore be to bring the North-South conflict more strongly into public awareness

> again, and in the midst of the dispute about rearmament and the deployment of new weapons Christians must become the advocates of the silent and dying peoples.
>
> *To become a church of peace*. The more the church becomes a free church, no longer tied to the state, the clearer its witness to peace can be, and the more unequivocal its intervention on behalf of peace. We believe that the church of Jesus Christ can become a church of peace without any sectarian separation from the world. It will become a church of peace to the extent to which it acknowledges Christ, and Christ alone, as its peace and the peace of the whole world, and draws the necessary conclusions from this acknowledgement.[15]

When we published our peace declaration, about ten members of the society resigned, among them Bishop Harms of Oldenburg. They wanted to abide by the Lutheran doctrine of the two kingdoms and—as a well-known Lutheran pastor from Barmen wrote to me—did not want to let themselves be drawn into politics. For there had also, after all, been highly varying reasons for belonging to the Confessing Church in the Nazi era. Some wished to defend the church against political influences; others were drawn into political resistance, for example, against the persecution of the Jews. But in this respect the Barmen Theological Declaration had not offered any orientation.

After the Arnoldshain conference on Discipleship and the Sermon on the Mount, we prepared for the next theological conference two years later. It took place in 1983, in 'Haus Stapelage' in Lippe. The peace movement had inevitably brought us up against the question of public resistance to the arms build-up and the threat of universal annihilation through weapons of mass destruction which was used against the enemy. There is the passive resistance of personal denial, the 'count me out' stance. But wholesale rejection does not of itself offer a politically viable alternative. One must enter into a situation in order to discover other possibilities and find new ways out. Acceptance does not mean conformity or acquiescence. Consequently, we called our conference 'Acceptance and Resistance' and wanted to discuss first of all the Christian traditions about the right to resistance, secondly the principle of non-violent resistance, and thirdly a politics based on love of our enemy.[16] I myself offered a fairly extensive introduction to the history of the right to resistance, especially in the Reformed tradition of the Scots

Confession of 1560, Article 14; Luise Schottroff gave us an interpretations of Romans 13; Hans-Eckehard Bahr, who had once accompanied Martin Luther King on a protest march through the streets of Chicago, presented 'Style Elements and Social Ethos of Non-violent Peace Processes'; and the political scientist Rainer Eckertz expounded a 'Criticism of the Self-Legitimation of the State'.

At the end of the stimulating discussions we acquired 15 new members for the society. These made good the losses I have mentioned. But the society was also moving farther to the left politically, away from the neutral centre. This evidently distressed Fritz Viering—though not me. Intervention on behalf of 'a piece of pacified, fear-free, viable world' (Konrad Stock) seemed to us enjoined by the gospel, and to belong to the discipleship of Christ.

The year 1984 was the fiftieth anniversary of the Barmen Theological Declaration. Together with the board of the Alliance of Reformed Churches and the Leuenberg Karl Barth Conference, the society issued an invitation to a theological conference to be held from 27 February to 1 March 1984 in Wuppertal-Barmen. The co-operation between the different bodies came about through my friendship with the moderator of the Alliance, Hans-Joachim Kraus. We had met by chance on the beach at Ravenna and had soon hatched our plans for this event. We wanted neither Barmen nostalgia nor Barmen orthodoxy. We wanted to view the Barmen Declaration as a call to the church and theology to go forward. We wanted to view the present of the Evangelical church critically in its light, and also to look back to the Declaration critically under the aspect of new experiences and perceptions of faith. So in the invitation I wrote, 'We need theological perspectives and criteria so that the Evangelical church can turn back from the undertow of bourgeois religion to the liberty of a confessing community. What does the Barmen Theological Declaration mean "after Auschwitz"? What does it mean in view of the threat of world annihilation through nuclear weapons?'[17]

The first question was answered impressively in the Bible studies of the theologians who came from the struggle between church and state, Joachim Beckmann, president of the church in the Rhineland; Wilhelm Niesel, president of the World Alliance of Reformed Churches; and Kurt Scharf, bishop of Berlin-Brandenburg, for they set the churches of the post-war period in the light of the Confessing Church. To answer the second question was the task of the younger generation: Bertold Klappert looked at the Barmen Declaration 'after Auschwitz', found a mention of the persecution of the Jews lacking, and revised the theses along the lines of the Rhenish synod's resolution on the new relationship between Christians and Jews: this is the acknowledgment of Jesus Christ the Jew, and his God as the God of Israel according to the testimony of Holy Scripture, the Old and the New Testament. Ulrich Duchrow tried, as he had already done in 1934 in Barmen, to determine the confessional situation today, in order to proclaim the *status confessionis*. He began with the developing Confessing Church in the apartheid state of South Africa, then went into 'the situation of the mass-murdering worldwide economic system'. He sought the 'conciliar confessional process in God's covenant people' and out of his ecumenical experience—he had long worked for the Lutheran World Federation in Geneva—presented many facts and examples of the political persecution of Christians in the US-directed dictatorships of Latin America. Helmut Simon, judge at the federal constitutional court, belongs to the middle generation. He looked at the state's use of force in the light of the second and fifth Barmen theses and defined afresh the tie to the constitutional state of the state's monopoly of force in view of modern means of force. Martin Rohkrämer, brotherhood pastor from the Rhineland and member of the society's board, took us historically into the situation of the Barmen synod in 1934.

At the end we passed a powerful declaration, 'Becoming a Confessing Church—the Barmen Confession Today'.[18] We set Barmen I in the context of the relationship between the church and Israel 'after Auschwitz', saw Barmen III in the context of the impoverishment of the Third World in the present worldwide economic system, and viewed Barmen II and V in the context of the church's witness to peace, in the face of weapons of mass destruction, and the attitude of Christians in the constitutional democracy and welfare state.

This theological conference was also full to overflowing. The main hall in the teacher training college on the 'Heiliger Berg' in Barmen seated 500 people. On 29 February we sent Martin Niemöller a greetings telegram on his birthday. He died a few days later, on 6 March 1984. We had illustrious guests. Johannes Hamel came from the GDR, and we had others from Austria, Hungary, Holland, and Switzerland. The Revd Nancy Vandenburgh brought from America the greetings of the Presbyterian Church there.

The discussions about the lectures given by Klappert and Duchrow were extremely controversial. I had ceased to believe that we would succeed in arriving at a joint final declaration, and grumbled over my task as president of the society half the night, until I told myself that things would have to take their course, and finally fell asleep. And the morning brought success. Hannelore Hansch had written and duplicated the proposals for the final declaration on the very same night. Without her optimism and her commitment, we should never have arrived at a result. Manfred Weber, editor in chief of Chr. Kaiser, wanted to print the conference papers immediately, so I had to drag the manuscripts, ready for the press, from all the speakers. This, too, was accomplished, and we presented the results in the same year.

I shall not go on to describe the other theological conferences for which I was responsible in such detail, but shall confine myself to indicating their general trend. In 1986 we were in Bad Herrenalb, the subject being 'Reconciliation with Nature?'; in 1988 a conference in Pfortzheim-Hohewart dealt with 'Theology of Peace and Theology of Liberation'; and in 1990 in Wildbad, near Rothenburg ob der Tauber, we discussed 'Religion of Freedom: Protestantism in the Modern Era'. We accompanied the political 'turning point' with a theological conference in Berlin in 1991, the subject being 'Christian Existence in the New Democratic Beginnings in Europe'.[19]

This list of the subjects for our conferences shows that we were working on the topical relevance of theology, not so much on an extension of our inner-theological perceptions. In comparison with earlier and later conferences, this was certainly one-sided and could well be criticized as the attempt always to surf theologically on the last wave of the *Zeitgeist*. But we already found ourselves in a situation in which political and social forces were trying to push critical theology back again into the inner sanctum of the churches. In Germany, the public was strongly orientated towards the Catholic church, and so 'Christian' was interpreted as meaning 'churchly', and 'churchly' as meaning 'the Catholic church', and the Catholic church as meaning the church of the bishops—and that of course meant the Roman church. Against this, Protestantism had difficulty holding its own. Prophetic theology was caught between the upper and the nether millstones of church theology on the one hand and state theology on the other. Consequently, I thought it was right to work theologically on subjects of public interest before they became a part of general awareness. Whether this always succeeded is another question. But we wanted to offer a *public* theology and to avoid letting ourselves be pushed off into a ghetto. Protestant theology is prophetic when it asks about the 'right word' at the 'right time' and seeks for the word that binds and looses in a given situation.

The new problems that arose from the changed world situation also demanded a revision of the theological traditions, for these included answers to questions that no one was now asking, and addressed only a few of the questions that had to be answered afresh. In 1986 we went into the ecological problems of the modern world and came upon ideas and rituals of harmonization between human beings and nature in Israel's Sabbath doctrine of creation and the cosmic Christology of the New Testament—ideas which had been pushed aside. The awakening of a new awareness of the environment relativized the anthropocentricism of modern times and the Western churches.

In our attempt to bring together a European theology of peace and an American theology of liberation, feminist ideas came to the surface for the first time in a working party led by Deborah and Heinrich Bedford-Strohm on the question of 'the peaceable woman'. These ideas were reinforced by Elisabeth Moltmann-Wendel at the next conference on the religion of freedom when she surprisingly introduced the dimension of bodiliness into theology and talked about the typically Protestant 'serving body' (*Dienstleib*).[20] Flight from the body, the subjugation of the body, the laying claim to the bodies of other people—do we not have to overcome these Gnostic traditions and slave-owning notions in Christianity if we seriously want to grasp God's incarnation and bodily indwelling through the life-giving Spirit?

Today, when I look through the Kaiser paperbacks published at that time, I am surprised to find so many new ideas there, some of which have still not been fully worked out. Those years were a very creative time for theology. Our conferences were a kind of study workshop with sectors in which we could experiment with new ideas.

In 1991 the 'turning point' brought us to a special theological conference in Berlin, the first which we could put on together with the (East German) Arbeitskreis für Evangelische Theologie in what was now a united Germany. Our joint conference was not intended to lead to the pocketing of the one side by the other, but was designed to let us get to know and appreciate each other. We needed time to tell one another what had been happening in our own lives, and to exchange different experiences. The committees of the two societies had decided on the subject of the conference: 'Christian Existence in the New Democratic Beginnings in Europe: Problems—Chances—Orientations'. But those of us from the West who participated were first deeply stirred by the demolition experiences of the sisters and brothers as the GDR was wound up. What a female doctor told us at the conference was appalling—how many people in East Germany are tired of life, the rising suicide figures, and the abortions undertaken by women out of fear of unemployment. One participant from the East wrote to me, 'To some extent the conference depressed more than it encouraged me. The situation among us is too dreadful, and the cleft between East and West, the new and the old is simply too great.' The major lectures ranged far afield, but the people were suffering from having to switch over every day to another way of life. The conference was open enough to take up the cry from the depths and to give it a hearing.

This Berlin conference was also my last as president of the Gesellschaft für Evangelische Theologie. Dr Rudolf Weth, once my assistant in Tübingen and afterwards director of the Neukirchener Erziehungsverein, was chosen to be my successor, and I remained on the board. I had gladly performed the work of a president, but now also gladly passed it on into good hands. I thanked the board, the society, and all its members, but especially my treasurer, Superintendent Werner Lauff, Remscheid, who always managed to finance great conferences with empty coffers.

TWENTY

IN CHRISTIAN-JEWISH DIALOGUE

I have never taken part in official Christian-Jewish dialogues, either at the German Protestant Lay Assembly (*Kirchentag*) or in the framework of the Evangelical church in Germany; and yet Jewish philosophers have put a greater mark on me than other contemporaries. Ernst Bloch, Franz Rosenzweig, Martin Buber, Abraham Heschel, and Gershom Scholem have all given me new ideas in the course of my theological work. The new Jewish thinking of Emil Fackenheim, Elie Wiesel, Richard Rubenstein, and others has influenced me deeply in the search for a post-Holocaust theology. I therefore gladly took the opportunity to meet Emil Fackenheim, Schalom Ben-Chorin, and Pinchas Lapide, but I am not one of the Christian-Jewish dialogue specialists, nor do I belong to the party of new Christian Zionists in post-war Germany.

For me the dialogue began in 1950, when Elisabeth, returning from a period of study in Amsterdam, brought back with her the new *Kerkorde* of the Dutch Reformed Church. I have never been able to summon up much enthusiasm for church orders, but here, in Article VIII, 'The Apostolate of the Church', I found a wise division. According to this, the apostolate exists

1. in conversation with Israel,
2. in the work of mission, and
3. in continuing work on the Christian reformation of one's own people.

The term *dialogue* was still restricted to the relationship to Israel and was not, as is the case today, inflated to include all religions; for with Israel, with the synagogue and with all who belong to the chosen people, the church has Holy Scripture in common. The dialogue with Israel goes forward over the open book of the Tenach/Old Testament. In the mission to the Gentiles, on the other hand, the gospel of the kingdom of God brings into the world of their religions something new which is without any preconditions. That distinguishes this mission from the relationship to Israel. Finally, the Christianization (*Kerstening*) of one's own people means placing the whole of life under the freedom of God and winning acceptance for his commandments.

In 1950, in Otto Weber's graduate group, we read the new Confession of the Hervormde Kerk (the Durch Reformed Church) which he had just translated, and which is entitled *Fundamenten en Perspektieven von Belijden*; and in Article 17 we found the first Christian appreciation after almost 2,000 years of 'the presence and future of Israel'.[1] This Christian acknowledgement of Israel had a lasting influence on me. The name Israel never meant for me only the Israel of the Old Testament, *before* the time of the church, but always at the same time the people of God who exist *parallel* to the church and who testify to the church the promises of the kingdom of God which have not yet been fulfilled through the coming of Christ. Israel and Church are two different forms of the kingdom of God in history, and they must recognize one another in their difference and respect one another in their common ground if they want to bring the hope for the coming of God to the peoples of the earth. At that time the Dutch theologian Arnold van Ruler helped us greatly with his book *Die christliche Kirche und das Alte Testament* (The Christian Church and the Old Testament).[2]

In the *Theology of Hope* (1964) I brought two principles to bear:

1. It is *Yahweh*, the God of Abraham, of Isaac, and of Jacob, the God of the promise, who raised Jesus from the dead. Who the God is who is revealed in and by Jesus emerges only in his difference from, and identity with, the God of the Old Testament.
2. *Jesus was a Jew*. Who Jesus is, and what the human nature is which is revealed by him, emerges from his conflict with the law and the promise of the Old Testament.[3]

For me, the continuity between *promise* and gospel was always more important than the difference between *law* and gospel, and I knew that in this I was in line with the Reformed tradition, although not with the Lutheran one. So I have always read the Old and the New Testaments parallel to one another, and not one after the other, as if the Old had been superseded by the New and only served as a sombre background for what is supposed to hold good now. The Scriptures will only be 'fulfilled' in the kingdom of God, towards which both testaments point. So it is inadmissible to use the name Old Testament disparagingly, or the name New Testament arrogantly.

With Emil Fackenheim

I took part in my first Christian-Jewish dialogue with Emil Fackenheim, whom I met at the Centennial Symposium of the University of California in Santa Barbara, from 1 to 3 April 1968. My friend Walter Capps had organized this memorable conference and opened it with his own 'Mapping the Hope-Movement'. The subject under discussion was 'The Future of Hope'.[4] Johann Baptist Metz expounded his 'political theology', while I spread myself with considerable enthusiasm on 'Religion, Revolution, and the Future'; and then Emil Fackenheim came and realistically proclaimed 'The Commandment to Hope: A Response to Contemporary Jewish Experience'—that is to say, after Auschwitz.

He began with the Jewish religion of hope, naming the expectation of the Messiah and entering into discussion with Ernst Bloch's views. But then came the existential Jewish question of today: 'After the holocaust of Auschwitz, can one still put Jewish children into this world, or bring up one's children as Jews?' Richard Rubinstein had taken his leave of 'the God of history' and wanted to revert to the pagan deities of nature. But Fackenheim heard out of Auschwitz the clear *commandment to hope* and to affirm Jewish existence: 'A Jew has to be witness against Hitler and all his works. A Jew is not permitted to give Hitler any belated or posthumous victories.'[5] For Jews voluntarily to give up their Jewish existence after Auschwitz would be blasphemy. The surrender of Jewish faith in God would even be a vindication of Hitler: 'I think a Jew is forbidden to despair of God. Hitler tried to destroy the Jewish belief in God as well as Jewish existence.' To say I despair of the God of history because Hitler has proved his absence from history would give Hitler a belated victory, a victory over Israel's God. And if anyone says, 'After Auschwitz it is too late to go on hoping for the Messiah, who could come but who has not in fact come'—then, said Fackenheim, he would reply, 'It is precisely because it is too late that we are commanded to hope.'[6]

I was deeply impressed, because I had never thought about a *commandment* to hope in the situation of despair and grief. The fact that belief in God after Auschwitz is a protest against Hitler was not clear to us either in post-war Germany. We were all still much impressed by Adorno's dictum: 'After Auschwitz there can be no more poetry'—and then how much less can there be belief in God; or so we thought. I therefore began the dialogue with the doubt, 'Perhaps we will never find an answer if we think about *God and Auschwitz*. But one should remember that in Auschwitz and these death camps, the "Shema Israel" and the "Our Father" were prayed. And so, perhaps, there was *God in Auschwitz*. We must not forget the martyrs or those who prayed in Auschwitz. To hope after Auschwitz and Hiroshima is just this: don't leave the future to hell because hell is always with us. To survive as a human being is already an act of hope. Perhaps not only for a Jew, but as a human being too, to survive is already an act of hope.'[7]

Metz agreed emphatically with me, and the two of us then talked about the shame and the pain in the country of the perpetrators 'after Auschwitz'. Emil Fackenheim met us more than halfway when he explained how painful the discussion between Jews and Germans was for him, as a German Jew who had grown up with Goethe and before 1939 had written a book on Hegel. In pre-war Germany, he had studied at Berlin University, in 1938 had been subjected for weeks to humiliating conditions in a German concentration camp, and had then emigrated to Canada via Scotland. His wife, Rose, whom I later met in Toronto, was a passionate Barthian. The rift between Germans and Jews went through Emil's own soul: 'Nothing human can redeem Auschwitz. But I think that the German soul might be revived and purified by encountering through an act of repentance instead of trying to sweep it under the carpet. Speaking of hope, repentance is the greatest renewal there is.'[8] Metz and I found Fackenheim helpful in the search for that repenting turn to the future which we were seeking in the depressing German post-war mentality.

In the same month, April 1968, I met Richard Rubinstein at a conference in Princeton. In 1966 with his book *After Auschwitz* he had provided the catchword for a wide discussion and a widely varying literature. It had taken all this time for the spell of silence about the unspeakableness of the Shoah to be broken. Rubinstein had been captivated by the God-is-dead theology of Thomas Altizer and Bill Hamilton which was en vogue at that time, and at first he only looked for a Jewish analogue. In discussion I found him erratic, and unlike Emil Fackenheim, he failed to keep to the point very consistently. The content of his book did not for Jews as yet offer the convincing answer to its correct title. At that time he was teaching at the University of Tallahassee, Florida. Some people were disappointed that he should have spoken out in the Southern states in favour of the death penalty which was the rule there. Others were surprised when he was later to be found in the camp of the Moon sect. I soon lost sight of him.

In 1969 in New York (where I had been invited by B'nai Berith), I then had my first conversation with Michael Wyschogrod and did not have the impression that we were at cross purposes. Then, in preparation for my theology of the cross, I read for the first time Abraham Heschel's book about 'the pathos of God' in the prophets and felt confirmed in my rejection of the metaphysical apathy axiom in the philosophical doctrine of God.[9] In the Institutum Judaicum in Tübingen, I even discovered the original German version of this famous book, which had been written in Berlin in 1936 and published in Cracow, and felt saddened by Heschel's expulsion. Elie Wiesel's Auschwitz book *Night* moved me deeply, and in my own book I quoted the famous scene with the question 'Where is God?' and the answer that was then heard: 'He's there, hanging on the gallows.' Through Elie Wiesel and Franz Rosenzweig, and not least Isaak Singer's novels, I came on the track of Jewish Shekinah thinking, which perceives God in his indwelling as companion on the way and fellow sufferer with his people in exile and in persecutions.[10]

In order to give a particular emphasis to my theology of the cross, which I had set in this Jewish framework, I gave it as title words which had occasionally been used ever since Luther: *The Crucified God.* But Pinchas Lapide later admitted to me that for Jewish ears this sounded so objectionable that he neither wanted to read the book nor even to pick it up.

That was probably also one reason why soon after the appearance of the English translation in America, a certain Roy Eckhardt launched a first attack on me, accusing me of 'anti-Judaism'.[11] He was not a Jew, though he no doubt still believed he was a Christian, but in the main he seemed to me like a neo-English re-education officer in what was supposedly still Nazi Germany. He came to Tübingen with his wife, all innocence, and asked for some talks, which I found perfectly pleasant. He had not revealed that every word 'could be used as evidence against me', any more than he had declared his true intentions. He had nothing else in mind when he met Helmut Gollwitzer, in Berlin. His reproach was that I presented Jesus as in conflict with the law of Israel, and had thus denigrated the law. This, he maintained, was typical German 'anti-Judaism', which replaced Israel's law by the gospel of Christ, thereby withdrawing from the Jews their right to religious existence, and ultimately speaking to physical existence as well. He waved aside my objection that in the passages he referred to in my book I was only citing the apostle Paul: Paul was a Jew, but I was not, so I was not permitted even to quote him; my intention could only be to 'expropriate' him. Since Barth, Gollwitzer and Bonhoeffer had also quoted Paul, they fell under the same condemnation, according to Eckhardt: theologians in Germany are quite simply German theologians; their thinking and judgements are still overshadowed by Hitler and require re-education by the America of the United States.

Through this 'Auschwitz cudgel', as Martin Walser not unjustly called it, in the hands of a Christian Zionist from America, I was of course supposed to more or less lose my credibility. He was right in saying that we were living in the country of the perpetrators and that he was not. But we had no more chosen the country we were born in than he had chosen his. Yet he preened himself on having been graced with American birth, and set himself up above our depths, with the dark shadows cast by Nazism.

I did not enter into discussion with Roy Eckhardt, but of course his anti-Judaism reproach stuck to me among all the people who did not like my theology. Fortunately, I found a wise and decent-minded defender in Robert McAfee Brown, who rebuked my persecutor and set the record straight.[12] But the reproach of anti-Judaism naturally ate into my soul and made me sensitive to self-righteous slurs in post-Auschwitz Germany.

With Pinchas Lapide

In public dialogues in Germany my partner was Pinchas Lapide. Professor Lapide was clever, witty, and easy to get on with. During the war he had fought in the Jewish Brigade in North Africa and had later been Israel's consul in Havana, but for a number of years he and his wife, Ruth, had been living in Frankfurt. Lapide was an Orthodox Jew but not a Jewish scholar. Professionally he was a talented journalist. That always made conversations with him very lively.

On 22 May 1978 our first dialogue took place before a conference of Protestant clergy in Niefern near Pforzheim. The subject we had been given was a demanding one: 'Jewish Monotheism and the Christian Doctrine of the Trinity'. When the dean introduced Pinchas Lapide as the only Jew in the room, Lapide jumped up and cried, 'I am not the only Jew in the room: the other one is hanging on the cross over there,' and he pointed to the crucifix on the wall. The dean and the clergy present visibly collapsed; they had never thought of that. But this prepared the ground for the dialogue. The lectures and the discussion that followed were full of surprises. Where one had expected profound divisions, one found bridges; where one had assumed that understanding would be lacking, agreements emerged. After my book *The Crucified God*, I had developed the doctrine of the Trinity out of the self-surrender of Christ and God's suffering over his death on the cross. Lapide could enter into this by way of the Old Testament Jewish doctrine of God's Shekinah. The doctrine of the Trinity by no means has to be formulated by turning one's back on Israel, and with the terminology of neo-Platonic metaphysics. Israel's 'living God' is also the God of Jesus Christ, who is love (1 John 4.16), and the God who 'is' love is the triune God.

At the end of our discussion we formulated a joint declaration on the dialogue: 'What is needed for such a dialogue? Three things—no more: "an understanding heart", such as Solomon once asked for (1 Kings 3.9); Paul's humble insight that all our thinking, doing and speaking is still only "in part" (1 Cor. 13.9ff.); and acceptance of the universal message of the Bible that "God desires all men to be saved" (1 Tim. 2.4).'

We were all surprised when Pinchas Lapide joined with us in the 'Our Father'. Ever since then, its first three petitions have been for me the prayer for Christian-Jewish dialogue. Our first dialogue was printed in 1979 in Munich as a Kaiser Traktat (with a second edition in 1982) and was then translated, first into Italian, then into English (as *Jewish and Christian Trinitarian Doctrine*, Philadelphia 1981), and afterwards into Dutch and Japanese.

On 7 January 1980 the Reformed congregation in Hamburg invited us to a dialogue on 'Church and Israel: A Common Way?'[13] When we entered into this conversation we did not yet know that our theme was to become the subject of a fierce dispute in the West German churches. On 11 January the synod of the Evangelical church in the Rhineland resolved on principles 'for the renewal of the relationship between Christians and Jews', and this resolution of the Rhenish synod still causes feelings to run high even today. The theological faculty in Bonn took up a critical position towards the theses, and fundamentalist groups reinforced their conviction that there should be a 'mission to Israel—today too!' In May, the Catholic Bishops' conference in Germany published a declaration on 'Church and Judaism'.

Our dialogue in Hamburg was well attended. Critical questions were raised on the one hand about the attitude of the churches to Judaism and about the politics of the state of Israel on the other. The people present did not indicate that what was wanted was neutral detachment, but rather critical solidarity. It also emerged, however, that the dialogue is difficult because the partners do not stand in a symmetrical position to one another. On the one side we have a Christian community of faith—on the other a Jewish community of faith *and* a Jewish nation; on the one side Christians, on the other side Jews *and* Israelis. The resolution of the Rhenish synod was based on the conclusion that 'the continuing existence of the Jewish people, its homecoming to the land of the promise, and also the establishment of the state of Israel, are signs of God's faithfulness towards his people.'[14]

At that time I supported this declaration, because I do indeed see 'the continuing existence of the Jewish people' as a sign of God's faithfulness to his covenant; but I became increasingly critical towards the view that it is only 'the homecoming to the land of the promise' that should be seen as the sign of God's faithfulness, and not Jewish existence in exile and diaspora as well. It was the old apocalyptic idea of Christian Zionists in England and the United States that the return of all the Jews to the land of their fathers was the precondition for the coming of the Messiah, Jesus, and that all Jews must therefore be urged to return. In the nineteenth century American Jews vehemently rejected this Christian notion. Today it is fundamentalist groups in Israel and the 'Christian Embassy' in Jerusalem that work towards this goal and that want to follow the homecoming of all the Jews by building the Third Temple, on whose pinnacle Jesus will one day appear.

When I discovered this, it became clear to me that, ultimately speaking, this would mean that every country would be made 'free of Jews', just as Hitler wanted. Absurd though it is, in the end Christian Zionism and anti-Semitism lead to the same result. But for me the presence of Jews and the synagogue in post-war Germany is a sign of God's faithfulness and of undeserved grace. In Ernst Bloch's view, Judaism in the diaspora has a prophetic mission to humanity, the aim of which is to bring to the nations the passion of hope. That was also the argument with which the chief rabbi of Amsterdam, Manassah ben Israel, persuaded Oliver Cromwell, the Lord Protector, to allow the re-entry of the Jews to England in 1650.[15] Pinchas Lapide agreed with me and maintained 'the age-old, twofold form of Judaism, which emphasizes both the link between land and people, and the missionary significance of the diaspora'.[16]

In our 'Joint Declaration' we confined ourselves to the relationship between the two religious communities, the Christian and the Jewish, and set the community between us in the context of the first three petitions of the 'Our Father'.

Joint Declaration

1. For centuries the relationship between Christians and Jews was determined by their mutual delimitation. The Christian churches cut themselves off from Judaism in order to maintain their own ground. As 'the new people of God' they saw themselves as superseding 'the old people of God', and tried to oust Israel from God's history with the world. This was a wrong turning. It is now at an end. Christians are turning back, and discovering the irrevocable promises to Israel, and God's unswerving faithfulness to his people. The dialogue between Christians and Jews does not serve mutual delimitation, to the end that each side may maintain its own ground. It is a sign of the wish to understand the other in his unique character. Christians need the dialogue with the Jews, not only in order to understand the Jews but also in order to understand themselves as Christians.

2. After having taken the step away from mutual delimitation to dialogue, the next move forward leads from understanding those who believe differently to community in difference. This community requires respect and sympathy. It does not merely respect the other's calling but also shares his suffering. Christians read Scripture together with the Jews. In dialogue about the understanding and interpretation of Scrip-

ture, Jews and Christians become witnesses to each other of the Lord. In wholehearted acceptance of the partner's religious independence they help one another to a better fulfilment of the task divinely committed to them. Towards the Jews, witness to the gospel of Jesus Christ does not take the form of mission. We wish neither to missionize nor to convert the other, but we do wish to give mutual testimony to the special mission to which the One God has called Israel and the Church. In order to become more faithful servants of God, Jews and Christians should 'provoke', spur and encourage each other to a purer faith, a more active love, and a greater hope.

3. We discover the community of Jews and Christians in the hallowing, or sanctification, of the name, in the hope for God's kingdom, and in the doing of his will. Where the name of our Lord is hallowed, salvation and blessing are brought to the peoples of the earth. Where hope for the kingdom of God is spread, people wake up out of resignation and apathy and become co-workers with God in his continuing work in creation. Where the will of the Lord is done, the new world of righteousness and peace on earth begins.

4. Jews and Christians are the Lord's witnesses, each in their own way. Although their pilgrimage through history takes different paths, they are united in their hope for a messianic kingdom in which their confidence will prove to be well-founded. The star of redemption points them to a common future, and its radiance already illumines our present. The person who hopes in common with another also hopes for the other. The Christian hope embraces the Jews, just as Israel's hope comprehends the salvation of all the peoples.

When we put on a joint seminar in Tübingen in the 1980s, we became closer personally, but the understandable limits of his scholarship also became evident. Pinchas Lapide often met with hostility—in Germany, but from the side of Jerusalem too. Schalom Ben-Chorin fiercely rejected him. Nor did he ever again visit Israel. But in those years Pinchas Lapide and his wife, Ruth, were a great help to us, and I think of him with gratitude.

I met Emil Fackenheim again at the conference 'Christian-Jewish Dialogue in the Shadow of the Holocaust' in December 1983 in Bangor, Maine. Each of us gave two lectures, and a dialogue followed. The conference was inspired by Sharon Lehmann (who wanted to address her own family history and for a while had elected me to be her 'rebbe') and by Warren Green, the director of the Holocaust Studies in St Louis. Again I got on very well with Fackenheim, but what impressed me was not what we had to say but what Gerda Haas, a survivor of the Theresienstadt concentration camp, had to tell. As a young girl she had been extradited to Switzerland by Himmler in exchange for a consignment of trucks, and so had survived. When I heard her account, I became terribly conscious that in post-war Germany we had taken the second step before the first: before beginning the Christian-Jewish dialogue, we should have listened to the stories of survivors in conferences on the Holocaust.

At that time Emil Fackenheim was on his way to Jerusalem, to the Hebrew University. He told me proudly that his son was a colonel in the Israeli army. He came to Germany from Jerusalem once more, in 2002, shortly before his death, in order to speak in Berlin and in Denkendorf near Tübingen. Unfortunately, I was not in the country at the time, so we were unable to meet again, as he had wished.

As I flew from Bangor, the newspapers were carrying the story that two Jewish synagogues there had been burnt down during the night by American Nazis. That weighed heavily on me, and I donated my fee towards the rebuilding.

The Anti-Judaism Reproach

In the German Federal Republic, theological groups had formed which demanded a radical about-turn in church and theology in their thinking about Judaism, and down to the present day these groups exert a great and problematical influence on the lay church assemblies (*Kirchentage*) and on some publishers. The periodical *Kirche und Israel*, excellently edited by Rolf Rendtorff, was formed out of the will for just such a reversal. As far as I could observe, there was a group round Friedrich-Wilhelm Marquardt in Berlin, and another in the Rhineland which had been involved in the resolution of the Rhenish synod. There were others, like Rolf Rendtorff in Heidelberg, who tried to find their own way in post-Auschwitz Germany, in order to arrive at the truth. I had friendly ties with the Rhenish theologians, such as Hans-Joachim 'Johnny' Kraus, Jürgen Seim, Bertold Klappert, Frank Crüsemann, and others. In the periodical *Evangelische Theologie* we were at pains to encourage this reversal with numerous contributions. In

May 1994 we held a memorable conference together with Jewish scholars in the Ausgustinian monastery in Erfurt on 'Jesus Christ between Jews and Christians'. On the Jewish side, participants were Michael Wyschogrod, Edna Brocke, and Ernst Ludwig Ehrlich.[17] The dialogue broke down when Edna Brocke reacted very vehemently to my report about our journey to Jerusalem and Hebron in 1994.

I agree completely with the goals of these groups. I already said in 1975 that 'after Auschwitz the Christian church … is bound to revolutionize its thinking.'[18] All my theological outlines and proposals, especially on the doctrine of creation and Christology, serve this turn to a new community with Judaism. The new Jewish thinking influenced me far too deeply for me to be able to distance myself from it. At first it was the prophetic kingdom of God theology; later and increasingly it was Jewish Shekinah theology and the Sabbath mysticism and legislation. The Jewish culture of remembrance, and remembrance theology, embodies truths which we still have to discover where our own culture and theology are concerned.

But this German reversal theology 'after Auschwitz' is often maintained in a typically German ill-mannered style, which I dislike, and which has also hurt me personally. It is probably due to the psychological pressure of having forefathers in the land of the perpetrators; for in America this turnabout is pursued in a more relaxed atmosphere, and Jews come to meet it halfway, as the liberating declaration 'Dabru Emet' shows.[19] What disturbs me about some representatives of post-war German conversion theology is the following:

The turn from the earlier self-exalting anti-Judaism to self-exalting pro-Judaism

The recognition of Israel as the root of Christianity cannot after all lead to the denial of one's own Christian identity or to its disparagement as an identity merely lent to it by the Jews. Anyone who discredits Judaism in order to elevate Christianity has no assurance of his own Christian faith. But anyone who elevates Judaism by discrediting Christianity has this assurance even less.

In the presence of Israel now perceived in a new way, what is at issue is authentic Christian identity, for this now has to be perceived in a new way too. Why should Jews enter into dialogue with Christians who are ashamed of being Christians, and have nothing of their own to say to them? There is no new relationship of Christians to the Jews if Christians give up the assurance of their own faith. An about-turn does not come about by denying one's own self but out of joy in God (Luke 15). In this process the self-doubt and introspection which are so typically Protestant seem for Jews to be something like paying off an obligation which they have neither required nor welcome, and the effect of which, as Ignaz Bubis said, is merely embarrassing. The cause is often merely a necessary but essentially only internal process, the coming to terms of those born later with their SS forefathers, or with their own Hitler Youth past.

Self-righteousness

It is self-evident that progress has been made in the necessary rethinking process, but when the 'progressives' look down on others as if they are people who have been left behind, saying, 'They are not as far advanced as us,' this is nothing but narrow-minded self-righteousness and contributes nothing to the matter itself. This is merely ideological obstinacy and the over-hasty judgements of a sectarian narrow-mindedness. The aim is then no longer to convince but only to profess one's standpoint, with the demand, familiar from the days of the Inquisition, that the others 'recant'.

Anti-Judaism?

One should be especially cautious about employing the reproach of anti-Judaism, because in post-war Germany it always implies the reproach of guilt for Auschwitz.[20] What does the reproach say, and what does it not say? 'Judaism' means Judaism as a whole and at all times. 'Anti-Judaism' therefore means the total rejection of Judaism as a whole and at all times. Anyone who rejects Judaism as a whole will not have anything against the extermination of the Jews. In certain circumstances, he or she will even welcome it. But on the other hand, the person who criticizes something or other in contemporary Judaism, or in the Judaism of another time, is not an 'anti-Judaist'. For the criticism can spring from a love of true, authentic Judaism. Or are Jesus and Paul now to count as 'anti-Jewish' too?

One can certainly distinguish further between internal Jewish criticism and criticism from outside, but one cannot go on to conclude that only Jews are permitted to criticize their Judaism; for then only Christians will be permitted to criticize their Christianity, and only Muslims their Islam.

But in the name of human rights, everyone has the right to put a name to inhumanity, whoever the target may be.

In post-war Germany the reproach of anti-Judaism belongs within a particular context, inasmuch as it is connected with accusations of guilt and with the exoneration from guilt of the people who are accusing the others. The reproach of anti-Judaism is often misused for other purposes, as a way of reducing opponents to silence. But that is a particularly shameful game to play at Judaism's expense.

Distinctions

Finally, Christians in post-war Germany should follow the Jewish Holocaust researcher Steven T. Katz and distinguish between Christian anti-Semitism and racist anti-Semitism.[21] The annihilation of the Jews in death camps such as Treblinka took place in the name of the Nuremberg race laws, not on the grounds of religion. Consequently, Jewish Christians were murdered as well—Edith Stein, for example—people to whom the churches had formerly always offered protection. This is not to excuse traditional Christian anti-Semitism. It was not responsible for the Nazi Holocaust, but it *was* the cause of the quite inexcusable silence of most Christians and the official churches, and for the refusal to stand by the Jews during the Nazi persecution. Theology and the church must surmount their traditional anti-Semitism but should avoid the typically Protestant 'arrogant assumption of guilt', as Margaret Mitscherlich called it. The person who believes he is responsible for everything also thinks that he must really have control over everything.

Attacks on Elisabeth and Myself

In 1988 Leonore Siegele-Wenschkewitz published an essay by the American Jewish feminist Susannah Heschel, Abraham Heschel's daughter, in which she fiercely attacked Elisabeth.[22] In her famous book *The Women around Jesus* (1980; ET 1982), Elisabeth had pointed to Jesus' special, unconventional dealings with the women round him and—following recent exegesis of the Epistles to the Corinthians—had said that it was Greek women who brought ideas of freedom into the congregation.[23] Susannah Heschel generalizes this historically correct comment and turns it into an alleged method: 'Once again, any positive elements which can be found in Christianity with regard to women are traced back to the Gentile world, whereas everything negative is put down as Jewish.'[24] A little later she generalizes once more: 'But it is not only Moltmann-Wendel's individual assertions which are false and misleading; the whole undertaking—to rescue Christianity by denigrating Judaism—must be rejected in principle.' Of course, this would have to be rejected, but no such undertaking can be found either in Elisabeth's 1977 book *Freiheit, Gleichheit, Schwesterlichkeit* (Liberty, Equality, Sisterliness) or in *The Women around Jesus*, the book which Susannah Heschel cites. Elisabeth is concerned with Jesus as the one born, the one crucified, and the friend.

It is an undisputed fact, according to both Jewish and non-Jewish sources, that in Israel at the time of Jesus, patriarchal family orders were the rule such as probably otherwise existed in the ancient world of that time only in Rome, and that Jesus—as Schalom Ben-Chorin put it—gave the preference to the 'elective affinities' of his men and women disciples rather than to the bonds of family and clan. Schalom Ben-Chorin even supposes that Jesus' deliberate breach of the fourth commandment was the reason for his condemnation by leading Jewish groups of the time. In these comments I can find neither a general reproach that Rabbinic Judaism was sexist, nor an anti-Jewish prejudice. Anyone who says that Jesus was something special is not thereby 'denigrating' Judaism; after all, Jesus himself was a Jew. Anyone who compares the situation of women in the Corinth of the time with the situation of women in Jerusalem is not thereby asserting that everything Gentile is positive and everything Jewish negative. One must be pursuing an exaggerated hermeneutics of suspicion if one presumes that this is a 'whole undertaking' of anti-Jewish provenance. But a number of German feminists have fallen all the more voraciously on Susannah Heschel's reproach that Elisabeth's observations are anti-Jewish, and have gone on repeating it for the last 20 years, undoubtedly with a defamatory intention.[25] One can harbour the gloomiest suspicions about this intention, but what is at least evident is that in post-war Germany people who accuse others of anti-Judaism are intending to show that they themselves are not anti-Jewish. They are accusing others in order to exonerate themselves. Against the grim background of Auschwitz, these are the signs of a neurotic German mentality.

In 1998 T. R. Peters published *Thesen zu einer Christologie nach Auschwitz*, criticizing me in the ninth of these theses: 'Auschwitz cannot be "understood" christologically either—for example along the lines of the scene in Elie Wiesel's book, which Jürgen Moltmann took up. Every premature christological interpretation is a misappropriation.'[26] But I had no intention of 'understanding' Auschwitz christologically, and would be unable to give it a christological interpretation. My point was the presence of God in Auschwitz: 'Though I make my bed in hell, thou art there.' That was why I had interpreted Elie Wiesel's scene about the murder as an echo of Golgotha—as Elie Wiesel's teacher François Mauriac had already done. In my answer to Peters, I tried to bring the God-in-Asuchwitz home to him by imagining what would have happened to Jesus if he had lived in Nazi Germany in 1940. He would have been gassed 'in Auschwitz'. Earlier I had written, 'God was in Auschwitz—Auschwitz is in God.'[27] Many people saw that, too, as an appropriation. But the second idea—that Auschwitz is in God—is just as irrefutable. All the murdered are etched into the memory of God and remain in him. Or is God also supposed to forget the victims, as so many people do in the country of the perpetrators? Peters' warning about a 'premature' christological interpretation is not convincing, for that would mean that a 'subsequent' interpretation of that kind would be possible.

The whole misunderstanding arises from the fact that my critics understand the theology of the cross as an 'answer' to their theodicy question. But I have never maintained that it is—only that the theology of the cross is the power to live with the open wound of the unanswerable but unrelinquishable question to God: 'My God, why have you forsaken me?' No one can live with negative theology alone without falling victim to the negation of theology.

Herbert Vorgrimler, who was a pupil of Rahner's, introduced a particularly infamous note into the discussion. In 2002 he asserted, contrary to Richard of St Victor, Hans Urs von Balthasar, Jürgen Moltmann, Walter Kasper, and Gisbert Greshake, that 'the way of speaking which describes God as a community of three Persons testifies in its own way to the division—indeed the terrible enmity—between Jews and Christians, which in the ultimate analysis led to Auschwitz. It springs from an insensitive, self-righteous belief which has turned its back on Israel and hence on Jesus.'[28]

Since the living God of the Bible is unknown to him, he also fails to understand the new Trinitarian thinking of the people he attacks and, with a misunderstood respect for the divine mystery, takes his leave both of Jesus and of Jewish belief.

Anyone who wishes to do away with the difference between Christianity and Judaism does not only lead Christians to Jews but also makes it easy for Jews to become Christians. The re-Judaizing of Christianity makes Christianity a Jewish possibility. Believing Jews will view this attempt with scepticism.

PLATE 31: Meeting with Jimmy Carter at Emory University, December 1983

PLATE 32 (TOP): In front of the Confucius Temple, Taiwan, 1984

PLATE 33: Dumitru Staniloae

PLATE 34: Elisabeth Moltmann-Wendel

PLATES 35 AND 36: With our first grandchild, Jonas

PLATE 37 (TOP): With Professor and Mrs Pannenberg at Hans Küng's sixtieth birthday party

PLATE 38: In the classroom, February 1990

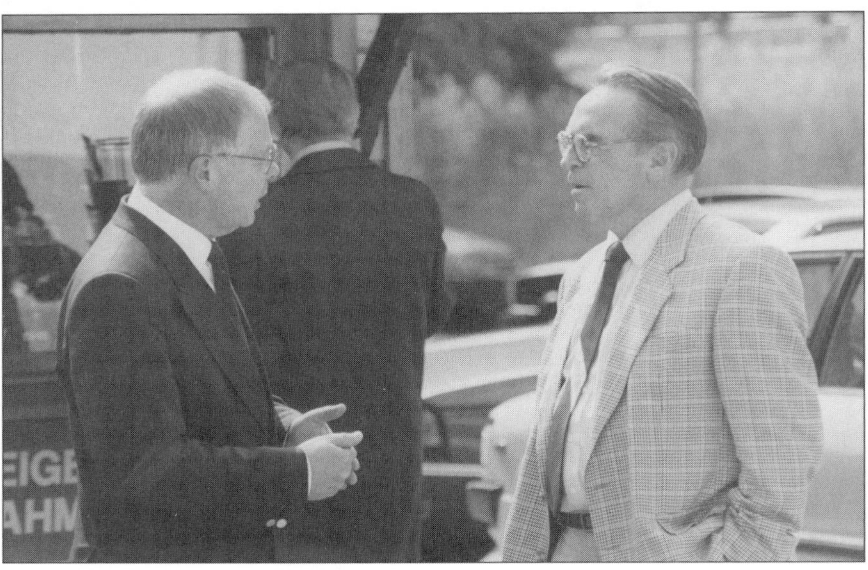

PLATE 39 (TOP): With our four grandchildren, 1990

PLATE 40: With Professor Mehlhausen at the symposium celebrating the fiftieth year of the periodical *Evangelische Theologie*, June 1990

PLATE 41: With Dr Lin Hong-Hsin in Taipeh, Taiwan, September 1992

PLATE 42 (TOP): With Ernesto Cardenal in Managua, March 1994

PLATE 43: Harvest Thanksgiving in Managua

PLATE 44 (TOP): With the Archbishop of Canterbury, George Carey, January 1995

PLATE 45: With members of the institute staff, Gisela Hauber and Carmen Krieg

PLATE 46 (TOP): With Eberhard Jüngel and Dorothee Sölle at the symposium 'How I Have Changed', July 1996

PLATE 47: At home in Tübingen, autumn 2000

PLATE 48 (TOP): With the president of the Chung Yuan University in Jongli, Taiwan

PLATE 49: With the pentecostal preacher Yonggi Cho in Seoul

PLATE 50: The presentation of the Grawemeyer Award, 2000

PLATE 51 (TOP): With Elisabeth, Marianne Saur, Eberhard Jüngel, and Hans Küng

PLATE 52: My seventy-fifth birthday, Bad Boll

PLATE 53 (TOP): Congratulations from Johannes Rau on my seventy-fifth birthday

PLATE 54: With two of our four daughters

PLATE 55 (TOP): Symposium in Peking, 2004

PLATE 56: With the children on 8 April 2006, my eightieth birthday

PLATE 57: The extended family

part VII

Uncompleted Completions—the Challenges of Life

TWENTY-ONE

THE NEW TRINITARIAN THINKING

I have often asked myself what really happened to me during the years from 1980 until 1994, the last 15 years of my life as a professor of theology. Were these the high spots of my 'career', or was this the autumn of middle age? High noon or the beginning of the farewell? Did I become older or younger?

At that time I tried theologically to follow up the new approaches of the theology of hope, the theology of the cross, and Trinitarian thinking by sorting out my various fragments—trying to put them together and to come to systematic conclusions. That was the beginning of my Systematic Contributions to Theology. They are provisionally final configurations of an ongoing work, uncompleted—perhaps even uncompletable—completions of beginnings which may well have held more than emerged at the end. Behind the existing realities there are always still unrealized possibilities which are an invitation to new ways forward.

In those years I experienced this personally too. Behind the life that has been lived there is always the wealth of possible life still unlived. The older one becomes, the more one senses this wealth. Whether we are young in years or are growing older, we are always standing on the threshold of our possibilities. Sometimes it takes a little longer to become young and to seize the possibilities with delight and love. But to do so is to feel as if newborn, and in this sense 'young' and full of hope. These are the challenges of the life that has not yet been lived. The possibilities really demand nothing, but are an invitation to go out of ourselves and to live out the fullness of life which is in us and round about. If one becomes older in terms of years, this can even help one to become younger, for one loses the fear for one's self, and threats from outside cease to be threatening. 'Ist der Ruf mal ruiniert, lebt man gänzlich ungeniert,' wrote Wilhelm Busch rightly—once reputation's gone, one is free as a bird. But in order to be 'free as a bird' we don't even have to lose our reputation; we only need to stop bothering about it, or to keep polishing up our image; for life doesn't depend on what other people think of us. Age frees us for untrammelled self-confidence. Perhaps that was the challenge to my life in the 1980s: 'They still bring forth fruit in old age, they are ever full of sap and green' (Ps. 92.14).

Going forward means continually beginning afresh. That was true of my theological work as well. The *Theology of Hope* (1964; ET 1967) and *The Crucified God* (1972; ET 1974) were written programmatically: the whole of theology was to be newly conceived from a single point. The key words were 'hope theology' and 'theology of the cross'. But even in *The Church in the Power of the Spirit* (1975; ET 1977), I no longer found it possible to arrive at a concentration on a single focus in the same way. A whole series of themes presented themselves, and these had to be treated from more than a single perspective.

In 1980 I then began to present a new series of systematic contributions to theology with a different method. This series was designed to differ from the previous books in several ways. My intention was now to treat important theological doctrines in a particular systematic sequence.

I had no wish to say yet again everything that other people had said already. I wanted only to treat subjects about which I believed that I had discovered something new and could suggest something fresh. My intention was not a new system and not a dogmatics of my own or another theological textbook; I wanted to make my 'contributions' to the ongoing dialogue of theology over the centuries and continents.

My contributions to theology presuppose an intensive *conversation* between theologians past and present, and take part in this conversation with proposals of my own. Human theology is theology on the road and theology in time. In my contributions I have recognized the limitations of the place where I stand and have not made the impossible attempt to present the whole of theology. I have tried to set myself, in my own time and in my own place, within the wider and yet still uncompleted whole of theology.

I also wanted to resolve critically the naive self-centredness of one's thinking. Of course I am a European, but European theology no longer has to be *eurocentric.* Of course I am a man, but my theology does not have to be *androcentric* in its emphasis. Of course I am living in the so-called First World, but my theology does not therefore have to reflect the ideas of those at the top, but should make the voice of the oppressed heard. By choosing the word 'contributions', and with the style of the theological 'suggestion', I wanted to express this suspension of the absoluteness of one's own standpoint which is otherwise tacitly presupposed.

Behind this is the conviction that humanly speaking truth is to be found in unhindered *dialogue*—dialogue which, if it is not already 'domination free', is at least truth-seeking. In this dialogue, community and freedom are joined: community in mutual respect and reciprocal participation, and freedom in the right to have one's own opinion and to give one's own assent.

And not least, with the phrase 'systematic contributions to theology' I am acknowledging that theology is more than systematic theology. There is historical, exegetical, and practical theology, and other theological fields still. Systematic theology is only one sector and should no longer be understood as the crown of theological studies, to which all the other forms of theology are ancillary. Systematic theology is at best what the Dutch theologian Kornelis Heilo Miskotte described in a nice image as 'a soloist and conductor' of the theological orchestra.

I began this new theological series with a social doctrine of the Trinity.[1] My concern here was to perceive the relationships of sociality in God and to practise a new 'Trinitarian thinking'. By that I meant thinking in relationships, in communities, and in transitions. I wanted to put an end to the old thinking in terms of substances and determining subjects, a method which cannot work without dividing and isolating its objects. We are accustomed to think of the substances as primary and the relationships as secondary. That is why the individual takes first place in Western and modern thinking, and the community, of which the individual is only a part, comes second. Private property is protected; common property is held cheap. We perceive the objective world in a similar way. Atoms are primary; their molecular combinations are secondary.[2] When we look for the 'elementary particles' out of which the world is supposed to subsist, we have to split the atoms and finally take the atomic nucleus apart. Today we distinguish quarks and strings. That has become method. We divide and isolate, and later, if we can, we put things together again according to our own design. Really this cognitive method simply applies to nature the ancient Roman principle: *divide et impera*—divide and rule—and this can rightly be termed the science of domination. Its goal is clear: 'Knowledge is power.'

In Trinitarian thinking, however, substances and relations are equally primary. According to the new ecological understanding, everything has its time, and every activity its occasion, and every living thing its environment among other living things. Consequently, individual and community are equally primal too. In processual thinking, finally, individual things can only be understood appropriately in their transitions in time to other states. There are no fixable facts and circumstances; there are only fluid transitions. All fixations are abstractions from these temporal processes. Neither this world nor anything in it is finished and done with, and we are not finished and done with either. We do not stand over against the world in a transcendent relationship to it, but are ourselves a part of the world and belong within its developing processes. As this became clearer to me, I departed from the decisional dialectic of my earlier writings, with its Yes or No, and Either-Or, and practised thinking in relationships, sociality, and transitions. I called this generally *Trinitarian thinking,* and in particular *perichoretic thinking.*[3]

Perichoresis means reciprocal indwelling and mutual interpenetration. For me, the archetypal image for perichoretic thinking in Trinitarian theology became the following passage from Jesus' high priestly prayer, John 17.21:

> That they may all be one,
> even as thou, Father, art in me, and I in thee,
> that they also may be in us.

Here the unity of Jesus with God his Father consists not only of a relationship—the relationship, perhaps, of his absolute dependence, or of his self-differentiation from God the Father—but also in their reciprocal indwelling: the Son *in* the Father, the Father *in* the Son. It follows from this that the unity of God has to be understood as a Trinitarian unity, and this unity as a perichoretic unity. If that is correct, then all monadic and all monarchical concepts of unity must be excluded from the Deity. Unity by virtue of reciprocal indwelling is the profoundest form of community, unity as sociality.

This perichoretic unity of Jesus with God the Father is not an exclusive unity; it is a community so open, inviting, and embracing that the community of the disciples can exist *in* the triune God: 'that they also may be *in us*'.

By virtue of this indwelling in the community of God through community with Christ, the earthly community of the disciples also *corresponds to* the eternal Trinitarian community of the Son with the Father. They become '*one, even as …*' So they will be present not merely with one another and for one another, but in love also in one another, and in this way testify to the eternal love of the triune God. Acts 4.32 shows how this can happen: they were of one heart and soul and had everything in common, and none of them suffered want. There was enough for everyone.

Perichoretic theology therefore comprehends the Trinitarian unity of the eternal God, the community of believers in God, and the community shared by those who love one another. The concept of reciprocal indwelling and the mutual opening of spaces for living describes both the community or fellowship of like with like, and the fellowship of the unlike. In this way, perichoretic thinking absorbs dialectical thinking into itself and goes beyond it. The contrasts become transitions, and the differences are preserved in the unities.

Now, the doctrine of the Trinity has often been reproached with having grown up on the foundation of Greek thinking. It is said to have departed from biblical thought and to be fundamentally speaking anti-Jewish, since there is no bond connecting it with Old Testament 'monotheism'. But my access to the doctrine of the Trinity came from the doctrine of the Shekinah in the Old Testament.[4] The God of Israel is not just the one and only God and Lord of his people. He is also the God of the covenant with his people, which is what he determines himself to be: 'I will be your God and you shall be my people.' He is thus not at all the Lord who like a distancing potentate makes fearing servants of his people. The promise of the covenant carries with it the promise 'I will dwell in the midst of the Israelites.' God's 'indwelling', which is called the Shekinah, follows from *God's descent* to his oppressed people in Egypt

(Exod. 3.8). In the pillar of cloud by day and the pillar of fire by night, God's Shekinah goes ahead of his people and leads them out of slavery into the land of liberty.

After the destruction of Jerusalem and the Temple in 687 BCE, this divine Shekinah moves with the deported people to Babylon, and then with the scattered Jews into the exile of the world. Everything that happens to them happens to the divine Shekinah too. In his Shekinah God becomes the companion on the way and the fellow sufferer of his people, and in this way will one day bring them home from the dispersion into the land of the fathers. God 'dwells in the high and holy place, and also with him who is of a contrite and humble spirit' (Isa. 57.15). That indicates God's double presence—in heaven and, according to Abraham Heschel's interpretation, in the misery of his people.[5] Franz Rosenzweig even spoke about a *self-differentiation* in God, who 'gives himself away to his people, he suffers with their sufferings, he goes with them into the misery of the foreign land, he wanders with their wanderings'.[6]

However we may interpret the Exodus and the exile history of God's indwelling among his people, the Christian history of God's incarnation in Jesus Christ and the indwelling of the Holy Spirit must be read against the background of the Shekinah histories in the Old Testament. The final vista of these histories in both Jewish and Christian terms points towards the universal indwelling of God in his creation, which will thereby be renewed and eternal: 'Behold, the dwelling of God is with men. He will dwell with them, and they shall be his people, and God himself will be with them' (Rev. 21.3; cf. Ezek. 37.27). Then the One God of Israel will become the One God of all, and God's incarnation in Jesus Christ will become the cosmic incarnation. It is true that the Old Testament concept of God's Shekinah among his people is as yet only the notion of an immanent transcendence. The New Testament perichoresis idea embodies a mutual indwelling—God in the human being and human beings in God—that is to say a transcendent immanence as well.

Anyone in the West today who is concerned with the doctrine of the Trinity and with Trinitarian thinking cannot ignore Orthodox theology, as the Fathers did, with the exception of Hans Urs von Balthasar. The tradition of the Western church, essentially moulded by Augustine, has cultivated a *psychological* doctrine of the Trinity, according to which Father, Son, and Spirit are reflected in every human psyche, as the self, the understanding, and the will. But the doctrine of the Trinity in the Eastern Church has always been directed to the community of the church, *sobornost*, and must rather be called a *social* doctrine of the Trinity.

In 1094 East and West split over the Western church's interpolation of the *filioque* into the Nicene Creed, and this resulted in fundamentally different developments of the Trinitarian foundations of Christian theology in the two churches. I have already touched on this in the context of my work in the ecumenical commission Faith and Order. In that framework, a specialist conference was arranged in 1978 in Schloss Klingenthal in Alsace, with distinguished participants. Because I myself was concerned with drafting a doctrine of the Trinity for the Western church without the *filioque*, in April 1978 the Romanian patriarchy invited me to visit the theological institute in Bucharest and Sibiu/Hermannstadt. Afterwards the patriarch sent me on the VIP tour of the famous, gloriously painted Moldavian monasteries, and to Iasi. A wholly new world opened up for me. The monasteries were all full to overflowing, the evening singing was deeply moving, and people thronged into the cathedrals for worship.

In Bucharest I made friends with the venerable doyen of Orthodox theology in Romania, Dumitru Staniloae. After my lectures, everyone first waited respectfully for him to give his opinion; it was only after that that the discussion began. And his contributions were always excellent. He picked out the best in what I had said and in his wisdom took it further. His *Theologia Dogmatica Ortodoxa* moulded generations of priests and theologians after the war in Romania. He himself was imprisoned for five years, having been condemned because of his 'mysticism'. He found that my *Theology of Hope* and his 'theology of love' were kindred spirits. We later invited him to Tübingen and conferred the Leopold Lukas Prize on him. At my insistance his *Orthodox Dogmatics* was translated into German by the Lutheran Professor Pitters in Hermannstadt and was published in Germany with financial help from the Protestant and Catholic churches.[7] That allowed an important Orthodox voice to be heard in the Western theological concert, and it is a voice very much worth listening to, for it opens up new theological ways of thinking. Professor Staniloae was accompanied at Klingenthal by his assistant, who is now Metropolitan Daniel of Iasi. I visited the theological faculty in Iasi, gave lectures there, and was awarded an honorary doctorate by the 'Al. I. Cuza' Universitas Iassiensis in 1996—which made me truly 'ecumenical' for the first time.

But it was also an Orthodox theologian who first impelled me to develop a social doctrine of the Trinity. When we met at the World Mission conference in Bangkok in 1972–73 (where we belonged to the same working party), he was still called Father George; a little later he became the Metropolitan Geevarghese Mar Osthathios in Kerala, India. We talked about the immanent Trinity and a classless and casteless society, joined together in truly spiritual dancing on New Year's Eve, and liked one another. He came to Tübingen and I went to Kottayam, to his Orthodox seminary. His illuminating application of Trinitarian doctrine to life impelled us to have his book on a classless society translated into German and published.[8]

At this point I should like to repudiate a hasty and stereotyped criticism. Whenever one draws practical conclusions from a theological insight, one is suspected of doing so in the interests of some political option. In this case, the assumption is that, first being convinced of the need for a classless and casteless society, one has then constructed a social doctrine of the Trinity in order to substantiate it. This reproach is nonsense and rebounds on the critic, since it could equally well suggest that he is against a social doctrine of the Trinity because he is in favour of a class and caste society and wants to defend it.

My book on *The Trinity and the Kingdom of God* came out in 1980 (ET 1981). It set the pattern for the other volumes in my series of systematic contributions to theology. Perichoretic thinking proved for me to be particularly fruitful in the doctrine of creation (*God in Creation,* 1985; ET also 1985) and in the theology of the Holy Spirit (*The Spirit of Life,* 1991; ET 1992). The book on the Trinity was translated into Swedish and Romanian as well as into other languages, and went through a number of editions. Some of my colleagues and friends were disappointed because what they had expected from me at this point and at this moment was an ethics of hope, a book which unfortunately still remains unwritten. But, through Leonardo Boff, my social doctrine of the Trinity had a very fruitful influence on the fusion between Latin American liberation theology and the base-congregation movement.[9] In the feminist theology of the United States, a number of well-known, mainly Catholic, women theologians followed my thinking, for example, Catherine LaCugna and Elizabeth Johnson, because it helped them to think in relationships and networks.[10]

Soon some people were talking about a 'new Trinitarian thinking' which—according to Wolfhart Pannenberg's kindly accolade—had begun with my book. This Trinitarian thinking, which started with Pannenberg and myself, is also new over against Karl Barth and Karl Rahner inasmuch as it does not start from the triadic concept of the self-consciousness of the absolute subject (thereby following Hegel), but begins with the biblical divine history and its three protagonists, Jesus, God, whom he calls 'Abba, dear Father', and the vital energies of the divine Spirit.[11] Karl Barth and Karl Rahner had already begun this inception of Christian theology with itself, without any presuppositions.[12]

My diaries show that 1980 and the years that followed were busy and full of stimulating experiences. I lectured on my social doctrine of the Trinity to the Baptists in Rüschlikon, near Zurich, and—in the Warfield Lectures—to the Presbyterians in Princeton. In 1981 I then took the lectures to Korea and Japan, and afterwards returned to Budapest and Debrecen, to my Reformed brethren. These were the years of rearmament, with the stationing of nuclear missiles in both parts of Germany, and it was therefore the era of the peace movement. With the Gesellschaft für Evangelische Theologie I came out strongly on behalf of 'creating peace without weapons', and not only arranged the conferences in Arnoldshain and Stapellage, but also travelled the world with our statement about peace. Visits in 1982 to the Mennonites in Elkhart, USA, and Winnipeg, Canada, were especially impressive. We could learn from these ancient peace churches—not just conscientious objection and the costs of the discipleship of Jesus which that involves, but also active intervention for peace in a world beset by natural and political catastrophes. In America the Mennonite relief service is always the first on the spot. Peace also demands commitment and sacrifice, not just war. In lectures in various places I also tried out the initial draft of my ecological doctrine of creation, which I was working on for the Gifford Lectures. In 1980 I even got above myself: I accepted a lecture tour through Italy arranged by the Associazione Culturale Italiana, and talked about 'Dio e Libertà' in small theatres in Turin, Milan, Florence, Rome, and Bari. True, I knew no Italian, but with the help of a translation, a tape recording, and a grappa, it all went quite well, at least as far as I was concerned. My friend Professor Nikos Nissiotis, whom I had got to know in the Faith and Order commission, persuaded me to give a lecture on 'Olympia and religion' in the Olympic Academy in Olympia in June 1980. He was the chairman of the Greek Olympic committee. So when I came home, I was able to say, 'I, too, started in Olympia.'

In the same year, the head of the Goethe Institute in Rome, Michael Marshall von Bieberstein, took me to Delphi so that I could take part in a discussion about the European Charter of Culture. But I found that this was already firmly in French possession, so that nothing much could be done to combat French laicism. I became powerfully aware of the neglects of German governments, neglects which are taking their toll today in the collapse of the draft for a European constitution. The reduction of politics to economics, and the undervaluation of culture and religion, have moved Germany to a back seat in the European theatre.

In 1983 I spent a free semester as visiting professor at Emory University, Atlanta. At first I was alone, but later Elisabeth joined me, and together we visited the Mayan ruins in Palenque, Mexico, so that we could also see pre-Columbian America. In 1981 and 1984 I was in Korea again. And meanwhile, parallel to all this, normal academic work took its normal course.

For me there were three high spots during the 1980s: first of all the Gifford Lectures in 1985; then the world tour with Elisabeth—America, Hawaii, Hong Kong, and China, and back to Tübingen; and finally my theological discovery of the Spirit, 'the giver of life', which led to a new love for life, a culture of life, and not least a new spirituality of the senses, the body, and the earth. In this part 7 I shall concentrate on these three peak experiences and shall begin with an account that I wrote directly after the Gifford Lectures, when these weeks were still fresh in my mind.

TWENTY-TWO

THE 1985 GIFFORD LECTURES IN EDINBURGH

God in Creation

As early as 1980 the principal of Edinburgh University wrote, telling me that the Gifford Committee had proposed me for the Gifford Lectures 1984–85. This invitation put me on cloud nine, for the only German theologians who had given these famous lectures before me were Karl Barth in 1938, Paul Tillich in 1948, Emil Brunner in 1950, and Rudolf Bultmann in 1957. Because Lord Gifford intended these lectures to be devoted to 'natural theology', I suggested the doctrine of creation and a theology of nature. This topic was welcomed as highly appropriate. It worked out well, because I had in any case intended the doctrine of creation to be the subject of my next book in the series which I had begun in 1980 with *The Trinity and the Kingdom of God*. But the closer the time came for giving these lectures, the less I was conscious of the honour, and the heavier the burden which I felt rested on my small shoulders, as I remembered that series of my theological forebears.

In order to try out the lectures beforehand in English, too, I took this doctrine of creation for my lectures at Emory University, Atlanta, during my visiting semester there in 1983. Dustin Anderson and Margaret Kohl translated the chapters I had ready, and I then revised them again in Atlanta, adding English and American literature on the problems to be considered. In the winter semester of 1984–85, I then used the finished book manuscript for lectures in Tübingen and at the same time read the proofs for the book. This was to be published by KaiserVerlag in March 1985, immediately after the Gifford Lectures, under the title *Gott in der Schöpfung. Ökologische Schöpfungslehre* (ET *God in Creation: An Ecological Doctrine of Creation*). The title *Gott in der Schöpfung* came from Elisabeth.

Between Christmas and New Year I then turned to the lectures, ten in number, drawing them from the various chapters in the book. In the last weeks of the semester I gave them a final polish. So, well prepared, I arrived in Edinburgh on 20 February 1985.

In addition to the lectures, I had to preach at the university service in Greyfriars Church on 3 March, and I had agreed to give lectures in St Andrews and Aberdeen. The two-hundred-year-old students' Theological Society had chosen me as its honorary president for the academic year 1984–85, so I had to deliver my inaugural address on 27 February in New College, my subject being 'Alienation and Liberation of Nature'. There was also an invitation for 23 February from the Fiona Hulbert group (which was concerned with feminism and peace) and one for the same day from the theological faculty—a seminar with Duncan Forrester and a class meeting about my book *The Church in the Power of the Spirit.* So I was well booked up for the three weeks.

John McIntyre met me at the Edinburgh airport. He had grown grey and was close to retirement. I had met him 16 years before on my first visit to Edinburgh, when he was dean. He drove me in the university car to the George Hotel in George Street, where I was to stay for three weeks, a quiet, distinguished, and well-kept hotel. Unfortunately, at first I was given a small, cold, dark single attic room, but this was rectified the next morning without any difficulty by Agnes Dougall, the dean's secretary. 'All expenses paid' was the generous offer of the Gifford Foundation.

On the afternoon of 21 February, at 4.50, the university car drew up and took me to the first lecture in the Appleton Tower. About 300 people were present. John McIntyre introduced me as a theological 'star' from the continent, a successor of Barth and Bultmann. I began by thanking the university: the Gifford Lectures were first of all an honour, then a burden, and now a pleasure. Then I thanked the Scots for their hospitality to the young prisoner of war who had been brought to their country in 1945. After the lecture 'God in the Creation', there was the inevitable sherry party. Tom Torrance, Bill Shaw, Hugh Anderson, and, in addition, our former au pair girl Alison and her husband came, and there was a great reunion.

The next day began quietly in the hotel. I walked through the streets to Stockbridge and admired 'the stony city' with its red granite. I had lunch at the 'carver's table' with roast beef and lamb. In the afternoon a taxi appeared and took me to the Appleton Tower. The second lecture was on 'natural theology' and Lord Gifford's will, which was very similar to that of my Freemason grandfather, Johannes Moltmann: the immature child's faith is followed by the independent faith of reason, and the particular theology of revelation is succeeded by universal natural theology as its consummation. There was again a large and very attentive audience, and I was able to hold my listeners throughout the lectures.

On Saturday, 23 February, I then went to the Fiona Hulbert group. Clergy, women, and interested students, about 60 to 70 people in all, had collected in the university chaplaincy. Allan Lewis and Ruth Page, the junior lecturers at New College, interviewed me, and then there was a very lively discussion on themes ranging from 'the motherhood of God' (a controversial subject at the previous synod of the Church of Scotland) down to questions about congregational structures. In the evening Jim Mackey, the liberal Catholic successor of Tom Torrance, then collected me and took me to dinner with Hugh and Jean Anderson. There was too much wine and whisky, and I was completely exhausted.

On Sunday morning I rushed to the bus station in order to gain my Sabbath liberty somewhere or other, and so as to escape all possible claims on me. At nine o'clock there was a bus to Dunbar, and that was a lucky choice. I found a little town with castle ruins at the sea, wonderful sun, a glorious promenade along the cliffs, a play of colours on the water—and endless quiet. Off the coast, steep cliffs towered out of the water, the Bass Rock and others. I had lunch in a shabby coffee shop and in the afternoon travelled contentedly back to Edinburgh. In the evening I looked through the lecture for the following day again, and then watched a *Miss Marple* episode on the BBC.

On Monday morning a journalist came for a radio interview. His tape recorder didn't work, so after an hour he came back again. In the afternoon no car arrived: I was now probably supposed to be able to find the way for myself. So I got hold of a taxi. I had worried about the subject of this lecture, 'Creation Out of Nothing', because it seemed so abstract. But it went down well, with the outlook on the annihilations of world history and the apocalyptic Nothingness. Afterwards Tom Torrance took me to his men's club (the New Town Club), where we dined very agreeably by candlelight in a panelled room, and evidently came closer to each other in questions about theology and science: 16 years earlier, we had clashed over 'the theology of revolution'.

On the morning of Tuesday 26 February, I still had to add an existential touch to the end of my lecture 'The Trinitarian Concept of Creation'. During the afternoon I wandered past the Mound and New College, crossed the High Street, and directed my steps to the university. There Mrs Dougall was waiting for me to make sure that everything was in order. After the lecture I went back to the hotel with Gordon Strachan, finding that in ecology he was a kindred spirit and that he had also discovered the wisdom of the Sabbath. In the evening I watched the third instalment of *Miss Marple*.

Wednesday, 27 February, was a full day. At two o'clock I met the Faculty of Divinity in New College. I talked without notes about the changing problems in German theology between 1969 and 1985: from the critical demythologization of Feuerbach, Marx, and Freud to the religion of C. G. Jung, from Marxism to neo-conservatism. After that I outlined the necessary transitions theology has to make today: from Eurocentricism to polycentricism, from denominationalism to ecumenism, from masculine theology via feminist theology to a truly human, shared theology. The older colleagues, such as Porteous and Anderson, were startled that the Bultmann school should have so silently disappeared. Then I had an interval of an hour until the inaugural lecture at the Theological Society. The 'large lecture room' (which admittedly by German standards was not very large) was packed. Through the windows opposite, the lecturer looked out at the sea. The lecture was followed by a brief but good discussion. Dinner in the somewhat run-down Faculty Club was only moderate. I spent the evening with Duncan Forrester's seminar in his house, and debated vigorously with a Brazilian about the weal and woe of liberation theology. I brought up the subject of unemployment in our countries, but the British students were more interested in 'the right way of dealing with the Bible'. Strange! At the end, to help us unwind, Duncan Forrester opened a bottle of whisky. That helped, me at least, at the end of this exceptional day.

Thursday, 28 February, began at twelve o'clock with the class meeting in New College. Throughout the term the students had been reading *The Church in the Power of the Spirit*, and now came up with detailed questions: What do you mean on page 217? Why do you say that on page 55? And so forth. With the help of a little imagination I was able to remember and reply. In the afternoon I walked through Edinburgh in the accustomed way and gave my lecture 'The Time of Creation', which I had prepared very thoroughly. Afterwards Gordon Strachan again accompanied me home, an independent spirit with a mind of his own. His wife, Elspeth, had already struck me during the lectures because of her intelligent face. She worked in a vegetarian restaurant. The two had just published a book of Jungian theology called *Freeing the Feminine*.

Friday, 1 March, began more quietly. During the morning I took a walk as usual up and down George Street, admired the Victorian facades, and enquired about a silver teapot, as a souvenir. In the afternoon I gave my lecture 'The Space of Creation'. Afterwards I tried to spend a relaxing evening in the solitariness of the hotel. But I was the only solitary person there. The hotel filled up with Welshmen, drinking and singing, because they were intending to beat Scotland at rugby the next day. The whole city was full of Welshmen, and the Welshmen were full of Scotch.

On Saturday, 2 March, I again celebrated my Sabbath at the sea, this time in North Berwick. I walked along the long sandy beach, listened to the roar of the waves, smelled the seaweed, and admired the play of light, clouds, and water. After lunch in another equally poor tea room, I got back to Edinburgh in good time to watch the famous rugby match on TV. The Scots lost 21:26, so at night long rows of Welshmen wandered singing through the streets from one pub to the next.

On Sunday, 3 March, Principal Burnett collected me in the car and took me to Greyfriars Church, the church of the covenant, with its wealth of tradition. At eleven o'clock the choir, the faculties, the president, and, bringing up the rear, the university chaplain, Fergus Smith, and myself processed into the church. The congregation was a good one by Scottish standards, in my opinion middling. The principal read the Gospel, and after a long liturgy I delivered my Pentecostal social sermon: 'There is enough for everyone.' Afterwards there was more than enough church music, and we slowly arrived at the end after one and a half hours.

On Monday, March 4, I had to prescribe a quiet morning for myself, because there was so much on the programme for the afternoon and evening. So after my morning walk, I took a sleep. After an early lunch, the Congregationalist pastor Nelson collected me, and Jim Mackey conducted a half-hour television interview with me. With the help of a good cup of coffee, I was able to summon up all the English I was capable of, and the interview went off effortlessly. But then I had to rush to the Appleton Tower in order to give lecture 7 'Heaven and Earth'. Afterwards John

MacIntyre pinned a black bow tie onto the collar of my white shirt, and off we went to the 276th dinner of the Royal Society of Edinburgh. All the members—lords and professors—appeared in the same uniform: dinner jacket, white shirt, black (bow) tie, tartan cummerbund. The venerable forefathers gazed down in oils from the walls, largest of all Sir Walter Scott. After sherry and whisky, we moved to the upstairs room. The quality of the wine exceeded the quality of the food. The first toast was to the Queen: 'The Queen, the Queen …' we all murmured to each other. At the end I even had the presumption to make a speech of thanks for Scottish hospitality, first in 1945 among the miners in Kilmarnock, where our prisoner of war camp was situated, and now in the Royal Society. It made quite an impression. After dinner snuff was passed round in silver snuff boxes, but I didn't venture to take any. The age-old port was also very good.

On the morning of Tuesday, 5 March, I bought an 1815 silver teapot as a souvenir. Then I gathered together my papers and my thoughts for the big trip to the north. This time Penny Prophit, a Franciscan nun and professor of nursing, introduced me, the subject being 'Evolution and Creation'. Afterwards I rushed to Waverley Station in order to catch the train to Leuchars Station for St Andrews. However, the train was an hour late, and I passed the time by drinking tea. Bill Shaw met me and took me to dinner in a remote but choice restaurant, then brought me back to the Golf Hotel. When I opened the curtains the next morning, the sea was spread out before me, wide and still. A mystical thrill ran through me, and I felt myself 'one with the universe'. But not for long; for at ten o'clock I had to give my lecture in St Mary's, as a fitting thank-you to my *alma mater honoris causa*. The lecture hall was full. The professors sat in the first row, among them Matthew Black, whom I had heard speak on 'the Son of man' in 1947 in Norton Camp. During the tea and coffee break, we were joined by students, professors, and some old acquaintances.

However, soon after lunch with Bill Shaw in the Royal Golf Club, Allan Torrance arrived—James Torrance's son and Tom's nephew. He drove me through the Scottish Highlands to Aberdeen, where I was put to bed with hot water bottles in the icy guest room by James Torrance, so that I would be fit again at 7.30. Curiously enough, I was; and I gave my first Gifford lecture once more. But then I was more or less finished. The next morning I was delighted to exchange the cold guest room for the warm train to

Edinburgh, and enjoyed the marvellous view of the North Sea, for the train follows the coast almost the whole way.

Thursday, 7 March: Duncan Forrester introduced the last lecture but one. Its subject was 'Soul and Body', and it took in aspects of Gestalt therapy. Afterwards I went back to the hotel with the pleasant couple Elspeth and Gordon Strachan.

Friday, 8 March, the last day: I had lunch with Alison and admired the baby which had arrived during these weeks. The three-year-old William was being energetically brought up. In the afternoon Principal Burnett introduced the lecture. He is a biologist and the son of a Methodist minister, was an exchange pupil at one of the German elite Napola schools, and otherwise, too, was widely travelled. My Sabbath theology was a fitting conclusion for the series Creation and the Spirit of God. The applause was never-ending, and I was probably red in the face with pleasure and embarrassment. My confusion abated during the beautifully appointed dinner in Abden House. The ten members of the Gifford committee were present, with their wives. I sat next to Penny Prophit. We dined well by candlelight at a polished table without a tablecloth. Principal Burnett gave a brief speech and presented me with the university tie, and I thanked him and the members of the committee with the finest words I could muster. I then let the day draw to a close in the hotel bar, where I thought over the events of the previous weeks.

On the morning of Saturday, 9 March, I again tried to find Lord Gifford's grave, but unfortunately in vain. Then John McIntyre took me to the airport. At 6.30 I landed with all my considerable luggage in Stuttgart, where Elisabeth and I fell into each others arms.

These three weeks were full of experiences, the peak, one might say, of what could be called a theological career. But it was also a time of lonely hotel rooms, which preyed on the spirits. In the preceding years I had always only thought as far as these Gifford Lectures, and the publication of the book *God in Creation* which had been prepared with them in mind. It was difficult to imagine the time afterwards and to take up something new.

TWENTY-THREE

OUR LONG WALK TO CHINA, 1985

We decided that we would celebrate our sixtieth birthdays with a special journey. I had agreed to go again to the Candler School of Theology, Emory University, Atlanta, for a brief visiting professorship. This time Elisabeth had also been invited to go as visiting professor for seven weeks. Then our friend Charles McCoy came up with the idea that our joint birthday year should be celebrated with a trans-continental conference in our honour. He had got Fred Burnham of Trinity Church, New York, to put on the Seventeenth National Conference of Trinity Institute with the two of us, to take place in three places: New York, St Louis, and San Francisco. This was to follow our time in Atlanta, in April 1986. Once we were in San Francisco, we thought, we could just as well fly home in the opposite direction and visit China.

When we studied the China travel literature, we found a tour that attracted Elisabeth particularly. It included a five-day voyage on the Yangze Kiang from Wuhan to Chungking. But this tour was only planned to begin on 6 May, in Hong Kong. That gave us 14 days between. Should we fly home and then start out again? It was Anne-Ruth who finally gave the casting vote and convinced us that it would be better to spend a holiday on Hawaii and then fly on. So one section of the journey was added to another, and at the end we were faced with a journey of nearly four months. We were supposed to start on 10 February and only come back on 29 May. That made us somewhat dizzy and put us in situations in which we were inclined to break off this 'long walk' to China prematurely. But we often reminded each other of the old Danish student song about the elephant: 'Slowly he moves, foot by foot, for he is no omnibus.' So we, too, moved forward from day to day, and in the end we reached China and came back home again without having 'dropped dead' first, as we had occasionally ironically feared. So my account of our journey will move forward step by step too.

Guests in Atlanta Once More

In January and February Elisabeth still had a good many lectures to give, and I had to fulfil my final examination obligations on Saturday. But on Monday, 10 February, we flew somewhat exhausted (and hence business class) from Frankfurt to Atlanta. We left Germany's snow flurries and arrived in Georgia's warm rain. On Wednesday my lectures and Elisabeth's seminar were already due to begin. Don Salier met us and took us to our old quarters again, 1212 Clifton Road. During the first three weeks we lived a quiet life and tried to gather up our strength again, so we took on no outside lectures and made hardly any excursions. For us this was a kind of retreat. But on the first Sunday, as always, we climbed the splendid granite Stone Mountain and admired the skyline of Atlanta, like a Jerusalem come down from heaven in the midst of the pine-tree-wooded plains.

Work with Don Salier in the lectures on eschatology proved to be extremely fruitful. His commentaries and contributions drawn from the liturgical traditions were the best possible supplement to my lectures, which often led over to political implications. Since all the lectures had already been translated, they did not give me much trouble. The seminar on political theology was more difficult. The participants were a very mixed bunch, old and young, beginners and advanced, American and foreign students, and the discussions were accordingly diffuse and diverging. I often didn't know whether I should address the theme or the participants. For the first time I sensed among the people present a diminishing theological interest in the political problems in the world, and a growing interest in their own denominational identity, as well as the need to assert themselves nationally. Nevertheless, a seminar with 15 participants and 10 guests was the purest leisure compared with the struggle with 180 students in my seminar during the winter semester in Tübingen. With the American students one could go to 'Jaggers' after the session and carry on the discussion in a cheerful group, which the large numbers in Tübingen simply made impossible.

Elisabeth had a much harder time with her lectures or seminars. Every weekend she had to start revising her lectures on feminist theology to make them suitable for her group of men and women students, so that she found this the hardest work of her whole life. Her group was very mixed. Common presuppositions were lacking, and the personal concerns of those participating were extremely diverse. Even after an hour's lecture, the discussion always strayed into many directions simultaneously, so that it was hardly possible to draw it together. She had valuable help from an American student called Larry, and from a German student who had once been second in command to a ship's captain but had now turned into a feminist. At the end of our time, on 6 March, she then gave a public lecture, with slides, titled 'Women—Snake—Sexuality', which attracted a large audience and met with an excellent response.

On 20 February we made our first expedition to the north Georgia mountains. It was a warm early spring day. We drove to Helen, a terribly funny imitation of a Bavarian village in the midst of the American South, a pure tourist attraction but, like Disneyland, still typically American. Beyond Helen we found the national park Unicoi, with reservoirs and a spacious lodge. We lay there in the warm sun on a landing stage and felt extremely contented.

On 23 February I preached in the university chapel, and in the evening we visited the open-door community with Ed Loring and Murphy Davis. He preached a heart-rending sermon, like a black enthusiast, and we were deeply impressed by him, by the work of this little congregation with the 'street people' in Atlanta, and by Murphy's pastoral work with the people in the prisons who had been sentenced to death. A child in the community nearly reduced us to tears by his resemblance to our little grandson Jonas in Tübingen. On 2 March we went to Martin Luther King's church, the Ebenezer Church. The Revd Roberts, an especially gifted enthusiast, greeted us effusively and preached impressively with many theatrical effects. We also greeted Coretta King, who was in the congregation. Black congregational worship is full of emotion and life, and one is tempted to warm one's cold, white hands at it, which of course helps no one.

I got an unpleasant touch of flu, which somewhat impeded me when on Monday, 3 March, I began my Caldwell Lectures in the Presbyterian Theological Seminary in Louisville, Kentucky. Harold Nebelsiek met me in Louisville and took me to a motel—unheated during the day. My lectures were held in the seminary chapel, and it was full to overflowing. I gave five lectures on 'Love, Death, and Eternal Life: The Personal Eschatology' and was well received, with a standing ovation at the end.

On Saturday, 8 March, we again made a whole-day excursion, this time to the sites commemorating the Indians in Georgia. We had asked colleagues about them but had never been given any clear information. We viewed the Indian mounds, mounds of earth which are laid out similarly to the Mayan temples in Yucatan and testify to a rich Indian culture. Then we drove to the last capital of the Cherokee Indians. In 1838 they were all illegally driven out of Georgia to Oklahoma by the white people with the help of the US Army, many of them dying on this 'trail of tears'.

And then Elisabeth fell ill. She went down with the American influenza, a virus against which we feeble Europeans are evidently powerless. We therefore had to cancel our planned flight to New Orleans, the jazz capital, and had to keep quietly to the house, living off take-away food. On Tuesday, 18 March, we thought the infection was over and flew in good spirits to our friends Kristin and Fred Herzog and our old Duke University, Durham, North Carolina, where we had lived with the whole family for a year from 1967 to 1968. We also got through the unavoidable dinner parties and our lectures without any problems. But then in the night from Wednesday to Thursday, Elisabeth became really ill with pneumonia. We took a very early flight to Atlanta, and she arrived with a high temperature. Our salvation was Marilyn Washburn, a doctor and student of theology in our seminars. She came immediately and took over the treatment. She visited Elisabeth most faithfully three times a day and actually managed to keep her from having to go to hospital, nursing her until she was well again. It was a tedious process because the infection was obstinate. It was a real relief that Anne-Ruth had planned to visit us, and on 2 March she arrived at Hartfield Airport in Atlanta.

From that point things improved. With Anne-Ruth we went up Stone Mountain; drove to Madison, Georgia, and viewed the ante-bellum houses; and finally celebrated Easter together with Cindy and Ted Runyon in the revolving restaurant in the Peachtree Hotel with an opulent dinner of lobster tails and steaks. On 31 March Dean Jim Waits invited the faculty to a spring party in honour of our sixtieth birthdays, which had fallen in that year. He had engaged a band to play old New Orleans jazz, which provided an idyllic background; colleagues gave delightful personal speeches; and then the great birthday cake arrived, with 60 candles which we blew out together. Candler Faculty and Atlanta have become something of a second home for us. In the last days of March, spring then arrived with a rush. The dogwoods and redbuds bloomed under Atlanta's great trees, and the magnolias and tulip trees opened. It was a magical atmosphere, for everything was still fresh and without the sultry humidity which can otherwise weigh on the spirits in the southern states of America.

On 3 April we flew to New York with Anne-Ruth, and the second stage of our 'long walk' to China began.

The Transatlantic Conference in New York, St Louis, and San Francisco

When this conference had been planned a year previously, I just happened to have on my writing desk an essay 'Love, Death, and Eternal Life: Outline of a Personal Eschatology'. Elisabeth was lecturing in various places on her thesis 'I am good, whole, and beautiful', which roused a good deal of attention and, in North Germany, Episcopal contradiction. My concern was the personal hope, hers self-acceptance and self-love. How could the two be reduced to a common denominator? The suggestion that occurred to me was 'Love: The Foundation of Hope'. And this was what we then took over the Atlantic.

Well-known theologians and friends of ours were invited to the three parts of the conference as respondents, and in this way a highly impressive conference-sequence came into being. In New York Christopher Morse of Union Theological Seminary came; he had written a doctoral thesis in 1970 titled *The Logic of Promise in Moltmann's Theology of Hope*; others were our old friend Letty Russell, the biblical-feminist theologian from Yale University, and the Anglican theologian Stephen Sykes from Cambridge. Bishop Kauluma, Namibia, opened all three individual conferences with a powerful liberation theology sermon in the context of high church liturgical services in the Episcopal churches. In St Louis we were joined by José Míguez Bonino from Buenos Aires (with whom ten years before I had carried on a critical open correspondence about liberation theology and Marxism) and also by our old friend Doug Meeks from Eden Seminary, St Louis. In San Francisco, finally, Charles McCoy came, my oldest American friend and co-admirer of federal theology, as well as Hans Frei from Yale, with his kind but also highly critical voice.

To see New York again was particularly enjoyable because we had the company of Anne-Ruth, who had lived there for a year and knew every corner round about Central Station. We were put up in the old Roosevelt

Hotel: great splendour downstairs but somewhat run-down bedrooms. They looked out on Madison Avenue and 45th Street and were accordingly unbearably noisy. I took part in the reception in Trinity Church and in the church service. The church is near Wall Street. During the evening rush hour, more than half an hour was needed for the three kilometres. The next morning Elisabeth had to speak first. But it went off fabulously well. She became livelier and livelier, the audience of 400 responded splendidly, and at the end she received a standing ovation. The same thing happened in St Louis and San Francisco. Her lecture was the 'hit' of these conferences. During the afternoon I walked through the renovated centre of St Louis and in a coffee house listened to a pleasant jazz band, all the players being 'seniors'. The next day we found about 300 people waiting in the Episcopal church and gave our lectures there.

In the evening, Eden Seminary put on a splendid birthday banquet. Walter Brueggemann made a sparkling and witty speech with serious points. Then Douglas Meeks talked about me as a fabulous theological Proteus, as a preliminary to presenting me with a book about Charlie Chaplin. At the end he said that, in his opinion, in an earlier life I had undoubtedly been a Mississippi river boat gambler. I agreed fervently with him and felt like Rhett Butler in *Gone with the Wind*. During dinner, a small orchestra played classical music, and candles and flowers decorated the long tables. In my thank-you speech, I talked about our love for America, our sympathy with her, and our hope for her. Everyone rose, and there was a lot of embracing. The next evening we moved to St Louis' huge Union Station, which had been very cleverly rebuilt as a shopping and recreation centre. Doug and I smoked our traditional, obligatory, one-dollar cigars, and Elisabeth enjoyed lobster tails and steaks. But nonetheless we realized the degree to which these conferences—and dinners—were a drain on our strength.

In San Francisco we had some initial difficulties because the Fairmont Hotel—my dream hotel for many years—was completely booked up. We had to switch to the smaller but elegant Canterbury Hotel. As a compensation, we took two rooms there, so that each of us could enjoy complete peace. For the first time we were living in San Francisco itself, and we enjoyed this wonderful city to the full. The next morning I took the famous old cable car from Market Street to Fisherman's Wharf and back again, simply for fun and because it was so romantic. In the afternoon Charles came with the car and we visited the classic old places again—the Golden

Gate Bridge, the great park, the seaside, and Seal Rock—and then sat over dinner in the restaurant at the top of the Hilton, with a superb panoramic view of the city and the bay. On Sunday we were at last able to move into the Fairmont. At first Elisabeth found it ostentatious, but she then came to enjoy the good beds and elegant surroundings as if she had always been at home there. For 'sundowners' we had invited the Rittberger family to the top restaurant of the Fairmont Hotel; we knew them from Tübingen, and for the moment they were at Stanford University. We sat there with them and their children and watched the sun go down behind the Golden Gate Bridge, with the ships sailing out and in: the world's dream view. It was a delightful 'Tübingen evening' in California.

On Tuesday, 15 April, the good Fred Burnham, who had conducted all these conferences with great patience and wisdom, invited the speaker to dinner. It was a very merry meal. Then came our last day on the American continent. Elisabeth gave the first Marjorie Casebier McCoy Memorial Lecture in Berkeley, and I was free. As usual, her lecture, with her slides on the history of 'Woman–Snake–Sexuality', was very well received. I celebrated my departure from America by myself up in the Fairmont restaurant with an opulent dinner, dreaming happily in the twilight as the bay slowly veiled itself and the Golden Gate Bridge stood out in the radiance of its lights.

Holiday on Maui, Hawaii

After a five-hour flight we finally arrived on 17 April at the island of Maui, which belongs to the Hawaii group. Tropical heat already met us at the airport. The apartment in the condominium we had booked proved to be an exceedingly stylishly furnished idyll: one bedroom had two bathrooms, the large living room was lavishly equipped with soft sofas, and the wide balcony ran right round the whole apartment. When we woke up in the morning, the blue sea was spread out in front of us, with the island of Lanai beyond and above it the sun. A red-headed bird, a cardinal, came every morning and demanded a share in our breakfast. The holiday apartment was situated in a garden complex with swimming pools, beach, and flowering trees wherever one looked. It was a retreat from history to nature, from time divided linear-wise into purposeful sections to the eternal return of the same thing, from working and doing to pure being, and to harmony with the earth, water, air, and sun. Consequently, there is nothing special to say about it. Every day was sunny, the wind caressed us, and the clear water repeatedly invited us to swim in it. We became lazy and brown and lived wholly in the present, without remembrance and without expectation. In the evening we often dined on the terrace of the Intercontinental, eating well and drinking a Mai Thai, the Hawaiian fruit cocktail, as the sun went down. Then the stars came out and the palms stood out against the dark blue background of the night.

On 2 April we drove up the huge crater mountain, 3,000 metres in 90 minutes from sea level to the top. Having arrived there one first of all passes through eucalyptus woods, then through meadows reminiscent of upper Bavaria, with the appropriate grazing cows. Then comes a kind of mountain moorland, and finally the grey fields of lava. The clouds boiled beneath, and at the top there was a very cold wind. The crater is so huge that the whole of Manhattan could fit into it. From above the volcano on Hawaii could also be seen.

Apart from that we did nothing special. At all events I cannot remember whether I read anything or how many letters I wrote. Our sparse postcards undoubtedly became sparser and sparser in content. In other words, we recuperated and gathered up our strength for 'the long walk' to China.

Singapore Airlines flew direct from Honolulu to Hong Kong, though unfortunately at four o'clock in the morning. The eleven-hour flight over the Pacific seemed utterly endless. Luckily, we could both sleep a little. We skipped a day in the calendar and reached Hong Kong on Sunday morning, 4 May. The aircraft circled round adventurously between mountains and skyscrapers, and finally landed in the old airport in the centre of the city. In the Hong Kong hotel we had booked a room 'with harbour view', and the outlook over Victoria, the ships in the harbour and the bustling ferries plying backwards and forwards, was breathtaking. One could sit for hours at the window and look out. In the streets it was tropically close and the air was polluted by the traffic. On Monday, 5 May, Dr Peter Lee of the Tao Fong Shan Ecumenical Centre collected me for a lecture which I had agreed to give.[1] We drove to Shatin, New Territories, a satellite town with high-rise buildings of 20 and 30 storeys. In spite of Hong Kong's return to China in 1999, milliards are being invested here, not only in housing and industry, but in the universities too. The next day it rained. We celebrated Jonas's first birthday with 'high tea' in the old English colonial hotel Peninsula, with at least as much style as in St Andrews, where Elisabeth had developed a taste for it. But then we were overtaken—or at least I was—by a compulsive shopping spree. We bought lamps and furniture, kimonos and cameras, even a portable electric typewriter. Luckily, we could send cases home by way of my brother's air-freight office, as we had already done in Atlanta and San Francisco.

On Tuesday the Kuoni party from Zurich appeared—the group with which we were going to tour China. Our individual liberty was at an end, and for the next three weeks Kuoni group socialism took possession of us, and was as hard to bear as China's 'socialism as it really exists', which is what we had set out to visit. We left Hong Kong on 7 May with the train and jogged unhurriedly to Canton. Once we had left the hyper-modern world of Hong Kong behind, we found ourselves in the prehistoric era. People were working in the rice fields as they had done thousands of years before, led around their water buffalos, and looked after their little villages under the palm trees. There were no more cars and no agricultural machinery, only people, people, people, with untold diligent hands. In the train the backs of the seats were furnished with lace antimacassars in true socialist fashion. Everyone had his glass, and the guard came and poured in hot water for the green tea. We had made it. We were in China.

Across China—1986 and Later

In Canton we were lodged in an extravagant luxury hotel which had been built for visitors from the West and for the industrial fair. In the evening there were Cantonese specialities in an exclusive restaurant. The high spot was a whole sucking pig, but we only ate small slices of the crackling. On the first day we visited the Buddhist temple in the centre of the city. It had just been restored after the ravages of the cultural revolution, and worshippers, women and a few young monks, were prostrating themselves in prayer. In a lesser temple I discovered the quite realistic statue of the ninth-century sixth Chinese Buddhist master. In 1986 the city was for us a real cultural shock: all the streets were thronged with people, while on every footpath people were hammering, washing, cooking, eating, and bargaining. All the houses and trees were hung with washing. In place of cars, the bicycle dominated the traffic. The 'free market' offered a wide variety of vegetables; meat, with flies buzzing round it; living, twitching toads; rotten eggs; young turtles; dead rats; and other delicacies. 'The

Chinese,' we were told by the Chinese themselves, 'eat everything that crawls, creeps or flies.'

The next day we flew to Guilin in the province of Guangxi, the garden city in the karst mountains with their improbable formations, an attraction for many Chinese painters. We sailed for a whole day on the Li River with a pleasure steamer through this wonder world. The river lay peacefully in the quiet of the morning; peasants fished with the help of chained cormorants, and in the villages along the banks, girls fetched water from the river, while the Chinese cargo boats glided lazily along: an oasis of tranquillity in a hectic world. But at the end of the tour we were greeted by a village with noisy markets designed for tourists. On the evening of the third day, we joined the train that was to take us to Wuhan, a 17-hour journey. Since the temperature was well up in the 80s, we had to keep the window open, the result being an enormous draught, so that the next morning Elisabeth had a temperature. Luckily there was a Chinese doctor, a general practitioner, in the high-rise hotel in Wuhan, direct on the Yangtze Kiang; he helped her with gentle pills and gave her a soothing head massage.

On 13 May we joined the river boat which was to take us up the Yangtze to Chungking, a journey of five days and four nights. This was the high spot of the whole journey. At first I had been afraid that a boat trip of this kind would be bound to be deadly boring, but it proved to be a poem, not to say a Chinese epic. The outside cabin was roomy, and one could watch the banks slipping by as one lay. Admittedly, for two days we travelled through a flat countryside, the dykes right and left stretching away monotonously. People sunned themselves on deck and took photographs of each other. But then at three o'clock in the morning we passed through the great Yangtze lock and entered the fantastic Yangtze gorges. All the passengers sat or stood at the rail and gazed in astonishment. The most monstrous cliffs closed in and pushed themselves apart again. Charming villages and towns set on projecting rocks lined the banks. Every patch of earth right up the cliff was cultivated. Fishermen sat on the bank in the cool of the morning. There were hardly any ships. At every bend one wanted to cry out, Stop! It's too beautiful! Luckily, the ship's microphone talked about the stretches which were not so interesting; otherwise we would have forgotten to eat and would have starved in the midst of all this beauty. In Siboazhai we visited a pagoda, which leaned against a steep cliff. But otherwise we let China glide past us—the beautiful, romantic China preserved in so many scroll paintings—and were totally absorbed in the sight. On the morning of 17 May we arrived in Chungking, the city on the rocks, high above the Yangtze.

This was 'the Chungking hell' already described by Han Suyin, the well-known Chinese writer, this over-populated, clammy-hot, and unhealthy city. More than six million people thronged the narrow mountain alleyways. The air stagnates in this deep basin, and the smell is indescribable. We had been warned by Kuoni about the 'modest hotel' in which we were to be put up. But the hotel was not in the city; it was 40 kilometres away, in a deep valley with a tropical forest, and it was not a hotel at all but a camp made up of huts, which was used to train party functionaries. It rained torrentially. We lay on the plank beds, there being no mattresses, and restricted ourselves to breathing, otherwise not moving our limbs at all. The food was indefinable. We were glad when morning dawned.

At the Shanghai airport we were met by German industry, for Volkswagen and Siemens had branches there. Whole streets had often been dug up, and in the city throngs of people jostled one another. One member of our party, a Swiss, asked anxiously if we had now seen half the Chinese. But it was only a fraction. In Shanghai the wheeled traffic often breaks down altogether, and so does the pedestrian traffic whenever ten thousand people from one side of the street and ten thousand people from the other side meet in the middle. The broad harbour promenade reminded me of Hamburg. At night we were put up in 'the government guesthouse' and slept well again in the wide beds. Unfortunately, we had to make much too early a start the next morning. The train to Wuxi left at eight o'clock, and we had to leave the hotel at 6.30.

Wuxi is beautifully situated. It is crossed by the Imperial Canal and its side canals and lies on the great Taihu Lake. After we had viewed porcelain factories, a silk farm and a farmhouse, we were put up in the beautiful hotel on the bank of the lake, and in the evening wandered through a winding Chinese park with a great many lotus pools and pavilions. The next morning a boat took us to the famous 'three floating islands' and to the 'turtle hill'. The Taihu Lake is bigger than Lake Constance. It is bordered by gentle hills and by pavilions, temples, and pagodas with soaring roofs. And the little cargo ships sail in and out of Wuxi as if in a procession.

Nanking was another high spot of our journey, because I had accepted a long-standing invitation from Bishop Ting to give a lecture in his theological seminary. For the first time we really came together with Chinese people. But when we were still in the foyer of the fabulous Golden Tower Hotel, I already fell into the hands of a group of American theologians and church people, who recognized me. It was a delegation of the National Christian Council, who had more or less invited themselves to Nanking and had then tried to invite Chinese pastors and theologians to their conference in the luxury hotel.

I sat next to Bishop Ting and immediately fell into interesting conversation with him. The next day we let our Kuoni group go off on their own, while we were fetched in a car and taken to Bishop Ting's seminar. What we experienced and saw there was truly astonishing. After long and intensive missionary endeavours during the nineteenth century, in 1949, when the revolution triumphed, there were about 700,000 Protestant Christians in China belonging to countless denominations. The Communists expelled the foreign missionaries and cut off all foreign influence. They were helped by the earlier Three-Self Patriotic Movement (Dr Wu and other Christians). With the patriotic principles 'self-sustaining, self-governing, self-propagating', the Chinese church stood on its own (that is to say, Chinese) feet. There were no more 'rice Christians'. It was no longer possible to say 'one Christian more—one Chinese less'. The barbarism of the Cultural Revolution meant severe persecution for the Christian congregations too. All the churches were closed and used for other purposes. All the pastors were taken to the country and subjected to forced labour. Many leading Christians were publicly disgraced and thrown into prison, many of them dying from their ill treatment. We heard stories of individual fates that were very moving, but they were told without bitterness and accusation. Bishop Ting's own sons went to the 'Red Guard', and the seminary building became the headquarters of the Red Guard of Nanking. And yet the older, ill-treated people talked only about their misled children, a sovereign attitude which greatly impressed us.

Because the Band of Four persecuted Christians with particular rigour, the Christians who had survived in house churches were particularly highly thought of after 1976, when the Cultural Revolution came to an end. Now, for the first time in its history, Christianity had become a purely Chinese possibility. Since 1975 the church in China has undergone a real resurrection. Four thousand new churches were built by the congregations, and there are numerous theological seminaries. The one in Nanking is the largest and has 180 students. It was calculated that there were about 4 to 6 million Protestant Christians in 1986, and in 2006 about 60 million.

It is thanks not least to the Three-Self Patriotic Movement that the Protestant church in China has overcome the denominational divisions we know in the West. These no longer exist, and all foreign missions that reintroduce them are forbidden. In this connection Bishop Ting lamented the visits of American Mormons. The church in China exists in the local congregations. The 'little flock' movement and the 'Yellers' are strictly congregationalist in their orientation and are suspicious of any supra-congregational church bodies. The loosely organized Chinese Council therefore does not wish to join the World Council of Churches either. For one thing, there are not enough qualified people who could be sent to the many ecumenical conferences. Nor is any importance attached to the theories of clever people who no longer have any contact with their own grass roots. Moreover, there is no wish to expose the church in China to the influence of the denominational divisions of Western Christendom again. I heard this criticism for the first time and found it entirely convincing. Christians in China need only one thing from the West: to be left in peace, and no longer to be 'over-visited'.

The seminary's difficulty is that for more than 12 years there was no theological training. Most of the professors are very old, and young ones are only slowly coming to take their place. In 1985 the first students graduated. The Chinese church has a catechism of its own, and a small press; and the first theological yearbook has just appeared.

We remained in the seminary until the late afternoon and then, in spite of the time, were quickly driven to the museum of the Taiping revolution and to the glorious street of tombs of the Ming emperors. Nanking is a beautiful city. It is crossed by broad avenues of plane trees and cedars, the houses and temples are well looked after, and the charm of the old imperial capital makes itself felt.

From Nanking we flew to Xian, China's oldest imperial city, from which, between 230 and 221 BCE, the famous—and for his cruelty notorious—Qin Shihuangdi unified and centralized China. The central Chinese city is still surrounded by a high rectangular city wall, with gates on the east, west, north, and south sides. In the centre are the typical high old towers, the bell tower and drum tower, from which the hours used to be announced. The modern Golden Flower Hotel, which is under Swedish management, is situated a little outside, and its glass façade stands out in glaring disharmony with the city. At its fence people continually stopped in order to admire this Western horror. Its only purpose is to minister to the tourists, who come to Xian simply in order to marvel over the terracotta army of China's first great emperor. This was discovered in 1979 and lies 30 kilometres away from Xian.

We visited the great Wild Goose pagoda, which was the centre of Buddhism in China in the seventh century. From here a monk set out and spent 12 years collecting and studying the Buddhist writings in India, for which his emperor built this glorious pagoda. We found beautiful Buddha statues and discovered the Yin-Yang sign on the temple. In 1986 we still saw with horror a number of old women limping on sticks because their feet had been bound in childhood and were completely crippled. In Peking we saw others to whom the same thing had been done. One shivers when one sees these traces of patriarchal cruelty with one's own eyes. We walked through the narrow alleys to the twelfth-century mosque, which was built in the style of a Chinese temple. Xian was the beginning of the famous Silk Road, so there were many lodgings for foreigners. The mosque is a harmonious complex of beautiful buildings. Ancient steles with Arabic and Persian script are to be seen everywhere. There were a number of Christian churches here, too, and one stele in the city museum is adorned with the Nestorian cross. The seminary in Nanking has a copy in its chapel.

In Peking the luxury Great Wall Hotel (which belongs to the American Sheraton chain) took us in. Here, too, the West flaunts itself in chromium and glass. But since the hotel was only open to Western visitors, no one was particularly impressed. The next day we drove to the real Great Wall. The closer we came, the more buses converged. When we arrived, the famous wall was once again being stormed by the masses: 10,000 were on the wall itself; 10,000 were waiting at the bottom. All the same, it is an imposing structure, which runs from mountain peak to mountain peak. It probably impressed the barbarians more than it really kept them out. The Qin emperor from Xian had it built by forced labour. Millions worked on it, and hundreds of thousands died during the building. We also visited the beautiful tomb of the Ming emperor: a round mausoleum on a square base, symbolizing the round heavens on the rectangular earth. This emperor also made provision for life after death and had a subterranean cathedral built for himself. The street lined with animals and ministers leads to the imperial tombs in the valleys round about and is reminiscent of the Egyptian Luxor. In the evening we spent an hour at the Peking opera, to us a strange artistic spectacle.

We visited the emperor's palace twice. The Gate of Heavenly Peace leads to the halls of Supreme, Medium, and Heavenly Harmony. This harmony is the mark of the whole conception. Everything corresponds—left and right, height and breadth, walls and roofs—and everything is laid out with geometrical precision. In the layout of this palace, the style shows no history, nor are there any abrupt changes of style; there is only a harmony unified to the point of monotony. Until the 1920s it was here that the emperors and empresses of China received foreign delegations in a prescribed ceremony, which included the kowtow of the guests. It was here that the highest state examinations were held. It was from here that the 'Middle Kingdom', the greatest and most populated country of the world, was ruled. The visitor is struck by the wide periphery of this centre, but even more impressive are the Temple of Heaven, the Temple of Agriculture, and the Altar of Heaven. This complex lies in the south city. Here the scene is dominated by the circle and the number three. The temple rises on three steps with three curved roofs, a formation of complete (Trinitarian) harmony. The Altar of Heaven consists of three times three flights of steps, nine steps in each flight, with nine tiles or stones on each. In the centre is the stone on which at New Year the emperor had to render to heaven an account of the past year. The echo is so cunningly contrived that it was not only heaven that could hear it.

Here it became clear that the Chinese emperor was responsible to heaven not only for the culture of his people, but also for nature on the earth that was his. He was also China's high priest, praying for the harvest and in spring ploughing the symbolical eight furrows: a truly ecological emperor. In the West, in contrast, the separation between church and state divided the functions of priest and emperor. Now the emperor was responsible only for the political welfare of the country, while the church cared for its religious salvation. Nature was left out altogether.

Anyone who comes to China for the first time knows afterwards that he or she at best still knows nothing. Our picture of China, the one passed on to us by Pearl Buck, Confucius, and the book *Tao te King*, was permanently changed. The religion, philosophy, and culture of 'equilibrium', of Yin and Yang, heaven and earth, civilization and nature, can hardly be detected any more. Instead we were everywhere confronted by the Western faith in progress, imported via Marx and socialism: China was 'backward', then came 'the great leap forward'—the industrialization and, today, the 'modernization' of China. What now dominates the mind of China and moulds its life is no longer 'the heavenly harmony' but modern ideas of 'progress', no longer the rhythms of 'nature' but the purposeful goal of 'history'. The industrial pollution of the atmosphere in the mass cities, of the water in the rivers (which are the arteries of the country's life), and of the soil is rapidly increasing. It is true that in China nature is almost boundlessly fertile—two and more harvests per year are the norm—and also endlessly patient; but even here there are 'limits of growth'.

One waits for the time when the Chinese will rediscover the wisdom of the 'Tao' of nature and when 'progress' and 'equilibrium', civilization and nature, will once more be reconciled.[2] It is paradoxical but true that whereas in the West the harmony of 'Tao te King', with its ecological wisdom, is being rediscovered, China's enthusiasm is concentrated on the faith in progress to be found in Karl Marx and Adam Smith. In 1986 we came back from China not endorsed in our views of the country but changed. Almost everything was—quite different. But that was precisely the fascinating thing, and that was why we have returned to China again and again.

In 1997 our oldest grandson, Jonas, suddenly stood in front of me and said, 'Granddad, I want to go to China with you.' So we studied the travel literature and found an attractive, eight-day journey to Peking. I took Jonas's mother, Susanne, with us so that I would not be alone with the 14-year-old. In China I admired the progress that had been made since 1986, but in the parks hairdressers were still cutting hair on chairs set up in the open air, and palm-readers were still telling fortunes. One day I left the group and gave a lecture in Peking University among the philosophers on 'The Change of Values in the West'. I no longer heard anything about Marx or Mao, but found only a great searching and questioning.

Because things went so well with daughter and grandson, and because they were so enthusiastic, we toured the country once more in 1999. The Sino-Christian Institute in Hong Kong had co-ordinated my lectures in such a way that they fitted in exactly with our projected tour. We began by sailing round the Hong Kong islands in a junk—and I gave my first lecture. By way of Guilin and the continually fascinating trip on the Li River, we arrived in Xian. The tour sought out the famous terracotta army—and

I talked to the philosophers. We repeated this in Shanghai and Peking. Grandson and daughter were well occupied with sightseeing, and I was kept busy with lectures. Mao had generously set up chairs in all the philosophical faculties in order to disseminate 'ML' (Marxist-Leninism). After Mao's fall, however, this state ideology was no longer so much in demand. There are still obligatory courses in Marxism, but the other philosophers must look for a place in other subjects, and there are courses in Western thought, Confucianism, Buddhism, and Christianity. So anyone who looks for Christian theology in Chinese universities will find it in the philosophy faculty. One question that was often put to me was, Can one study theology if one is not a Christian? I always replied in the affirmative. After all, centuries ago the Chinese also studied Buddhist literature before they became Buddhists. People talk about 'literature Christians', meaning intellectuals who have arrived at Christian faith through Western literature and theology, but who seldom have any ties with the local Christian congregations, because these are always made up of poor and uneducated people. Our grandson Jonas was again so much impressed by the Chinese world that he wanted to study computer science and sinology. Since he is very blond, the Chinese girls found him attractive. They came and wanted to stroke his hair, which was not always to his liking.

I had already got to know the Sino-Christian Institute in Hong Kong on our first journey to China. There people were beginning to translate Christian literature for China. Consequently, some of my books were available in China. The first was *The Crucified God*, and it was followed by *God in Creation*, and so on. The books were always first printed in Hong Kong in complex Chinese characters, and then in Shanghai in a simpler Chinese script. I was fortunate enough to find an excellent translator in Tübingen in the theology student Thomas Tseng. He comes from Taiwan and intends to go back there. With his help, ten of my books are now available in Chinese.

Daniel Yeung of the Institute urged me to come to China for a time as visiting professor, but I felt that I was already too old. So a compact seminar for professors and graduate students was arranged in the famous Ching Yuan University in Peking, and we flew there in October 2004. Elisabeth had accepted lectures in Peking University and at the Academy of Social Science. We stayed in the venerable Peking Hotel, right by the imperial palace, and enjoyed whatever was left of the imperial splendour. My graduate student Lin Hong-Hsin came over from Taipeh to translate. Daniel Yeung came from Hong Kong and showed us round, always taking us to the best restaurants. Whereas in 1986 a student had come to me at the end of my lecture and had only whispered, 'I am a Christian,' Christianity and theology were now publicly recognized and discussed, and we were received with great goodwill. Of course, in Christianity people were looking for the religious secret of the Western world with its scientific-technological progress, but anti-modern, fundamentalist missionary theology had not been forgotten either. Because Marxist ideology evidently now offers little stimulus to the modern Chinese world, and since pure capitalism also lends life no meaning, reflective intellectuals are questioning further. I offered them the philosophy and theology of hope, but then came back to the ecological wisdom of their own Tao Te Ching, in order to combine the scientific progress of modernity with the wisdom of life and practical reason. But I undoubtedly sensed that in Chinese thinking the dimension 'future' is not so strongly anchored as it is in the West, which has learnt to read life through the Bible. Ever since Confucius, the ancestor cult not only has dominated the relationship to a person's forefathers, but is also the foundation of a thinking in terms of origin which dominates everything. Many people give themselves up pragmatically to modern, Western thinking, but not to its visions of the future, such as the humanity of human rights, the realm of freedom and eternal peace, the consummation of creation, and the kingdom of God.

In October 2004 we spent ten days in Peking. Where 20 years earlier millions of cyclists had dominated the streets, now thousands of cars travelled on new city motorways and caused an appalling traffic chaos from morning to evening. High-rise buildings with fantastic roofs had pushed out the old hutongs. Wonderful flowers grew along the city motorways, but the air was poisoned. The whole progress of the modern world seems to have become concentrated in Peking and Shanghai. We again visited the beautiful Tao Temple, sat reflectively on the Behai island, and as a farewell bought a beautiful old Kwanjin statue in Lungshan Street. If I were young again, I would found a theological centre in the university quarter of Peking, in order to establish 'the principle of hope' there.

Finally, what is China without Taiwan, or Taiwan without China? Through Thomas Tseng and the philosophy professor Luh, I made contact with the Chung Yuan Christian University in Chung-Li, an hour south of

Taipeh. They invited me to a conference in 2002 on 'my thinking', with twelve Chinese scholars. These memorable meetings took place in November. The participants came from the United States and Hong Kong and from many parts of Taiwan. I replied to each contribution as best I could. Since this was one of the first encounters between European and Chinese theology and philosophy, we then issued two publications, one in Germany, the other in Chinese in Hong Kong. Apparently the meetings were so well received that Elisabeth and I were invited to the fiftieth anniversary of the university in 2005, and I was made an honorary Doctor of Science. I received the honour, with cap and hood, together with the genetic scientist Craig Venter and the star architect Meinhard von Gerkhan. We had taken our daughter Anne-Ruth with us. With Elisabeth and me she visited the tallest tower in the world, '101', in Taipeh, and the Taroko Gorge (which had unfortunately suffered somewhat from a typhoon), and conversed industriously at the completely endless Chinese dinner parties.

Taiwan exists at present in a curious state of suspension, and this can be sensed everywhere: diplomatically no longer recognized, economically remarkably successful, threatened by China with military intervention, and not securely protected by the USA, many of its people are emigrating to America, have a second passport, or, poised to leave, are there to earn money. It is only slowly that there is coming to be a general conviction that something must be done to renovate the city and protect the environment, if long-term living in Taiwan is to be possible. The Chung Yuan University has its sights set on remaining, and that means being pledged to the future of life in Taiwan. This roused our admiration and won our support.

TWENTY-FOUR

GOD—HIS AND HERS

Joint Theology with Elisabeth

My Parents Die—the Children Leave Home: The House Is Empty

In the 1980s my life changed radically. My parents died, and our children grew up and went their own ways. The house was empty and life became quiet. But in a new way Elisabeth and I found a joint task. Masculine and feminist theology, in spite of their own particular characters, became a 'joint theology'. We began to develop joint lectures and to learn to talk about God as a woman and a man, with mutual respect and sufficient self-respect. That goes beyond the old, traditional theology and the new feminist theology, and anticipates a future of which at present we can still see but little.

But first I should like to talk personally about my experiences with the death of my father and mother. My father died very suddenly, after a heart attack, on 16 July 1982 in Hamburg. He was 85 years old. Four years earlier, my parents had had to give up the house that they had built in 1928 with their own work and much sacrifice, and had moved into a one-room apartment in an old people's home. They gave up gracefully and without fuss what had made up their lives for 50 years. When I wanted to encourage my father, and told him that in this home he would have a new life without worries, he waved me aside with cheerful irony: 'One life is enough for me.' He had a feeling for the proper time. Difficult though it was, I took his funeral in Volksdorf and preached at it. I had to struggle with my tears, but I felt that it was my duty as his son.

Shortly after he died I wrote down my thoughts: 'Father, you died two weeks ago. With Mummy I visited you afterwards and saw your body.

Father, where are you? Up to now for me you were a matter of course. I knew you were in Hamburg, that you were sitting at your writing desk, smoking a cigarette and pondering. I knew that you were becoming older, feebler and quieter. But you were there, always there, reliable, unnoticeable and always attentive: my father. Now I can't find you there any more, but you haven't gone away and disappeared. You are more present to me than ever you were—present everywhere, you have escaped from limited space and restricted time. You are looking over my shoulder, kindly and critically as always. When I think of you I see you before me, not just as you were in old age but as you were when you were at the height of your strength, as you were when I was a small child, when I rode on your shoulders and put my hands over your eyes, and also as you were as a young man, when you went to the war in 1914 as a 17-year-old, as I did too in 1944; and I see you, too, as a child, as you played alone with building blocks and draughts or checkers and forgot the world, as you so often did. I hear you, I see you, I feel your nearness. Did you go away from me so that you could come to me now in this way? You died bodily so as to be beside us in spirit.'

It is the miracle of this transformation of the dead which I experienced so intensively after my father's death. But it is not only consoling. It is demanding, too, for whenever we four brothers and sisters meet, we discuss our father and wrestle with the way he brought us up, as if he were present among us and listening to us.

The dead are not 'dead', far away and without any further meaning, so that they can be quickly forgotten. They are beside us and in us, and our life is a continual dialogue with them. We live in their past, which is now present, and they exist in our present. We live with what the dead owe us and with what we owe them. We exist in the space of their blessing, their unforgotten suffering, and their unforgiven guilt. Their light and their shadow are part of our lives. It was only later that I came to understand that better, when I studied the ancestor cults in Asia, in Korea, on Okinawa, and in China.[1] The modern shutting out of the dead from the lives of those who come after makes their presence at most silent, but does not do away with it. In America, the first name is everything, and the family name is quickly dropped. But in Asia the family name is more important than the personal first name. The name invokes not just a single person, but a life-history as well. Every individual life is embedded in the life of the family, and does the family name credit or disgraces it. The individualism of the modern world certainly brings freedom from family ties, but it also destroys the wider network of life and abbreviates life to the individual's own particular time, without past and without future.

My mother died on 3 November 1987, after she had lived alone for five years in the one-room apartment in the old people's home. Fortunately, my sister Marianne lived close by, so she was not isolated. But these years were hard for her because my father had really made all the decisions in their lives. I couldn't take my mother's funeral. She was too close. So I only took part in the funeral. The day before, I baptized our second grandson, Christoph. Dying and being born again were very close to each other in these days.

My mother was my first great love. Perhaps as son I was something like the light of her eyes. At all events I grew up in a special mother-son relationship. It did me good and astonishingly enough never made me dependent in any way. I didn't cling, and my mother didn't cling either. When my father was called up in 1939, I was 13 years old and gladly took over some of the things he had done, shopped, looked after the garden, felt responsible for my little sister and brother, and turned from being a playful child into a little adult. My mother was the first woman whom I perceived as woman, when as a small child, after a bath, she rubbed my head dry, cuddled me, or went for walks with me on which we invented stories full of fantasy. She was my goddess, and occasionally I was something like her little hero. Looking back, I realize that she was probably also the image I was unconsciously looking for when later I fell in love and married. But that is probably true of every boy who has experienced a profound motherly love. In the case of my mother, I had no problems with her death. She was, and is, present to me, as if it were a matter of course, in everything I experience and do, like a great basic trust.

When parents are no longer there, there is no one ahead of one any more. When one looks ahead to death, one is lonelier and more unprotected. There is no longer any fatherly and motherly care; one is oneself only a father or mother who has to care for children and grandchildren. One is next in the sequence of the generations, and next time it is one's own turn. That is an unusual experience. One moves into a position for which one has not prepared oneself. For so many years my father was the family 'patriarch' and made all the birthday speeches. My mother was the warm-hearted, sympathetic, and encouraging mother of the family. But now I had to take over these roles, or at least some of them—bless newly born grandchildren, perform the wedding when children marry, and bury the dead in the family. This family responsibility was not to my liking; it ran counter to my fundamental drive for liberty. But what could I do? The generation contract demands it, and it is good and right that this should be so. This is what one has received—this is what one has to pass on.

When we moved into our new house in Tübingen in 1975, we had furnished a room for each of our four children. The family was still complete. But then the daughters finished their schooling one after another and went off to the university. First Susanne went to Freiburg, and only seldom appeared, because there were certain friends there; then Anne-Ruth left home and went away as far as it was possible to go—to Kiel, the remotest of the German universities; Esther studied in Hohenheim near Stuttgart, but of course wanted to live by herself in a student's room. Friederike studied in Berlin and Munich and then in 1987 moved to Amherst, before finally going to MIT in Boston to study linguistics with Noam Chomski and to do her doctorate under him. And with this our house was empty. For a while we kept the children's rooms free, hoping they would occasionally come back, and so that they could feel at home somewhere in the world; but three of them married and then only came 'on visits'. Often in the evenings I went through the empty rooms which had once been so full of life, and even today I still have withdrawal symptoms. I realized that I had depended on them much more, and was more accustomed to their presence (even if it was not always a quiet presence), than I had been aware of. It was not so much the feeling of a 'childless father'; it was more the feeling of a friendship that one could no longer live with and experience close by, but only at a distance.

It Began in Sheffield in 1981

In the summer of 1980 the Revd Con Parvey telephoned from the World Council of Churches in Geneva and asked whether Elisabeth and I would be prepared to give a joint opening lecture at the ecumenical conference in Sheffield in July 1981. The subject was to be 'Becoming Human in a New Community of Women and Men'. We had never done anything of the kind before, and after all there were better-known theologian couples in the ecumenical community—Annemarie and Joos Aargard in Denmark, for instance, or Dorothee Sölle and Fulbert Steffensky in Hamburg. But Con Parvey was insistent, and so nothing was left to us but to make the attempt.[2]

Ever since 1974 Elisabeth had developed her own feminist theology and had spoken together with other feminist theologians at large congresses, for example, in Berlin and Brussels. She had given feminist Bible studies at the German Protestant lay assemblies (*Kirchentage*) with an excellent response and had published very successful books about human rights for women and about the women round Jesus.[3] With my theology of hope, my theology of the cross, and my doctrine of the Trinity, I was not specially in demand in this new camp of feminist theology—on the contrary: ever since Dorothee Sölle had stigmatized my *Crucified God* as 'sadistic', I counted rather as bogeyman in the circles of the new feminist theology. Elisabeth often had to suffer under this criticism of me. She has described that in some detail, so I need not go into it here.[4] I myself could follow her with sympathy and curiosity along the new paths of feminist theology, but as a man I was of course always still 'an outsider'. Because, being in the same house, I was the 'male theologian' closest at hand, I often even served as 'type of male thinking' and representative of dominating theology, reproaches which I gladly accepted, with readiness to learn.

So what should we be letting ourselves in for, if we were to produce a joint theological lecture in the name of 'the new community of women and men'? Because from our youth onwards neither of us had been disinclined to undertake adventures, we decided to take a leap onto the thin ice. A long and not always easy discussion process was needed before we were able to produce the joint lecture. We tried to find statements we could make in common, with respect for each other while preserving our self-respect. But the situation was undoubtedly asymmetrical: on the one hand, a new theological movement, with enthusiasm and wonderful new discoveries, a new plant with unexpected blossoms; on the other, an ancient tree with a patriarchal tradition stretching back two thousand years and with the weight of many great names; on the one hand, feminist theology, on the other, traditional theology. We tried to shape the encounter as a confrontation, as a dialogue, and as a common witness to Christ, as an alteration of mainstream theology, our aim being to serve ecumenically a new, non-hierarchical, egalitarian community of men and women in Christianity, in line with Galatians 3.28. What did we want? At that time we wrote the following:

> A process of new thought, related to life, is taking place today in feminist theology. Unfortunately, in many circles in the church and theology, feminist theology is still feared, because it seems to conjure up images of 'man' or 'patriarchy' as enemies. There is no doubt that in fact in many instances there is reason for this fear. We therefore feel it all the more important to point out differences between women and men which are not to be seen as oppositions. Dualistic thought—thinking in exclusive opposites—has a fatal tradition in Christianity. It is still difficult for us to perceive the wealth of distinctions and differences, because the certainty of faith usually thinks that it has to entrench itself behind rigid dogmas. Nor is feminist theology by any means free of absolutist claims. That makes us feel it all the more necessary to turn the distinctive approach of feminism into an interconnected way of thinking and to take cautious steps towards a dialogue which takes our differences seriously. The power of patriarchal structures which women keep experiencing in the church and theology will not be removed by that alone. But it can be made more evident, and the painful way to justice in the church and society can be straightened out. The reciprocal recognition of human justice and human dignity in the structures of the church and also in theological statements will ultimately be the only basis on which the church can become a community of women and men.[5]

The conference in Sheffield was marked by the feeling that this was a new departure. Even the head of the Church of England, Archbishop Runcie, felt that, and thought about the ordination of women, which then only became possible under his successor. Philip Potter gave a powerful meditation on Galatians 3.28, and in the evening we sat among self-confident younger women and tried in interviews to demonstrate the liberation of women and men for a new community with equal rights. 'You two are making history with a theological dialogue such as this,' Catharina Halkes wrote to Elisabeth. We went back feeling good about the conference; but it was after all only a beginning, and what was to come was by no means already a harmonious 'community of men and women', but a multiplicity of conflicts, anxieties, and conservative reactions.[6]

Thematically, our attempt to find a new, joint theology began with the feminist analyses of the patriarchy, as a cultural form going back thousands of years, as a masculine way of thinking, and as an authoritarian theology rooted in the picture of God. This patriarchalism was not invented by Christianity, but early Christianity adapted itself to this culture, its legal system and ways of thinking in the Roman Empire. It is easy to see the chain of legitimation: from God the Father to the Father of his country, to the pope as father of the church, to the father of the family. God was thought of in masculine terms as king, judge, lord, and authority, and men took their bearings from this picture. With this, the lower place assigned to women was predestined. These archaic structures of superiority and subordination in God and world, heaven and earth, soul and body—and man and woman—reach right down to the modern *Church Dogmatics* of Karl Barth. For, according to Barth, the super-ordination and subordination of the commanding father and the obedient son are already to be found in God.[7] But Christian feminist theology assumes that this was not so, and should not be so, in the fellowship of Jesus with women and men. For this theology, the feminist movement for the dignity and human rights of the woman is based on the gospel. It therefore aims at nothing less than a reformation of the church of Jesus, and of Christian theology, in the name of the original gospel.

In the years immediately following 1980, I was busy with the 'new Trinitarian thinking', whose purpose is to overcome the monarchical monotheism of the 'Lord God' in Christian theology in favour of the insight that God is a 'God of community', with a wealth of relationships. 'Is God a man?' asked critical women at that time. My answer was not, 'God is both man and woman,' or 'God is neither man nor women,' but "God is a wonderful community." That is what is brought out by the expression 'the triune God'. It is not the individual Persons who can be reflected in the human world; it is the mutual relationships in God, as John 17.21 says: 'That they may all be one, even as thou, Father, art in me, and I in thee, that they also may be in us.' That 'even as' of the resonance of the divine in the human refers exclusively to the mutual 'indwellings' of the Father and the Son. Through the feministic thinking in relationships and networks of relationships, I was prompted to put the ancient idea of *perichoresis* in the foreground of the doctrine of the Trinity.

With the help of my graduate student Mathias Meyer, who comes from the Moravian Brethren, we then discovered the age-old Christian tradition about *the motherly ministry of the Holy Spirit*.[8] The Syrian Fathers already saw the Holy Spirit and its efficacy as feminine: the Spirit comforts as a mother comforts, and those who are born again are born out of the motherly Spirit of God. When the community of brothers and sisters was founded in Bethlehem, Pennsylvania, Count Zinzendorf solemnly proclaimed in 1741 'the motherly ministry of the Holy Spirit' as a congregational doctrine. He was sensitive enough to write later that it was not right for him to have proclaimed this; a sister should have done it. In the little chapel in Urschalling in Bavaria, women discovered a picture of the Trinity with the Spirit as woman between the Father and the Son. Certainly these are hints of the varied wealth of Christian traditions, which cannot be reduced to God as Lord and Father, but they do not mean that the concern of feminist theology is an integral part of the tradition of the mainline churches. Nothing about the patriarchal papacy changed just because Pope John Paul I once talked about God 'our Father and our Mother'. The whole hierarchical, authoritarian system and the way of thinking has to be changed.

Oppression always has two sides: on the one hand the master, on the other the slave; on the one hand the ruling man, on the other the serving woman. But oppressions of this kind destroy humanity on both sides. The oppressed are robbed of their human dignity, and the oppressors lose their humanity. Both are alienated from their true being; it is just that the one side suffers under the fact, while the other side is quite content with the situation. But if the oppressors were also to recognize themselves for what they are, they would discover how much their dominating position cheats them of their true human happiness. How are children brought up to be 'men'? In my generation the process was undoubtedly extreme. We were turned into soldiers in order to die for our country as sacrificial victims. In other generations, too, boys are brought up to be men after the pattern of their fathers. They have to learn to control themselves in order one day to be able to control others. For this they are made to live in constant fear of being a nonentity, who 'has to make something of himself'. The patriarchy halved the man and elevated him into a determining subject of understanding and will (with which he had to identify himself), and degraded him to an object of heart, feeling, and needs (from which he had to detach himself). This distorted relationship to himself was then reflected in his distorted relationship to the woman and to nature. When today women set out to break out of the roles assigned to them in the patriarchy and to 'be persons in their own right', men are also freed to shake off the repressions assigned to them, which cut them off from true life, and are able to become true human beings. The way to a 'new community of women and men' is still a long journey, for men too. At that time I wrote, 'The master in the man must die so that the brother prepared for open friendship can be born.'[9] This sentence from the Sheffield Report was often quoted.

Finally, in contrast to an authoritarian theology 'from above', the new feminist theology presents itself emphatically as a theology of experience 'from below'. It discovered in the divine Spirit the source of life and the fullness of life's energies. The feminists liked to talk about the Holy Spirit as feminine. This in itself counted in episcopal circles as 'enthusiastic and sentimental'. In order to combat such 'speculations', the Western church had already, long before, inserted into the Nicene Creed the *filioque* to describe the procession of the Holy Spirit, putting it at the end of the Christology. Then the Holy Spirit is nothing other than the subjective efficacy of the objective Word of God: the objective Word of God is the person Jesus Christ; the person Christ is the Son of God, the Father. In this sequence the Spirit proceeds from Christ, and Christ from God. So the Spirit is always only the third person of the Trinity in heaven, and in the Church the 'spiritual' leader—priest, pastor, or minister—stands in front of the congregation, which receives the Spirit through him alone. In orthodox Lutheranism, extemporary prayer in the pulpit was frowned upon. Prayers had to be read 'so as to avoid enthusiasm'. What a theological and practical liberation it is if, with the Eastern church, we eliminate the *filioque* from the creed and let the Holy Spirit proceed from the Father and dwell in the Son! Then we would understand that Christ comes from the Father and from the Spirit, and that the Spirit of God is the subject in Jesus' life until his death. It is only after his resurrection that Christ sends the Spirit from the Father. In the life of the Christian community, this would mean that every Christian is a 'spiritual' leader (not just the congregation's 'spiritual' leader), and that the preacher, pastor, or priest simply exercises the function of proclaiming the word and administering the sacraments, thereby representing the many; but that 'everyone who has crept out of baptism is consecrated priest and pope,' as Luther once put it. We must get away from the official and established church and become an everywhere-vital Pentecostal community. The true Christian community is a 'charismatic congregation' which lays hold of everyone and uses everyone. By this I am thinking of the vision of the apostle Paul in 1 Corinthians 12–14, not necessarily of the contemporary movements which call themselves Pentecostal.

At the end of our first joint speech in Sheffield, Elisabeth said, 'One thing seems to me important, and it is something we share: it is that we should again trust ourselves, and trust the renewing power of our experience of God; that we should trust ourselves to communicate life with all our senses and capabilities.'

Looking back, I was evidently concerned in this Sheffield lecture to open the doors of traditional dogmatic theology for this new theological movement; on the one hand to open a door for feminist theologians for their own visions, and on the other to open windows for traditional theologians for this fresh wind from outside. We both tried our honest best to promote the new dialogue and the bridge between the two. We did not experience much success, or even awaken curiosity, either in the one camp or in the other. Perhaps it was, and is still, too early. A new path always runs: separation—the finding of oneself—new community. On this path it is a particularly perfidious trick when the old and established say to those who are new and searching, 'Feminist theology—good for women. Give them an institute, and then they will leave us in peace.' When black theology grew up in the United States, many white theologians also responded to it in just this way: 'How good for them. Let's give them an institute and they will leave us alone.'

Personally, the discussions with Elisabeth about a joint theology taught me to say 'I' and to withdraw my seemingly objective professorial language—'this is the way it is'—reducing it to my own conviction. Whatever we see and perceive is limited by the conditions of the place where we stand. If we want to communicate our perception to other people, we must be aware of our perspectives. Male and female existence in their respective socio-cultural forms are part of these conditions for possible perceptions. This does not at all mean putting what has been perceived down to existential conditions, as Feuerbach and Marx thought. Not every objective perception is 'nothing other than' a self-perception, but every perception is a link between the perceiver and the perceived, and creates community between the two. Consequently, the subjective perception of one's self belongs to every perception of God, even if this leads to a self-forgetting astonishment. I have learnt to introduce theological questions and perceptions into the context of the life in which I myself am living together with others. For this path 'out of ideas into life' I have to thank Elisabeth and her feminist theology.

After this beginning in Sheffield we were increasingly prepared to offer dialogues. These usually appeared in *Publik Forum* and were very sensitively presented either by Hartmut Messmann or Doris Weber. Whereas earlier I had thought that personal considerations had no place in theology, I now found it agreeable to think theologically about personal things, and to think personally about theological topics. In the time that followed, we probably did not discuss the conflicts between feminist and traditional theology as directly as we had done in Sheffield, but rather entered with our different perspectives into subjects we both had at heart. At the General Assembly of the World Alliance of Reformed Churches in Seoul, Korea, in August 1989, we gave a joint Bible study, comparing the confession of Peter according to Matthew with the confession of Martha according to John, dividing the roles between us. What was to some extent a high spot was a joint television appearance in Zurich in 2002. We received numerous letters, and the programme was repeated. Meanwhile, we were no longer the only ones who ventured to do something of this kind. Dorothee Sölle and Fulbert Steffensky put forward publicly their common ground and their very different views. Everywhere we met with emphatic assent from the congregations but unfortunately hardly any official reactions on the part of theologians.

Our last joint theological lecture for the time being took place in the summer of 2005 in St Louis, at the suggestion and invitation of the Catholic Society of Theology in America. We talked about hope for 'the resurrection of the body' and how it could prepare us to believe 'with all the senses' in life here and now.[10] In front of us sat Catholic priests, theologians, and nuns. The community of our marriage was for them a double novelty, but celibacy did not prevent them from appreciating it. The conversations with Rosemary Ruether, who wanted to be buried and recycled in the earth after her death, and Elisabeth Johnson, who rather wanted to enter into the communion of saints, were extremely interesting and like all important theological discussions today did not run along denominational lines, with which they only seldom have anything in common. The new feminist theology is trans-confessional and calls new fellowships to life.

We have tried to bring the new feminist theology into the public forum of traditional theology. In 1980 Elisabeth joined the editorial committee of

Evangelische Theologie and saw to it that feminist theology was represented in individual contributions and theme numbers. Then Ina Prätorius, Margot Kässmann, Ute Grümbel, and Isolde Karle joined the committee. Women increasingly took over leading positions in the Protestant churches. Margot Kässmann became a bishop, Isolde Karle a professor. About 40 percent of all Protestant clergy are women, and in the universities more and more women are presenting post-doctoral theses (*Habilitationen*), which enable them to apply for professorial chairs. But this certainly does not mean that feminist theology could be called established or even successful. Positions that had to be fought for in the first generation are already a matter of course for the succeeding generations. Women are already represented in the traditional theological disciplines—but this is not true of feminist theology, as a tendency in its own right.

Has the new potential of theological thinking already been exhausted? Is nothing more to be expected there, when after all ever since 1991 there has been a powerful *Wörterbuch der Feministischen Theologie* (Dictionary of Feminist Theology)? I need not rack my brains about this because Elisabeth is already writing about it.[11] What causes me more concern is the regrettable fact that only a few male theologians in my generation, and almost none at all in the following generation, have taken up ideas from feminist theology. Kurt Lüthi in Vienna and Uwe Gerber in Darmstadt, and in the United Sates Leonard Swidler, have remained exceptions. Women are accepted as sisters in the monastery and as colleagues in the university faculties, but not this unsettling or strange 'feminist theology'. My attempt to present it for men remained almost without response.[12] On the German theological scene there is silence on this front. I experienced something rather different in America. Here the pluralism is perceived gladly by seminar participants (women and men) as a wealth of perspectives. When looking at a shared problem, one calls upon the perspective of black theology, or process theology, or feminist theology, so that one also learns something from the other viewpoint. I have not experienced this form of integration in Germany, but my horizon was also restricted to Tübingen.

Of course, feminist theology reached me through our marriage, so I have to put the critical question to myself: should I have been interested in it otherwise? At the same time, my interest in it is not only motivated by private circumstances. When we began with political theology at the end of the 1960s, we rapidly arrived at a stimulating exchange with

Latin American liberation theology, and this did not remain excluded from mainstream Catholic and Protestant theology but left marked traces behind it, positive and negative. Its fundamental ideas and guiding visions were absorbed. This does not mean that traditional theology as a whole became liberation theology, but it was changed, and one cannot say that it would have been what it is now without liberation theology. My objective interest in feminist theology derives from participation in liberation theology, but my interest has unfortunately not been infectious.

TWENTY-FIVE

NEW LOVE FOR LIFE

After I had become 60, I looked into the future with a kind of happy resignation. The children were grown up and had gone their own ways, and were also already standing on their own feet. The theological books I wanted to write had for the most part been published; my professional work was drawing to a close. At that time professors could already retire at 65, and had to do so when they were 68. During the last five years I was able to see my last 12 graduate students through their doctorates, complete lectures and seminars, put the presidency of the Gesellschaft für Evangelische Theologie in other hands, and grow old tranquilly.

But then something unexpected happened to me: I became young and lively again. On the meadows in the Swabian alps where the windfalls lie, a wonderful phenomenon can be seen in the springtime. Age-old trees, gnarled, deformed, and as if dead, begin to blossom and put forth the wealth of an exuberant bloom which one could never have expected of them. On spring walks I took that as a symbol for myself: there is life after 60! I went willingly again to my lectures, the longer the better. I once more enjoyed the seminar discussions. My graduate seminar took on new life, and new ideas occurred to me. Round my university chair a seminar family formed: my secretary, Gisela Hauber, with my assistants, Claudia Rehberger, Carmen Krieg, and Thomas Kucharz. I enjoyed my active years until I was 68 to the full.

I shall now talk first about the highlights of the years between 1987 and 1990, then about our joint journey of discovery in India, and finally about my new 'theology of life'.

Highlights in a Life after Sixty

As visiting professor at the Gregorian

In the academic year 1987–88 I was again dean of our faculty. Then came the surprising invitation to go as visiting professor to the Gregorian University in Rome. My old friend Gerald O'Collins SJ, who at that time was *decanus theologicus* there, had initiated it. Elisabeth and I really wanted to go together to Rome for four weeks, and prepared for it with a short holiday in Lugano. But then Elisabeth was ill and had to return to Tübingen, and we decided that I should go alone. Gerry received me with some of his colleagues in the famous restaurant Dodeci Apostoli, then settled me in the Germanicum. The Jesuit fathers looked after me with touching solicitude. So every morning I walked past the Trevi Fountain to the Gregoriana in order to lecture in English on eschatology. I had armed myself for Rome with many Latin phrases, but unfortunately in vain, because when I began in Latin, my listeners called out, 'Please put it in English!' They didn't know any Latin. There were many students from India and the Caribbean, for whom English had taken over the role of universal language. They all seemed to me intelligent and lively, but were always looking to see when the lecture became Protestant and therefore for them 'heretical'. However, they found very little.

Well looked after as I was in the Germanicum, I also visited the other faculties in Rome, first of all of course the Waldensians, then San Anselmo, the American College and the Irish College, Regina Mundi, and the Bellarminum. In addition, there was a shared event with Johann Baptist Metz in Naples, with a joint trip to Capri, and a lecture in Urbino. Together with Philip Rosato SJ, who had studied with me, I visited the famous Monte Cassino, and with Gerry O'Collins Castel Gandolfo. In Nettuno I enjoyed walking along the beach by myself. But at the end of March Rome can be cold and very wet, so after two weeks I returned to Tübingen for a weekend. My vice-dean, Professor Hofius, was kind enough to stand in for me during these four weeks.

During the weeks when I was living in Rome not just as a visitor, I came to love the ancient city, especially the part behind the Piazza Navona. I often thought that I could become a Roman, but not a Roman Catholic. On the other hand, I acquired a great respect for the centre of the worldwide Roman Catholic Church. The international gatherings on St Peter's

Square, the two-thousand-year-old tradition, the ability to keep together such a far-reaching organization, the many ancient religious orders which have their mother houses here, the boundless patience of the Romans with the Vatican hurly-burly of the worldwide church—all that in itself radiates a unique splendour. I did not waver in my Protestant faith, but I did feel impatient with the provincial narrowness of the regional Protestant churches in Germany, and the divided denominationalism of Protestant Christianity in general. I often thought that although I could not become Roman in the Vatican sense, I am nonetheless catholic. Everywhere, and in Rome, too, I have pleaded for a Protestant *communio cum Petro*, but in the interests of freedom of belief and theology have rejected any *communio sub Petro*—that is to say, I am in favour of communion *with* Rome but not *under* Rome. Unfortunately, in the Vatican I found little interest in such a *communio cum Petro.* It is evidently not sufficient for the Catholic Church community. I said goodbye to the Germanicum with a lecture, and in enduring friendship, which also extended over later visits.

Comprehensible theology in Sexau

In November 1988 something curious happened to me. A Protestant congregation in Sexau, near Freiburg, which up to then had been completely unknown to me, conferred on me the Congregational Prize for Comprehensible Theology, the prize having been established by their former pastor Landau. It was endowed with 2,000 DM and crates of red wine from the Sexau wine country. For an academically spoiled theologian like myself, this was of course a special honour, and an incentive to remain comprehensible in the future. So we drove through the Black Forest and reached this little congregation in the midst of the great vineyards. I gave a lecture to the congregation about peace, and on Sunday preached in their church. A farmer's wife read a long eulogy, and then we addressed ourselves to lunch (with local specialities) and to the wine.

The following year, Elisabeth and I arranged for a service to be televised from the Sexau church. The theme was Jesus' healing of the crippled woman, and I added the healing of the crippled man. The women in the congregation took an active part and had constructed huge figures as an illustration. It was only then that it really began to be 'comprehensible theology'.

A peace conference in America

Emory University had invited me to a chair at the Candler School of Theology. If I had been 20 years younger, we might have accepted, but at over 60 I had to refuse. Instead I had promised the dean, Jim Waits, that I would often come over. In April 1988 the time had come to fulfil my promise, and I gave an intensive course on the theology of peace, two seminar sessions every day. Then the faculty, together with the Carter Center in Atlanta, organized an international conference on 'Theology, Politics, and Peace', with Jimmy Carter and myself as key speakers. José Míguez Bonino came from Argentina, Kurt Biedenkopf from Germany, and Manuel Antonio Garreton from Chile. Andrew Young, meanwhile mayor of Atlanta, talked about Martin Luther King; Clarke Chapman from the Moravians spoke about Bonhoeffer; John Yoder, the Mennonite, criticized military training; Rebecca Chopp spoke on behalf of feminist theology; Mark Ellis spoke for Jewish liberation theology; and Castillo-Cardenas spoke for the Indian perspective. Ted Runyan, our old friend at Emory University, organized and published the whole. It was one of the few conferences on peace in the United States at that time. Jimmy Carter wrote about it: 'Politicians and theologians owe it to each other to be in dialogue … the avowed desire of both is to promote peace—not only individually and internally, but internationally.' The second edition of the volume that documented the conference already appeared only a year after the publication of the first edition.[1]

April 1988 brought the most beautiful spring weeks I had ever experienced in America. When I arrived, the dogwood was already in bloom all over the city, and when I left, the azaleas were coming out with a rush. The weather was still pleasant. I walked through President Park and Stone Mountain Park and absorbed all the blossoming into myself.

A 'Festival of Creation' in Washington

In May 1990, environmental policy was a burning question even in Washington, and the National Cathedral laid on a conference of experts. So I arrived at this conference of scientists and politicians together with the theologian Langdon Gilkey, from Chicago. Like myself, he had been a prisoner of war in his youth, in his case in a Japanese camp in China, and in his later years he had also become 'green'. In the theological division of the World Alliance of Reformed Churches, we were just trying in Seoul to find the bridge between human rights and the rights of nature. So 'Human

Rights and the Rights of Nature' was what I talked about. Langdon Gilkey supported me strongly, but I don't know whether we made any impression on the bureaucrats from the Washington ministries. Nor is it for that reason that the visit to Washington has remained in my memory. But after the conference there was a 'Festival of Creation' in the cathedral, with Jessica Tuchman Matthews, president of the World Resources Institute; His Royal Highness Prince Philip, president of the World Wildlife Fund for Nature; and myself. I was the last speaker and talked about 'Reconciliation with Nature'. Because this took place in the church, I gave a benediction at the end, and blessed the land: 'And the peace of God be with the land and the sea, with the forests and the meadows, with the flowers and the animals. The peace of God be with us in the community with all our fellow-creatures.'[2] The response was fantastic. There was a long standing ovation. Prince Philip came and congratulated me and took me with him to the ceremony he had to perform. He was to plant a British oak tree in front of the cathedral. His grandfather had already used the same spade forty years previously, and I was to help him; and we gave a demonstration of hard work. I hope the tree has taken good root and is showing Washington the way to global environmental protection. Afterwards I enjoyed the quiet beauty in the rose garden of the National Cathedral, and felt 'reconciled' with nature in its May blossoming. I think that after my long academic work at my writing desk, my senses were slowly awakening again to the beauties of the world, and a 'spirituality of the awakened senses' was developing in me.

In the Wonderland of India

Kottayam and Madurai, Jaffna and Sri Lanka

In 1978 the next Faith and Order conference took place, this time in Bangalore. The subject was 'The Responsibility of Hope', but for this Lukas Vischer invited Jan Lochman, not me. At that time I felt brushed aside and was annoyed. So I did not take part in the conference but accepted an invitation of the metropolitan of the Syrian-Orthodox church in Kerala, Mar Osthathios, and went to India on my own. Through Bishop Ambalavarnar, a visit to Sri Lanka followed.

It was like immersing oneself in a quite different, alien world. The wonderful temples were as fascinating as the importunate begging of the sick and poor was horrifying. Mar Osthathios received me in Trivandrum and immediately on my arrival demanded a lecture in his seminary. Then he took me to Mount Tabor, to hermit monks. During the night some animal or other gnawed at my hut. On the journey through his diocese, one saw what over-population means: behind every tree and every bush sat a family. But the land is fertile and rich. In Kottayam a large Orthodox seminary took me in, and I expressed my thanks with three lectures. I came to know this church's history, which is one of suffering. When the Portuguese arrived, they demanded that the church join Rome, but after a short time a section of the church became independent and Orthodox again. When missionaries came from the London Bible Society, they forbade prayers for the dead—and again part of the church broke away and once more became Orthodox. At the time of my visit there was a conflict between the Katholikos of the east and the Patriarchy in Damascus.

Through Mar Gregorios and Mar Osthathios, this ancient church, which was allegedly founded by the apostle Thomas himself in the first century, has become strongly ecumenically committed. I felt honoured at also being permitted to give the Philoxenos of Mabugg Lecture. I knew the name only vaguely, from my early study of church history. On 9 September we celebrated a missionary festival in the village of Umayattukara. We were hung round with garlands of flowers, protected with huge sunshades, and attempted to give fiery missionary speeches.

Over the weekend, the Orthodox theologians took me over the mountains, with their great tea plantations, to Tamil Nadu, to the theological seminary of Madurai. The drive through the open country was beautiful, and at evening, the craftsmen in the villages could be seen working in front of their doors in the dim light of oil lamps. In Madurai every visitor is flabbergasted by the fantastic Hindu temple, in which Ganesh is worshipped—Ganesh, the son of Shiva and Parvati, with his great belly and elephant head, who rides on a fat rat. But I was also fascinated by Shiva Nataraja, who creates the worlds in dance and destroys them again. Mar Osthathios gave me a wooden figure of him, which I often ponder over. In the hall of a thousand pillars, each pillar has a different, musically harmonizing sound. This Sri Menaskshi Sundareswarar temple was the first I had seen that was full of life—and what life! In Greece and Egypt one sees only the ruins, but not the people who used the temple. In India everything is alive, full of sound and every conceivable smell, and overflowing with people.

The next day I had planned to fly on from Madras to Jaffna, but Air Ceylon had for the moment broken down. Consequently, I had to fly to Colombo and then see how to get to the north of Sri Lanka from there. So in Colombo I was able to see the first Buddhist stupas, before an ancient locomotive drew a lethargic train very slowly and endlessly to Jaffna. When we arrived, all the passengers were black with smoke from the engine.

In Jaffna I did not lecture in a room but in the open air, under palm trees, and the audience sat round me on the ground. They were especially interested in human rights, for on the island the Tamil separatist movement was just beginning. Then Ambalavarnar sent me with a car and driver on a sightseeing tour. In Anuradjapura I saw the offshoot of the tree under which Buddha received enlightenment, and also the fourth-century Samadhi Buddha. In Polonaruwa I admired the reclining Buddha, and finally arrived in the ancient royal Singhalese city of Kandy. There I sat for a whole morning in the Buddhist temple, marvelling at its flower-bedecked stillness and beauty.

Madras and the temples of South India

Ten years later I convinced Elisabeth that we ought to follow the temple roads in South India together. For that hot country we chose the coolest season, and spent the Christmas of 1988 in Madras and south of the city. In Madras I visited the Lutheran seminary and gave a lecture there, and we climbed St Thomas's mountain, on which the apostle is supposed to have been killed. Then we flew to Tiruchirapalli in order to see the fantastic Srirangam temple. It was so full of pilgrims that at first Elisabeth shrank back, but then we simply let ourselves go with the crowd and absorbed this strange Hindu world with all our senses. Vishnu on the eagle, Shiva united with Parvati, the plump Genash, and the temple with the ascending horses, and the whole on a square kilometre: it was overwhelming. In the evening we climbed up to the Rock Fort, above the Cauveri River, on which the town lies. The next day we saw what was for me the most beautiful of the temples, in Tanjuvur. We were the only visitors. Behind the great Nandi bull made of black basalt, the interior of the temple opened. There a priest sat at the fire, quite alone. He painted a sign on my forehead. We spent Christmas itself in Fisherman's Cove, on the Gulf of Bengal. In the fishing village we visited a church, and on Christmas Eve looked out over the moonlit sea. In Mahalibapuram we saw the oldest sculptures hewn out of the rock of the Ganges, and the gods who came flying on bended knee. Kanchipuram was a whole city of temples. Admiration for the art of the sculpture is exceeded only by the delight in the dancing and moving figures. Whether or not one may make 'no graven image', or produce images in such an utterly unending profusion, reverence for the indescribable and incomparable divine mystery can very well be the same.

We spent our last days in the centre of Madras in old Indian splendour, in the Connemara Hotel. After we had visited the garden of the Theosophical Society, with places for all existing religions, my asthma took over and on the flight home I had to fight for air. On our arrival in Stuttgart, Esther met us with the sad news that our brother-in-law Gerhard had died the evening before.

Elephanta, Ajanta, and Ellura

The next time we went to India, we went directly, and well prepared, to Bombay. We wanted to see the cave temples in Ajanta and Ellura, which can be reached from Aurangabad. We took a week for this in February 1992. In Bombay (now called Mumbai) we stayed in the old Taj Mahal Hotel, opposite the Gateway of India, and enjoyed its colonial splendour. The next day we took the ship to the island of Elephanta, about an hour away from the city. There one climbs up the mountain by way of a great many steps and then finds oneself at the entrance to the caves, which date from the seventh century. The temples and all the sculptures have been hewn out of the rock, an endlessly laborious but timeless work. There, in the semi-darkness, the Indian gods gaze at one and radiate a tranquil majesty. It is a Shiva temple, and Shiva is shown in the trinitarian form of Mahesamurti, as creator, preserver, and destroyer of the worlds; one sees him as the 'Lord of the Dance', as Nataraja, as the 'Lord of the Yogis', with his divine spouse, Parvati, accompanied by her son, Ganesh, and even as hermaphrodite with only one breast. On the walls, angels and lesser gods on bended knee fly between them, and mythical lions guard the entrances. The atmosphere is sublime and mysterious, and lays hold of everyone who gives himself up to it.

Because our flight left early the next day, in the evening we moved into the elegant Leela Kempinski Hotel, near the airport. Araugabad is a Muslim city with mosques, gardens, and artificial lakes and fountains. The cave temples of Ajanta are not far away in a crescent-shaped mountain ridge. Buddhist monks dug these temples into the rock between the second and the seventh centuries. The mural paintings depict the life of Buddha and also the life of the men and women of that time, their clothes, their jewels, their faces. One is enchanted and transported into that period. As well as the fantastic flower and bird decorations, it is the presentation of human beings which is impressive. There is no more beautiful museum for that period in India. While in Elephanta it is the nobility of the figures that is impressive, in Ajanta it is their beauty, from which something redemptive emanates.

Ellora is a little farther away. One arrives at the towering mountain fortress of Daulatabad, and at the burial place of the terrible Aurangzeb. The 34 cultic caves have been chiselled out of the rock. The temples of the Hindus, the Jains, and the Buddhists are peacefully united. Outside they are adorned with countless figures from Indian mythology. In time one comes to recognize the patterns, and the stories they are depicting. The Kailasa temple is the most impressive: this cultic building, hewn out of the rock, is said to be the largest monolithic building in the world. In Ellora, too, the protean wealth of the Shiva figures fascinated me. Although they are very much later than those in Elephanta, they have the same elegant sweep and communicate the same sovereign tranquillity.

On the way back we again spent the night in the Leela Kempinski, and flew home through the night.

Agra, Jaipur, and Udaipur

All this gave us a taste for India, and three years later we took the more classic tour to Delhi, Agra, and Jaipur, so that we could marvel over the Taj Mahal as well. We chose November 1995 for our journey. Having arrived in Agra, we immediately hailed a three-wheel taxi with open seats and were taken to India's most famous building. The park, with its flowers and reflecting sheets of water, was so beautiful that we had ourselves photographed on a bench in front of this monument to love. The building itself is at least as beautiful as the park on the Yamuna River. Even the tiniest marble surfaces are embellished with inlaid semi-precious stones, which form decorative flower patterns. Today hardly anyone can read the Arabic verses from the Koran, but they are wonderfully decorative in design. If the whole is seen as the Mogul's song for his beloved wife, Mumta, one is roused to admiration for a great love that has achieved immortality.

In Agra we hired a car with a driver and drove to Jaipur by way of Fatepur Sikri. The Mogul Akbar had this palace built for himself and initiated his religious discussions here, with the aim of creating a monotheistic religion of his own, which admittedly endured no more than has his palace. When Fatepur Sikri was built, the city was already once more deserted. We really did encounter Jaipur as the 'pink city', for it is built entirely of pink sandstone. We spent the night in a palace hotel on hard beds. Elisabeth was only able to sleep after we had had a second mattress brought. We greatly enjoyed sightseeing tours with the open three-wheel taxi, which allows one to see, hear, and smell more. The halls of mirrors in the city palace, the pink Palace of the Winds, the Maharajah's old astronomical instruments, the wealth of jewellery and art—one doesn't know where to begin. We also drove up to the old palace fortress of Amber, which at sundown looked extremely picturesque in the autumn colourings.

The next morning we wanted to fly farther inland to Rajasthan, but when we got to the airport no flight to Udaipur was available. It had simply been cancelled because not enough passengers had booked. So we went back to the car and engaged a driver for the long stretch. That gave me the opportunity to re-route our journey by way of Mount Abu. At that time I was fascinated by the Jain temples with their dancing figures, especially on the heavenly vaulted ceilings. After a long drive through Rajasthan, we arrived in the evening at the place of pilgrimage. All the hotels were full; we were given a room under the roof and froze miserably. But as compensation the next morning the Dilvara temple complex was spread out before us, one of the most important Jain temples in India. A wonder-world in marble opened up before our eyes; one could not get one's fill of it. All the walls, pillars, and domed ceilings are peopled over and over with meditating and dancing figures. It is incredible that anything of the kind could be fashioned out of stone. The ceilings are like a reflection of heaven, filled with musicians and dancers. The 24 Tirhankaras of the Jains (literally 'ford-makers', who have escaped from the cycle of rebirth), with their glassy eyes and the sign of enlightenment on their foreheads, look quite modest in comparison. I have never again seen anything so beautiful and harmonious.

On the way from Mount Abu to Udaipur, we also visited the other famous Jain temple in Ranakpur, built with royal support at the time of the Mewar kingdom in the fifteenth century. It is just as breathtaking as the temple in Mount Abu, but is specially characterized by particular light effects, which are brought about by stepped storeys. That gives the interior a transparent splendour. The centre is conceived with geometrical precision in the form of a Latin cross. In addition to the ornamental motifs and those taken from nature, the whole Hindu pictorial world is displayed, figures of gods, musicians and dancers, elephants and pairs of lovers, stories from the great epics such as the Ramayana, and cosmogrammes hard to interpret. Here, too, one could sit for hours and days and would continually discover something new. What one can see surpasses everything one feels capable of imagining. Unfortunately, we were only passing through, and I had to tear myself away so that we could get to Udaipur by evening.

In southern Udaipur we had booked at the Lake Palace Hotel, which lies like an island in the middle of the lake and can only be reached by boat. But we were two days early. We spent the first night in an expensive 'president's suite', and the second in a palace hotel on the shore, in an 'imperial suite', which was all in silver and had a fountain in the bedroom. It was only afterwards that we could settle down for a few days in the Lake Palace Hotel. We were cut off from Indian life by the lake and could swim in the marble pool, dine in princely fashion, and admire the surrounding mountains. We drove to a little abandoned mountain castle, inhabited only by monkeys, viewed the Maharajah's palace on the shore and his summer residence on the lake, and enjoyed India's sunny sides. The Lake Palace Hotel is a dream within a dream, excellently suited as a place for digesting the host of new impressions gained on a journey through India. When we flew back via Bombay, we promised ourselves that we would come back to Udaipur.

Jodpur, Jaisalmer, and then Udaipur again

Three years later we fulfilled the promise we had made to ourselves. In 1998 we planned to go to Jodpur and into the Thar Desert to Jaisalmer, and finally to the Lake Palace Hotel in Udaipur. We again spent the night in Bombay at the fine Leela Kempinski hotel, so that we could fly the next morning to Jodpur. There we had booked a room at the Umaid Bhawan Palace Hotel. Unfortunately, this turned out to be a gloomy building; it was only the sunrise on the terrace, with the view of the high cliffs and the Mekeragath Fort, that was magical. We again viewed the town from the tried and tested three-wheel taxi. We only let ourselves be driven by car if we wanted to gain an impression of the delightful surroundings. In Ossian and Mandore I again discovered Jain temples with the enchanting dancers. For the long journey through the desert to Jaisalmer, we once more hired a car and a driver. On the road we met herds of trotting camels and also military vehicles, for the desert borders on hostile Pakistan. Jaisalmer is a rocky fortress in the middle of the desert. It was once a trading centre, so there are picturesque havellis in the old city, and it has a medieval flair. We drove back by way of Jodpur.

This third Indian journey was an anticlimax. The excitement of the unique had abated. Jodpur was not as interesting as Jaipur; the desert fortress Jaisalmer, though certainly unique, is situated in dreary countryside; and the Lake Palace Hotel in Udaipur was an old acquaintance. Since I could not persuade Elisabeth to visit Madurai, because she thought it would be too hot there, we have simply never got round to visiting India again. But the dream remains, and in all my theological thinking this religious continent is present, especially Shiva Nataraja and the dancing heaven of the Jains. Although all Indian religions wish to redeem human beings from the cycle of being born and dying, the ardent love for life and the unbounded joy in life, which find expression in the figures in the temples, exhilarate me. Birth is more than death, being comes before not-being, and before the negation stands invincibly the affirmation of life. It seemed to me that this could be the Christian gospel for India.

A New Theology of Life

From Christology to Pneumatology

The Volkswagenwerk Foundation granted me an academic bursary for the academic year 1988–89, and this gave me the opportunity to write the third book in my series of systematic contributions to theology. In 1980 I had announced a 'Christology'. I had, of course, submitted one already in *The Crucified God*, but there my central purpose was only the theological significance of Christ's death on the cross. Now I wanted to give a broader account. Consequently, I chose as a title *The Way of Jesus Christ*, and as subtitle *Christology in Messianic Dimensions*; for a 'way' can involve a number of stages and stopping points.[3] As unusual stopping places on the way of Christ, I took a Protestant view of the virgin birth as 'birth in the Spirit', developed from the resurrection a 'cosmic Christology', and pointed the way of Jesus Christ in the direction of 'Christ's parousia'. Because this book did not develop just a single theme but was more broadly conceived, it did not attract as much attention as *The Crucified God*.

The various new theological movements, such as liberation theology, feminist theology, and ecological theology, had added many new perspectives to the history of Christ, and these had to be integrated. For me, one of them was particularly important: In the 1980s the Christian-Jewish dialogue had come to be focused on a dispute about Jesus. Whereas in the nineteenth century liberal theology had discovered 'the historical Jesus', while conservative theology had adhered to 'the Christ of faith', in the twentieth century it became clear that the historical Jesus was the Jewish Jesus. How did the Jewish Jesus become the Christian Jesus? Must we not in the Christian Christ rediscover the Jewish Jesus? But what did we know about 'Rabbi Jesus'? Did the men and women disciples not proclaim his resurrection from the dead, and hope for his parousia? Since the first Christians were all Jews, one cannot reproach them with anti-Judaism or consider belief in Christ to be *per se* anti-Semitic. Not everyone who believes in Jesus Christ is therefore anti-Jewish. That can only be said of people who link this faith with a denigration of Judaism. In the same way, not everyone who recognizes Jesus as a Jew is therefore anti-Christian; this is only true of those who by doing so deny Christianity its right to exist and its own identity.

This free year, 1988–89, left me enough time to bring out what had long been in my mind: a theology of the Holy Spirit that dispenses with the *filioque*—that is, one that recognizes the relative independence of God's Spirit. In order not to keep the divine Spirit remote from human beings by always using the term 'Holy', I called him or her 'the Spirit of Life', the power who is 'the giver of life'. I fitted in the book between the Christology and the eschatology, as I had originally intended, and in doing so found the link between the remembrance and the expectation of Christ in the experience of his presence in God's life-giving Spirit. The book interrupted the planned series, but I wrote it with great enthusiasm and new love for life, because the subject led me to sectors of theology and spirituality which until then had been unknown to me. I gave it the subtitle *A Holistic Pneumatology*,[4] because I did not want to separate the spiritual from the physical life, or spirituality from vitality, in the traditional manner.

Where the content was concerned, my prime purpose was to acquire once more a concept of theological experience, after dialectical theology had set the revelation of God over against human experiences. In presenting 'life in the Spirit' of God, I then followed the old Protestant *ordo salutis* (order of salvation) and talked about the liberation, the justification, the rebirth, the sanctification, and the mystical experience of life. I rediscovered 'the fellowship of the Holy Spirit' in the experiences of community between human beings and talked about a 'theology of the social experience of God'. The Holy Spirit is 'the Go-Between God', the Deity who is sociality. When I arrived at the body language of the social experience of God, I came upon the ancient tradition of 'the holy kiss', which 1 Peter 5.14 calls 'the kiss of love'. While it expresses the fellowship of the Holy Spirit, it also has to do with the awakening and communication of the energies of life and an inner community of soul. Other forms of body language are the hand clasp, the embrace, the foot-washing, and the fellowship at the table. These are sensory perceptions of social experiences of God. At the end I tried once more to grasp the Trinitarian personhood of the Holy Spirit, which is after all different from the Trinitarian personhood of the Father and the Son, because each Trinitarian person is unique. I had particularly come to like the Pentecostal verses of Rabanus Maurus:

> Our senses with thy light inflame,
> Our hearts to heavenly love reclaim;
> Our bodies poor infirmity
> With strength perpetual fortify.

A culture of life

The book appeared in 1991. Afterwards I laid more and more weight on *a culture of life* because I sensed the deadly dangers of the increasing nihilism. After the mass murders in the Second World War, Albert Camus wrote, 'It is Europe's mystery that life is no longer loved.' The twenty-first century began with the terror of the Islamic suicide murderers. In Afghanistan Mullah Omar told Western journalists, 'You love life—we love death.' That was reminiscent of the Spanish civil war, when the old Fascist general cried, 'Viva la muerte!' Whatever these terrorists may love, Christians love life, for God is love, and with Christ the loved, the true and eternal life has come into this world of death. But it is not just a question of the spectacular death which terrorists spread; we have also got accustomed again to quite normal killing—as in Iraq, in Israel, in African countries. Among us this is a kind of emotional nihilism. In addition, there is the nuclear nihilism, and the ecological nihilism, and not least the growing social nihilism which affects the millions of 'superfluous' people, whom no one needs and no one wants. Behind these forms of modern nihilism there is a growing apocalyptic nihilism, which gives the future of life up for lost. A new culture of life certainly does not have to do only with questions about abortion and genetic and stem cell research. A culture of life follows with inner cogency from belief in the living God, and from the experiences of the divine energies of life. Elie Wiesel, a survivor of Auschwitz, was right when he said, 'In order to praise God one must live. In order to live one must love life—in spite of everything.'

The spirituality of the awakened senses

After the full-scale book *The Spirit of Life* (1991; ET 1992), in 1997 I again published a paperback for the general reader on the same subject, called *The Source of Life*.[5] In this I wanted to explain—without a plethora of references, footnotes, and learned discussions—why reverence for the life of all the living and why spirituality of the body and the earth had become important for me. If one says in one's own words only what one wants to say, the learned chapters quickly shrink from twenty pages to five! My concern was to turn the traditional spirituality of the soul, which in its love for God is orientated towards the world beyond, into a spirituality of the senses, of the body, and of the earth.

'Close the gateways of thy senses and seek God deep within.' That was the recommendation of the seventeenth-century Protestant mystic Gerhard Tersteegen. That is the path of the spirituality of the soul. One abandons the sensory experiences of the outer world and suppresses all bodily needs and signals. The way to God does not lead outwards but inwards, not into the world but out of it. One must arrive at the innermost depths of the soul, for it is in its innermost depths that every soul comes close to the Deity. That is its divine secret. 'Turn back into thyself: truth is to be found in the innermost man,' said Augustine, from whom this Western mysticism of the soul derives. On the seventh step this withdrawal arrives at the innermost sanctum of the heart; it is there that the mystic marriage of the soul with God takes place. Teresa of Avila describes this in the book of her inner experiences: *The Castle of the Soul* (1577); in our own time, Thomas Merton depicts it under the title *The Seven-Storey Mountain* (1948).

But spirituality is determined solely by what is sought and experienced as the Spirit of God. In the spirituality of the soul, men and women seek the other-worldly Spirit of the wholly other God. But what Spirit did the people experience in the biblical stories? In the creation account we are told:

> Then the Lord God formed man from the dust of the ground, and breathed into his nostrils the breath of life; and man became a living being. (Gen. 2.7)

Here the breath of God becomes the human being's power to live. So human beings sense the divine Spirit when they sense their own vitality with all their senses. In the Easter story, the dead Jesus is made alive through God's resurrection Spirit. In the Pentecost story, 'God's Spirit is poured out on all flesh' (Acts 2.1–21). The Spirit always comes from above to below, from God to human beings, from heaven to earth. All the works of God always end in bodiliness, as the eighteenth-century Friedrich Ötinger already knew. In their evening prayers little children pray, 'Take me when I die to heaven / happy there with thee to dwell.' But the kingdom of God comes '*on earth* as it is in heaven'. In order to experience that with the life we live here, we need a spirituality of the wakened senses, a new mysticism of bodily life, and a new reverence for the earth. The motto of this new spirituality of the loved life is this:

> Open the gateways of thy senses
> And seek God in all things.

What do I love when I love God?

One evening I read the following passage in Augustine's *Confessions*:

> But what do I love when I love you? Not the beauty of any body or the rhythm of time in its movement; not the radiance of light, so dear to our eyes; not the sweet melodies in the world of manifold sounds; not the perfume of flowers, ointments and spices; not manna and not honey; not the limbs so delightful to the body's embrace: it is none of those things

> that I love when I love my God. And yet when I love my God I do indeed love a light and a sound and a perfume and a food and an embrace—a light and sound and perfume and food and embrace in my inward self. There my soul is flooded with a radiance which no space can contain; there a music sounds which time never bears away; there I smell a perfume which no wind disperses; there I taste a food that no surfeit embitters; there is an embrace which no satiety severs. It is this that I love when I love my God.

And that night I answered him:

> When I love God I love the beauty of bodies, the rhythm of movements, the shining of eyes, the embraces, the feelings, the scents, the sounds of all this protean creation. When I love you, my God, I want to embrace it all, for I love you with all my senses in the creations of your love. In all the things that encounter me, you are waiting for me.
>
> For a long time I looked for you within myself and crept into the shell of my soul, shielding myself with an armour of inapproachability. But you were outside—outside myself—and enticed me out of the narrowness of my heart into the broad place of love for life. So I came out of myself and found my soul in my senses, and my own self in others.
>
> The experience of God deepens the experiences of life. It does not reduce them. For it awakens the unconditional Yes to life. The more I love God, the more gladly I exist. The more immediately and wholly I exist, the more I sense the living God, the inexhaustible source of life and eternal livingness.

Paths to the Pentecostal Movement

When the English translation of *The Spirit of Life* appeared in 2002, six theologians belonging to the Pentecostal movement coming from five continents addressed themselves to the book. The new *Journal of Pentecostal Theology* published their commentaries with a summarizing reply from me. This established the (by no means uncritical) link with the developing theology of the Pentecostal churches. The organizer was the famous Pastor Yonggi Cho, the head of the Yoidoo Full Gospel Church in Seoul, Korea, and the connection came about in the following way.

In 1995 my graduate student Dr Yong-Wha Park, who was at that time the general secretary of the resisting Presbyterian church in Korea (PROK), took me with him to a breakfast with Yonggi Cho. From seven o'clock in the morning until ten, we carried on an astonishingly good theological discussion. I got to know and appreciate the revival preacher and healer as a thoughtful theologian. He comes from a non-Christian, Buddhist family and arrived at Christian faith when he was 17, during a severe illness. After the Korean War, he began to preach—at that time in a tent. Now his Full Gospel Church has more than 600,000 members in South Korea. In Seoul he built a huge atrium church, with room for 20,000 visitors. This Pentecostal church supports missions in many countries in Asia and Africa. When I visited him, I was again suffering from asthma. He took my hand and prayed; and when I flew home, the asthma was in abeyance and remained so for some weeks. I do not want to make a miraculous healing out of this, but it was certainly unusual. I then gave a lecture to 400 pastors and 400 women missionaries belonging to his church.

In 2000 Yonggi Cho invited me to an international theological seminary belonging to his church and the university he had just founded. I spoke to an overflowing house about the Holy Spirit and the church, and replied in friendly terms to the sometimes critical questions of a phalanx of Pentecostal theologians.

In 2004 he sent me a series of basic theological declarations for his church: 1. The Seven Theological Foundations of the Full Gospel; 2. The Threefold Blessing; 3. The Fivefold Gospel; 4. The Gospel of Advent. I was supposed to comment on these declarations and, if necessary, improve them. When I discovered that these texts contained a powerful theology of the cross and an extensive Pentecostal theology, but were curiously silent about Easter resurrection theology, I knew what I had to say. My lecture appeared in the *Journal of Pentecostal Theology* in April 2005 under the title 'The Blessing of Hope: The Theology of Hope and the Full Gospel of Life'.[6] I took up a common forerunner of dialectical theology, the theology of hope, and the Pentecostal movement in Germany—Christoph Blumhardt. Among the younger theologians of the Pentecostal movement, such as Frank Macchia and Peter Althouse, Blumhardt's influence can be felt: they have moved from rigid dispensational eschatology—that is, a salvation-history calculation of the end-time—to a dynamic eschatology, according to which the gifts and energies of the Holy Spirit which can be experienced here and now are 'the powers of the future world' (Heb. 6.3) and are not supernatural gifts like 'fire from heaven'.[7] With this dynamic eschatology these theologians also open themselves for the social concerns of the theology of liberation and the critical tasks of political theology.

A moving sign of this new openness on the part of Pentecostal theology is the speech which Pastor Yonggi Cho gave at New Year 2005. He criticized himself for having interpreted the meaning of the cross of Christ too small-mindedly, reducing it to the salvation of human beings, and of reducing the salvation of human beings to the salvation of their souls, and he proclaimed 'the year of social redemption' and the redemption of the whole sighing creation. 'I have neglected social evil. I had no interest in the catastrophe of nature,' and 'We must remember that God's redemption also includes nature.' At the same time, he established a foundation for social help and for the protection of nature. His church newspaper asked me for a contribution along these lines, and I wrote it with joy and gratitude.[8]

part VIII

In the End—the Beginning

TWENTY-SIX

THE FESTIVAL OF THE END AND THE BEGINNING

Because I still had an old contract with the ministry of education (things changed later), I was able to go on teaching for three years after I reached the age of 65, and I only retired at 68. But in 1994 this point was reached. I was also given a document commemorating 50 years' service, because my years as prisoner of war were included, and indeed counted double. The certificate for 'faithful service' went along with 'one day's holiday' and a bonus of 1,000 DM.

I found saying goodbye to the professorship more difficult than I had envisaged. At the end I still hastened with great anticipation through Tübingen's old city to the *Theologicum*, in order to give lectures and seminars, and my last 'seminar family' looked after me very well. Earlier, I had often supposed that hope enables a person's mind and spirit to live in the future, in expectations and projects. Later on I realized that hope is the living power to find the new beginning in what is at present an end.[1] A poem by T. S. Eliot concludes, 'In my end is my beginning,' and I found this very illuminating. When I came to the end of my active academic career, I began to look forward to the new beginning and to let go of what had enthralled me all my life up to then. But I have to admit that at the beginning of a semester I often phoned my earlier assistant Michael Welker (who had become professor in Heidelberg) and asked him how the beginning had gone. This tense excitement at the beginning of a new semester—how many will come, who will come, shall I be able to awaken their interest and hold it to the end?—all this was deeply engrained in me. Every semester was a new project and a new adventure.

However, my retirement in 1994 was not a real end, but only a transition from what in ice-skating is called the compulsory figures to free skating, or the change from what one wants to do because one has to do it, to what one wants to do because one feels like it. My life changed very little. Suddenly my time was my own, but I also became my own employer, and the demands of that employer were far from easy. I went on reading and writing (*nulla dies sine linea*, no day without a line written!) and continued to travel and speak, really just as I had done before. For scientists and people in the medical profession, retirement often means an end and a severance. For people in the humanities it is easier, because apart from their own minds they do not require much in the way of instruments, such as laboratories and hospitals. The new beginning, which I found after my academic end in 1994, had after all already been prepared for over many years in my old academic life. I could now develop it without scruples or feelings of guilt.

The Farewell Party 1994

The end and the beginning were also made easy for me through a wonderful festivity which my assistants and former graduate students gave for me on 12 and 13 February 1994 in the theological seminary. I have always enjoyed parties as a way of expressing freely and with friends an uninhibited joy in life. So I have always invited friends to special birthdays in order to celebrate for myself and with others, not me myself but our friendship, and to let others share in the celebration. For me these parties are unforgettable: for my sixtieth birthday, a foregathering in the Evangelische Akademie in Bad Segeberg, followed by a symposium on my doctrine of creation, with Nordic theologians; on my sixty-fifth, a get-together in Tübingen, with dancing; for my seventieth, another celebration, with a symposium of prominent theologians, also in Tübingen; and for my seventy-fifth, a gathering in Bad Boll with Johannes Rau, the president of the German Federal Republic; Erwin Teufel, the prime minister of Baden-Württemberg; and my former graduate students. But the high spot of my festive life was the generous 'rights of passage' ceremony on my retirement in 1994, in the halls of the Tübingen *Theologicum* which are otherwise so quiet.

I already took leave of the faculty on 10 February with a little theological biography. The room was overcrowded, many colleagues had come, and the dean, Eberhard Jüngel, gave a delightful farewell speech: J. M. existed in this faculty as a citizen of the world—as a contemporary witness of the times—as someone always full of ideas (who was probably often himself surprised at what had just occurred to him!). He presented me with a yard-long red rose and hoped that I would now blossom 'without a why', as Angelus Silesius said in his poem, so that without a why and wherefore I could say, 'I am blossoming just because I am blossoming.' I answered briefly and—citing Goethe—said that now I was just a human being, and was permitted to be one.*

On Friday evening the real farewell symposium began, the subject being 'The Moment'. The invitations had been sent out by my assistants Carmen Krieg and Thomas Kucharz, and by my former assistants and former graduate students. What was meant was the moment 'between the times, past and future, as well as time and eternity', but there were other associations, too, some of them surprising. As a motto they had put on the invitations Heinrich Heine's saying: 'Every moment is for me an eternity: I do not measure time with the little Hamburg yardstick.' In the evening my American graduate students spoke—Lyle Dabney on 'What Has Jürgen Moltmann Got to Do with John Wesley?' and Bob Cornelison on 'Jürgen Moltmann and Modernity'. On Saturday morning Hermann Deuser then presented 'The Joy of the Lived Moment' and Marcel Martin 'Moment II' (wherever 'Moment I' may have been). Afterwards there was a plenary discussion, to which I contributed an introductory suggestion on 'Moment and Eschaton'. Thomas Kucharz set the moment over against the clock and the time of festival. It was a fireworks display of invention, a real brainstorming.[2]

I began the evening festivities in the seminary hall somewhat formally with a little autobiography, '35 Years in 35 Minutes', and kept within my time. Then the surprise guest appeared. It was Reinhard Dobbert, dean in Nuremberg, whom I had known from my youth up in Volksdorf and with whom I had studied in Göttingen during my first semesters. Elisabeth had secretly got hold of him. I had not seen him and his wife, Anne, for such a

*Goethe, *Faust*, pt 1: 'Hier bin ich Mensch, hier darf ich sein.' Cf. R. Burns, 'A man's a man for a' that.'

long time that I was left speechless. My Korean graduate students came, as well as my Belgian friend Herman-Emiel Mertens; Imgard Rittberger spoke on behalf of our Rainbow Bar Gang (which I shall talk about later); my Norwegian graduate student sang in a hoarse voice and gave me a brightly coloured knitted cap, with bobble, against the winter cold. Heino Falcke had come from Erfurt. One of my first assistants, Reiner Strunk, gave me a wooden carving of a sleeping Chinese for my 'retirement'. Witty speeches followed as well as imaginative sketches, much that made sense and much that didn't; and finally we danced late into the night. The next morning, the American and Koreans came to our house in order to say goodbye. With all this I was given a send-off into 'an endless Sabbath', as Strunk said in a poem. The farewell party was so splendid an expression of friendship that it forbade any looking back, in either anger or nostalgia.

For the next ten years I gave no lectures or anything of the kind in Tübingen. It was only much later that I held concentrated seminars with my Old Testament colleague Janowski, and in 2004 also gave a course on the *Theology of Hope* with Thomas Baun, in order to see how, after 40 years, 'hope' struck a new generation in its different circumstances.

'How I Have Changed': A Symposium of Theologians 1996

In 1996 I actually celebrated my seventieth birthday twice, first in Tübingen and then in Los Angeles. On 8 April 1996 everyone came to our house. Carmen Krieg and Thomas Kurcharz presented me with a German Festschrift with the title 'Theology on the Way to the Third Millennium'; Miroslav Volf was the third editor.[3] Faculty, university, and church were all represented. Our grandchildren served, and sang a song on the model of a current hit:

> You must be grandpa in the world, grandpa.
> As grandpa you must travel the world, grandpa.
> For to live life on the sofa—let's be honest:
> so much could happen without you, GRANDPA.

My translator Kazuo Hasumi presented me with the Japanese translation of *The Coming of God*, which had just been published. Good wishes and letters flowed in to such an extent that I could hardly answer them, including greetings from the president of the Federal Republic, the prime minister of Baden-Württemberg, the chairman of the Catholic Bishops' Conference, the Archbishop of Canterbury, and Bob Schuller of Crystal Cathedral. The *Rheinische Merkur* newspaper thought I was already 80. Eberhard Jüngel sent a telegram from Venice saying that my life had not only been 'toil and trouble', and Wolfhart Pannenberg reminded me that, earlier, we had hindered rather than encouraged each other 'through rivalry and dispute': both were right. The *Washington Post* put my birthday and Elisabeth's together and wrote, 'Husband-wife team has joint account in theology debate'. A German radio and television station even thought that 'in this recent dispute, feminist theology, the Moltmanns are at their best as a couple, and for public appearances it is often only as a couple that they are to be had.'

On 19 April we continued our celebrations at Fuller Theological Seminary in Pasadena, California. We came to Los Angeles via Washington, where our friends the Meekses, of Wesley Seminary, were waiting for us; then via Birmingham, Alabama, where Elisabeth preached in Paul Zahl's Cathedral of Advent; and finally—by way of a detour—via the Grand Canyon, which shone in all its colours in the morning and evening sun, like a spectacle put on by nature. In Los Angeles my American pupils had organized a conference at Fuller Seminary with Nicholas Wolterstorff and James McClendon, then inviting us to a festive banquet on 19 April.[4] Nancy Bedford, Lyle Dabney, Reinerio Arce, and Miroslav Volf found kind words for me and presented me with the American Festschrift *The Future of Theology*.[5] And then, as surprise guest, our old friend Walter Capps from Santa Barbara appeared, with his wife, Lois. He was now a member of Congress. To meet them again was a very special pleasure. Sadly, Walter died soon afterwards, as he left the plane in Washington. Lois Capps succeeded him as member for Congress. The next morning we enjoyed a wonderful sunrise in Santa Monica, and in the evening visited the famous television preacher Bob Schuller and his wife, Arvella, in his Crystal Cathedral, the tower of which he had called 'Tower of Hope'. We found him to be a good theologian, when one talked to him privately. He was heart and soul at one with Elisabeth's doctrine of justification—'I am good, whole, and beautiful'—for he always preached powerful self-confidence to his listeners in this society of competitive struggle, with its fear of 'not making it'. Every year he sends me a telegram on my birthday saying, 'God loves you and so do I.' My contribution to this American celebration was a little speech titled 'My American Dream—a Confession of Love', in which I summed up my hopes and our experiences with this country of 'unlimited possibilities'—and unfortunately impossibilities—and looked for the promise of equality to follow the promise of freedom. We flew home happy and full of America.

For the year in which we both turned 70, Elisabeth had thought out something special. We invited ten well-known theologians from our own generation to come to Tübingen. Each of them was to talk biographically, telling a little about his theological development. 'Theology as biography' or 'biographical theology' were not new perspectives, but we wanted to know, and make public, the way our generation came to theology during the war years and the post-war era, and hear how they had lived with theology, our idea being that we might then see the direction in which we wanted theology to move in the future. We issued our invitation for Saturday, 8 June 1996, and envisaged three rounds of discussion, each of them with three people, with a plenary discussion at the end, to be followed by a festive evening at the Hirsch restaurant in Bebenhausen, just outside Tübingen. We invited Hans-Eckehard Bahr, Norbert Greinacher, Eberhard Jüngel, Fred Herzog, Johann Baptist Metz, Wolfhart Pannenberg, Philip Potter, Hans Küng, Dorothee Sölle, and Jörg Zink, and we ourselves joined them. They all accepted our invitation, but unfortunately in the event not all were able to come. Fred Herzog died unexpectedly in the autumn of 1995, Hans-Eckehard Bahr sent his greetings from hospital, and Wolfhart Pannenberg, who was so influential in our generation, withdrew at the last minute.

In my introductory greetings I said:

> We should like to look back on the last thirty years or so, and ask ourselves what has come of our new beginnings, after Barth and Rahner, Bultmann and Tillich, or whoever our teachers were. With what expectations did we begin at that time? Why did we react so variously to the challenges of the time? What has changed in our perspectives of theology in these years, and what has remained unchanged? And what unsolved problems are we leaving for the next theological generation? What questions move us at the deepest level, and what questions do we want to put to one another? We have deliberately refrained from inviting only theologians who are working in academic faculties, for we are convinced that theology is not made at universities alone.

> 'How I have changed': that is of course a feeble translation of the question circulated every ten years by *Christian Century* in Chicago, for which some of us have written. But behind it is also Bert Brecht's well-known story: 'Herr Keuner met an old friend on the street whom he hadn't seen for many years. "But you haven't changed at all", the friend greeted him. And Herr Keuner turned pale.' So we will now see which of us turns pale.

Everyone had 20 minutes for his or her biography and for his or her theological message, and then there was half an hour for a back-and-forth between the three participants. The last of the discussions took place in a lecture room and was televised. Hans Norbert Janowski, a well-known Protestant journalist, took the chair. The first group consisted of Eberhard Jüngel, Dorothee Sölle, and myself; the second of Johann Baptist Metz, Elisabeth, and Norbert Greinacher; and the third of Jörg Zink, Philip Potter, and Hanz Küng. A convivial evening in Bebenhausen followed. There were lively speeches, and at the end of the evening we sang folk songs with Dorothee Sölle, for these had just become her great love. Fortunately, by that time there was no one else left in the Gasthaus.

We published our speeches in a Kaiser paperback in 1997, with nice photographs, and translations into Italian, English, and Korean followed.[6]

Spaces of God—Living Spaces: The Seventy-fifth Birthday Celebration in Bad Boll

From 6 to 8 April 2001 the Evangelische Akademie Bad Boll sent out invitations to a symposium and a celebration. We chose as subject 'space', in its theological and anthropological dimensions. Ever since Augustine, there have been countless theological meditations and studies on the relation between God and time, but since Leibniz and Newton in the eighteenth century, little has been thought about God and space. But Einstein has made such reflection unavoidable. Again we were treated to a fireworks display of stimulating ideas and suggestions: Reiner Strunk opened our proceedings with morning devotions and compared Psalm 31.8, 'Thou hast set my feet in a broad place,' with the end of *Faust II*: Faust, the winner of space, and the narrow grave for his body. Marcel Martin added to this a prologue taken from practical theology, 'Living Spaces—Spaces of

God'. I myself described my progress from the restless God of hope to the 'indwelling' and 'inhabitable' God. Claudia Rehberger described feminine spaces for living as spaces for dreaming. Carmen Rivuzumwami developed the experiences of space in the movement of the dance. Geiko Müller-Fahrenholz put forward his ecological vision of 'the earth as living space'. Bob Cornelison discussed the slogan 'God's own country', and Thomas Kucharz presented the virtual worlds of cyberspace. The last to enter these 'spaces for thought' were the Belgian Herman-Emiel Mertens, the Japanese Kazuo Hasumi, and the American JoyAnn McDougall, all with critically helpful comments on my ideas about space.[7]

Johannes Rau, the president of the Federal Republic, had come to our gathering together with his wife and had already taken part in the symposium. That shed high political glamour from Berlin on Bad Boll's provincial huts; but Rau had not come as president but as an old friend (our friendship dating from our time in Wuppertal), as a brother and a comrade. However, his security officials saw well and truly to the appropriate respect, and his presence awakened the interest of the newspapers. I was deeply touched that he should have made time for me in this way, in spite of his breathtakingly full diary of official engagements. But Johannes was always faithful and dependable in his friendships.

The evening of 7 April was ceremonious. Erhard Eppler greeted his old comrade in the name of the German socialist party (the SPD); Eilert Herms came as dean, but also found repentant words for having once in his youth severely criticized my theology of hope, and for having thereby done me an injustice. Benjamin Cortes had flown in from Nicaragua, and—after Uwe Martini had translated his fine speech—conferred on me the George Casalis Award. JoyAnn McDougall talked amusingly on behalf of my American faculty (the Candler School of Theology, Emory University, Atlanta) about my subversive doings there. And finally, Frank Crüsemann let off lightning shafts of wit on behalf of the periodical *Evangelische Theologie*. Before the high spot was reached in the Café Heuss, Rudolf Weth took the floor on behalf of the Gesellschaft für Evangelische Theologie. And then there was midnight champagne to accompany the congratulations and embraces—and Elisabeth and I sank into bed, dead tired.

The next morning we wrote our names in the Golden Book of the little town Boll, and attended church with Rau and Teufel. Carmen and Reinerio preached liberation theology sermons, not much to the liking of all the politicians. Eppler's face darkened visibly. The so-called 'official ceremony' followed in the Academy. After some excellent music by a trumpet ensemble conducted by Professor Bosin from Stuttgart, Johannes Rau and Erwin Teufel gave laudatory speeches, and finally Prelate Paul Dieterich entitled me 'Swabian Father' in the name of the church in Württemberg, putting me side by side with Albrecht Bengel, Friedrich Ötinger, and Christoph Blumhardt, whom I had come to admire but beside whom I had never deemed myself worthy to stand. I stammered some words of thanks, as far as I was able to do so after so much overwhelming and friendly acclaim. Our four daughters were present as well, and attracted the attention of other guests because of a certain family resemblance. On this occasion we also quite unexpectedly met our friend Charles McCoy from Berkeley, alas for the last time.

TWENTY-SEVEN

NEW EMPHASES

Joachim Ringelnatz once wrote a delightful skit on the folksong 'If I were a little bird and had two wings, I would fly to thee …', his version being, 'If I were two little birds, I would fly after myself.' In writing one's own biography, one seems like two people and cannot catch up with oneself. So it is time to bring the story to an end, and I shall do so in this last chapter. I shall only describe the main emphases or focuses of my present international interests, and talk about the groups of people in Tübingen which have become important to me; and then I shall stop flying after myself.

In the Asiatic World

My Japanese translator Hasumi had told the preparatory committee in Nahe, Okinawa, that it would be impossible to get me to come to Okinawa. But they nevertheless tried, and so in April 2003 I arrived on the island which I only knew as the place where the last battle of the Second World War was fought. A reading group had been formed among Christians on the island under the leadership of the cultivated Revd Yohane and Professor Kenjo, and they had studied my books in Japanese translation and therefore invited me—the first theologian to be invited from abroad. And the adventure tempted me. Hasumi and his wife, Sachie, were flown from Tokyo, and everything was thoroughly planned. In the Christian college I had to speak to clergy and a large group of Christian laity, and in the city hall I was to address non-Christians. In addition, I was to preach on Sunday in Nahe's central church.

Okinawa counts as 'the Japanese Hawai', but it was originally the independent kingdom of Ryokyo, and orientated towards China. Then the Japanese came and in 1878 made the islands a Japanese prefecture. After the Second World War they were 'Americanized'. Large parts are given over to American air force and naval bases. The airfield in the middle of the island is much larger than Frankfurt Airport, and rows of B-52 bombers equipped with nuclear weapons stand there. The marines contaminate the coasts with uranium-enriched ammunition. The southern part of the island is completely built up with concrete houses. It is quite right that the island inhabitants on what was once a battlefield now want to make this American military island a 'heart of peace' for the Pacific; and the Christian message of peace falls on fruitful ground.

But there is a deeper reason for this as well. Okinawa counts as a centre of the Asian ancestor cult. Everywhere in the mountains one sees graves with benches in front of them where families can gather. I gave the main lecture of my tour in a Catholic church, taking as my subject 'Ancestor cult and the Resurrection Hope'. My listeners were very moved, and for the first time I saw Japanese people weeping. For them, the dead are not 'dead and gone' as they are for us. As ancestors, they are indeed very much present, and as good spirits can bless and as suffering spirits torment. Down to the present day, the battle of Okinawa has left behind it long shadows in families. The stories they tell are terrible beyond all imaginings. During a long car journey, Professor Kinjo, who is today 80 years old and pastor of the central church, told me how defeated Japanese soldiers on the island of Tokashiki drove families in his village into the caves to mass suicide, in order to save 'the Tenno's honour'. He himself and his brother were forced to kill their own mother, and he only survived by chance. On the southern tip of Okinawa, whole classes of Japanese schoolchildren threw themselves down the precipice. Finally, Admiral Ota committed ritual suicide. On the black marble tablets in the Peace Park, the names of 250,000 people who died in that battle are engraved. The souls of these dead find no peace, because they have received no justice, and to find peace with the dead belongs to the reverence for ancestors.

Christian missionaries condemned this Asiatic reverence for ancestors as idolatry and demanded that Christians abandon it. But that was the non-culture of the Western world rather than Christian faith. It is better to develop a Christian form of reverence for ancestors, springing from the shared Christian resurrection hope, as has happened in Korea. And for us in the West, it is important to learn again how to deal with the burdens and blessings of our forefathers instead of letting them disappear in anonymous graves; for whether we like it or not, we live in their light and in their shadow. I came back very thoughtfully from Okinawa.[1]

In October 2004 Elisabeth and I were in Peking again. Daniel Yeung of the Sino-Christian Institute in Hong Kong had organized for me an academically recognized seminar for lecturers and graduate students at the Tsinghua University. I wanted to give an introduction to 'The Philosophy and Theology of Hope', and the seminar was intended to end with a conference with professors about 'The Role of Religion in a Globalized World'. Elisabeth was invited to talk about feminist theology at Peking University, and about 'Mary Magdalene and Jesus' at the Academy for Social Sciences. We flew Air France, because that had the cheapest business class offer. Time was short, so I held my first seminar meeting, somewhat breathlessly, the day we arrived. We were lodged in the old Beijing Hotel, right next to the Forbidden City, and could always quickly go over through the park. My old graduate student Lin Hong-Hsin had come from Taiwan in order to translate for Elisabeth and me. Then Daniel Yeung also joined us. After two lectures and three seminar sessions, we relaxed over the weekend in the summer palace, took a boat to the Bridge of the Seventeen Arches, and followed Daniel Yeung along the Liulichang shopping street. Here glorious illustrated books were to be had. At the end of lectures and seminars, the participants always went to lunch or dinner together. This social custom is part of Peking's academic life and is nothing special, as it is with us. One only needs a strong stomach. Daniel Yeung took us to the most exquisite restaurants, one after another, and we followed him with pleasure.

The second week I was invited to a new Protestant theological seminary on the outskirts of the city, and there about 200 students were waiting. In the middle of the campus there is a wooden church with gothic windows, the gift of a congregation in Texas. After I had talked personally about my faith and the task of theology, the questions came, and they all had to do with Satan. That was no doubt the legacy of fundamentalist missions from Korea.

The symposium with the professors was astonishing in another respect. Most of them were non-Christians—one of them even came from the Party college—but they were all extremely interested. In spite of the conference title, they were not much concerned about 'globalization', but they asked whether one could study and understand Christian theology even if one were not a Christian. For me, curiosity and interest were a sufficient motive. That contented them. But the question shows how far Christian thinking reaches beyond the circle of believers and the Christian congregations, and how it attracts intelligent Chinese people.

On the last day but one we walked round the island in the Beihai Park and enjoyed the quiet of the lake and the weeping willows in the midst of this hectic metropolis. We also went once more through the imperial palace and let ourselves be taken back to a hotel on the back seat of a motor rickshaw. I feared for my life in the murderous traffic, but Elisabeth found it gloriously exciting. We also saw the old lanes with the hutongs, which are now giving way to the new high-rise buildings. It means the loss of a piece of old China. But the architecture of the new Peking is fantastic. The roofs of the skyscrapers are astonishingly beautiful in their form. Flowerbeds have been planted along the six-lane main roads and are carefully tended. It is as if most of the investment capital in the globalized world today is going to China. Everywhere one senses the mood of a new departure. Beside it, Europe appears somewhat antiquated. Occasionally I thought that if I were 40 years younger, I would go to China for a few years.

In the Country of Volcanoes and Lagoons: Nicaragua

In 1991 the German Goethe Institute sent me on another trip through Latin America, which took me to Lima, Bogota, San Jose, Managua, and Mexico City. In Lima I met my old friend Gustavo Gutiérrez, who was involved in a clash with the theological faculty in Lima. The Goethe Institute, where I held my lectures, was the first neutral ground where the conflicting parties met. From Gustavo I heard the astonishing comment that although his people work on the outskirts of the slums, the evangelical Pentecostal preachers go into the slums themselves. After that, the need to bring liberation theology and Pentecostal theology together in Latin America became increasingly important for me.

In Costa Rica I found my graduate student and friend Geiko Müller-Fahrenholz at the UNESCO peace university, and met other liberation theologians grouped round Elsa Támez. But then the moment came when I had simply had enough of this whole conference and travel theology, because it is a superficial hovering in universal categories. I looked for a specific place where I could be involved and for which I could be responsible. And I found it in Nicaragua.

In Managua there is a large Protestant theological seminary called (abbreviated) CIEETS, which at that time already had about 600 students from many denominations. I was surprised at the size and vitality of this seminary with its straw-roofed huts, until I learnt that on the Atlantic coast of Nicaragua about 25 percent of the whole population is Protestant. The Miskito Indians in the north are Moravians, having been missionized by the Moravian Brethren. The blacks in Bluefield are Anglicans, since in the nineteenth century this area was still British, like British Honduras, today Belize. But otherwise, too, in nearly every village there is an *Iglesia Bautista*, and Pentecostal churches are springing up everywhere. There are no roads linking the Protestant Atlantic coast with the Catholic Pacific region, and the people on the Atlantic coast also do not speak Spanish, and had never paid taxes. The dictator Somoza viewed them as his private property and sold off timber felled from the forests to Taiwan, and land for dumps for nuclear waste to Canada. Unfortunately, in their literacy campaign the Sandinists took Spanish to the Miskitos, too, and because they were afraid of foreign influence, the Miskitos accordingly supported the 'Contras'. In September 1991 the Contra war was still raging along the frontier to Honduras. In Managua electricity was cut off in the evening, and all day there was no water. It was a critical situation, because the Sandinista front—where Christians and socialists joined together in opposition to Samoza's cruel (US-supported) military dictatorship—threatened to fall apart because of inner tensions.[2] Protestant Christians now suffered much less under the Communists than under Catholic repressions, which originated in the political Catholicism of Archbishop Obando y Bravo.

The picture showing Pope John Paul II shaking an admonitory finger at the minister of education, Father Ernesto Cardenal, as he gives him a dressing down went round the world. His admonition that priests had to prepare people for eternal life, not interfere in the politics of this one, was theologically so erroneous that even Poland, thank God, did not adhere to it, but supported Solidarno in its criticism of the government. Unfortunately, after his visit, the central square, the Plaza de la Revolucion, was renamed after him: political Catholicism had to be victorious over the Sandinista revolution.

At the CIEETS seminary I met the charismatic and inspired leader Benjamin Cortes and the German theologian Uwe Martini, who had worked in the seminary for a number of years. With both of them I at once struck up a friendship which still endures and deepens. Uwe became my translator and companion whenever I came to Nicaragua. I thought highly of this seminary, which had to fight for its existence, and at last I found the place in Latin America where I could settle, or to which I at least often wanted to return.

The students did not come from well-to-do homes and had to work to keep themselves. The theological lecturers included a French woman and a Dutchman. George Casalis had devoted the last years of his life to the Sandinista revolution and to this theological seminary, and the library rightly bears his name. My lectures on Jesus and the kingdom of God, and the meaning of his passion and his resurrection, were published in Managua in 1992.[3] Uwe Martini had translated them. I also drove to Matagalpa with him. There hundreds of Protestant campesinos had gathered on the marketplace and cheered on my address 'The Day of the Bible' with enthusiastic cries of 'Amen' and 'Hallelujah'; so it turned into a real missionary occasion, which is otherwise not my style. Afterwards we visited the coffee farm and the restaurant Selva Negra in the mountains (once called in German *Schwarzwald*, or Black Forest). As late as 1945 Somoza entered the war against Germany, but only in order to rob the German settlers of their property. His estate in Montilemar on the Pacific coast had also once belonged to a German. Now it had been converted into a beach hotel, with many bungalows. The sunsets were wonderful, and the sea, too—only the beach was volcanically dark. Nicaragua is poor but beautiful. The volcanoes, such as the Momotombo, tower impressively into the sky, and the lakes glitter in the burning sun. It is a wonderful country, with people who are poets through and through. The names of Gioconda Belli and Ernesto Cardenal stand out, but almost everyone sings political and erotic songs to the guitar.

In February 1994 I was back in Nicaragua. CIEETS had organized a great Middle American conference on ecology and theology, and seminary students had come from far afield, from Costa Rica to Guatemala. The Indios among them talked about their special and even personal relation to animals such as the jaguar. A woman poet devised a ritual praying to the earth for forgiveness for our human depredations. And then there was the evening with Brother Ernesto Cardenal. With thrilling pathos he recited lines from his 500-page poem *Cantico Cosmico*. Even someone who understood no Spanish was moved. I knew him from a meeting in Prague, and he knew my books. So we made avowals of friendship with many embraces. Afterwards I drove with Uwe to Montilemar again, to jump into the water there, and then preached in Benjamin's church between mountains of harvest thanksgiving fruits. After six days I was on my flight home again.

In February 1996 I was in Managua once more, in order to take part in the founding of the first Protestant university in Middle America. This was a bold undertaking, for the UCA, the private Jesuit university, stands directly next to CIETTS. But Benjamin Cortes was both circumspect and courageous, and the foundation was accomplished and proved successful. Today more than 5,000 students study in Managua, Matagalpa, and Masaya at this Universidad Evangelica Nicaraguense. I talked about the idea of a Christian university that cuts free from both politicizing and economic pressure, in order to serve truth and the liberty of the people. I also brought with me greetings which I had collected in Europe, among others, one from the Archbishop of Canterbury and one from my friend Johannes Rau, at that time prime minister of North Rhine Westphalia. This gave a considerable fillip to the new foundation, at least in the eyes of the foreign ambassadors. Johannes Rau did not stop at friendly words, but also sent 30 computers for the first teaching courses at the UENIC. Afterwards I drove with Uwe to Lake Nicaragua near Granada and hired a boat in order to sail round the world of the little and yet inhabited islands. We then drove to the sea near La Boquita and enjoyed not only the waves but the fresh shrimp afterwards too. I had to give my lecture again in Matagalpa. We once more stayed overnight in Selva Negra, and during the night Uwe heard mountain lions prowling round the huts. After eight days I was home again.

In March 1999 the university of Miami invited me to give some lectures, and I thought I could easily add on a visit to Managua in order to open the academic year in the university with some lectures. All went well in Miami, but things didn't work out in Managua. Instead of Uwe Martini, I was given a German pastor as translator, whose Spanish was inadequate and his theology too.

Then in July 2002 came what was up to then the high spot. The Universidad Evangelica Nicaraguense had developed so well and was so fully recognized in Nicaragua that it was given the right to confer doctorates;

and it wanted to give the first honorary doctorate to me. In addition, it wanted to combine the beginning of its academic year with a *Cathedra Internacional*, to which they wished to give my name. I was, of course, greatly touched by these honours. Uwe Martini came with me, as well as my former assistant Carmen Rivuzumwami, who is a Latin America fan. I opened the first *Cathedra* with the lecture 'God and Human Rights'.[4] Then came the official ceremony, in the People's Palace of Culture. The huge hall was lavishly adorned with the UENIC symbol and with my name. I was robed in cap and gown. Then the presidents, Benjamin Cortes and Hamlet Garcia, conferred on me an honorary doctorate, and I gave a lecture titled 'Freedom in the Modern World'. When I criticized neo-liberal capitalism in not particularly sharp words, the representative of the German embassy left the room. But the Spanish and Mexican ambassadors came to me later and expressed their understanding. In this Catholic country, this public demonstration was important for the Protestant university, and I gladly played a part in it.

Afterwards we drove with Benjamin and Hamlet to Catarina, a village with a fantastic view of Granada, Lake Nicaragua, and the Mombacho volcano. For the first time in my life I ate turtles' eggs, and did not enjoy them. An evening in Montilemar ended this—for the time being—last visit, or I should rather say homecoming, to a place, a people, and a Christian community that I have learnt greatly to respect and love.

The Meeting of Systematic Theologians in Tübingen, the Tübingen 'Table Round', Friendship with Hans Küng and Eberhard Jüngel in Contrapuntal Harmony

It is not very easy to describe what really grew up over a period of more than 35 years. When, soon after me, Eberhard Jüngel moved from tranquil Zurich to turbulent and restless Tübingen, taking the place of Gerhard Ebeling, who—tired of Tübingen—exchanged posts with him, we met regularly with the Catholic dogmatic theologian Hans Küng, and from 1971 with Walter Kasper, too, and decided that, denominationally divided professional colleagues as we were, we would set up a regular ecumenical meeting. On 15 December 1969 Elisabeth and I invited them for the first time to the dinner which then became a firmly established custom for the next 43 years. At this dinner and afterwards, we always went at it hammer and tongs over controversial theology as well as the theology we shared. Küng and Kasper were completely enthralled by the new start in church and theology initiated by the Second Vatican Council; Jüngel contributed Barthian and post-Barthian hermeneutics; and I offered revolutionary and political theology. Elisabeth was present from the beginning and later brought her own perspectives in the context of feminist theology. Last but not least, Marianne Saur, who worked together with Hans Küng, brought a little sparkle and some critical comments to our sometimes harsh controversies. Sometimes the atmosphere was electric, but the unruly spirit was only 'the ghost of Geiselmann', whose house Walter Kasper and his sister had taken over.

Our theological passions were not aroused along the denominational alignment. Controversies arose between Kasper and Küng in the conflict between the curia and the Council, and worlds separated me from Jüngel in political theology, or so Jüngel believed. Just because we were so close, we often became heated, but after the pleasures of the table and with the accompaniment of good wine, how could personal differences make themselves felt? Later on there were other systematic theologians, too, in the Catholic and Protestant faculties, but it never occurred to us to expand our circle by adding their names. In mutual respect, both personally and for the direction of the others' theological work, we had become friends without our having become conscious of it. Of course, rumours about our meetings were rife. It was said, for example, that 'Küng and Moltmann first tick off the continents they have just visited before they get down to business.' For me these meetings were always important, because they drew me out of my isolation and relativized my own positions.

Küng's conflict with the Congregation for the Doctrine of the Faith in Rome dragged on for years and concerned us deeply. Because of good contacts with the great international dailies, for a long time he was able to parry successfully every attack from Rome. I always admired his readiness to react at once to all criticism, and never to become resigned. But then his opponents prepared a surprise attack. At the end of 1979 he had already gone off for a skiing holiday when his *missio canonica* (his permision to teach) was withdrawn, so he was unable to reply immediately. Up to Christmas, if I remember rightly, most of his Catholic faculty put themselves on his side, acknowledging him as a 'Catholic theologian'. Jüngel and I organized a declaration of our Protestant faculty in his defence, and at midnight already took it to the local newspaper, the *Schwäbisches Tagblatt*.

But after the Christmas holidays things looked different. Küng lost the support of the majority of his faculty, which hurt him most of all, and Walter Kasper no longer supported him either. Because after the withdrawal of the *missio* Küng was no longer supposed to count as a 'Catholic theologian', Walter Kasper was lost to our circle of systematic theologians. He had decided in favour of the curia, later left the theological faculty, became bishop in Rottenburg, and is now curia cardinal in the Vatican. Jüngel and I have always viewed the outcast Küng as a 'Catholic theologian'. When I was in Rome I always said that Küng was very good, only he was unfortunately a 'Catholic theologian'. It is true that Karl Rahner had termed him a 'liberal Protestant', but that was an error, as every upright Protestant can show.

Afterwards, Jüngel and I continually encouraged Küng to go on giving his dogmatic lectures in spite of everything, even though only a few Catholic students would come. But he shifted the emphasis of his work, initially to the *Studium generale*, the course of general studies in which, together with Walter Jens, he gave splendid public lectures. Then inter-religious dialogue became important for him, and he built up his knowledge of Indian and Chinese religions. He was most interested in Islam and was a pioneer in his demand for dialogue with this religion. Out of these inter-religious dialogues he then developed his 'Global Ethics Project', for which he is known all over the world today. Elisabeth, Jüngel, and I accompanied him respectfully along this path, but also very critically, whether he liked it or not.

In Küng's house there was as aperitif always an especially good champagne with the name 'Philipponat', which he had sent from Switzerland. One day in the summer of 1987 we decided to drive to Rheims in order to seek out the source of this delicacy. We raced over the French motorway to Verdun (a race which I of course lost, for Küng was always faster), and after a long search found in Champagne the vineyard in question, where we let ourselves be initiated into the art of making this famous wine. Jüngel proved himself a particularly ready pupil. Then we made our purchases and spent the night in Rheims in the light of the floodlit cathedral. When the next day Elisabeth discovered in the museum the over-sized Eve with the serpent in her arm, and stopped in front of it, Küng urged her to hurry; we had to follow him 'smartly, smartly'. In Verdun the meal was again so extensive and the conversation so interesting that we saw nothing of what was left after the battle of the First World War.

Two years later, in 1989—again in July—red Burgundy and white Mersault drew us. So we drove off, descended into the wine cellars, and listened to lectures (which I found endless). We visited Autun and Baune. In one of the churches I suddenly stood in front of the skull of the Lazarus whom Jesus had once raised from the dead. According to the legend, he had come to the south of France with Mary and Martha on their missionary journey (even if, probably, not as far as the St Lazare railway station in Paris). I stood startled in front of his skull, and thought of his resurrection from the dead.

Only a year later we were again together for a week, having flown to Taormina in order to explore Sicily. In Catania Küng and I hired cars with which we then tore through the island. We drove to Agrigent, Selinunt, and Segeste, admired the fantastic mosaics of Monreale, and stood for a long time on the hill of Enna. When at dinner Küng lamented the now extinct Rome protest of 'the Protestants', we challenged him to become a Protestant himself. But that was a bit too much. For a whole day he stayed in the hotel and wanted to see nothing of us. But then, after a clarifying discussion, the matter was laid to rest, and we went on together. I tell this not as an anecdote but in order to show the enjoyment of conflict and the readiness for reconciliation which we had developed.

We undertook what was our last journey for the time being in October 2002, to Bari, in order to see Emperor Frederick II's lonely and proud Castel del Monte. It towers in a mysterious pentagon out of a silent landscape and is a testimony to medieval encounters between the cultures of East and West. We also visited Monte San Angelo in Gargano, where the archangel Michael protects the Christian West from the Eastern dragon—a counterpart to the Western Mont Saint Michel on the French coast. I myself found the Norman churches in Apulia the most beautiful.

In this way the meeting of systematic theologians became a 'table round' of friends, and a pleasant travel group. We remained pugnacious and clung to our mutual self-distinctions, but respect for the achievement of the others, and personal sympathetic participation in whatever happened to them, increased. And in any event, what we all had at heart was the truth of the Christian faith. Here we spared each other nothing out of politeness, as when Jüngel once called the Koran 'a frightful book' and I agreed with him, or when Elisabeth disputed the doctrine of original sin, or when I was forced to defend Calvin and Puritanism, or when Küng attacked the weaknesses of Protestantism. After 20 years we then reached the point of addressing each other as 'Du', the familiar form of address used for family and close friends.

The Rainbow Bar Gang

The other group of our Tübingen friends began unplanned and grew of itself. I shall explain presently why we occasionally called ourselves after the Rainbow Bar in New York, for we are a worthy group of professors from different faculties, and their independent wives. A first enduring contact grew up between Elisabeth and me and Imgard and Volker Rittberger, who came to Tübingen from America. He became Theodor Eschenburg's successor in the new chair for political science; she is a pharmacist, trains other pharmacists, and has been for some time a city councillor in Tübingen. Through our youngest daughter, Friederike, we came into contact with her headmistress, Linde Liegle, and her husband, Ludwig, who was professor of general educational theory in Tübingen. Through them we got to know the doctor couple Inge and Richard Michaelis. For many years we had already met in the so-called Österberg circle, an association of liberal professors in the Great Senate of the university, and had celebrated the annual Lili Festival together.

Something like a formal foundation of this group of friends came about in Bad Teinach on 8 April 1989. Bad Teinach is an old spa belonging to the royal Württemberg family, with a famous spring and—even more famous—Princess Antonia's kabbalistic-Christian-feminist teaching tablet or painting, dating from the seventeenth century, which can be seen in the village church and which Elisabeth greatly loved and liked to expound. After we had been accordingly instructed, and after a relaxing bathe in the thermal pool, we sat in the noble spa hotel and reinforced our mutual sympathy through the 'Du', the familiar form of address used between friends. Then it occurred to us that we might visit all the different places we came from, letting ourselves be shown them by the one who had been born there.

Accordingly, we set out on our travels together. Already in May of the same year, Inge and Richard Michaelis invited us to Schwäbish Hall. She is a psychotherapist, he is professor at the children's hospital in Tübingen, and they have their roots in Gaildorf and Schwäbisch Hall. Since we were strangers to this countryside, they introduced us to the secrets of the Würtemberg region. I remember the splendid steps in front of the Michaelskirche. On a later occasion we saw Dumas's *Three Musketeers* performed on these steps.

At the end of August 1989 we visited Elisabeth's home, Potsdam. It was the year of German reunification, and we wanted to see what was left of Prussia's glory after war and socialism. We stayed in Schloss Cecilienhof, wandered through the glorious Sanssouci Park, and saw on one side of the castle the grave of Frederick the Great's greyhounds, and on the other the memorable bench where Elisabeth and I had exchanged our engagement rings in 1950. We came closer to each other and learnt to appreciate each other, each in his or her own way.

In October 1991 Richard Michaelis showed us 'his' Swabian baroque. Up to then I had always only felt that baroque was very Catholic and smacked of the Counter-Reformation; but now he taught me to look closer and to appreciate it from aesthetic perspectives—and lo and behold, the playful and ebullient baroque began to fascinate me.

In the winter semester of 1992–93, Volker Rittberger was visiting professor at the Institute for Social Science in New York. Like him, we were attracted by the New World, so we decided to visit him and his family over New Year. Norbert Greinacher also joined the party. He was professor for practical theology in the Catholic-Protestant faculty in Tübingen, and a social democrat. He and I had both taken part in a demonstration at the nuclear missile base in Grossengstingen. So Norbert joined our family circle as a Catholic 'single'. We flew to New York on 28 December, stayed in the Hilton and the Tower Hotel, and carried out a full New York programme—for example, the Broadway Musical *Crazy for You*, the Metropolitan Opera, the Metropolitan and Guggenheim Museums, the Empire State Building, the Statue of Liberty, and other things. Elisabeth and I saw the film *Malcom X* and the musical *Cats*. With the Rittbergers we ate seafood on Pier 17, and with Greinacher I indulged in 'surf and turf'—steak with lobster—a delicacy which soon brought us to the limits of our capacity. The hotel was close to the Rockefeller Center. Above the walled courtyard below hovers the golden Prometheus, under which Elisabeth and I had eaten a long and leisurely meal on the first evening after our first arrival in 1967. High up under the roof is the Rainbow Bar I have already mentioned, from which there are glorious views of Lower Manhattan on the one side and Central

Park on the other. One is only admitted in jacket and tie, but if need be these can be hired in the cloakroom. We often went there in the late morning or early evening for drinks, and it is from there that we took the name 'the Rainbow Bar Gang'. On New Year's Eve we tried to get to Times Square, but it was already full of jostling, no longer quite sober people, who wanted to greet the New Year when the hour struck. So we did the same from a distance.

In 1993 Ludwig and Linde Liegle took us through Schwäbisch Gmünd. Under the guidance of a supervising architect, we explored the great church and climbed up to the roof. There one can see an old crane, no longer in operation, with which, once upon a time, during the service on Ascension Day, a figure of Jesus was drawn up out of the church into the heavenly roof. This blatant realism was a bit too much for my Reformed heart. The old goldsmiths' city had already turned into an artists' town, and a good deal of modern art was displayed in the squares and on the streets.

In 1994 we first travelled to Norbert's home town, Freiburg, and to Baden's wine towns, such as Staufe, where Mephisto is supposed to have taken Faust off to hell, and to the gardens of the countess Zeppelin. In July Greinacher then invited us to the Bregenz Festival, for he was on good terms with one of the directors. In the lakeside theatre we saw *Nabucco* and heard the prisoners' chorus, which rang out far over Lake Constance. Norbert also enjoyed introducing us to his artist friends in the Black Forest and the Swabian Alb. He is a well-known figure in these parts. The two of us also held an ecumenical service at the opening of a Socialist Party (SPD) conference, where we harmonized very well.

In 1995 we prepared for a more extended journey to Rome, where we stayed for five days in the Hotel Santa Chiara on the square with Bernini's little elephant. We ate truffle ice in the Tres Scalini on the Piazza Navona, wandered through the remains of the old Roman Forum, descended to the Christian underworld of the catacombs, and were shown the new excavations beneath St Peter's by a Jesuit Father whom I knew. After we had admired the Vatican Museum and Michelangelo's Sistine Chapel, we also paid tribute to Giordano Bruno, who was executed as a heretic in 1600. His monument stands on what is today the flower market. We also drifted at random through wonderful ancient Rome. My old friend Gerald O'Collins, theological dean at the Gregoriana, joined us, and we celebrated the meeting in the well-known restaurant Dodeci Apostoli. I also gave a lecture in the priestly college at the Chiesa del Gesùs. Then an awkward situation cropped up. The director of the Germanicum invited Elisabeth and me to a formal discussion, since I had lived there during my visiting professorship at the Gregoriana. But he had no wish to include the reform Catholic theologian Greinacher: to us he was bound by ecumenical friendship, but he had no ties of the kind with the reformers in his own camp. That was a blow for our friend, but we didn't want to refuse because, with Elisabeth, the first feminist theologian was invited to the Germanicum.

I shall leave out a journey to St Petersburg in 1998, because we were there together with a larger group under the leadership of Nora Bierig. A particular high spot during the year—quite literally so—was a visit to the holiday home of Inge and Richard Michaelis on Lake Maggiore. The house lies above the lake on the top of a mountain, like an eagle's nest, and is built on the slope. It is not easy to find, but then offers a glorious view of the west side of the lake.

This brings me to our great Andalusian journey, which was thought out and organized by Linde Liegle. On this journey we were joined by Eva and Uli Herrmann, and they remained members of our group of friends. Her field is the Romance languages, while he is professor of pedagogics in Ulm, and a high-ranking cultural historian. We viewed Moorish Granada, with the courts in the castle which looked to me Indian, and the long gardens of the Generalife, with their artistic fountains. We explored Christianized Cordoba, with the church that towers up in the midst of the widely spreading mosque. In Seville my acquaintance Professor Garrido Luceno took us on and brought us close to the altar wall in the great church, which is supposed to be adorned with the first gold that Columbus brought back from America. The tiled Old City was scented with countless orange trees, and the Spanish Square, which was left over from the World Fair, impressed us greatly. We saw neither *Carmen* nor the *Barber of Seville*, but both reflect the European culture which originated in this city in southern Spain. In Ronda one is shown the hotel where Rilke wrote when he did not happen to be in one of diverse European castles. Elisabeth and I skipped the famous bull-fighting arena and instead took a coach drive through the quiet city. In Marbella we celebrated Uli Herrmann's birthday and then, culturally sated, flew home.

In July 2002 the time had finally come for me to invite the 'Gang' to my own home town of Hamburg. For once it was not raining, and the Alster and the harbour were bathed in glorious sunshine. We sailed through the canals, which are more numerous than those in Venice. But then the group was determined to see the church of my old congregation in Wasserhorst. We borrowed cars from our daughter Susanne and her husband, Wilhelm, and drove in the direction of Bremen. We viewed not only my old village church, which dates from the twelfth century, but Worpswede as well. Our friend Tamen Köhler came and told the story of Heinrich Vogeler in the garden belonging to his house. I was relieved that I had been able to show my North German home from its best side.

The following year, 2003, it was the Herrmanns' turn. They took us to their home in Velbert, in the Rhineland. In Altenberg Cathedral, which was restored by Prussia and was consecrated bi-confessionally, we discovered the heavenly Jerusalem in the huge, round stained-glass window. I was especially moved by a modern sculpture: the crucified Christ is leaning down from the cross and embracing Bernard of Clairvaux and Martin Luther. Beneath his cross the denominational divisions end: that was the message. We also visited the little Reformed villages of Gruiten and Schöller, where I had preached during my time in Wuppertal.

This group of friends is, of course, more than a travel group. We celebrate our retirements and our birthdays together. We discuss theological and political, medical and educational, local and universal questions, and appreciate the variety of faculties and personalities we represent. For each and every one of us, it is good to be drawn out of our own circle and to look beyond our own backyard. And when the professional deformations which make one unilateral and solitary recede and disappear, free, human friendships grow. These are wonderful experiences as one grows older, because they make one come completely alive in a new way. As the Chinese proverb says, 'With maturity one becomes ever younger.'

POSTSCRIPT

A great deal that is worth thinking about has been written about truth and fiction in biographies, and in autobiographies especially. Who knows anyone else? And who can know himself? But I shall dispense with these reflections and in this postscript shall only say why I have written this story of my life.

To put it simply: I enjoy telling, and I want to thank—which is why I am thinking back.

The fearful question 'Who am I really?' has never tormented me since I was young. It is a lonely question. That question has left me since I experienced the love of a beloved person: 'Wie sie sich mir zugewendet, / bin ich mir ein wertes Ich,' wrote Goethe in his *Westöstlichen Diwan*—'In that she turned to me, I became for myself a valued I.' And so I have found it down to the present day.

For the most part I have been able to answer with gratitude the question about divine guidance in my own life, even though so much was at the time incomprehensible and remained obscure. But what I have been sure of ever since my early experiences of death in the firestorm in Hamburg in 1943 was, and still is, the need to find an answer to the question, Why am I alive, and not dead like the others? Everything I have begun in my life was an attempt to answer this question.

What finally impelled me to write this autobiography was not the wish to draw up a balance sheet of my life—what was positive, what negative; what were the gains and the losses. No one is bound to be his own judge, even if his own accuser is still his own defender. That we can confidently leave to the one who knows us better than we know ourselves, and who awaits us with love. But as I wrote, I went through my life with increasing gratitude. After those early experiences of death, life has for me always been a wonderful alternative, and every morning a surprise to be welcomed.

But I have not only lived myself; I have also been given life, and 'by goodly powers wondrously safeguarded', as Dietrich Bonhoeffer wrote in his poem. The people to whom I owe my life are unforgotten. They are present to me, because in their love I became free and can breathe in wide spaces. Unforgotten for me are people to whom I am bound in affection and respect. They have entered into my life, and I perhaps a little into theirs. Unforgotten for me are the dead whom I miss. They are always especially present to me. Nothing that has been, is no more; everything that has happened remains. We cannot make anything undone, not the ill, but not the good either. What was lovely and successful, and the happiness we have experienced, no one can take from us, neither transitory time nor death.

I have written this story of my life for all those to whom I am bound in life's closer circles and its less close ones: for Elisabeth, with whom I have shared life for 54 years, for our children and grandchildren, for those who have accompanied me on the path I have travelled, those who have shared its pains and have been my neighbours in my joys in theology and church, in the faculties here and in seminaries and universities all over the world, for the students who listened to me assentingly or with a frown, who read my books or had to read them, for my more than 200 doctoral candidates who were supposed to solve the riddles in my theology and explain its obscurities, and not least for the unknown readers who take up this book. But in the end I have to admit that in writing I simply had delight in the telling, and pleasure in the writing.

NOTES

Chapter One. The Settlement

1. Johannes Moltmann, *Vom künftigen Gott oder Psychotheismus statt Kosmotheismus*, Leipzig 1905; and many other titles.

2. The later federal chancellor and his wife.

Chapter Two. July 1943: Operation Gomorrah

1. H. Brunswig, *Feuersturm über Hamburg. Die Luftangriffe auf Hamburg im 2. Weltkrieg und ihre Folgen*, Stuttgart 2003; M. Middlebrook, *The Battle of Hamburg: Allied Bomber Forces against a German City in 1943*, London 1980.

2. The school-leaving examination which is the necessary qualification for study at the university.

Chapter Three. Prisoner of War, 1945–47

1. *Norton Camp. Die Universität hinter Stacheldraht. Cuckney/Nottinghamshire, England. Kriegsgefangenenhilfe des Weltbundes der Christlichen Vereine Junge Männer 1945–1948. Bericht über eine Reise nach 50 Jahre 1995*, Pfullendorf 1995.

2. My sermon preached on the occasion of that journey after 50 years to the old site of Norton Camp was a personal meditation on Jacob's wrestling with God on the Jabbok, according to Genesis 32.25–32. It was preached on 13 August 1995 in the Bonhoeffer Church in Forest Hill, London. See J. Moltmann, *The Source of Life*, trans. Margaret Kohl, London and Minneapolis 1997, 1–9.

Chapter Four. Theology Student in Göttingen, 1948–52

1. H.-G. Ulrichs (ed.), *Hellmut Traub, 'Unerschrocken zur Zeit und zur Unzeit'*, Wuppertal 1997.

2. In some of the Protestant regional churches in Germany, 'superintendent' is the equivalent of what in other parts of Germany is called 'regional bishop'.

3. J. Seim, *Hans-Joachim Iwand. Eine Biographie*, Gütersloh 1999; id., *Iwand-Studien. Aufsätze und Briefwechsel mit Georg Eichholz und Heinrich Held*, SVRKG 135, Cologne 1999.

4. H. J. Iwand, *Predigt-Meditationen*, Göttingen 1963.

5. These had the reputation of being right-wing and nationalist.

6. V. von Bülow, *Otto Weber (1902–1966). Reformierter Theologe und Kirchenpolitiker*, Göttingen 1999.

7. ET *Foundations of Dogmatics*, trans. and annotated D. L. Guder, Grand Rapids 1981–83.

8. O. Weber, *Karl Barths Kirchliche Dogmatik. Ein einführender Bericht zu den Bänden I/1–IV/3.2*, 6th ed., Neukirchen 1967. ET *Karl Barth's Church Dogmatics: An Introductory Report on Volumes I:1 to III:4*, trans. A. C. Cochrane, Philadelphia 1953.

9. E. Wolf, *Peregrinatio. Studien zur reformatorischen Theologie und zum Kirchenproblem*, Munich 1954; *Peregrinatio II. Studien zur reformatorischen Theologie, zum Kirchenrecht und zur Sozialethik*, Munich 1965; also *Barmen. Kirche zwischen Versuchung und Gnade*, Munich 1957.

CHAPTER FIVE. PASTOR IN WASSERHORST, 1953–58

1. J. Moltmann, 'Prädestination und Heilsgeschichte bei Moyse Amyraut. Ein Beitrag zur Geschichte der reformierten Theologie zwischen Orthodoxie und Aufklärung', *Zeitschrift für Kirchengeschichte*, 4th series III, vol. 65/3, 270–303.

2. Later president of the German Federal Republic.

3. Later president of West Germany.

4. Johannes Kuhn, *So war's—mein Leben. Biographische Notizen*, Stuttgart 1996.

5. 'Zur Bedeutung des Petrus Ramus für Philosophie und Theologie im Calvinismus', *ZKG* 68, 1957, 295–318. My examination thesis 'Grundzüge mystischer Theologie bei Gerhard Tersteegens' was published in *EvTh* 16, 1956, 205–24.

6. 'Christoph Pezel (1539–1604) und der Calvinismus in Bremen', *Hospitium Ecclesiae, Forschungen zur bremischen Kirchengeschichte* 2, Bremen 1958.

7. 'Johannes Molanus und der Übergang Bremens zum Calvinismus', *Jahrbuch der Wittheit zu Bremen*, vol. 1, Bremen 1957, 119–41.

8. A. A. van Ruler, *Theologie van het Apostolaat*, Nijkerk 1954; id., *Gestaltwerdung Christi in der Welt. Über das Verhältnis von Kirche und Kultur*, Neukirchen 1956.

CHAPTER SIX. THE CHURCH SEMINARY IN WUPPERTAL, 1958–64

1. H. Aschermann and W. Schneider, *Studium im Auftrag der Kirche. Die Anfänge der kirchlichen Hochschule Wuppertal 1935 bis 1945*, Cologne 1985.

2. Ehrentraut und Rudolf Bohren, *Das Gesicht des Theologen in Porträts photographiert von Georg Eichholz*, Neukirchen 1984.

3. M. Breidert und H.-G. Ulrichs (eds), *Wilhelm Niesel—Theologe und Kirchenpolitiker*, Emder Beiträge zum reformierten Protestantismus 7, Wuppertal 2003.

4. J. Harder, *Aufbruch ohne Ende*, with a foreword by Johannes Rau, Wuppertal and Zurich 1992.

5. Later president of the Federal Republic.

6. *Anfänge Dialektischer Theologie*, pt I: Karl Barth, Heinrich Barth, Emil Brunner, Theologische Bücherei 17, Munich 1962; pt II: Rudolf Bultmann, Friedrich

Gogarten, Eduard Thurneysen, Munich 1963. Abbreviated Eng. trans., ed. J. M. Robinson, *The Beginnings of Dialectic Theology*, Richmond 1968–.

7. 'Die "Weltoffenheit des Menschen." Zur neueren philosophischen Anthropologie', *Verkündigung und Forschung* 1960–61, 115–34.

8. 'Geschichtstheologie und pietistisches Menschenbild bei Johann Coccejus und Theodor Undereyck', *EvTh* 19, 1959, 343–61.

9. 'Jacob Brocard als Vorläufer der Reich-Gottes-Theologie und der symbolisch-prophetischen Schriftauslegung des Johann Coccejus', *ZKG* 71, 1960, 110–29.

10. O. Weber, *Die Treue Gottes und die Kontinuität der menschlichen Existenz, Gesammelte Aufsätze*, Neukirchen 1967.

11. 'Erwählung und Beharrung der Gläubigen nach Calvin', *Calvinstudien* 1959, Neukirchen 1960, 43–61.

12. H. A. Obermann, *Zwei Reformationen. Luther und Calvin. Alte und Neue Welt*, Berlin 2000, 227 (cf. ET ed. D. Weinstein, *The Two Reformations: The Journey from the Last Days to the New World*, Newhaven and London 2003).

13. Published in the series *Beiträge zur Geschichte und Lehre der Reformierten Kirche*, vol. 12, Neukirchen 1961.

14. 'Herrschaft Christi und soziale Wirklichkeit nach Dietrich Bonhoeffer', *Theologische Existenz heute* 71, Munich 1959.

15. 'The Lordship of Christ and Human Society', in J. Moltmann and J. Weissbach, *Two Studies in the Theology of Dietrich Bonhoeffer*, New York 1967, 19–94.

16. 'Die Wirklichkeit der Welt und Gottes konkretes Gebot nach Dietrich Bonhoeffer', in E. Bethge (ed.), *Die mündige Welt*, vol III, Munich 1960, 42–67.

17. J. Mehlhausen (ed.), *Zeugen des Widerstandes*, Tübingen 1996, 194–216.

18. Clarke G. Chapman, 'Hope and the Ethics of Formation: Moltmann as an Interpreter of Bonhoeffer', *Studies in Religion/Sciences Religieuses* 12, no. 4, 183, 449–60.

19. 'Die Gemeinde im Horizont der Herrschaft Christi. Neue Perspektiven in der protestantischen Theologie', Erkenntnis und Bekennen 5, Neukirchen 1959; M. Dröge, 'Über Moltmanns Frühschriften', *EvTh* 66, 2006, 173–85.

20. Speech on the conferral of the Ernst Bloch Prize in Ludwigshafen 1994; 'Über Ernst Bloch', in *Publik Forum* 1995, 24, 63–65.

21. ET *The Principle of Hope*, trans. N. and S. Plaice and P. Knight, Cambridge, Mass., and Oxford, 1986.

22. Messianismus und Marxismus. Einführende Bemerkungen zum "Prinzip Hoffnung" von Ernst Bloch', *Kirche in der Zeit* 15, 1960, 291–95. See also Elke Kruttschnitt, *Ernst Bloch und das Christentum*, Mainz 1993.

23. ET *The Spirit of Utopia*, trans. A. Nassar, Stanford 2000.

24. *Gedenkbuch für Else Bloch-von Stritzki*, in *Tendenz—Latenz—Utopie*, Frankfurt 1978, 3–50.

25. 'Messianismus und Marxismus. Einführende Bemerkungen zum "Prinzip Hoffnung" von Ernst Bloch', in *Kirche in der Zeit*, 1960, 291–95; M. Walser (ed.), *Über Ernst Bloch*, Frankfurt 1968, 42–60; *Im Gesprach mit Ernst Bloch*, KT 18, Munich 1976.

26. ET *Natural Law and Human Dignity*, trans. D. J. Schmidt, Cambridge, Mass., and London 1986.

27. 'Die Menschenrechte und der Marxismus. Einführende Bemerkungen und kritische Reflexionen zu Ernst Bloch "Naturrecht und menschliche Würde"', *Kirche in der Zeit*, 1962, 122–26; *Im Gespräch mit Ernst Bloch*, KT 18, Munich 1976.

28. 'Exegese und Eschatologie der Geschichte', *EvTh* 22, 1992, 31–66. ET 'Exegesis and the Eschatology of History', in *Hope and Planning*, trans. Margaret Clarkson, London and New York 1971, 56–98.

CHAPTER SEVEN. PUBLIC THEOLOGY

1. 'Schrift, Tradition, Traditionen. Bericht über die Arbeit der Sektion II der 4. Weltkonferenz für Glauben und Kirchenverfassung in Montreal', *Ökumenische Rundschau* 13, 1964, 104–11.

2. See E. Käsemann, 'Unity and Multiplicity in the New Testament Doctrine of the Church', in *New Testament Questions of Today*, trans. W. J. Montague, London 1969, 252–59 (being selections from *Exegetische Versuche und Besinnungen*, vol. 2, Göttingen 1964).

3. See 'The Ecumenical Church under the Cross', in *The Passion for Life: A Messianic Lifestyle*, trans. D. Meeks, Philadelphia 1978 (= *The Open Church: Invitation to a Messianic Lifestyle*, London 1978). W. Visser't Hooft presents an autobiographical approach to the ecumenical movement in *Die Welt war meine Gemeinde*, Munich 1972.

4. L. Vischer, *Die Einheit der Kirche. Materialien der ökumenischen Bewegung*, Munich 1965; G. Gassmann (ed.), *Documentary History of Faith and Order 1963–1993*, Geneva 1993; G. Müller-Fahrenholz, *Einheit der Kirche—Einheit der Menschheit*, Frankfurt 1978.

5. L. Vischer (ed.), *Geist Gottes—Geist Christi, Ökumenische Überlegungen zur Filioque-Kontroverse*, Ökumenische Rundschau Beiheft 39, 1981.

6. *Credo in Spiritum Sanctum*, Rome 1984.

7. Special number Regensburg 1963; *Bayerisches Ärzteblatt* 1964; *EvTh* 1955.

8. R. Kunz and H. Fehr (eds), *The Challenge of Life: Biomedical Progress and Human Values, Roche Anniversary Symposium*, Basel and Stuttgart 1972.

9. Ibid., 316–34.

10. See *Science and Wisdom*, trans. Margaret Kohl, Minneapolis and London 2002; also Celia E. Deane-Drummond's excellent book *Creation through Wisdom: Theology and the New Biology*, Edinburgh 2000.

11. Summarized in *Diakonie im Horizont des Reiches Gottes. Schritte zu einem Diakonentum aller Gläubigen*, Neukirchen 1983. See also T. Runyon (ed.), *Hope for the Church: Jürgen Moltmann in Dialogue with Practical Theology*, Nashville 1979.

12. First published in *Gott kommt und der Mensch wird frei*, KT 17, Munich 1975, 51–63.

13. For example, by Nancy I. Eiesland, *The Disabled God*, Nashville 1997; Nancy I. Eiesland and Eon E. Salier (eds), *Human Disability and the Service of God: Reassessing Religious Practice*, Nashville 1998; R. D. Hitching, *The Church and Deaf People*, London 2004.

14. J. Polkinghorne, *Belief in God in an Age of Science*, New Haven and London 1998; A. R. Peacocke, *Creation in the World of Science*, Oxford 1979; I. G. Barbour, *Issues in Science and Religion*, New York 1966.

15. See n. 6 above.

16. K. Koschorke (ed.), *Wege zu einer trinitarischen Theologie. Festakt zur Feier des 75. Geburtstag von Wolfhart Pannenberg*, Munich 2004. Pannenberg replied at the academic celebration of my eightieth birthday in April 2006 with a lecture on 'Der Offenbarungstheologische Ansatz in der Trinitätslehre'. See M. Welker and M. Volf, *Der lebendige Gott als Trinität, Festschrift für J. Moltmann*, Gütersloh 2006, 13–22.

17. *Hoffnung jenseits von Glauben und Skepsis. Fontane und die bürgerliche Welt*, Munich 1964.

18. *Sinnflut und Arche. Biblische Motive bei Wilhelm Raabe.*

19. W. Kreck, *Grundfragen der Dogmatik*, Munich 1970; *Grundfragen der Ethik*, Munich 1975; *Grundfragen der Ekklesiologie*, Munich 1981; *Grundfragen der Eschatologie*, Munich 1961.

20. Universities in Germany are not autonomous institutions but come under the ministries of education in their respective states.

21. Required of civil servants in Germany.

CHAPTER EIGHT. THE THEOLOGY OF HOPE, 1964

1. *Heute: Theologie der Hoffnung. Untersuchungen zur Begründung und zu den Konsequenzen einer christlichen Eschatologie*, Gütersloh 2005.

2. Major J. Jones, *Black Awareness: A Theology of Hope*, Nashville 1971; J. H. Cone, *Martin and Malcolm. America: A Dream or a Nightmare?* New York 1991.

3. G. von Rad, *Old Testament Theology*, trans. D. M. G. Stalker, 2 vols, Edinburgh and London 1962, 1965.

4. C. Hinz, '"Feuer und Wolke im Exodus", Kritisch-assistierende Bemerkungen zu Jürgen Moltmanns Theologie der Hoffnung', *EvTh* 27, 1967, 76–109; also in W. D. Marsch (ed.), *Diskussion über die Theologie der Hoffnung*, Munich 1967, 125–61.

5. B. Janowski, *Gottes Gegenwart in Israel. Beiträge zur Theologie des Alten Testaments*, Neukirchen 1993, 119–49.

6. For more detail, cf. *The Way of Jesus Christ: Christology in Messianic Dimensions*, trans. Margaret Kohl, London and San Francisco 1990.

7. F. Herzog (ed.), *The Future of Hope: Theology as Eschatology*, New York 1970.

8. K. Barth, 'The Christian Community and the Civil Community', in id., *Against the Stream: Shorter Post-War Writings 1946–1952*, ed. R.G. Smith, trans. E. M. Delacour and S. Goodman, London 1954.

9. *Uppsala 68 spricht. Sektionsberichte der Vierten Vollversammlung des Ökumenischen Rates der Kirchen Uppsala 1968*, Geneva 1968, 1–2.

10. See Paul Ricoeur, *The Conflict of Interpretations*, ET ed. Don Ihde, new ed., London 2004.

11. Ibid.

12. J. B. Metz, *Zur Theologie der Welt*, Mainz and Munich 1968, 83 (cf. ET *Theology of the World*, trans. W. Glen-Doepel, London and New York 1969).

13. Ibid., 106.

14. K. Rahner, 'Zur Theologie der Hoffnung', in *Zur Theologie der Zukunft*, Munich 1971, 160–76. This is a lecture that Rahner gave in America in 1967. He called the Godness of God 'the absolute future' and discussed it in relation to the relative future of secular thinking. See also E. Schillebeeckx, *God, the Future of Man*, trans. N. D. Smith, London 1969.

15. Hans Urs von Balthasar, 'Der Versuch Moltmanns', in *Theodramatik* IV. *Das Endspiel*, Einsiedeln 1983, 148–67 (*Theodrama: A Theological Dramatic Theory*, trans. G. Harrison, San Francisco 1988, vol. 5 [German vol. 4]: *The Last Act*).

16. J. B. Metz, 'Nachwort', in R. Garaudy, J. B. Metz, and K. Rahner, *Der Dialog oder Ändert sich das Verhältnis zwschen Katholizismus und Marxismus?* Hamburg 1966, 121–38.

17. Göttingen 1967 (ET *Basic Questions in Theology*, trans. G. H. Kehm, 3 vols, London 1970–).

Chapter Nine. The Christian-Marxist Dialogue

1. *Marxismusstudien*, vol. 1, Schriften der Studiengemeinschaft der Evangelischen Akademien, Tübingen 1954, with a foreword by Erwin Metzke. At least five volumes appeared.

2. E. Kellner (ed.), *Christentum und Marxismus—Heute. Gespräche der Paulus-Gesellschaft*, Vienna, Frankfurt, and Zurich 1966.

3. Hamburg 1966.

4. K. Rahner, *Christentum* (see n.19), 204; *Dialog* (see n.16), 12.

5. R. Garaudy, *Dialog*, 89.

6. Ibid., 95–97.

7. E. Kellner (ed.), *Schöpfertum und Freiheit in einer humanen Gesell-schaft. Marienbader Protokolle*, Vienna, Frankfurt, and Zurich 1969; J. Moltmann, 'Marxismus und Christen in Marienbad 27.4–30.4', *EvTh* 27, 1967, 398–400.

8. 'Die Revolution der Freiheit'; reprinted in *Perspektiven der Theologie*, Munich and Mainz 1968, 189–211; in revised form, trans. D. Meeks, in *Religion, Revolution, and the Future*, New York 1969.

9. R. Garaudy, *Dialog*, 98.

10. Ibid.

11. Cf. R. Garaudy, *The Alternative Future: A Vision of Christian Marxism*, trans. from the French by L. Mahew, Harmondsworth 1976.

12. J. B. Metz, *Dialog*, 128.

13. Ibid., 131.

14. R. Garaudy, *Parole d'homme*, Paris 1975.

15. 'The Revolution of Freedom: The Christian and Marxist Struggle', in T. W. Ogletree (ed.), *Openings for Marxist-Christian Dialogue*, Nashville 1968, 47–72.

16. ET 'God in the Revolution', *Student World* 61, no. 3, 1968, 241–52; also in *Religion, Revolution, and the Future*, New York 1969, 129–47.

17. R. Garaudy, *Parole d'homme*, op. cit.

18. That already comes out very clearly in his book *Jesus für Atheisten*, with a foreword by Helmut Gollwitzer, Stuttgart 1972, which went through many editions (ET *Jesus for Atheists*, London 1976).

19. V. Gardavsky, *Gott ist nicht ganz tot—Ein Marxist über Bibel, Religion und Atheismus*, Munich 1968, with an introduction by J. Moltmann (ET *God Is Not Yet Dead*, trans. from German by V. Menkes, Harmondsworth 1973).

20. Garaudy, *Parole d'homme*.

21. Ibid.

22. R. Garaudy, *Plädoyer für einen Dialog der Zivilisationen*, Vienna 1980.

23. Cf. S. Ramirez, *Adios Muchachos! Eine Erinnerung an die sandinistische Revolution*, Wuppertal 2001.

CHAPTER TEN. MY AMERICAN DREAM

1. Cf. J. Moltmann, 'Der "Amerikanische Traum"', *EvTh* 37, 1977, 166–78; ET 'America as Dream', in *On Human Dignity: Political Theology and Ethics*, trans. M. D. Meeks, Philadelphia 1984, 147–62.

2. F. Herzog, *Liberation Theology: Liberation in the Light of the Fourth Gospel*, New York 1972.

3. For a general impression see Jörg Rieger (ed.), *Theology from the Belly of the Whale: A Frederick Herzog Reader*, Harrisburg 1999.

4. W. Capps (ed.), *The Future of Hope*, Philadelphia 1970.

5. New York 1964; London 1966.

6. W. Capps (ed.), *The Future of Hope*, Philadelphia 1970.

7. F. Herzog (ed.), *The Future of Hope: Theology as Eschatology*, New York 1970.

8. Maryleen Muckenhirn (ed.), *The Future as Presence of Shared Hope*, New York 1968.

9. E. Loring, *I Hear Hope Banging at My Back Door: The Open Door Community Atlanta*, Atlanta 2000; P. R. Gathje (ed.), *The Open Door Reader 1982–2002*, Atlanta 2004.

10. In 1970 I wrote for the series How My Mind Has Changed in *The Christian Century*: 'In a culture which glorifies success and happiness and which is blind to the suffering of others, the remembrance that at the centre of the Christian faith is an unsuccessful, suffering Christ dying in shame can open people's eyes for the truth.' Preface to the reprint *Umkehr zur Zukunft*, Munich 1970, 14. That was the turning point from the theology of hope to the theology of the cross. Cf. also D. Hall, 'Theology of Hope in an officially optimistic society', in *Religion in Life*, 1971; now *The Cross in Our Context*, Minneapolis 2003.

Chapter Eleven. A First Beginning in Tübingen, 1967

1. O. Michel, *Der Brief an die Hebräer*, Göttingen 1949.

2. E. Käsemann, *The Wandering People of God*, trans. R. A. Harrisville and I. L. Sandberg, Minneapolis 1984.

3. H. Oberman, *The Two Reformations: The Journey from the Last Days to the New World*, ed. D. Weinberg, New Haven and London 2003.

4. D. Rössler, 'Positionelle und kritische Theologie', *ZThK* 67, 1970, 215–31.

5. Frankfurt 1968. ET *Atheism in Christianity*, trans. J. T. Swann, New York 1972. My review in *Der Spiegel* of 30 September 1968 is also printed under the title 'Hat die Schlange doch recht?' in *In Gesprach mit Ernst Bloch*, Munich 1976, 49–62.

6. 'Annahme oder Abtreibung—Thesen zur Diskussion über §218 StBG von Eberhard Jüngel, Ernst Käsemann, Jürgen Moltmann, Dietrich Rössler', in Jürgen Baumann (ed.), *Das Abtreibungsverbot des §218,* Darmstadt Neuwied 1972, 135–43.

7. J. Moltmann, *Die Gemeinde im Horizont der Herrschaft Christi. Neue Perspektiven in der protestantischen Theologie*, Neukirchen 1959, 16–17.

8. G. Sauter, 'Die Zahl as Schlüssel zur Welt. Johann Albrecht Bengels "prophetische Zeitrechnung" im Zusammenhang seiner Theologie', *EvTh* 26, 1966, 1–36.

9. J. T. Beck, *Die Vollendung des Reiches Gottes. Separatdruck aus der Christlichen Glaubenslehre*, Gütersloh 1887.

10. J. B. Metz, *Zur Theologie der Welt*, Mainz 1968, 83 (ET *Theology of the World*, trans. W. Glen-Doepel, London 1969).

11. Ibid., 106.

12. A. Schindler (ed.), *Monotheismus als politisches Problem. Erik Peterson und die Kritik der politischen Theologie*, Gütersloh 1978, 172.

13. J. B. Metz, 'Zukunft aus dem Gedächtnis des Leidens. Zur Dialektik des Fortschritts', in *Glaube in Geschichte und Gesellschaft*, Mainz 1977, 87–103 (ET *Faith in History and Society*, trans. D. Smith, London 1980).

14. J. Moltmann, 'Theologische Kritik der politischen Religion', in J. B. Metz, J. Moltmann, and W. Oelmüller, *Kirche im Prozess der Aufklärung*, Mainz and Munich 1970, 11–52 (ET 'The Cross and Civil Religion', in *Religion and Political Society*, New York 1974, 9–48) .

15. C. Schmitt, *Politische Theologie. Vier Kapitel zur Lehre von der Souveränität*, Munich and Leipzig 1922, 1934. Still important here is E. Peterson, 'Der Monotheismus als politisches Problem', (1935) in *Theologische Traktate*, Munich 1951, 45–148.

16. J. B. Metz, *Zum Begriff der neuen Politischen Theologie 1967–1997*, Mainz 1997.

CHAPTER TWELVE. A SECOND BEGINNING IN TÜBINGEN

1. Joseph Cardinal Ratzinger, *Aus meinem Leben. Erinnerungen*, Stuttgart 1998, 139.

2. In *Perspektiven der Theologie. Gesammelte Aufsätze*, Munich 1968, 128–48.

3. Ibid., 36–56; ET 'God and Resurrection', in *Hope and Planning*, trans. M. Clarkson, London and New York 1971, 31–55.

4. See *The Church in the Power of the Spirit*, London and New York 1977, 242–60.

CHAPTER THIRTEEN. LECTURE TOURS WORLDWIDE, 1969–75

1. Cf. 'Versöhnung in Freiheit', in Studienbuch zur Vorbereitung der Konferenz, 1970; reprinted in *Umkehr zur Freiheit*, Gütersloh 1970, 89–104; 'Gott versöhnt und mach frei', *EvKomm* 3, 1970, 515–20; ET 'God Reconciles and Makes Free', *Reformed and Presbyterian World* 31, no. 3/4, 1970, 105–17.

2. See '"Where There Is Hope, There Is Religion": Ernst Bloch', in *History and the Triune God: Contributions to Trinitarian Theology*, trans. J. Bowden, London 1991, 143–55; also *The Experiment Hope*, trans. M. D. Meeks, Philadelphia 1975.

3. Cf. J. H. Cone, *The Spirituals and the Blues: An Interpretation*, New York 1972.

4. J. Moltmann, *Die ersten Freigelassenen der Schöpfung. Versuche über die Freude an der Freiheit und das Wohlgefallen am Spiel*, Munich 1971. ET *Theology of Play*, trans. R. Ulrich, New York 1972; British edition under the title *Theology of Joy*, London 1973.

5. *The Experiment Hope*, op. cit. (see n. 22).

6. Stuttgart 1970.

7. Op. cit.; see n. 4 above. This little book went through six editions and was translated into ten languages. It evidently had a liberating effect in the situation of the time.

8. R. Kunz and H. Fehr (eds), *The Challenge of Life: Biomedical Progress and Human Values; Roche Anniversary Symposium*, Basel 1972.

9. E. H. Cousins (ed.), *Hope and the Future of Man*, Philadelphia 1972, London 1973.

10. In *Das Experiment Hoffnung*, 93–111 (ET *The Experiment Hope*).

11. German version of this lecture in J. Moltmann and J. Stöhr (eds), *Begegnung mit Polen. Evangelische Kirchen und die Herausforderung durch Geschichte und Politik*, Munich 1974, 165–82.

Chapter Fourteen. World Mission Assembly in Bangkok, 1972–73

1. P. Potter (ed.), *Das Heil der Welt heute, Ende oder Beginn der Weltmission? Dokumente der Weltmissionskonferenz Bangkok 1973*, Stuttgart 1973 (World Conference on Salvation Today); K. Viehweger, *Weltmissionskonferenz Bangkok. Samudhprakaru-Kilometer 31*, Hamburg 1973.

2. 'Bangkok 1973: Eine Mission an uns', *EvTh* 33, 1973, 209–13. 'In Bangkok sagte Dr Jürgen Moltmann, Stellungnahme zur Arbeit der Sektion II: Heil und soziale Gerechtigkeit, der Weltmissionskonferenz Bangkok', in *Der Überblick* 9, 1973, no. 1, 21.

3. Mar Osthathios, *Theologie einer klassenlosen Gesellschaft, mit einem Geleitwort von Jürgen Moltmann*, Hamburg 1980.

4. *Das Heil der Welt heute*, op. cit., 196–208 (World Conference on Salvation Today. Cf. II/I A-c with *The Crucified God* [ET 1974], 329–38). Klaus Viehweger wrote (*Weltmissionskonferenz*, op. cit., 156): 'Since Bangkok there has been much talk about the theological introduction to the report of Section II/I, in which the German theologian Jürgen Moltmann played an essential part. People often speak of it as if it were *the* theology of Bangkok.'

5. *Das Heil der Welt heute*, op. cit., 1.

6. Minutes and Report of the Assembly of the Commission on World Mission and Evangelism of the World Council of Churches, December 31, 1972, and January 9–12, 1973, Bangkok Assembly 1973. Appendix E: World Conference on Salvation Today, Section II: Salvation and Social Justice.

Chapter Fifteen. Ways to the Far East, 1973 and 1975

1. *Das Heil der Welt heute*, op. cit., 1.

2. First published 1946; ET Richmond 1965, London 1966; in German, Göttingen 1972.

3. I have gone into this in *The Crucified God*, 14f., 153 n. 2.

4. See *The Passion for Life*, trans. M. D. Meeks, Philadelphia 1978, British edition under the title *The Open Church*, London 1978, 95–112.

5. *Evangelische Kommentare* 8, 1975, 288–93.

6. *Minjung. Theologie des Volkes Gottes in Südkorea*, Neukirchen 1984. My 'introduction' also appeared in Japanese in *Hukkkin to Sekai* 40, 1985, 53–57.

7. Gershom Scholem, *Judaica* I, Frankfurt 1969, 73.

Chapter Sixteen. The Crucified God, 1972

1. J. Moltmann, *The Crucified God*, trans. R. A.Wilson and J. Bowden, London and New York 1974; SCM Classics, London 2000, IX.

2. I have described this in 'A Personal Meditation on Jacob's Struggle at the Brook Jabbok, Following Genesis 32.25–32', in *The Source of Life*, trans. Margaret Kohl, London and Minneapolis 1997, 1–9.

3. I owe this to Hans Joachim Iwand.

4. *Theology of Hope*, 168–72.

5. J. B. Metz, J. Moltmann, and W. Oelmüller, *Kirche im Prozess der Aufklärung*, Mainz and Munich 1970, 11–52.

6. C. Schmitt, *Politische Theologie II. Die Legende von der Erledigung jeder Politischen Theologie*, Berlin 1970, 117, n. 3.

7. See J. Moltmann, *Umkehr zur Zukunft*, Munich 1970, 133–47.

8. An excellent account of this is given in J. K. Mozley, *The Impassibility of God: A Survey of Christian Thought*, Cambridge 1926. Cf. also A. van Egmond, *De Lijdende God in de Britse Theologie van de Negentiende Eeuw*, Amsterdam 1986.

9. A. Heschel, *The Prophets*, New York 1955, 221–31, starts from the 'pathos of God' in order to understand the God of Israel.

10. Mascha Kalécko has expressed this exactly in her poem 'Memento': 'Remember: in one's own death one only dies, but with the death of others one has to live.'

11. F. Buchheim, *Der Gnadenstuhl. Darstellung der Dreifaltigkeit*, Würzburg 1974.

12. A. E. Lewis, *Between Cross and Resurrection: A Theology of Holy Saturday*, Grand Rapids 2001.

13. H. Urs von Balthasar has described 'the theology of the three days'. See '*Mysterium Paschale*', in J. Feiner and M. Löhrer, *Mysterium Salutis* III/2, Einsiedeln 1970, 133–326. See also the comment in S. Lösel, *Kreuzwege. Ein ökumenisches Gespräch mit Hans Urs von Balthasar*, Paderborn 2001.

14. D. Bonhoeffer, *Letters and Papers from Prison*, ed. E. Bethge, trans. R. H. Fuller, (4th) enlarged edition, London and New York 1971, 361 (letter of 16 July 1944).

15. T. Rees, *Hymns and Psalms*, Peterborough 1983, no. 36, verse 2.

16. *K. Rahner im Gespräch*, ed. P. Imhoff and H. Biallowons, Munich 1982, 245f.

17. *History and the Triune God*, trans. J. Bowden, London 1991. I do not understand how negative theology knows what God *cannot do*. He cannot change, he cannot move, he cannot suffer. Is there no respect for the liberty of God to determine himself?

18. J. B. Metz, *Memoria Passionis. Ein provozierendes Gedächtnis in pluralistischer Gesellschaft*, Freiburg 2006.

19. H. Küng, *Das Judentum*, Munich 1991, 722 (ET *Judaism*, 1992).

20. D. Sölle, *Suffering*, trans. E. R. Kalin, London 1975. She also used my book as a treasure-trove for her quotations. Her reproach that this is a 'sadomasochistic

theology of the cross' is unfortunately not her own idea, but derives from the atheistic protest movement of 1968 in Tübingen. It was used against Ernst Käsemann and myself in order to discredit us, as the leaflets of that time show.

21. As, for example, J. Niewiadomski, *Die Zweideutigkeit von Gott und Welt in J. Moltmanns Theologien*, Innsbruck 1982, 58; J. O'Donnell, *Trinity and Temporality: The Christian Doctrine of God in the Light of Process Theology and the Theology of Hope*, Oxford 1982–83, 154; M. Steen, 'J. Moltmann's Critical Reception of K. Barth's Theopaschitism', *EthL* 67, 1991, 303; M. Murrmann-Kahl, *'Mysterium Trinitatis'? Fallstudien zur Trinitätslehre in der evangelischen Dogmatik des 20. Jahrhunderts*, Berlin 1997, 1955. I am indebted for this compilation to M. Remenyi, *Um der Hoffnung willen. Untersuchungen zur eschatologischen Theologie Jürgen Moltmanns*, Regensburg 2005, 99.

22. See *The Crucified God*, 192, 242f., passim.

23. Thus with particular lack of comprehension H. Vorgrimler, *Gott. Vater, Sohn und Heiliger Geist*, Münster 2002.

24. E.g., Millicent C. Feske, 'Christ and Suffering in Moltmann's Thought', *Asbury Theological Journal* 55, Spring 2000, 85–104. For a very different view see R. Bauckham, '"Only the Suffering God Can Help": Divine Passibility in Modern Theology', *Themelios* IX, 1984, 6–12; W. McWilliams, *The Passion of God: Divine Suffering in Contemporary Protestant Theology*, Macon 1985; M. Sarot,'De Passibilitas Dei in de Hedendaagen Westerse Theologie: Een Literaturverzicht', *Kerken Theologie* XL–XLIII, 1989, 196–206.

25. U. Ruh, 'Das unterscheidend christliche in der Gottesfrage', *Herder Korrespondenz* 1982, 185.

26. R. Goetz, 'The Suffering God. The Rise of a "New Orthodoxy"', *The Christian Century*, 1986, 385–89. He refers to Warren McWilliams, *The Passion of God: Divine Suffering in Contemporary Protestant Theology*, op. cit. I should also like to point to Paul S. Fiddes, *The Creative Suffering of God*, Oxford 1988; Douglas Hall, *God and Human Suffering*, Minneapolis 2003; and Jean-Louis Souletie, *La Croix de Dieu*, Paris 1997.

Chapter Seventeen. Theological Expansions of the Horizon

1. O. Weber, *Versammelte Gemeinde. Beiträge zum Gespräch über Kirche und Gottesdienst*, Neukirchen 1949.

2. H. Küng in J. Moltmann (ed.), *Wie ich mich verändert habe*, Gütersloh 1997, 99.

3. For more detail see 'Die Zukunft des Christentums', *EvTh* 63, 2003, 25–36.

4. Ahn Byung-Mu, *Draussen vor dem Tor. Kirche und Minjung in Korea*, Göttingen 1986.

5. J. Moltmann (ed.), *Minjung. Theologie des Volkes Gottes in Südkorea*, Göttingen 1986.

6. J. Moltmann, *Diakonie im Horizont des Reiches Gottes. Schritte zum allgemeinen Diakonentum aller Gläubigen*, Neukirchen 1984, 42–52.

7. N. L. Eiesland, *The Disabled God: Toward a Liberatory Theology of Disability*, Nashville 1994; N. L. Eiesland and Don Salier (eds), *Human Disability and the Service of God*, Nashville 1998; R. D. Hitching, *The Church and Deaf People: A Study of Identity, Communication, and Relationships with Special Reference to the Ecclesiology of Jürgen Moltmann*, Paternoster Monographs, Carlisle 2003.

8. In *Diakonie*, op. cit., 52–74.

9. J. Moltmann, 'A Pentecostal Theology of Life', *Journal of Pentecostal Theology*, 1996, 9, 3–15.

10. Gemeinschaft Sant'Egidio, *Jesus als Freund. Mit geistig behinderter Menschen auf dem Weg des Evangeliums*, Würzburg 2004. In Italian: *Gesu per amico. Un Percorso evangelico con i disabili mentali.*

11. *The Open Church: Invitation to a Messianic Life-Style*, trans. M. D. Meeks, London 1978, 84 (also as *The Passion for Life: A Messianic Life-Style*, Philadelphia 1978).

12. Ibid., 87 (trans. slightly altered).

13. E. Moltmann Wendel, *Wach auf, meine Freundin. Die Wiederkehr der Gottesfreundschaft*, Stuttgart 2000; ET *Rediscovering Friendship*, trans. J. Bowden, London 2000 (also as *Rediscovering Friendship: Awakening to the Power and Promise of Women's Friendship*, Minneapolis 2001). For a detailed study see Liz Carmichael, *Friendship: Interpreting Christian Love*, London 2004.

14. E. von Weizsäcker (ed.), *Offene Systeme I. Beiträge zur Zeitstruktur von Information, Entropie und Evolution*, Stuttgart 1974.

15. H. Wehrt, 'Über Zeitverständnisse und die Problematik von Möglichkeit und Offenheit', in A. M. K. Müller, *Zukunftsperspektiven in einem integrierten Verständnis der Lebenswelt*, Stuttgart 1976, 144–208.

16. 'Creation and Redemption', in R. McKinney (ed.), *Creation, Christ, and Culture: Studies in Honour of T. F. Torrance*, Edinburgh 1976, 119–34.

17. ET *The Future of Creation*, trans. Margaret Kohl, London and Philadelphia 1979, 115–30.

18. J. Moltmann, 'Cosmos and Theosis: Eschatological Perspectives on the Future of the Universe', in G. F. R. Ellis (ed.), *The Far-Future Universe. Eschatology from a Cosmic Perspective*, West Conshohocken 2002, 249–65.

19. 'Grundzüge mystischer Theologie bei Gerhard Tersteegen', *EvTh* 1956, 205–24.

20. T. Merton, *Seven-Storey Mountain: Elected Silence; The Autobiography of Thomas Merton*, London 1961; D. Sölle, *The Inward Road and the Way Back: Texts and Reflections on Religious Experience*, trans. D. L. Scheidt, London 1979.

21. J. Moltmann, 'The Theology of Mystical Experience', in *Experiences of God*, trans. Margaret Kohl, London and Philadelphia 1980.

22. J. B. Metz, *Followers of Christ: The Religious Life and the Church*, trans. T. Linton, London 1978.

23. I was later invited by the nuns of the Tübingen Edith Stein Carmel to give a lecture on Teresa of Avila, and in this tried once more to say what mystical experience means to me: see 'Die Wendung zur Christusmystik bei Teresa von Avila und Martin Luther', in W. Herbstrith (ed.), *Gott allein. Teresa von Avila heute*, Freiburg 1982, 184–208.

24. J. M. Lochman and J. Moltmann, *Gottes Recht und Menschenrechte. Studien und Empfehlungen des Reformierten Weltbundes*, Neukirchen 1977.

25. J. Bohatec, *England und die Geschichte der Menschen- und Bürgerrechte*, Graz 1956.

26. 'Die Menschenrechte. Entwurf für eine Studienarbeit des Reformierten Weltbundes', *EvKomm* 1972, 401. Also in *The Experiment Hope*, trans. M. D. Meeks, Philadelphia 1975.

27. J. Lochmann in *Gottes Recht*, op. cit., 16.

28. K. Barth, *Rechtfertigung und Recht*, Zurich 1938.

29. *Gottes Recht*, op. cit., 63–67.

30. *EvKomm* 1976, 282.

31. L. Vischer (ed.), *Rights of Future Generations—Rights of Nature: Studies from the World Alliance of Reformed Churches* 19, Geneva 1990.

32. J. Moltmann, 'Human Rights—Rights of Humanity—Rights of the Earth', in *God for a Secular Society*, trans. Margaret Kohl, London and Minneapolis 1999, 117–34.

33. W. Huber and H. E. Tödt, *Menschenrechte. Perspektiven einer menschlichen Welt*, Stuttgart 1977.

34. M. Honecker, *Christlicher Beitrag zur Weltverantwortung. Eine kritische Stellungnahme zu den beiden Hauptreferaten von Professor Tödt und Professor Moltmann auf den Tagungen des Lutherischen Weltbundes in Evian und des Reformierten Weltbundes in Nairobi*, Stuttgart 1971.

35. Justitia et Pax, *Die Kirche und die Menschenrechte*, 1974.

Chapter Eighteen. Ecumenical Expansions of the Horizon

1. See *The Passion for Life: A Messianic Lifestyle*, trans. M. D. Meeks, Philadelphia 1978 (also as *The Open Church: Invitation to a Messianic Lifestyle*, London 1978).

2. 'America as Dream', in *On Human Dignity, Political Theology, and Ethics*, trans. M. D. Meeks, Philadelphia 1984, 147–61.

3. Patricia Wilson-Kastner, *Faith, Feminism, and the Christ*, Philadelphia 1984; see now also Elizabeth Johnson, *She Who Is: The Mystery of God in Feminist Theology Discourse*, New York 1992.

4. *Temas para una Teologia de la Esperanza*, Buenos Aires 1978.

5. 'Hoffnung und Befreiung. Offener Brief an José Míguez-Bonino', *EvKomm* 9, 1976; ET 'On Latin American Liberation Theology: An Open Letter to José Míguez Bonino', *Christianity and Crisis* 36, 1976, 57–63.

6. G. Gutiérrez, *We Drink from Our Own Wells: The Spiritual Journey of a People*, trans. M. J. O'Connell, Maryknoll, NY, and London 1988.

7. In *EvTh* 38, 1978, 527–38; ET 'The Liberation of Oppressors', trans. M. D. Meeks in *Christianity and Crisis* 38, 1978, 310–17; trans. P. Hodgson in *Journal of the Interdenominational Theological Center* 6, 1979, 69–82; also in *Journal for Theology of South Africa* 26, 1979, 24–38.

8. My last exposition of these ideas can be found in my book *In the End—the Beginning*, trans. Margaret Kohl, London and Minneapolis 2004, 53–78.

Chapter Nineteen. In My Own Place

1. *Evangelische Kommentare* 1, 1968, 13–20.

2. E. Lohse has drawn a very fine portrait in '*Christus Rex*. Zum Gedenken an Ernst Wolf', *EvTh* 32, 1982, 277–91.

3. W. Fürst, 'Predigt am Sarge Ernst Wolfs', *EvTh* 31, 1971, 511–14.

4. I took over the declaration of principles E. Wolf made in 1946, and presented *Evangelische Theologie* as a *commitment* to the gospel, as a *promise* of breadth of theological discourse, and as a *call* to theologians, teachers, and congregational pastors to make common cause with each other.

5. *EvTh* 48, 1988, 488,

6. *EvTh* 54, 1944, 1.

7. For the best account of the beginnings and history of *Concilium*, see the special number on the preparation for the International Theological congress from 9 to 13 September 1990 in the University of Louvain, Belgium, the subject being 'On the Threshold of the Third Millennium', *Concilium* 26, 1990, February, no. 1.

8. For the history of the society from 1940 to 1971, see M. Rohkrämer in J. Moltmann, *Christliche Existenz im demokratischen Aufbruch Europas*, Munich 1991, 148–66. For more detail now A. Strohm, *Chronik der Gesellschaft für Evangelische Theologie im Überblick 1940–2005* (published by the society).

9. K. Barth, *Das Geschenk der Freiheit. Grundlegung evangelischer Ethik*, Theologische Studien no. 39, Zurich 1953.

10. E. Busch, *Karl Barth: His Life*, trans. J. Bowden, London 1976.

11. J. Moltmann (ed.), *Recht auf Arbeit—Sinn der Arbeit*, Munich 1979.

12. J. Moltmann (ed.), *Nachfolge und Bergpredigt*, with contributions by Helmut Gollwitzer, Rolf Heinrich, Ulrich Luz, and Werner H. Schmidt, Munich 1981, 2nd ed. 1982.

13. D. Bonhoeffer, *The Cost of Discipleship*, trans. R. H. Fuller, London 1951; new ed. and trans. with the title *Discipleship*, Minneapolis 1996. Cf. also R. Strunk, *Nachfolge Christi. Erinnerungen an eine evangelische Provokation*, Munich 1981.

14. J. Moltmann, *Nachfolge und Bergpredigt*, op. cit., 11.

15. B. Klappert and U. Weidner (eds), *Schritte zum Frieden. Theologische Texte zu Frieden und Abrüstung*, Wuppertal 1983, 260–63.

16. J. Moltmann, *Annahme und Widerstand*, with contributions by Hans-Eckehard Bahr, Rainer Eckertz, Werner Lauff, Luise Schottroff, and Konrad Stock, Munich 1984.

17. J. Moltmann (ed.), *Bekennende Kirche wagen. Barmen 1934–1984*, with contributions by J. Beckmann, U. Duchrow, B. Klappert, H.-J. Kraus, J. Moltmann, W. Niesel, M. Rohrkrämer, K. Scharf, and H. Simon, Munich 1984, 9.

18. J. Moltmann, *Bekennende Kirche* op. cit., 266–73.

19. *Versöhnung mit der Natur? Friedenstheologie—Befreiungstheologie. Analysen—Berichte—Meditationen*, Munich 1988; *Religion der Freiheit. Protestantismus in der Moderne*, Munich 1990; *Christliche Existenz im demokratischen Aufbruch Europas. Probleme—Chancen—Orientierungen*, Munich 1991.

20. E. Moltmann-Wendel in *Religion der Freiheit*, op. cit., 66–89.

Chapter Twenty. In Christian-Jewish Dialogue

1. *Lebendiges Bekenntnis. Die 'Grundlagen und Perspektiven des Bekennens' der Generalsynode der Niederländischen Reformierten Kirche von 1949, eingeleitet und übersetzt von Otto Weber*, Neukirchen 1951, 65–66.

2. The German translation was published in Munich in 1955.

3. J. Moltmann, *Theology of Hope*, trans. J. W. Leitch, London 1967, 141.

4. W. Capps (ed.), *The Future of Hope*, Philadelphia 1970.

5. Ibid., 89. Fackenheim developed a 'Jewish thinking' of his own, as can be seen from his chief work, *To Mend the World: Foundations of Future Jewish Thought*, New York 1982.

6. Ibid., 91.

7. Ibid., 96.

8. Ibid., 100.

9. A. Heschel, *The Prophets*, New York 1955.

10. Elie Wiesel, *Night*, trans. from French by S. Rodway, Harmonds-worth 1981.

11. R. Eckhardt, 'Jürgen Moltmann, the Jewish People, and the Holocaust', *Journal of the American Academy of Religion* 44, no. 4, 1976, 675–91.

12. R. McAfee Brown, 'The Holocaust: The Crisis of Indifference', *Conservative Judaism* 26, 1–2 (1976–77), 18–19.

13. P. Lapide and J. Moltmann, *Israel und Kirche: ein gemeinsamer Weg?* Kaiser Traktat 54, Munich 1980; 'Church and Israel: A Common Way of Hope?' trans. in part by S. Gehlert in J. Moltmann, *On Human Dignity*, ed. M. D. Meeks, Philadelphia 1984.

14. B. Klappert and H. Starck (eds), *Umkehr und Erneuerung, Erläuterungen zum Synodalbeschluss der Rheinischen Landessynode 1980: 'Zur*

Erneuerung des Verhältnisses von Christen und Juden', Neukirchen 1980; B. Klappert, 'Zeichen der Treue Gottes', 73–88.

15. Avihu Zakai, 'From Judgement to Salvation: The Image of the Jews in the English Renaissance', *WTJ* 59 (1997).

16. *Israel und Kirche*, op. cit., 85. (Lapide's contribution is not included in the ET [see n. 13]).

17. *EvTh* 55, 1994, 1.

18. *The Church in the Power of the Spirit*, trans. Margaret Kohl, London 1977, 136.

19. German text in *Kirche und Israel* 2003, 1, 77–79. See also R. Rendtorff, 'Versuch einer christlichen Stellungnahme', ibid., 4–7, and 2004, 61–67.

20. With reference to B. Klappert, 'Israel—Messias/Christus—Kirche. Kriterien einer nicht-antijüdischen Christologie', *EvTh* 55, 1995, 64–87.

21. S. T. Katz, *Kontinuität und Diskontinuität zwischen christlichem und nationalsozialistischem Antisemitismus*, Tübingen 2001.

22. L. Siegele-Wenschkewitz (ed.), *Verdrängte Vergangenheit, die uns bedrängt. Feministische Theologie in der Verantwortung für die Geschichte*, Munich 1988, 54–103.

23. E. Moltmann-Wendel, *Ein eigener Mensch werden. Frauen um Jesus*, Munich 1980, now 9th edition, 126; ET *The Women around Jesus: Reflections on Authentic Personhood*, trans. J. Bowden, London and New York 1982.

24. S. Heschel in Siegele-Wenschkewitz, 81. See here E. Moltmann-Wendel, *Autobiography*, trans. J. Bowden, London 1997.

25. Particularly crass is Eveline Valtink in R. Jost and E. Valtink (eds), *Ihr, aber, für wen haltet ihr mich? Auf dem Weg zu einer feministisch-befreiungstheologischen Revision von Christologie*, Gütersloh 1996, 81–88.

26. See J. Mannemann and J. B. Metz (eds), *Christologie nach Auschwitz. Stellungnahme im Anschluss an Thesen von Tiemo Rainer Peters*, Münster 1998, 4.

27. *The Crucified God*, 278.

28. H. Vorgrimler, *Gott, Vater, Sohn und Heiliger Geist*, Münster 2002, 122. One asks in some surprise, why 'between Jews …'? Cf. here the fierce discussion with M. Striet and G. Greshake in *Herder Korrespondenz* 56, 2002, 202–7, 534–37, and *Stimmen der Zeit* 6, 2002, 545ff. On Vorgrimler, see M. Scheuer's critical and rectifying comments in *Trierer Theologische Zeitschrift* 114, 2005, 82: 'The distinction between Father, Son and Spirit describes the divine reality which emerges in the event of revelation. The trinitarian difference in God permits us to think together the true nearness of God in us and his abiding transcendence. Contrary to a prominent feature of negative theology, it is theologically unavoidable to learn to understand God further in categories of personhood. In the New Testament God encounters us as communicative happening of three active Persons. If the one and only God realizes himself and is thought as relational unity, if communication and relation are not accidents but the highest form of unity, then it is not a self-

righteous faith which turns its back on Jesus but a form of thinking which accords with the biblical God.'

Chapter Twenty-one. The New Trinitarian Thinking

1. 1980. ET *The Trinity and the Kingdom of God: The Doctrine of God*, trans. Margaret Kohl, London 1981 (= *The Trinity and the Kingdom: The Doctrine of God*, San Francisco 1981).

2. G. Freudenthal, *Atom und Individuum im Zeitalter Newtons*, Frankfurt 1982.

3. Cf. J. Moltmann, *Experiences in Theology: Ways and Forms of Christian Theology*, trans. Margaret Kohl, London and Minneapolis 2000, pt 4: 'The "Broad Place" of the Trinity', 303–33. Also now C. Sorc, *Entwürfe einer perichoretischen Theologie*, Münster 2004; G. Buxton, *The Trinity, Creation, and Pastoral Ministry*, London 2005.

4. B. Janowski, *Gottes Gegenwart in Israel*, Neukirchen 1993; J. Moltmann, *The Spirit of Life*, trans. Margaret Kohl, London and Minneapolis 1992, chap. 2, §3, 'God's Spirit and His Shekinah', 47–51. For what I have to say about the term 'monotheism', see 'Kein Monotheismus gleicht dem anderen. Destruktion eines untauglichen Begriffs', *EvTh* 62, 2002, 112–22.

5. A. Heschel, *The Prophets*, New York 1962, 221–31. I have entered into this in *The Crucified God*, 267–74.

6. F. Rosenzweig, *Der Stern der Erlösung*, Heidelberg 1954, book 3, 192–94 (see *The Star of Redemption*, trans. W. W. Hallo, London 1971).

7. D. Staniloae, *Orthodoxe Dogmatik*, Zurich and Gütersloh, vol. 1 1985, vol. 2 1990, vol. 3 1995; ET *The Experience of God*, trans. and ed. I. Ionita and R. Barringer, Brookline, Mass., 1994–.

8. Hamburg 1980. ET *Theology of a Classless Society*, London 1979.

9. L. Boff, *Trinity and Society*, trans. from Portuguese by P. Burns, Maryknoll, NY, 1988.

10. Catherine M. LaCugna, *God for Us: The Trinity and Christian Life*, New York 1991; Elizabeth Johnson, *She Who Is: The Mystery of God in Feminist Theology Discourse*, New York 1992.

11. M. Volf, *After Our Likeness: The Church as the Image of the Trinity*, Grand Rapids 1998.

12. For the development of 'the new trinitarian thinking' at the present day see Stanley J. Grenz, *Rediscovering the Triune God: The Trinity in Contemporary Theology*, Minneapolis 2004.

Chapter Twenty-three. Our Long Walk to China, 1985

1. 'The Cosmic Community. A New Ecological Concept of Reality in Science and Religion', in *Ching Feng: Quarterly Notes on Christianity and Chinese Religion and Culture*, Hong Kong, vol. 29, nos. 2–3, September 1986, 93–106.

2. J. Moltmann, 'China zwischen Tao and Mao', in *Gerechtigkeit schafft Zukunft. Friedenspolitik und Schöpfungsethik in einer bedrohten Welt*, München and Mainz 1989, 112–29.

CHAPTER TWENTY-FOUR. GOD—HIS AND HERS

1. J. Moltmann, 'Ahnenkult und Auferstehungsglaube', *Orientierung* 67, June 2003, 141–44.

2. Elisabeth Moltmann-Wendel and Jürgen Moltmann, ET *God—His and Hers*, London 1991, 1–17.

3. *Menschenrechte für die Frau*, Munich 1974; *The Women around Jesus: Reflections on Authentic Personhood*, trans. J. Bowden, London 1982.

4. See E. Moltmann-Wendel, *Autobiography*, trans. J. Bowden, London 1977.

5. *God—His and Hers*, op. cit., xii–xiii.

6. See the detailed account in Elisabeth Moltmann-Wendel, *Autobiography*, op. cit.

7. J. Moltmann, 'Creation, Covenant, and Glory: A Conversation on Karl Barth's Doctrine of Creation', in *History and the Triune God: Contributions to Trinitarian Theology*, trans. J. Bowden, London 1991, 125–42.

8. M. Meyer, 'Das "Mutter-Amt" des Heiligen Geistes in der Theologie Zinzendorfs', *EvTh* 43, 1983, 415–30; see also J. Moltmann, *The Spirit of Life: A Universal Affirmation*, trans. Margaret Kohl, London and Minneapolis 1992, 58–160.

9. Op. cit., 26.

10. E. Moltmann-Wendel and J. Moltmann, 'Mit allen Sinnen glauben: Überlegungen zur Auferstehung des Fleisches', *Stimmen der Zeit* 223, no. 11, November 2005, 723–35.

11. E. Moltmann-Wendel, 'Nein danke, ich glaube selber', *EvTh* 66, 2006, 95–115.

12. J. Moltmann, 'Feminist Theology for Men', in *Experiences in Theology*, trans. Margaret Kohl, London and Minneapolis 2000, 268–92.

CHAPTER TWENTY-FIVE. NEW LOVE FOR LIFE

1. T. Runyon (ed.), *Theology, Politics, and Peace*, New York 1990.

2. *A Festival of Creation: Cathedral Papers*, vol. 2, Washington National Cathedral 1991.

3. German edition 1989. ET *The Way of Jesus Christ: Christianity in Messianic Dimensions*, trans. Margaret Kohl, London and San Francisco 1990; also *Jesus Christ for Today's World*, trans. Margaret Kohl, London and Minneapolis 1994.

4. ET *The Spirit of Life*, trans. Margaret Kohl, London and Minneapolis 1992. The subtitle of the English edition is *A Universal Affirmation*.

5. *The Source of Life*, trans. Margaret Kohl, London and Minneapolis 1997.

6. 'A Pentecostal Theology of Life', *Journal of Pentecostal Theology* 9, October 1996, 3–15; 'The Blessing of Hope: The Theology of Hope and the Full Gospel of Life', *JPT* 13, April 2005, 147–61.

7. Cf. P. Althouse, *Spirit of the Last Days: Pentecostal Eschatology in Conversation with Jürgen Moltmann*, London 2003.

8. *Full Gospel News* 13, February 2005 (in Korean).

CHAPTER TWENTY-SIX. THE FESTIVAL OF THE END AND THE BEGINNING

1. J. Moltmann, *In the End—the Beginning*, trans. Margaret Kohl, London and Minneapolis 2004.

2. See *EvTh* 56, 1996, 2, with the contributions of G. M. Martin under the heading 'Moment', and H. Deuser on 'Die Freude des gelebten Augenblicks'.

3. *Die Theologie auf dem Weg in das dritte Jahrausend*, ed. Carmen Kreig, Thomas Kucharza, and Miroslav Volf, together with Steffen Lösel, Gütersloh 1996.

4. M. Wolf (ed.), *A Passion for God's Reign: Theology, Christian Learning and the Christian Self; Jürgen Moltmann, Nicolas Woltersdorff, Ellen T. Charry*, Grand Rapids 1998.

5. M. Volf, C. Krieg, and T. Kucharz (eds), *The Future of Theology*, Grand Rapids 1996.

6. J. Moltmann (ed.), *Wie ich mich geändert habe*, Gütersloh 1997; *How I Have Changed: Reflections on Thirty Years of Theology*, trans. J. Bowden, London 1997.

7. J. Moltmann and C. Rivuzumwami, *Wo ist Gott? Gottesräume—Lebensräume*, Neukirchen 2002.

CHAPTER TWENTY-SEVEN. NEW EMPHASES

1. 'Ancestor Worship and Resurrection Hope', in Okinawa Lectures, published by Shinkyo Shuppansa, Tokyo 2005.

2. S. Ramirez, *Adios Muchachos! Eine Erinnerung an die sandinistische Revolution*, Wuppertal 2001.

3. J. Moltmann, *Sufrimiento de Dios—Esperanza del Mundo*, Managua 1992.

4. My lectures in CIETTS and UENIC were always published in the periodical *Sacuanjoche, Revista de pensamiento, cultura y desarrollo alternativo*. This is now in its sixth year.

INDEX OF NAMES